Sloan

A Paleoindian Dalton Cemetery in Arkansas

Dan F. Morse

With Contributions from

Glen Akridge
Bruce A. Bradley
Keith W. Condon
Hazel R. Delcourt
Paul A. Delcourt
Linda Gaertner
Jami L. Lockhart
Robert C. Mainfort Jr.
Phyllis A. Morse
Jerome C. Rose
P. Daniel Royall
Roger T. Saucier
Richard Yerkes

The University of Arkansas Press • Fayetteville • 2018

ISBN: 978-1-68226-049-4
eISBN: 978-1-61075-626-6

22 21 20 19 18 6 5 4 3 2

♾ The paper used in this publication meets the minimum requirements of the American National Standard for Permanence of Paper for Printed Library Materials Z39.48-1984.

Library of Congress Cataloging-in-Publication Data

Sloan . a paleoindian Dalton cemetery in Arkansas / [edited by] Dan F. Morse.
p. cm. —(Smithsonian series in archaeological inquiry)
Includes bibliographical references (p.) and index.
ISBN 1-56098-712-X (hard cover : alk. paper)
1. Sloan Site (Ark.) 2. Paleo-Indians—Arkansas—Greene County. 3. Indians of North America—Funeral customs and rites—Arkansas—Greene County. 4. Indians of North America—Arkansas—Greene County—Implements. 5. Indians of North America—Arkansas—Greene County—Antiquities. 6. Excavations (Archaeology)Arkansas—Greene County. 7. Stone implements—Arkansas—Greene County. 8. Projectile points—Arkansas—Greene County. 9. Greene County (Ark—Antiquities.
I. Morse, Dan F. II. Series.
E.78.A8S59 1997 96-54013
976.7'99301—dc21 CIP

On the opening pages, Sloan artifacts at one-half actual size. HALF TITLE PAGE: unbeveled Dalton points. TITLE SPREAD: large Dalton points at Sloan. DEDICATION PAGE: *left,* backed uniface; *right,* end scraper. CONTENTS PAGE: beveled Dalton point. Page facing contents: *left,* adze; *right,* beveled Dalton points. ON THE COVER: large Sloan-site Dalton points at actual size.

Publication was supported in part by the Arkansas Archeological Survey.

This book is dedicated to the memory of
Carl and Eleanor Chapman,
the first Dalton scholars

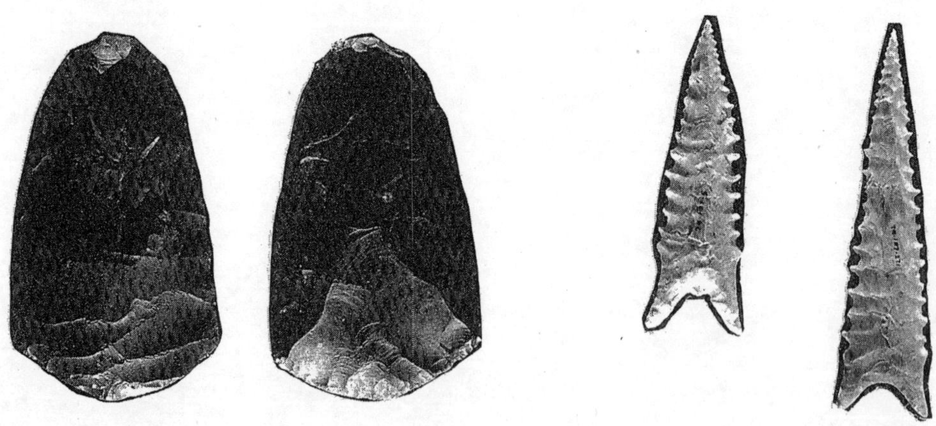

Contents

List of Illustrations ix

List of Tables xii

Preface xv

Acknowledgments xvii

1: Excavation of the Sloan Site 1
Dan F. Morse and Phyllis A. Morse

2: Bioarchaeology of the Sloan Site 8
Keith W. Condon and Jerome C. Rose

3: Description of the Artifacts 14
Dan F. Morse

4: Sloan Site Biface and Projectile Point Technology 53
Bruce A. Bradley

5: Microwear Analysis of Dalton Artifacts 58
Richard Yerkes and Linda M. Gaertner

6: Provenience of Artifacts 72
Dan F. Morse, Phyllis A. Morse, Robert C. Mainfort Jr., Jami J. Lockhart, and Glen Akridge

7: Late Quaternary Geologic History of the Western Lowlands 96
Roger T. Saucier

8: Late Quaternary Vegetational History of the Western Lowlands 103
Hazel R. Delcourt, Paul A. Delcourt, and P. Daniel Royall

9: An Overview of the Dalton Period in Northeastern Arkansas and in the Southeastern United States 123
Dan F. Morse

10: Summary 140
Dan F. Morse

References Cited 143

List of Contributors 153

Index 155

Illustrations

Figure 1.1 Frank Sloan and the first two Dalton points found at the Sloan site **2**
Figure 1.2 Excavations in progress at the Sloan site **4**
Figure 1.3 The Sloan site in relation to sand dunes **5**
Figure 1.4 Contour map of the Sloan site setting **6**
Figure 1.5 The Sloan site during excavation **7**
Figure 2.1 Breakdown of Sloan skeletal fragments by category **12**
Figure 2.2 Unquestionably human bone from the Sloan site **13**
Figure 3.1 Chert sources in northeastern Arkansas in relation to the Sloan site **16**
Figure 3.2 Large Dalton points at the Sloan site **18**
Figure 3.3 Beveled Dalton points at the Sloan site **19**
Figure 3.4 Unbeveled Dalton points at the Sloan site **20**
Figure 3.5 Other Dalton points at the Sloan site **22**
Figure 3.6 Sloan-site Dalton points: maximum length versus weight **30**
Figure 3.7 Sloan-site Dalton points: maximum width at base versus weight **30**
Figure 3.8 Sloan-site Dalton points: maximum length versus maximum width at base **31**
Figure 3.9 Sloan-site bifaces: maximum length versus maximum width **31**
Figure 3.10 Adzes and adze preforms at the Sloan site **32**

Figure 3.11 Sloan-site Dalton adzes: maximum length versus weight **34**
Figure 3.12 Sloan-site Dalton adzes: maximum length versus width at bit **34**
Figure 3.13 Bifaces at the Sloan site **35**
Figure 3.14 End scrapers at the Sloan site **38**
Figure 3.15 Other unifaces at the Sloan site **40**
Figure 3.16 Other artifacts at the Sloan site **44**
Figure 4.1 Idealized Sloan Dalton-point manufacture sequence **55**
Figure 4.2 Bruce Bradley manufacturing a Dalton point **56**
Figure 5.1 Experiments with replicas of Dalton adzes and bifaces **63**
Figure 5.2 Dalton adze from the Sloan site **64**
Figure 5.3 Dalton adze from site 3PO81 **65**
Figure 5.4 Advanced-stage Dalton point from the Brand site **67**
Figure 5.5 End scraper from the Brand site **69**
Figure 5.6 *Pièce esquillée* from the Brand site **70**
Figure 6.1 Distribution of artifacts used in spatial analysis and human bone fragments **73**
Figure 6.2 Distribution of artifacts at the Sloan site **83**
Figure 6.3 Distribution of artifacts at the Sloan site **84**
Figure 6.4 Distribution of artifacts used in spatial analysis **85**
Figure 6.5 Artifact concentrations indicative of possible graves **86**
Figure 6.6 Artifacts indicative of insignificant disturbance at the Sloan site **87**
Figure 6.7 Artifact clusters at the Sloan site **89**
Figure 6.8 Distribution of large Dalton points **92**
Figure 6.9 Distribution of adzes **93**
Figure 6.10 Distribution of normalized zinc/copper concentrations for the Sloan site soil samples **95**
Figure 7.1 Major physiographic elements and depositional units of the Western Lowlands and the St. Francis Basin, Lower Mississippi Valley **97**
Figure 7.2 Major landscape elements (landforms) in the vicinity of the Sloan site **101**
Figure 8.1 Location map of late Quaternary paleoecological sites and landforms in the central Mississippi Alluvial Valley and adjacent uplands **104**
Figure 8.2 Detailed location map for Hood Lake, Poinsett County, Arkansas **106**
Figure 8.3 Detailed location map for Powers Fort Swale, Butler County, Missouri **107**
Figure 8.4 Curve of net sediment accumulation rates at Hood Lake **109**
Figure 8.5 Percentage diagram for assemblages of pollen grains and spores from Hood Lake **110**
Figure 8.6 Plant-macrofossil diagram for Hood Lake **111**

Figure 8.7 Curve of net sediment accumulation rates at Powers Fort Swale **115**
Figure 8.8 Percentage diagram for pollen grains of selected taxa from Powers Fort Swale **116**
Figure 8.9 Paleovegetation map for the central Mississippi Alluvial Valley and adjacent uplands at 10,000 yr B.P. **121**
Figure 9.1 Distribution of Dalton-period sites in Arkansas **126**
Figure 9.2 Distribution of Dalton-period sites within the Cache River Basin, showing the location of the Sloan site **127**
Figure 9.3 Distribution of hypothesized Dalton local groups in northeastern Arkansas **129**
Figure 9.4 Distribution of hypothesized northeastern Arkansas settlements during the Dalton period **130**
Figure 9.5 Distribution of pre-Dalton fluted points in northeastern Arkansas **131**
Figure 9.6 Distribution of early notched and stemmed points in northeastern Arkansas **133**
Figure 9.7 Major Dalton-period sites in the eastern United States **138**

Tables

Table 2.1 Sloan site bone provenience **9**
Table 3.1 Summary of artifacts by basic artifact category **15**
Table 3.2 Measurements of points **24**
Table 3.3 Measurements of adzes **33**
Table 3.4 Measurements of bifaces **36**
Table 3.5 Measurements of broken biface tools **38**
Table 3.6 Measurements of end scrapers **39**
Table 3.7 Measurements of backed unifaces **41**
Table 3.8 Measurements of perforators **41**
Table 3.9 Measurements of retouched flakes **42**
Table 3.10 Measurements of other unifaces (utilized flakes) **43**
Table 3.11 Measurements of discoid hammers **45**
Table 3.12 Measurements of pebble cores **45**
Table 3.13 Measurements of grooved abraders **47**
Table 3.14 Measurements of notched abraders **49**
Table 3.15 Measurements of grooved and notched abraders **50**
Table 3.16 Measurements of other abraders **50**
Table 3.17 Measurements of cobble abraders **51**
Table 5.1 Summary of microwear analyses **60**
Table 6.1 Sloan site artifact provenience **74**
Table 6.2 Artifact clusters at the Sloan site **88**
Table 6.3 Results of selected soil samples **94**
Table 8.1 Lithologic description of the Hood Lake sediment core **109**

Table 8.2 Lithologic description of the Powers Fort Swale sediment core **115**
Table 9.1 Selected radiocarbon dates in the Southeast **135**
Table 9.2 Late Pleistocene–early Holocene sequence chart for the Southeast **137**

Preface

The Sloan site was created circa 8500 B.C., immediately before the end of the Pleistocene ("Ice Age"). The diagnostic late Paleoindian fluted point found at the Sloan site is known as Dalton. Based on the analyses summarized in this book, we know that the Dalton people made dugout canoes, hunted and butchered white-tailed deer, processed wild plant foods, lived in small villages, frequented temporary camps, traded with and/or visited peoples near present-day St. Louis and in the Ozark Mountains, and buried their dead in cemeteries such as Sloan.

When the Sloan site was brought to our attention on 13 March 1974, we were unprepared for the magnitude of the discovery (chapter 1). During a period of thirty-one days, 439 Dalton artifacts were recovered within a 12 by 12 meter excavation no deeper than 0.5 meter. The final soil samples were collected on 13 April and the site was backfilled. In total, 360 artifacts were photographed in situ, and 146 of the 439 artifacts found were Dalton points, mostly complete specimens.

The Sloan site is the earliest recognized cemetery in the New World. The existence of a cemetery in an American Paleolithic setting was not forecast in 1974 by anyone. When the Sloan site was excavated, most interpretations of hunter-gatherer-fisher populations involved a very high degree of nomadism over considerable distances and/or across significantly different ecotones. An understanding of the Dalton artifactual remains in northeastern Arkansas has forced a new emphasis on local resources and greater territorial and residential stability. Not all Dalton-complex expressions in the Southeast are being interpreted as homogeneous in settlement and economic behavior. But all Dalton complexes are held together by a point style and undoubtedly some degree of behavioral similarity (chapter 9).

We know Sloan was a cemetery, based on the presence of human bone (chapter 2), the kinds of artifacts recovered (chapters 3, 4), and the intrusive nature of the artifacts into an older soil (chapter 7). We can make a general guess at how many people were present and what constituted a typical grave lot (chapter 6). The immediate environment (chapters 7 and 8) will help give us clues as to why the terminal Pleistocene period in northeastern Arkansas witnessed an American Paleolithic climax. We wish to emphasize here that sophistication is not just seen in well-crafted lanceolate points (chapter 4). Some of these points are beyond the scope of mere function as butchering tools, measuring up to 189 millimeters in length. But it is tools such as the earliest known true adze in the New World (chapter 5) and a variety of hafted unifaces that help attest to the sophistication of northeastern Arkansas Dalton behavior.

The Sloan-site assemblage enables us to reconstruct functional technology to a great degree. Pristine examples of tool classes previously known only by worn-out and/or aborted artifacts were recovered at Sloan. It is as if a time traveler were able to grab an armful of unhafted stone tools from a single band over a period of about three generations, including some tools that were recently manufactured, others just resharpened or reshaped, and almost all of which were complete.

The actual excavation of the site occurred in the late winter and early spring of 1974. The first interruption in writing this book occurred when the focus of my sabbatical in the spring semester of 1975 was hastily shifted from the analyses of Sloan-site artifacts to the emergency salvage of the Zebree site, still the earliest Mississippi expression known. The focus on Zebree continued until 1980, when publication of that effort was stalled by a potential publisher while a new series was being contemplated. That was not actually resolved until 1989, and the Zebree volume still has not been formally published. Between 1980 and 1983, the focus of attention was on the writing of a major regional book for Academic Press (Morse and Morse 1983).

In 1984 I began to assemble a research team, and the Sloan-site artifacts were photographed and measured. Casts of selected specimens had already been made by Allen Eichenberger. In 1985 the research team was mainly assembled and a book prospectus written. After a two-year review, a contract was signed with the Smithsonian Institution Press for the publication of Sloan, and royalties were assigned to the Archaeological Conservancy.

By 1986 archaeologists and ethnohistorians in the southeastern United States realized that the 450th anniversary of the DeSoto expedition into La Florida would occur during 1989–1993, and that none of us would be around to observe the 500th anniversary. Because the expedition spent most of 1541–1543 in Arkansas and because the northeastern Arkansas route was crucial to our understanding of that route and of the complex chiefdoms that existed then, we were compelled to focus our main attention on something completely unrelated to Sloan. We accomplished a great deal of important new understanding of the expedition and of the route. In addition, the development of GIS computer analyses of that route were important in reexamining Dalton-site locations. In 1991 *Pictures of Record* published a slide set of selected artifacts to supplement this book (Morse 1991).

Finally, by 1994, we were once again able to concentrate fully on Sloan. Our procrastination is unfortunate, but actually many of the needed analyses were not possible until twenty years after the actual excavation. The dedication and patience of the research team and particularly of Daniel Goodwin, editor for the Smithsonian Institution Press, are very much appreciated.

Acknowledgments

Frank Sloan's father, W. C. Sloan, and the 3BF Sloan Ranch technically owned the site and artifacts, but it was Frank Sloan who unselfishly recommended that we excavate it, gave us constant encouragement during the late winter month of the excavation, and insisted that all artifacts belong to the state of Arkansas because of their importance. Frank Sloan is an avocational archaeologist and historian whose primary prehistoric interest is the Dalton period. He turned down the efforts of one local treasure hunter to buy digging rights and did not heed the advice of another to have us removed from the site.

Many collectors think they are archaeologists. An archaeologist attempts to increase the knowledge of the field of archaeology. An avocational archaeologist (one whose profession or job is nonarchaeological) consciously contributes to the understanding of the history and prehistory of a region. Collectors and treasure hunters vandalize the sites and artifacts of history, often motivated by greed and/or profit. They deface the monuments of history as surely as a painting is defaced by a knife or a spray can. Any contributions to archaeology by such people are accidental.

Scientific amateur archaeology is important. The local treasure hunter who sold two "6–7 inch long black Daltons" from the Sloan site defaced it. Frank Sloan by his actions revolutionized archaeological interpretation and immortalized the Sloan site.

A number of individuals helped us produce this book. The help of the Arkansas Archeological Survey under the direction of Thomas Green was invaluable. Marvin Jeter was kind enough to ensure that it was written in acceptable English. Lindi Holmes accomplished the final difficult tasks of making sure that final corrections were incorporated into the text and that the manuscript was in the form requested by the publisher. Jami Lockhart did the GIS maps that are Figures 9.1, 9.2, 9.5, and 9. 6. Mary L. Kennedy produced the map relating the Sloan site to its immediate environs on a computer (Figure 1.4) and also produced Figures 2.1, 3.1, 9.3, and 9.7 and cleaned up several others. Pam Ashford photographed the artifacts. Janie Kellett produced the prints used for illustrations and prepared them for the press.

Frank Sloan, Leonard Blake, Anna Parks, Cara Parks, Phyllis Morse, and the Northwest Arkansas Archaeological Society made it financially possible for Bruce Bradley to visit Jonesboro to examine the Sloan-site artifacts. Iris

Weaver, avocational archaeologist from Paragould, Arkansas, expertly numbered the Dalton-period artifacts from Sloan. Her numbers are small, neat, and legible. David Anderson, National Park Service, helped with the tables. He provided summary statistics and pinpointed possible errors to be checked. Dr. Anderson provided Figures 3.6, 3.7, 3.8, 3.9, 3.11, and 3.12.

The Sloan site was excavated by a mixed group of professional archaeologists and enthusiastic volunteers. The one-week Spring Break project in which students in an introductory class at Arkansas State University could gain extra credit by aiding Michael Schiffer and John House in test excavating a few pits in select sites developed into the complete excavation of a totally new type of site. The Cache River Archeological Project had to proceed as scheduled, but personnel from this project such as John House volunteered on their days off. Dan Morse had to resume teaching his classes on Monday, but fortunately these were only on Monday, Wednesday, and Friday mornings. He left for the field immediately thereafter and spent the remaining full four days of the week at the site. Sam Smith, the Arkansas State University survey station assistant, was able to devote much of his time to the excavation. John House, Michael Million, James Smith, and Sam Smith constituted the primary excavation crew chiefs. Dan's students recognized the importance of the site and were motivated to aid in the daily discovery of caches of artifacts. Jim Smith drove out early to the site most mornings to prevent incursions by the local treasure hunters. Michael Million and several other students went when their classes permitted. In fact, we suspect that many such classes were not attended during that one-month period. Phyllis Morse went out to the site when possible, juggling the needs of three young sons and the task of feeding hungry archaeologists and volunteers at the end of the day. Other volunteer excavators who were able to help at least one day included Mike Conine, Bill Davidson, Ann Early, Jacqueline Fehon, John Foltz, Norma Hoffrichter, John Johnson, Danny Kent, D. D. Million, Daniel Morse, John F. Morse, Michael Schiffer, Mary Shipley, Carol Spears, Nan Stiles, and Alfred Viscito.

Frank Sloan visited the site when he could, while supervising the spring cultivation of his family land holdings in Greene County. Frank loaned us equipment, made coffee for us, and encouraged us all the way without even a hint of interference or irritation. Mary Ann Sloan also lent considerable support (and a fifth of Scotch!). Frank's father, W. C. Sloan, also cooperated in every way and was most congenial at a time when he was approaching a hip replacement operation. The true unselfishness of the entire Sloan family and their intelligent realization that the artifacts recovered were of great scientific value and should be owned by the state cannot be overemphasized. The Sloan family formally donated all the artifacts to the Arkansas Archeological Survey in a legal document. The only small reward we could give was to suggest an artifact appraisal for a tax donation and to name the site after them. Frank Sloan was presented with the 1988 annual Preservationist Award by the Arkansas Archeological Society.

1
Excavation of the Sloan Site

DAN F. MORSE AND PHYLLIS A. MORSE

Site 3GE94 was recorded on 25 June 1968 by Mary Ann Sloan as part of a paper required in Sociology 2311: Introduction to Archaeology taught by Dan Morse at Arkansas State University. Six sand dunes on Sloan family land initially were mapped as 3GE94 and collectively were called "Dalton Field" and, later, "Dalton Hill." The site had been cultivated with small equipment and the dunes were surrounded by wooded areas. By 1970 the woods had been cleared, and in that year Larry Medford noted in his site destruction survey project field notes (see Medford 1972) that destruction due to clearing included wind erosion and erosion by farming. At about that time, unknown to us, large and well-crafted Dalton points began to be collected at the site and sold. A local treasure hunter (from Light, Arkansas) sold two Pitkin Chert Daltons measuring between "6 and 7 inches" in length for $75 apiece to a Corning dealer. Another three points were sold for $75 each, and five "5-inch" Daltons sold for higher prices. That treasure hunter intensively hunted the site for six years and sold other points he found for several hundred dollars. He was unsuccessful in trying to purchase digging rights. Other treasure hunters including the tenant were also finding points and selling them for large sums. By 1974 more than fifteen Daltons found at the Sloan site by the tenant had been sold to dealers in the nearby towns of Lafe and Egypt for no less than $100 each. That was when Frank Sloan became concerned about the loss of the historical value of the site and the greed of the collectors involved.

Dan Morse called Frank Sloan on 13 March 1974 in connection with the Cache River Archeological Project (Morse 1975; Schiffer and House 1975). In June and July 1973 John House had conducted a preliminary survey of the lower reaches of the 5,247-square-kilometer (2,018-square-mile) Cache River Basin. During March 1974 seven sites were tested, primarily to investigate the effects of cultivation on smaller sites, to understand the true nature of a site in relation to a surface collection, and to investigate the validity of pollen sampling at shallow sites.

Dan Morse was teaching two introductory courses that semester at Arkansas State University, the host university for the northeastern Arkansas station of the Arkansas Archeological Survey, and twenty-six students were allowed to spend three days each in the field during Spring Break week in lieu of writing a research paper. Arkansas State University offers neither an anthropology major nor a mi-

Figure 1.1 Frank Sloan and the first two Dalton points found at the Sloan site.

nor. In fact the only anthropology classes offered then were those taught by Morse. Fortunately, undergraduate students such as Jim Smith and Michael Million and his wife D. D. Million were volunteering in the archaeological laboratory and also had dedicated their spare time that year to the Cache River Archeological Project.

Morse called Frank Sloan to learn the positive identification of a Jonesboro land owner of a site in southwestern Craighead County (3CG230) and also requested that he recommend a site in Greene County to test in case permission could not be obtained to test the Craighead County site. Frank urged that 3GE94 be tested immediately and Dan agreed to do so because Frank was so insistent. On 15 March Dan and Jim Smith met Frank about noon, after collecting at three other sites, and put in three one-meter test pits where Frank had been told by his tenant that the points had been found. All three pits were sterile. Frank went to lunch, Dan's volunteer student assistant began to surface-collect on an adjacent knoll, and Dan placed test pit 4 in a convenient place on top of the dune. It was specifically placed to include a probable Dalton-period blade of Pitkin Chert. The placement of the test pit to the east of the blade was because that area had less cotton stubble. As Frank got out of his truck on returning from lunch, Dan uncovered a Dalton point and immediately afterward two more at the base of the cultivation zone in the northeastern corner of the test pit (Figure 1.1). We enlarged the pit north and east to measure about 2 meters square and uncovered three more Dalton points. After Dalton number 4 and a soil sample were collected, Dan called the Arkansas State University station laboratory to report on the discoveries. Michael Schiffer, John House, Michael Million, Mike Conine, and a student immediately visited the site in time to help recover Dalton numbers 5 and 6. Schiffer made a controlled surface collection in about a 3 by 4 meter area near the test pit.

The next day Million, House, Smith, and Morse recovered a seventh Dalton point and a cache of ten bifaces. Then we decided to establish a grid system. It was so windy that we could not use a transit. Point 50R50 and Datum was established at the northeastern corner of test pit 4. The excavation was then outlined as a 4 by 4 meter square. Each artifact below the cultivation zone was assigned a catalog number and a specific grid provenience that included a grid point and depth. Suspected Dalton-period artifacts in the cultivation zone were also cataloged and assigned a specific grid provenience.

During the third day the same crew found fifteen more Dalton points. No matter which direction we excavated, there were Dalton artifacts. Unknown to us at the time, the initial approximately 1-meter-square test pit 4 was almost exactly in the center of the cemetery.

It was obvious by then that we were not dealing with a single cache of Dalton-period artifacts, thought at that time to have been the situation with the reported Hawkins Cache (Morse 1971b). In the case of the Hawkins Cache, the discovery site was not accurately reported to us (reported as 3LW89), and we were never able to tell just what the find represented. We now think that the Hawkins Cache represented one of several burials at a single site, based on reports years later of numerous pits dug at a site (3LW505) thought to have been the real site by another informant. It was too late to halt the Sloan excavation to save it for a field school, because all arrangements had been made to excavate at the Nodena-phase Armorel site in June and July. But the local treasure seekers and dealers had begun to suspect something. We had to finish the Sloan excavation as quickly as possible to accommodate spring planting and to fulfill the necessary teaching obligations for that semester, an obligation to the Cache River Archeological Project and report, and the summer school commitments. We also had to protect the Sloan site against vandalism, a constant problem even today in northeastern Arkansas archaeology.

One of the coldest late winter–early springs on record occurred in 1974. Temperatures were often in the thirties and ranged from a low of –7°C to a high of 16°C (20–60°F). The wind blew constantly, causing lenses in cameras and glasses to abrade from the blasted sand grains. Occasionally we had to sit inside a vehicle until the wind calmed down. Visibility could be measured in meters during those times. The ground was often frozen in the morning and we even had snow storms as well as sleet and rain. The weather at times was more like our typical January than March and April. March normally is one of the most comfortable months of the year in northeastern Arkansas.

We had to devise a method of accomplishing the excavation quickly and efficiently, because of lack of funding and the adverse weather conditions. We did not screen. Weather, lack of personnel, inappropriateness of our screens, lack of time, lack of funding, and ignorance of the actual site extent constituted the major factors influencing our decision not to screen. Instead, we employed a method of shoveling units slowly on a horizontal plane with centimeter-deep slices with square-point shovels. That allowed us to find most artifacts in situ (Figure 1.2). Each shovelful of dirt was thrown on a dirt pile adjacent to the excavation so that the sandy soil would roll down the dirt pile, hence exposing artifacts missed by the shovel. Where possible, a second person troweled through soil thrown up on the dirt pile. Actually, very few artifacts were recovered from the back dirt.

Whenever an artifact was encountered, it was exposed using a bamboo pick and paintbrush. The area around the artifact was explored by troweling because many of the artifacts were clustered in groups. An area of a meter or more was carefully cleaned of any loose soil and excavated to the same plane as the artifact. Artifacts were readied for photographing by gently brushing them with a wet paintbrush. All artifacts found in undisturbed soil were cataloged in the field, and all possible Dalton artifacts found in disturbed deposits (e.g., the cultivation zone) were cataloged in the field. Caches were photographed and drawn as they were removed artifact by artifact. All individual cataloged artifacts were recorded by grid point and depth and also drawn on a floor plan. All in situ Dalton artifacts were to be photographed in black and white as well as in Kodachrome. A very few were not photographed. The camera lenses mandated at that time by the state agency were only 35-mm wide-angled ones. This caused distortion of artifacts photographed close-up in situ. Personal cameras, equipped with the normal 55-mm lens, were also used.

During the excavation, telephone and letter communication was initiated and continued with a number of individuals, including Roger Saucier, Vance Haynes, Dan Morse, M.D., Bob McGimsey, Hester Davis, Frank Livingstone, and Marie Wormington, to get information on specialized recovery techniques. Soil samples were taken where appropriate and at every half meter at a depth of 0.5 meter across the entire excavation. Over 450 separate soil samples were collected in all. Carol Spears did a preliminary test on a select few of the samples in the soil laboratory at the University of Arkansas, and the remainder was the basis for a study by Glen Akridge in 1993–1994 as partial credit for an undergraduate degree in chemistry at Arkansas State University.

Once the grid system and a 4 by 4 meter square were established, the excavation progressed by digging 1-meter-wide extensions in all four directions from the original test pit 4. A front-end loader moved the dirt piles out of our way. The excavation was eventually halted one month later when a one-meter extension on all sides did not produce definite Dalton artifacts.

The Sloan site occupied the summit of a sand dune (Figures 1.3, 1.4, 1.5). The Sloan site dune is part of a group of sand dunes (Figure 1.3, *bottom*) that occupy a substantial part of the Western Lowlands of northeastern Arkansas (see chapter 7). These dunes date approximately between 18,000 and 22,000 years ago (Saucier 1978:28). Evidently they have been stabilized for at least the last 10,500 years and probably longer. Grass cover and tree shelter probably account for that stability. Certainly modern clearing of these dunes for farming has allowed erosion to accelerate and the shallow intrusive deposits to be exposed. It was fortunate that we were able to salvage most of the site before it was destroyed. Today, much of this area has been leveled and filled for rice cultivation. The

a

b

c

d

Figure 1.2 Excavations in progress at the Sloan site: *a*, technique of shoveling (AAS neg. 742723); *b*, excavating a point and preparing it for photographing (AAS neg. 742357); *c*, recording (AAS neg. 742597); *d*, photographing (AAS neg. 742749).

area immediately east of Sloan has been excavated up to a couple of meters deep to use as fill in the slough connecting Sloan and a possible Dalton-period living site (3GE3).

On 17 March the first of the relic collectors, the tenant and two boys who lived near the site, visited the dig. We developed a strategy of moving back dirt until they finally left because we did not dare let them know that we had found fifteen Dalton points that day. In addition, Frank asked us to please keep the discovery secret. He was concerned about collectors converging on the farm and digging random holes. He also was very concerned that the artifacts should belong to the state of Arkansas and not

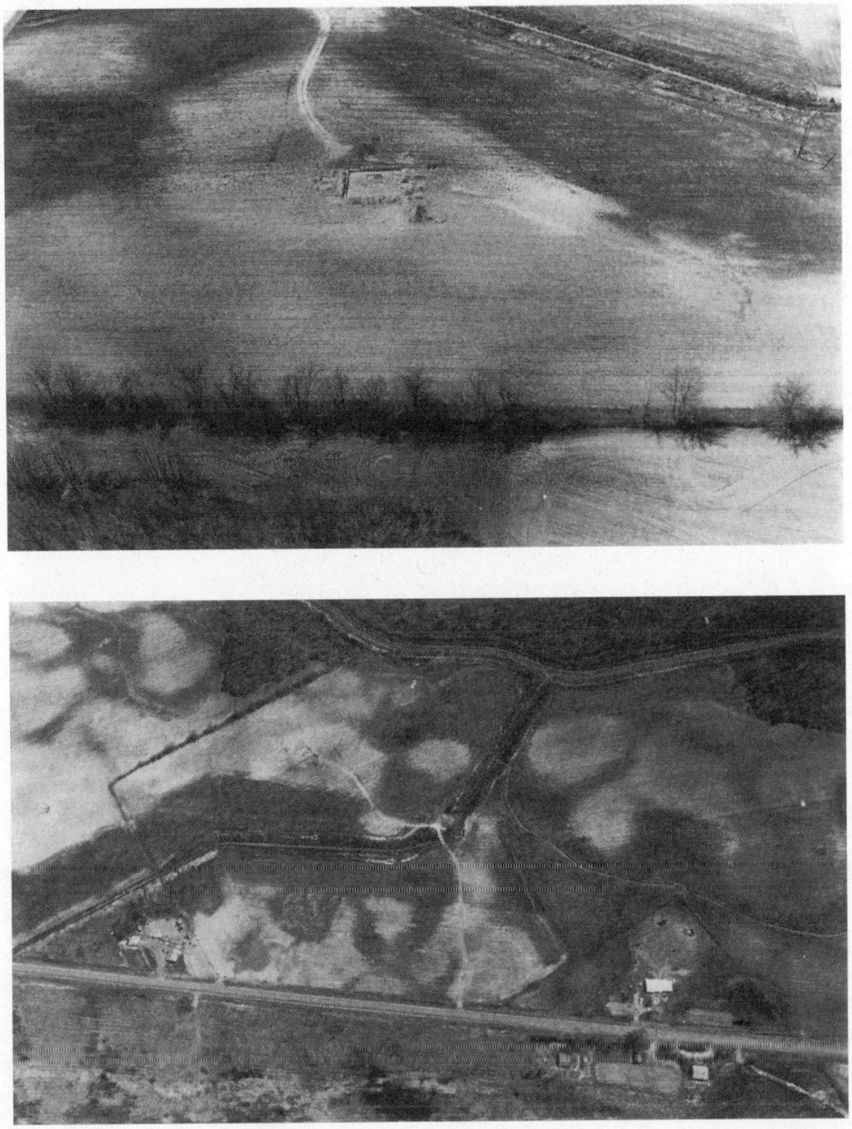

Figure 1.3 The Sloan site in relation to sand dunes: *top*, aerial view showing the site dune (AAS neg. 742770); *bottom*, aerial view showing surrounding dunes (AAS neg. 742764).

greedy collectors. That evening I called Hester Davis, state archaeologist, Roger Saucier, and Dan Morse, M.D., adjunct professor, Florida State University and forensic anthropological expert, to get advice and to begin informing colleagues what had been discovered.

On 19 March Dalton number 50 was discovered when one of the crew softly stated "I can't find any ends for this one." Within seconds everyone was there. He had uncovered the central portion of a Dalton point, 19 centimeters long and 6 centimeters wide, lying flat! By the end of 21 March the excavation measured 5 by 7 meters. We had found seventy-one Dalton points and 124 other field-cataloged artifacts. Included were abraders, adzes, bifaces, end scrapers, other unifaces, and a discoid hammerstone. We finally could set up a transit to map the excavation grid points and discovered that grid north was 7°7′40″ west of magnetic north and that some grid points were 6 centimeters off. Bill Davidson, cultural geographer at Arkansas State University then and at Louisiana State University now, visited and collected soil samples to test pH values to see if he could recover soil phosphorus values. It snowed that day, with winds at 35 kilometers (22 miles) per hour. The ground was frozen the next morning when we arrived at the site. In total, forty-five soil samples were

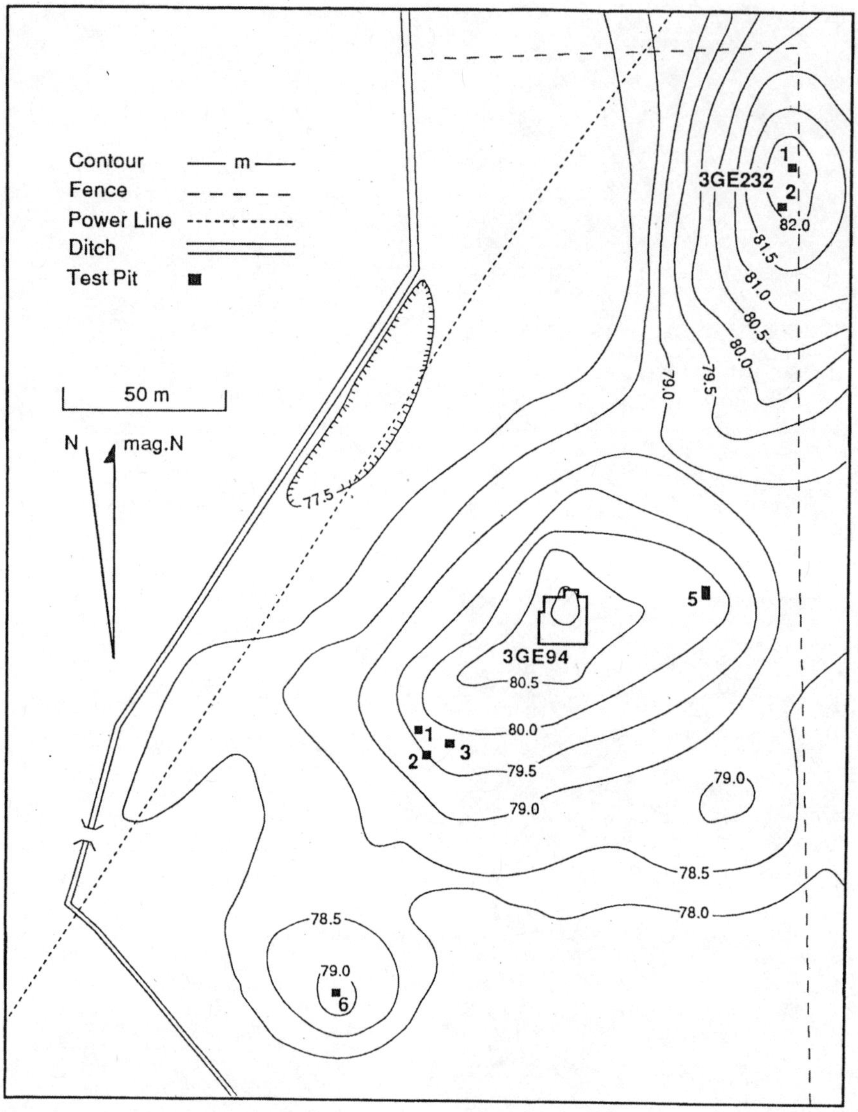

Figure 1.4 Contour map of the Sloan site setting.

collected by Davidson before a cold front with sleet arrived.

The next day, 24 March, a Sunday, the ground was frozen all day and we arrived at the site about noon. We found that all of our grid stakes had been pulled out and the excavation completely stomped. On Monday morning Jim Smith observed a two-tone black Chevy pickup hurriedly turn around when the driver realized that someone was there. The pickup returned with another person two days later when it rained all day and again turned and fled. D. Morse had spent the afternoon following a mastodon lead in Poinsett County and relieved Jim Smith at 5:30 P.M. We were lucky because that evening Morse found four Dalton points, which these collectors would have located with their stomping methodology, just in the edge of the excavation wall.

Dalton point number 100 was found on 28 March, and by 29 March the excavation measured 8 by 8 meters. On 30 March several collectors visited. We were able to see a strange cross section of the regional treasure hunters. Following the landowner's suggestion, we simply told them that we were collecting soil samples (actually a truthful statement). The first one squatted and spit tobacco so that the wind carried it into our faces. Another was on a motorcycle. Two collectors began to probe on an adjacent knoll without permission of the landowner. Two others

Figure 1.5 The Sloan site during excavation: *top*, ground-level view of the dune (AAS neg. 742388); *bottom*, block nature of the excavation (AAS neg. 742737).

surface-collected on the next knoll. The delays meant that we had to use a flashlight to do the final recording on a preform cache that night.

By 31 March the excavation almost measured 11 by 12 meters; the corners had not yet been removed. The next day there were more collectors in two pickups and rain and tornado warnings. On 2 April gas pipeline people (two carloads of them) arrived to check us out and then spent much of the day surface-collecting all around the dig. We began to collect the hundreds of soil samples. One group of people, running motorcycles on the sand dunes, avoided us politely. One older visitor, during a very windy 3 April, was a "picker" for a major Lafe artifact dealer. We had to endure his bragging of selling points including a "9½-inch" side-notched point for $300 for nearly half a day while concealing an in situ Dalton point and other artifacts under bags, shovels, dirt, and notebooks.

On 4 April after a foggy evening, a cold front with high winds arrived just as we discovered an Archaic skeleton at the edge of the Dalton cemetery. That afternoon, Carol Spears and Norma Hoffrichter arrived as volunteer help. Hester Davis arrived later. We collected soil samples over, around, and under the Archaic skeleton to use as a reference for any future soil analyses in the Paleoindian cemetery, where we did not have any skeletons. At that time, we did not know that the small bone fragments we had collected would eventually be identified as human.

By 6 April the final excavation unit was almost ready to be cleaned up for aerial photographs. Dalton numbers 133, 134, 135, 136, and 137 were found on that date. The excavation then measured 14 by 12 meters. On 7 April the excavation was ready for photographing, but another cold front with high winds and rain prevented Sam Smith from flying with Charles Scanlon, professor of mathematics, Arkansas State University, who was a member of the Osage tribe. He volunteered to fly his plane over the site for expenses. Sam was finally able to take the aerial photographs at 1:30 P.M. on 8 April. We took the opportunity to begin to set out bench marks and do a transit map of the general area. We also collected another two hundred soil samples. On 10 and 11 April the excavation was finally finished when we had excavated a 1-meter strip along all sides and found few or no Dalton-period artifacts. The last of the test pits excavated nearby was done. On 11 April the last Dalton point was found in the excavation. The finished excavation was 200 square meters in extent and measured essentially 14 by 14 meters. Artifacts were concentrated in a contiguous area of just over 100 square meters; squared off, the area of artifacts measured 11 by 12 meters. There was an average of three to four complete Dalton-period tools per square meter and just over one complete Dalton point per square meter. On 15 April the Dalton Hill excavation was closed down after thirty-two continuous days of working. Frank Sloan loaned us a front-end loader and a dirt buggy behind a tractor plus drivers for backfilling. When the backfilling took place, a Dalton point was recovered by Dan from the base of one of the dirt piles, and on 22 April the final Dalton point was recovered by Phyllis from an area where the base of another dirt pile had been spread. That point was stolen the next week by an Arkansas State University student working in our laboratory. Ten years later a plain brown envelope arrived at our home with that point enclosed. There was no explanation or apology.

2
Bioarchaeology of the Sloan Site

KEITH W. CONDON AND JEROME C. ROSE

The 1974 excavations of the Sloan site produced numerous artifacts and 211 small fragments of bone from 141 cataloged locations (Table 2.1). The patterning of the artifacts recovered suggests that the Sloan site represents a Dalton cemetery, but designation as a cemetery requires establishing the presence of human remains at the site. The small size of the fragments made this a difficult task requiring the use of atypical osteological techniques. Two approaches were employed. The first was to compare the histological structure of the Sloan fragments with a series of reference histological sections derived from a variety of known species including *Homo sapiens;* the second was visual comparison between the Sloan fragments and a comparative archaeological collection of known vertebrates including prehistoric humans. The visual comparisons ultimately led to establishing the presence of human bone at the Sloan site.

METHODOLOGY

A series of articles by Enlow and Brown (1956, 1957, 1958) indicated that it is possible to distinguish between various vertebrate taxonomic groups using histological observation of bone thin sections. They proposed that bone tissue features can be classified as primary vascular, Haversian, or nonvascular, with the first two categories containing nine and three subtypes, respectively (Enlow and Brown 1956). Furthermore, their research demonstrated that the various taxa differ in the proportions of the various tissue types and subtypes present. We postulated that both the comparative data presented in those articles and in the reference collection of histological sections from known archaeological bones could be used to classify the Sloan bone fragments as either human or nonhuman.

The Sloan bone fragments were examined and a list of potential nonhuman identifications was prepared. The following archaeological specimens were obtained for comparison: deer antler (two), box turtle carapace (two), bear vertebra, bear cranium, pond turtle carapace, bobcat ulna, dog tibia, fox humerus, and pig humerus. In addition, the following archaeological human bones were added to the reference collection: humerus, radius, ulna, rib, clavicle, and frontal. Five of the best-preserved and morphologically different Sloan fragments were selected for initial observation: 74-107-40, 74-107-524, 74-107-546, 74-107-

Table 2.1
Sloan site bone provenience

Specimen No.	Grid Point	Depth (cm)	Code[a]
74-107-10	48.44 R 49.33	13	1
74-107-40	47.82 R 48.64	22	3
74-107-505	49.60 R 48.21	32	1
74-107-505	49.62 R 48.16	32	1
74-107-505	49.63 R 48.32	32	1
74-107-505	49.31 R 48.17	21	1
74-107-505	49.13 R 48.35	28	1
74-107-505	49.25 R 48.19	28	1
74-107-506	49.56 R 49.60	0	3
74-107-507	49.94 R 47.62	30	3
74-107-508	49.90 R 47.29	21	2
74-107-509	49.49 R 47.22	36	1
74-107-510	49.85 R 48.37	17	1
74-107-511	49.29 R 48.56	16	2
74-107-512	49.56 R 48.25	14	1
74-107-513	49.76 R 46.37	21	1
74-107-514	49.29 R 48.24	15	1
74-107-515	50.10 R 47.24	19	1
74-107-515	50.64 R 45.64	23	1
74-107-516	48.68 R 48.4	14	1
74-107-517	49 R 43.5	38	2
74-107-518	49.67 R 50.08	10	1
74-107-518	49.30 R 51.03	13	1
74-107-518	49.89 R 49.95	16	1
74-107-519	48.41 R 49.79	27	1
74-107-519	48.30 R 49.42	28	1
74-107-519	48.17 R 49.86	30	1
74-107-519	48.63 R 49.65	38	1
74-107-520	53.00 R 49.13	17	1
74-107-521	53.16 R 49.26	17	1
74-107-522	53.33 R 48.64	23	1
74-107-522	52.87 R 49.06	17	1
74-107-522	52.91 R 49.25	20	1
74-107-522	53.24 R 49.90	17	1
74-107-522	53.29 R 49.69	18	1
74-107-523	53.55 R 44.20	25	2
74-107-524	46.56 R 51.00	16	1
74-107-525	50.20 R 47.71	23	1
74-107-526	50.80 R 48.73	19	4
74-107-527	53.42 R 52.04	15	1
74-107-528	53.30 R 53.25	16	1
74-107-528	53.12 R 52.04	0	1
74-107-529	49 R 45	0	1
74-107-530	54.81 R 49.89	11	1
74-107-530	54.01 R 49.70	12	1
74-107-531	49.05 R 43.72	0	1
74-107-532	48.50 R 43.60	0	4
74-107-533	50.14 R 48.69	0	1
74-107-534	46.70 R 49.80	42	3
74-107-535	45.44 R 53.70	0	2
74-107-536	45.85 R 52.145	12	2
74-107-537	45.64 R 52.33	22	3
74-107-538	45.37 R 47.62	16	4
74-107-539	44.54 R 48.35	18	2
74-107-540	52.15 R 51.47	15	1
74-107-541	52.63 R 51.40	16	2
74-107-542	52.30 R 51.42	16	2
74-107-543	52.63 R 51.51	16	2
74-107-544	52.82 R 51.84	17	2
74-107-545	52.20 R 51.56	26	1
74-107-546	52.24 R 48.55	0	1
74-107-547	52.25 R 49.00	20	1
74-107-548	52.62 R 48.92	20	1
74-107-549	52.37 R 48.53	26	1
74-107-550	52.18 R 48.65	25	1
74-107-551	52.33 R 49.57	30	1
74-107-552	52.12 R 48.86	43	1
74-107-553	52.33 R 48.92	19	1
74-107-553	52.16 R 48.87	19	1
74-107-553	52.37 R 49.03	18	1
74-107-553	52.54 R 49.38	18	1
74-107-553	52.17 R 49.39	17	1
74-107-553	52.38 R 49.09	25	1
74-107-553	52.24 R 48.95	26	1
74-107-554	52.65 R 51.45	0	4
74-107-555	52.54 R 51.52	0	2
74-107-556	52.24 R 51.50	10	1
74-107-557	52.60 R 51.76	9	1
74-107-558	52.66 R 51.72	9	4
74-107-559	52.46 R 51.50	14	4
74-107-560	52.00 R 51.75	15	1
74-107-560	53.15 R 50.04	16	1
74-107-560	53.28 R 50.07	16	1
74-107-560	53.61 R 50.14	16	1
74-107-560	52.21 R 51.78	8	1
74-107-561	52.08 R 49.07	14	1
74-107-562	52.29 R 49.29	15	4
74-107-563	52.00 R 49.20	15	1
74-107-564	52.10 R 49.55	14	2
74-107-565	52.10 R 49.23	18	2
74-107-566	52.50 R 48.49	19	4
74-107-567	52.18 R 48.89	20	1
74-107-568	52.06 R 48.89	18	1
74-107-569	52.31 R 49.37	20	1
74-107-570	52.31 R 49.25	14	1
74-107-570	52.17 R 48.79	18	1

Continued on next page

Table 2.1
Continued

Specimen No.	Grid Point	Depth (cm)	Code[a]	Specimen No.	Grid Point	Depth (cm)	Code[a]
74-107-570	52.46 R 48.88	18	1	74-107-600	46.26 R 50.57	28	1
74-107-570	52.36 R 49.34	15	1	74-107-600	46.0 R 50.59	27	1
74-107-570	52.27 R 48.39	21	1	74-107-601	48.28 R 50.20	36	1
74-107-570	52.46 R 48.67	20	1	74-107-601	48.43 R 50.24	27	1
74-107-570	52.34 R 48.84	22	1	74-107-601	48.57 R 50.0	26	1
74-107-570	52.33 R 49.15	20	1	74-107-602	49.33 R 53.60	0	1
74-107-571	54.28 R 50.0	16	1	74-107-603	49.62 R 53.03	19	2
74-107-572	54.50 R 50.63	16	4	74-107-603	48.18 R 52.20	20	2
74-107-573	54.77 R 50.90	22	2	74-107-603	49.56 R 52.25	28	2
74-107-574	54.15 R 50.75	19	1	74-107-603	47.96 R 52.51	22	2
74-107-575	54.20 R 50.50	16	1	74-107-604	50.35 R 52.70	0	2
74-107-576	50.68 R 46.78	21	1	74-107-605	50.53 R 52.83	0	1
74-107-576	50.46 R 46.12	43	1	74-107-606	50.89 R 53.41	0	1
74-107-577	50.81 R 48.97	19	1	74-107-607	51.68 R 51.31	29	1
74-107-578	51.20 R 48.56	14	4	74-107-608	51.36 R 48.66	17	1
74-107-579	49.97 R 50.00	34	4	74-107-609	51.50 R 49.20	16	1
74-107-580	50.43 R 48.98	19	4	74-107-610	51.65 R 48.43	17	1
74-107-581	50.90 R 49.89	14	1	74-107-611	51.51 R 48.45	17	1
74-107-582	51.22 R 48.83	17	3	74-107-612	51.35 R 51.10	17	2
74-107-583	51.06 R 48.05	27	3	74-107-613	51.5 R 48.5	0	1
74-107-584	51.86 R 48.80	27	1	74-107-614	51.34 R 48.02	14	1
74-107-584	51.45 R 48.53	29	1	74-107-615	51.16 R 48.92	16	1
74-107-584	51.52 R 42.75	36	1	74-107-616	51.88 R 48.76	22	1
74-107-584	51.95 R 48.20	46	1	74-107-617	51.60 R 48.27	12	1
74-107-585	52.82 R 50.84	21	1	74-107-617	51.37 R 48.35	12	1
74-107-586	53.35 R 50.48	21	1	74-107-617	51.03 R 48.22	13	1
74-107-587	52.84 R 50.12	21	2	74-107-617	51.06 R 48.50	9	1
74-107-588	52.98 R 50.82	21	1	74-107-617	51.08 R 48.58	11	1
74-107-589	50.32 R 50.50	20	1	74-107-617	51.26 R 48.93	9	1
74-107-590	50.78 R 49.48	19	1	74-107-618	51.13 R 48.34	0	1
74-107-591	47.17 R 51.23	23	1	74-107-619	51.50 R 48.70	26	3
74-107-592	45.7 R 49.35	15	2	74-107-620	51.27 R 46.67	13	1
74-107-593	45.53 R 49.90	14	1	74-107-621	51.18 R 49.70	16	1
74-107-594	50.44 R 49.88	33	1	74-107-622	51.25 R 49.68	16	1
74-107-595	54.73 R 50.51	16	1	74-107-623	52.07 R 51.17	0	2
74-107-595	54.14 R 50.56	20	1	74-107-623	51.38 R 51.0	0	2
74-107-595	54.20 R 51.85	43	1	74-107-624	51.05 R 48.54	21	1
74-107-596	54.60 R 51.22	21	1	74-107-625	51.7 R 48.5	16	1
74-107-597	46.23 R 51.90	16	1	74-107-626	51.46 R 48.82	13	3
74-107-598	46.56 R 51.62	17	2	74-107-627	51.45 R 47.24	100	1
74-107-598	47.55 R 51.49	0	2	74-107-628	51.29 R 49.05	0	1
74-107-599	47.14 R 50.07	19	2	74-107-629	51.19 R 48.64	16	3
74-107-599	48.25 R 50.40	19	2	74-107-630	51.15 R 48.59	16	1
74-107-599	47.95 R 51.78	20	2	74-107-631	51.27 R 48.56	16	2
74-107-599	48.14 R 50.88	26	2	74-107-632	51.12 R 48.88	16	1
74-107-600	47.75 R 50.79	40	1	74-107-633	51.02 R 48.58	15	4
74-107-600	47.12 R 50.92	30	1	74-107-634	51.34 R 48.65	18	2
74-107-600	47.09 R 50.42	39	1	74-107-635	51.5 R 48.5	18	1

Table 2.1
Continued

Specimen No.	Grid Point	Depth (cm)	Code[a]
74-107-636	51.5 R 48.5	18	1
74-107-637	51.05 R 49.0	11	1
74-107-638	51.33 R 49.0	14	4
74-107-639	51.22 R 49.12	11	1
74-107-640	51.83 R 49.83	13	1
74-107-640	51.90 R 49.76	13	1
74-107-640	51.95 R 49.50	14	1
74-107-640	51.50 R 49.60	21	1
74-107-640	51.80 R 49.10	13	1
74-107-640	51.88 R 49.0	13	1
74-107-640	51.16 R 49.12	12	1
74-107-640	51.83 R 49.18	14	1
74-107-640	51.90 R 49.22	15	1
74-107-640	51.35 R 49.17	22	1
74-107-640	51.0 R 49.21	24	1
74-107-640	51.17 R 49.28	24	1
74-107-641	52.0 R 48.40	32	1
74-107-642	52.0 R 49.15	29	2
74-107-643	49 R 48.5	0	3

[a]1, human bone; 2, probably human bone; 3, indeterminate; 4, possibly nonhuman bone.

549, and 74-107-597. Portions of each of these bones were processed using standard hard tissue embedding and thin sectioning procedures (Condon 1981). All thin sections were covered with cover slips and examined with both transmitted white light and transmitted polarized light microscopes at 100 magnifications.

The second technique employed for identification of the Sloan skeletal fragments was visual examination and sorting. The visual sorting of small bone fragments obtained from screening and flotation processing of archaeological feature fill is a standard task in bioarchaeological analysis. These small fragments are often very useful in the analysis of human skeletal material; the nonhuman bone fragments need to be identified and provided to a faunal analyst for identification and interpretation. Because this task is routinely performed with consistently reliable results, it was decided that the process could be systematized and applied to the Sloan material.

Three visual criteria were established for segregating human and nonhuman skeletal fragments. The first criterion was the absence of trabecular bone (matrix of bone spicules) along the medullary surface of nonhuman long-bone diaphyses (shaft) (Murray 1936). Observation of large known faunal collections indicated that the most commonly found mammalian species on archaeological sites exhibit few or no trabeculae along the medullary surfaces of the diaphyses except at the midshaft region. When trabeculae are present in nonhuman material, the ratio of trabeculae to compact bone thickness is very low and the spaces between the trabeculae are relatively large. The second criterion was that nonhuman bone appears relatively dense and solid in contrast to human bone, which appears porous when observed in cross section. This difference is due to the increased development of secondary osteons (Haversian systems) in adult human bone and a higher overall vascularity. The third criterion was that the cortical surfaces of nonhuman bone appear denser, smoother, and nonporous in contrast to human bone surfaces, which are rougher in texture and appear porous upon examination. This last criterion was the least usable because of the extensive weathering and degradation of the Sloan fragments.

The 141 groups of Sloan fragments were sorted into five categories: (1) human bone, fragments that met all of the criteria; (2) probably human bone, fragments that met only one or two of the criteria; (3) indeterminate; (4) possibly nonhuman bone, fragments that met only one or two of the criteria for nonhuman bone; and (5) nonhuman bone, fragments that met all of the criteria for nonhuman bone (Figure 2.1). Count was by cataloged group in case fragments from one locus were actually parts of a single bone. The sorting process was conducted a second time with special attention focused upon the probably human bone and indeterminate categories. All fragments in the probably human bone category were examined and reclassified as either human bone or indeterminate because of the small size of the fragments. Similarly, all fragments in the indeterminate category were reassigned to the other

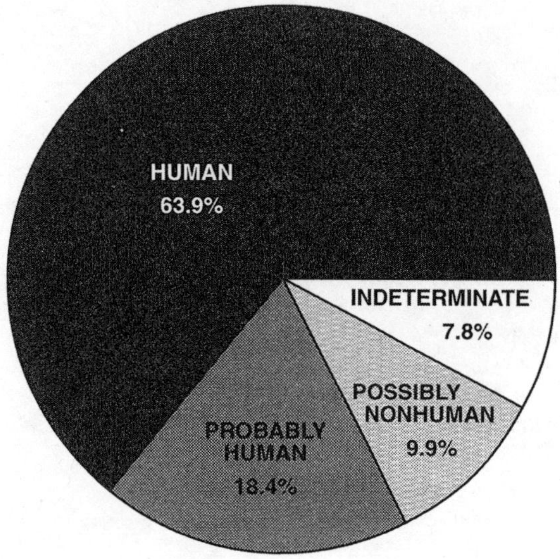

Figure 2.1 Breakdown of Sloan skeletal fragments by category.

categories or left indeterminate because of small size. The remaining categories were also restudied and reclassified where appropriate.

RESULTS

The Sloan bone fragments varied considerably in size, although they are all regarded as small (Figure 2.2). A typical large cranial fragment measures 2.03 by 1.87 by 0.28 centimeters, and a typical large long bone shaft fragment measures 3.03 by 1.06 by 0.60 centimeters. A typical small fragment measures 0.88 by 1.06 by 0.60 centimeters. All fragments exhibit a brownish tan color on the surface, and the interior bone is gray to white in color. The fragments are very friable and chalky in texture. Both the color and texture indicate that the entire organic matrix has been removed from the bone, which is consistent with burial in a sandy matrix with high water permeability.

The results of the histological observation of the selected five Sloan fragments are described individually. Sections from 74-107-40 display minimal histological structure, but a moderate number of osteons are present along with clearly defined circumferential lamellae. In all cases, the Haversian canals of the osteons are irregularly shaped and appear to be badly eroded. The periosteal surface is completely eroded and not observable.

Specimen 74-107-524 exhibits frequent osteons with good definition of the Haversian canals. Circumferential lamellae are observable, but again all periosteal lamellae have been lost to erosion.

No observations could be made of specimens 74-107-546 and 74-107-597 because of poor preservation, which prevented the preparation of usable thin sections.

Specimen 74-107-549 shows distinct circumferential lamellae and one distinct complete osteon. Again the periosteal region has been completely eroded. Fragments of what appear to be osteons were observed, but all of the Haversian canals are completely destroyed.

The results of the histological examinations were extremely disappointing. The bone was so poorly preserved that the histological structures were almost completely obscured by dense opaque staining, which is typical of poorly preserved bone. The opacity could not be removed by the standard oxidizing procedures employed, although they have produced satisfactory results in other skeletal analyses. There was no question that the three observable specimens were bone, and there were no features identified that suggested that these fragments were not human. On the other hand, the histological structures were not sufficiently preserved to enable histomorphological comparisons with the human and nonhuman reference histological collection.

Observational classification of the Sloan bone fragments produced more satisfactory results. Fragment 74-107-641 was identified as the right petrous portion of the temporal bone from a human skull. There is no question that at least one adult human skull was present at the Sloan site. In addition, there are five fragments that are unquestionably human: 74-107-608, a radius or ulna shaft; 74-107-609, a possible clavicle shaft; 74-107-613, clearly human long bone; 74-107-616, human cranial fragment; and 74-107-620, human cranial fragment. In total, ninety fragments (63.9%) were classified as human because they met all of the applicable criteria. An additional twenty-six fragments (18.4%) were classified as probably human because they met at least one or two of the appropriate criteria. With the exception of the right petrous bone, few of these fragments could be unquestionably identified as to their bone of origin. However, five fragments are cranial (74-107-553, 593, 616, 632, and 641), eight are probably juvenile cranial fragments (74-107-513, 533, 547, 549, 575, 577, 581, and 589), six are probably clavicle shaft fragments (74-107-509, 512, 521, 585, 609, and 622), six are from either radius or ulna shafts (74-107-514, 530, 608, 618, 627, and 639), four are probably ulna shafts (74-107-

Figure 2.2 Unquestionably human bone from the Sloan site: *a,* temporal, cat. no. 74-107-641 (AAS neg. 785553); *b,* radius or ulna, cat. no. 74-107-608 (AAS neg. 7855614); *c,* possibly a clavicle, cat. no. 74-107-609 (AAS neg. 785576); *d,* long bone, cat. no. 74-107-613 (AAS neg. 785583); *e,* cranial, cat. no. 74-107-616 (AAS neg. 785582); *f,* cranial, cat. no. 74-107-620 (AAS neg. 785589).

520, 524, 596, 636), two are probably from the tibia (74-107-546 and 624), one is either tibia or femur (74-107-611), and one is probably a femur shaft fragment (74-107-637). The variation in the thickness of the human cranial fragments suggests that both adults and juveniles (less than fourteen years of age) were interred at the Sloan site.

In total, eleven fragments (7.8%) are classified as indeterminate because they were too small to observe the required features. Possibly nonhuman fragments total fourteen (9.9%); they met one or two of the designated criteria. None are classified as definitely nonhuman by meeting all three criteria for that designation. The failure to identify at least one definitely nonhuman bone fragment strongly supports the conclusion that the Sloan site was a human cemetery.

CONCLUSION

The 141 Sloan groups of skeletal fragments are classified as human (63.9%), probably human (18.4%), indeterminate (7.8%), and possibly nonhuman (9.9%), and none as nonhuman (0.0%). Identification of one fragment as the right petrous portion of the temporal bone of a human skull indicates that at least one human skull was interred at the Sloan site. The identification of 63.9% of the fragments as human and the failure to identify any fragments as nonhuman clearly indicate that Sloan was a human burial area. The variation in thickness of the cranial fragments indicates the presence of both human adults and subadults younger than fourteen years of age. This observation has important ramifications for interpreting Dalton social organization.

3
Description of the Artifacts

DAN F. MORSE

In total, 439 artifacts were recovered in apparent Dalton deposits at the Sloan site. This number includes a very few found on the surface soon after the excavation had been backfilled. A detailed list by provenience is tabulated in chapter 6. A final summary by basic artifact category is given in Table 3.1.

The closest comparison we have is the Brand site. Brand was a living site, whether an extraction camp or a village. A total of 490 artifacts associated with Dalton features based on Goodyear (1974) helps indicate the uniqueness of Sloan. There are less bifaces (17), points (74), adzes (1), end scrapers (26), and abraders (17) at Brand. There are more point (116) and adze (40) fragments, retouched flakes (88), *pièces esquillées* (63), cobble tools (23), and pebble cores (25). Absent at Brand are backed unifaces, chert discoid hammers, and edge abraded cobbles. Debitage, probably including utilized flakes, was present in large numbers at the Brand site but has not been analyzed.

CHERT SOURCES

One of the most intriguing characteristics of Dalton sites in the central Mississippi Valley lowlands is the abundance of good-quality cherts. Not only is the quality good, but many discarded chert artifacts are large enough to be recycled. A site with a substantial Dalton assemblage is easily recognized because of the varieties of colors and the quality of workmanship. However chert is only available in the uplands.

Dalton knappers had easy access to outcrops that must have become increasingly less accessible to later occupations. In addition there were far fewer knappers at 10,500 B.P. than at 3,000 B.P., when quality of chert and of workmanship seems inferior to casual observers. However, high chert quality is also very evident in the Mississippian periods when population approached two hundred times that of the Dalton period.

Evidently there was a need for good cherts to be distributed throughout the central Mississippi Valley in the Dalton period. The chert debitage and discarded artifacts at Dalton sites include a variety of colorful stones that are high quality in texture. Because of what I interpret to be wasteful consumption of this resource, Dalton needs appear to have been as sociological as they were technological. There also seems to have been a constant need. If, as has been interpreted, there was a network (macroband) of

Table 3.1
Summary of artifacts by basic artifact category

Artifact	No. Recovered
Dalton point	146
Adze	42
Biface	92
Broken biface tool	3
End scraper	33
Backed uniface	9
Perforator	2
Retouched flake	22
Utilized flake	35
Chert discoid hammer	3
Pièce esquillée	1
Chert chopper/core	1
Pebble core	4
Sandstone abrader	35
Edge-abraded cobble	1
Cobble abrader	4
Ocher	5
Ironstone object	1
Total	439

a half dozen local groups (microbands) in the central valley, chert distribution may have been a means of keeping this network intact. Because the sites are mostly located within the delta (see Figure 9.1), chert was not immediately available to most of the population. Band territories have been equated to watersheds. Each watershed in the central valley is connected to an upland, and each watershed upland provides access to one or more major chert sources. The surface geology of the Ozark portion of the central valley is temporally sequential north to south so that a single chert formation usually outcrops in only one specific location (Figure 3.1).

CROWLEY'S RIDGE CHERT. The closest chert sources to the Sloan site are the gravels of Crowley's Ridge (Call 1891). Most gravel occurs in streambeds. The gravels are part of the Lafayette Formation, which varies in thickness and is located between Tertiary sands and clays and the Quaternary loesses that constitute the final deposit on the ridge. Most of the gravels are light colored and well rounded, usually brown and tan cherts, and also include gray quartzite. Some chert is quite colorful with mottled red, purple, and other bright shades. The ultimate source may be the Appalachian Highlands, possibly including some western Great Lakes stone sources. Similar gravels occur on the edge of the Ozarks, but it is logical to assume that cherts found at sites were most probably derived from the closest source. Light-colored cherts, particularly with evidence of cortex, at the Sloan site are assumed to have originated from Crowley's Ridge.

PITKIN CHERT. The Ozark Escarpment contains many cherts that can be obtained from formation outcrops or from nearby stream gravels. The most recognizable chert is a Mississippian formation, Pitkin Chert, which is plentiful immediately south and west of Oil Trough, located near the confluence of the White and Black Rivers. These cherts are various shades of black.

OZARK CHERT. Along the Ozark Escarpment and along streams that feed into the Black River in Arkansas are numerous cherts. They tend to be difficult to separate, with rare exceptions, and are little studied from the standpoint of recognition away from their outcrop position. North and northeast of Oil Trough are Mississippian, Devonian, and Ordovician formations that contain distinctive cherts: Boone, Penters, and Everton. Evidently the formations from just south of Oil Trough to about Black Rock were the sources of most of the Ozark chert for the people at the Sloan site.

Everton Cherts are often oolitic or brecciated, and colors range widely but are mostly blue-gray. Penters Chert is a white and mottled tan stone. Boone is extremely variable in color but generally light. Geologists consider it difficult to identify this chert away from its source. Wherever possible I identify or guess at the specific chert but mostly only differentiate it as "Ozark chert."

COTTER CHERT. Northward, near Pocahontas, are outcrops of a major Missouri chert called Cotter–Jefferson City, which is also Ordovician. It is not considered good for knapping purposes. Very few examples of that characteristically white-gray banded chert are represented in the Sloan-site assemblage.

CRESCENT QUARRY CHERT. Many of the artifacts are made of a white chert, often with tans, but occasionally including shades of reds, purples, and other colors, that matches the chert used in Emergent Mississippian (A.D. 800–1000) at the Zebree site in northeastern Arkansas and at Cahokia for microliths. I have visited the quarries south

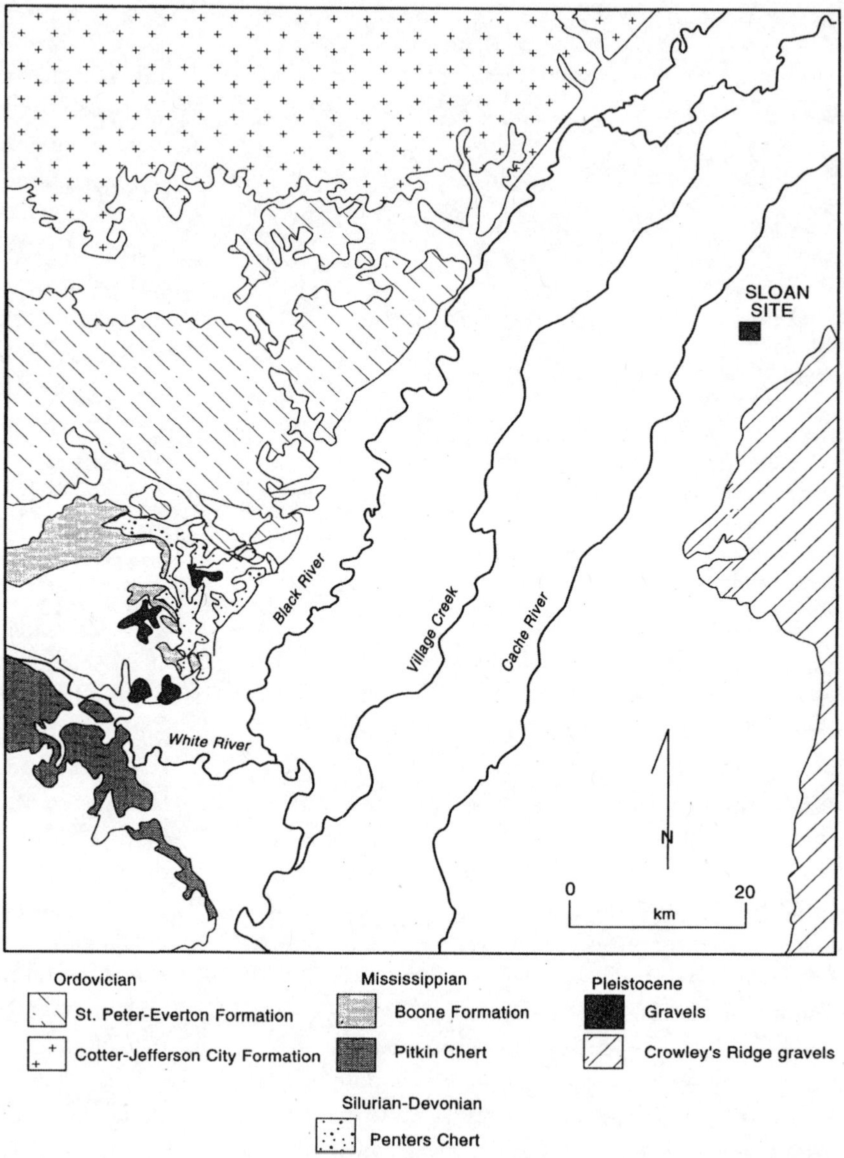

Figure 3.1 Chert sources in northeastern Arkansas in relation to the Sloan site (after Mathis 1980).

of St. Louis along the Meramec River with Leonard Blake of St. Louis (Morse and Morse 1983:205, fig. 10.3; see also Fowke 1928:533–536 and Ives 1975). To ensure that our identifications were correct and to broaden them, we invited Brad Koldehoff, lithic specialist who knows this chert best, to examine all of the artifacts found at Sloan. Crescent Quarry Chert is part of the Burlington Formation, which produces high-quality cherts in a much larger area of Missouri than where Crescent Quarry Chert outcrops.

The manufacture of large Dalton points was possible through the use of Burlington/Crescent Quarry Chert. The gravels of Crowley's Ridge and the Ozark chert outcrops did not produce enough good-quality stone of sufficient size to make the largest points. Although Crescent Quarry Chert undoubtedly was available through trade, there would probably have been minimal problems for Dalton knappers to visit the quarries and obtain their own material.

SLOAN ARTIFACTS WITH DALTON FEATURES

POINTS. A remarkable collection of 146 Dalton points ranging up to 19 centimeters in length was recovered from the excavation. This represents almost 15% of the Dalton points contained in our total northeastern Arkansas collection. It is amazing that only a very few of the points are incomplete. Two are missing minute tips that have broken off since excavation (131, 317). Two are artifacts made on broken points (221, 248). One has both ears missing (25), and three (4, 56, 185) have one ear missing. Four have small tips missing (173, 249, 264, 305). Specimen 249 appears to have sustained an impact fracture. Only three points are represented by fragments. One (491) consists of part of the base and midsection. One is a tip (183). The other (252) has lost an ear and the lateral edge of the base, probably as a result of an impact. No other Paleoindian deposit to my knowledge has produced such a large number of complete points.

SLOAN POINT. Specimen 133 (Figure 3.2) was named after Frank Sloan, who so unselfishly helped us excavate the Sloan site, which he discovered. In my opinion, only one Sloan point was found at the Sloan site. Sloan points have been reported from other locations in northeastern Arkansas, southeastern Missouri, and southern Illinois, and the largest one reported (unfortunately lost) measured 38 centimeters in length (Anonymous 1948). The Sloan-site specimen measures 19 centimeters in length.

Specimen 133 is made of Burlington Chert. It is essentially triangular and well thinned basally but is not noticeably ground on the base or laterally. I do not think it was intended to be hafted and probably was not meant to be used, at least as an ordinary butchering or cutting tool.

The 38-centimeter-long point mentioned above was found near Crab Orchard Lake in southern Illinois. Another Sloan point is pictured in an adjoining frame with six large Daltons (Anonymous 1948). It is from a site now under a reservoir located near Johnson City, Illinois, and must measure about 20 centimeters long. The six large Daltons must measure about 12–15 centimeters in length, although the distortion evident in the photograph makes it difficult to be very accurate. All other points pictured are Dalton or at least Pleistocene in age.

Sloan points have been found at other sites in northeastern Arkansas. One measuring 30 centimeters is from an unknown site in Jackson County (Morse and Morse 1983:fig. 4.5*a;* Gilcrease Collection). Two reportedly measuring about 30 centimeters in length were found together on an unknown site in White County (private collection). One found at an unknown site in Poinsett County measures about 25 centimeters long (private collection). The only one known to me from southeastern Missouri measures about 27 centimeters long and was found at an unknown site in St. Genevieve County (private collection).

LARGE DALTON POINTS. Although there is a clear continuity in size within this group of Dalton points from the Sloan site, some stand out as being much larger than normal (Figure 3.2). Without doubt, the most impressive is specimen 294, 18 centimeters in length and clearly made of Crescent Quarry Chert. It is heavily ground at the base. A tip (183) possibly from a point almost as large as 294 but probably no smaller than about 13 centimeters, is made of Ozark chert, probably from the Everton Formation.

Specimen 216 is made of Crescent Quarry Chert, and specimens 265 and 462 are made of Burlington Chert. These three are unresharpened points measuring 13 centimeters long. Other Burlington Chert points are numbers 138, 362, and 414. The first two have definitely been resharpened. Number 138 is beveled, and specimen 362, the shortest in the group, appears to have been broken and then resharpened. Three points with very similar outlines and made of a similar Ozark (possibly Everton) chert are numbers 113, 165, and 428. Another Ozark chert (possibly Everton) point is number 108. Specimens 118, 277, 278, and 403 appear to be Ozark chert (possibly Penters). Number 118 has been resharpened and is beveled. Points made of Ozark (possibly Boone) chert are numbers 174, 181, 275, 295, and 445. Specimens 174 and 295 are resharpened and beveled. They still measure 14 and 12 centimeters in length. Two points have been identified as possible Cotter Chert. They are numbers 23 (resharpened and beveled) and 314. Two points were identified as Crowley's Ridge chert. These points are numbers 6 and 128.

A total of twenty-five large points measure 8 to 18 centimeters in length. Average length is 11 centimeters. All but two are made of nonlocal chert. Seven are made of Burlington/Crescent Quarry Chert. Only six were obviously resharpened: one probably because of breakage and the rest as beveled knives.

BEVELED DALTON POINTS. The remaining 110 Dalton points measure 8 centimeters or less in length and appear to be typical of the points found at other Dalton-period sites in northeastern Arkansas. The only difference is that almost all of them are complete and unused. A basic separation is into beveled (Figure 3.3) and unbeveled points

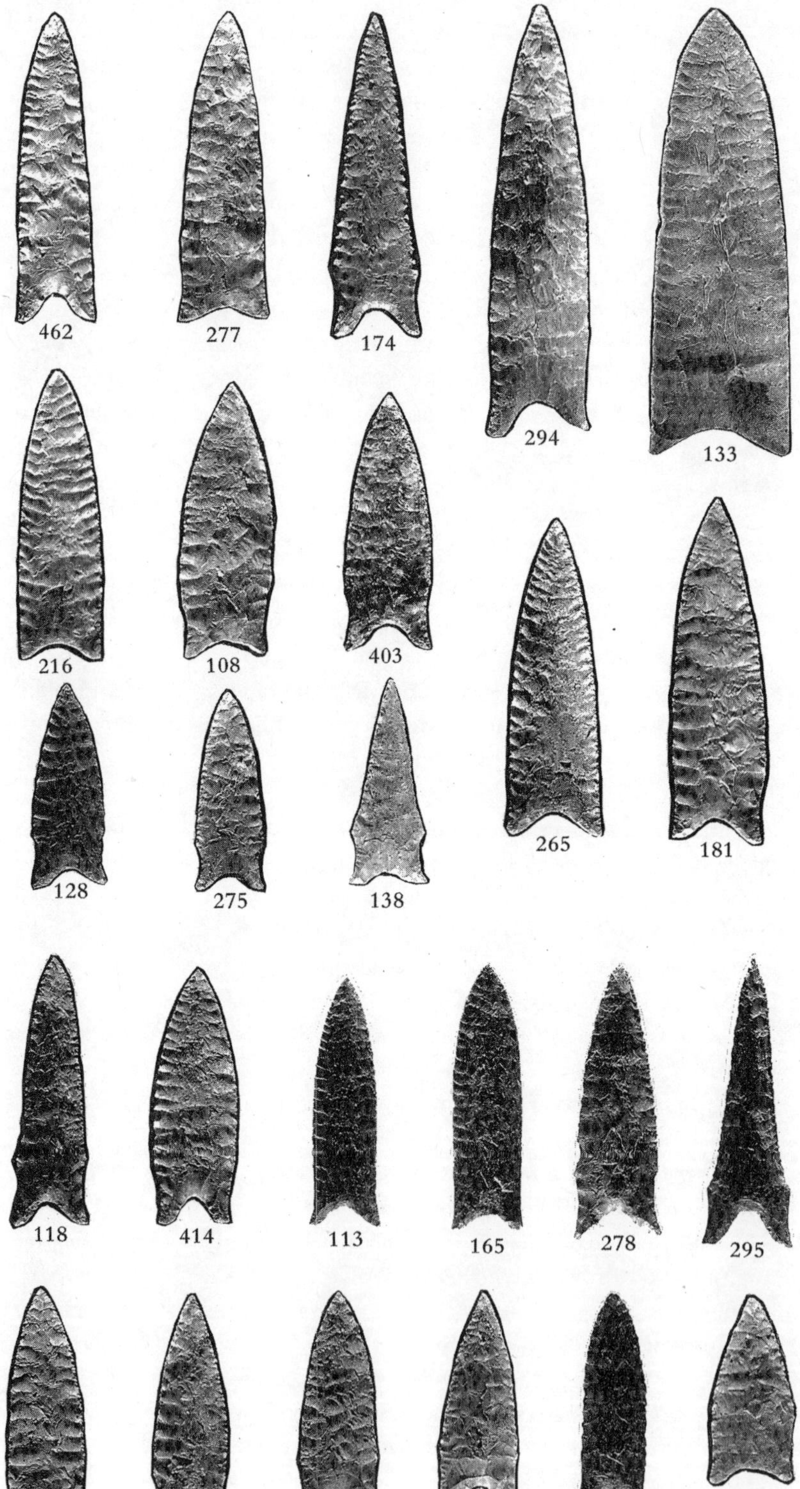

Figure 3.2 Large Dalton points and Sloan point (133) at the Sloan site. Numbers are catalog numbers keyed to tables. Artifacts are approximately one-fourth actual size.

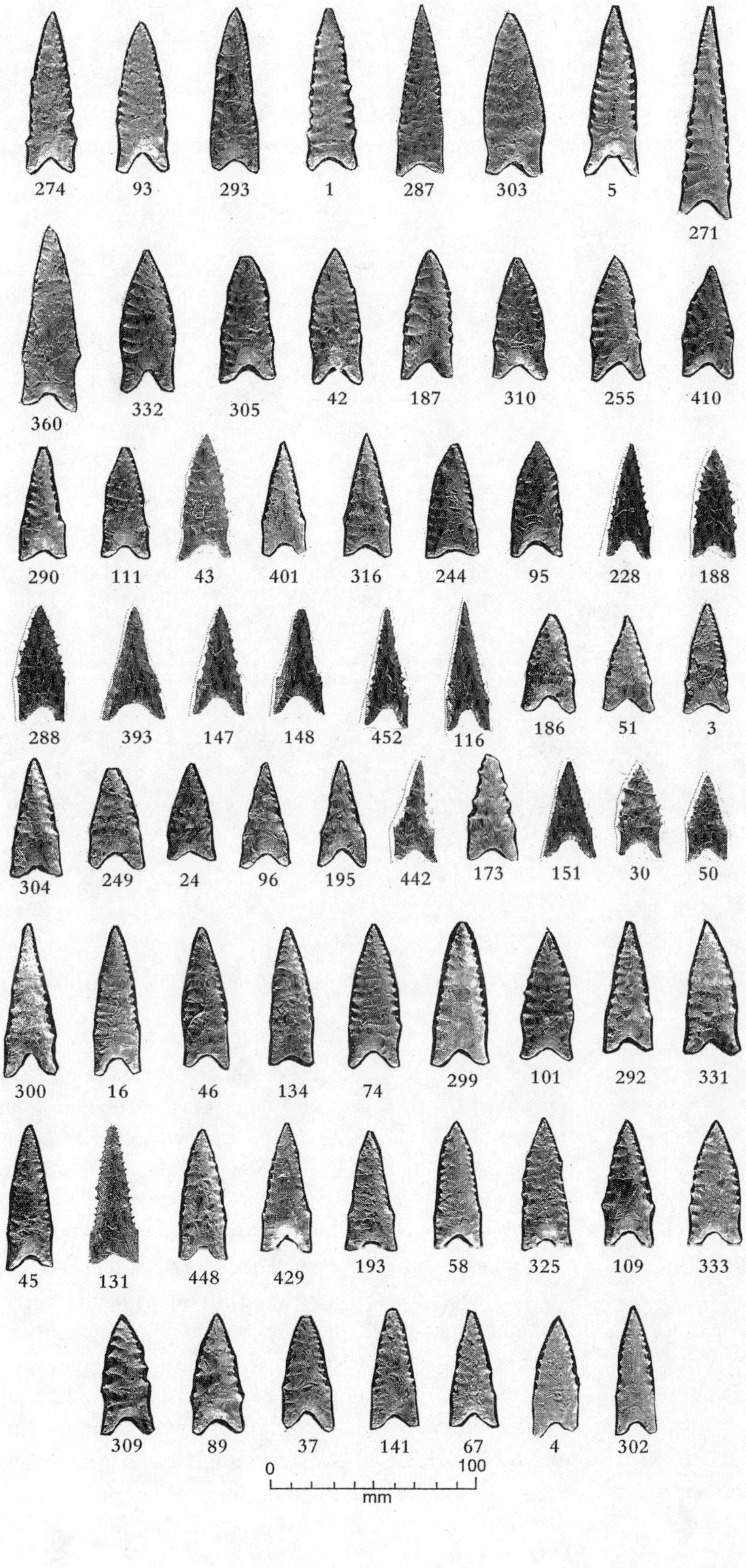

Figure 3.3 Beveled Dalton points at the Sloan site. Numbers are catalog numbers keyed to tables. Artifacts are approximately one-fourth actual size.

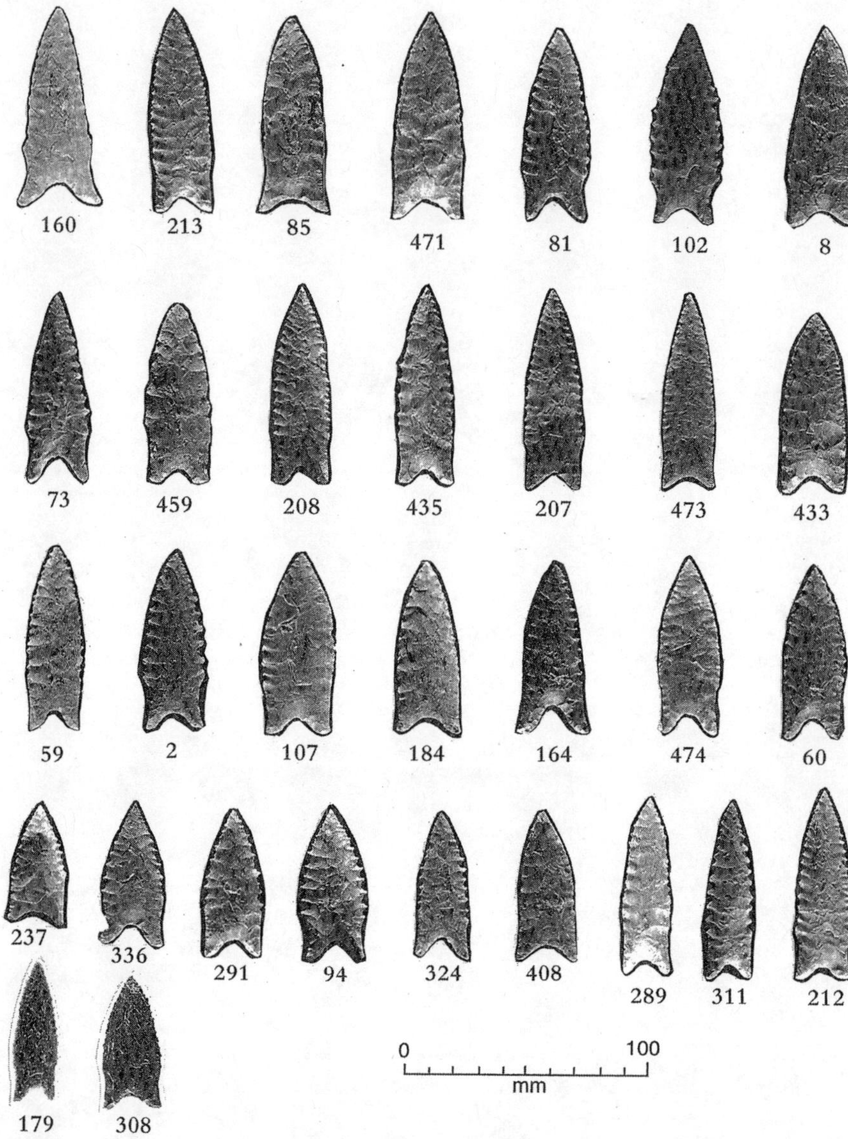

Figure 3.4 Unbeveled Dalton points at the Sloan site. Numbers are catalog numbers keyed to tables. Artifacts are approximately one-fourth actual size.

(Figure 3.4). Subcategories are serrated and unserrated. Unbeveled points can be further divided into unresharpened and probably resharpened. All beveled points appear to have been resharpened. This is the reason they are beveled with distinct shoulders. By unifacially resharpening edges off a platform made smooth through use, the knapper was able to extend the life span of a knife through more resharpening stages than if the resharpening had been bifacial. Serrations were advantageous because (1) the cutting edge was saw-toothed and (2) the worn-down serrations themselves could be used as the platforms for the new edge.

There are seventy-two typical serrated or denticulated beveled Dalton points in the collection. Another three points (148, 360, 393) are distinctly beveled but lack the prominent serrations. The large beveled Dalton points (23, 118, 138, 174, 278, 295) are not included in this discussion. Specimen 23 is not a typical beveled point; it is only beveled near the tip.

All of the seventy-two beveled serrated points exhibit what is known as a "right-hand" bevel. When the point is held with the tip away from the observer, the bevel is on the right-hand side. For the knapper to retouch a "right-hand" beveled point with pressure exerted downward, the tip would have to be oriented toward the knapper. It is interesting that almost all beveled Dalton points found in northeastern Arkansas are "right-hand" beveled. Early Holocene beveled points, on the other hand, are almost all "left-hand" beveled. The few exceptions to the rule are interpreted as indicating that the knapper was probably left-handed. One point (134) at Sloan is "left-hand" beveled near the base and "right-hand" beveled at the tip. Presumably this point was reoriented during the resharpening process or the knapper changed the pressure direction.

Two additional Pitkin Chert points (148, 393) have distinct bevels but lack prominent serrations. Both edges feel sharp with very fine serrations. A third point (360) of Ozark chert is beveled on the left side, and there were obvious problems in the resharpening process, with excessive bifacial retouch midway along one edge that was unsuccessful in thinning the edge at that location. The point is uneven as a result.

Twenty-two of the beveled points are probably made of Crowley's Ridge Chert. Very few are colorful. Eight points are made of Pitkin Chert (116, 131, 147, 148, 151, 228, 393, 452). Two points are probably made of Cotter Chert (173, 401). There are twelve points probably made of Ozark (Penters) chert (4, 5, 51, 74, 101, 271, 287, 290, 299, 302, 332, 448). There are eighteen points apparently made of Ozark (Everton) chert (30, 42, 43, 45, 50, 96, 185, 186, 264, 300, 304, 305, 316, 333, 360, 410, 442, 1414). Twelve points may be made from Ozark (Boone) chert (1, 16, 89, 188, 244, 249, 255, 274, 288, 293, 303, 331). One point (58) is made of Burlington Chert.

UNBEVELED DALTON POINTS. There are thirty-five unbeveled Dalton points, not including the nineteen large Daltons discussed earlier. Twenty-two are serrated, twenty of which are fairly typical of what I have interpreted newly made Daltons or Daltons only resharpened once should look like. When impact fractures are found on Dalton points in northeastern Arkansas, the points mostly look like those included in this group of twenty (Albert C. Goodyear, personal communication). One serrated point (237) appears to be a reworked broken Dalton point. Another serrated point (179) is much narrower than usual and would almost fit into a sort of miniature class. It is very well made.

Eleven points do not have prominent serrations. Five (107, 184, 408, 435, 459) would be classified as preforms were it not for the fact they are basally ground, two of them heavily. Three points (8, 85, 160) seem, based on the width of the base in comparison to the width and length of the point, to have been resharpened. One point (474) is almost stemmed, with long (34 mm) flutes on both faces. Similar points exist in our collections, and this may be a distinct category or type worth investigating. However, the Sloan assemblage makes it obvious that as a "type" it is rare. Two points are smaller broken specimens. One (317) was broken accidentally when it dropped onto the concrete laboratory floor. It is made of Pitkin Chert and may be unresharpened even though it is small. The other (25) is crude and missing two ears. It is made of Ozark (Cotter) chert.

Eighteen points appear to have been made from Crowley's Ridge Chert cobbles. Some (94, 102, 207, 208, 291, 435) are extremely colorful, a characteristic of Dalton debitage. Three points (160, 184, 473) are made of Burlington Chert and one (474) of Crescent Quarry Chert.

The remainder seem to be made of Ozark cherts. One (25) is Cotter Chert. Three are Pitkin Chert (56, 308, 317). Four appear to be Ozark (Everton) chert (73, 81, 179, 289). Three possibly may be Ozark (Boone) chert (207, 212, 324). Two (59, 60) are probably made of Ozark (Penters) chert.

AWLS (27, 68, 77, 122, 221, 420). All six are made on Dalton points (Figure 3.5). Each had been removed from its haft and rechipped into a drill-like shape. However all have sharp distal lateral edges and do not appear to have been used as drills. This same observation has been made on other drill-shaped artifacts made on Dalton points. It is interesting that specimen 221 is broken diagonally across its base. The break feels smooth to the touch and evidently has been treated lightly with an abrasive. We have postulated that these artifacts were hand-held and used as a sort of awl. Specimen 122 is made of Burlington Chert, and number 221 is made of Ozark chert (probably Boone). The other four Dalton-point awls are probably made of Crowley's Ridge Chert. All exhibit very slight tip wear and at least minute step fractures laterally, but this treatment could have been done deliberately by the knapper to minimize damage and/or to strengthen the awl during use.

BURINS (36, 120). Specimen 36 is made of Crowley's Ridge Chert (Figure 3.5). The Dalton point was made into a dihedral burin with a 2-millimeter-wide but skewed chisel tip. The very slight possible polish observed under magnification is concentrated on a tip that measures less than a millimeter wide. The other burin, also made of

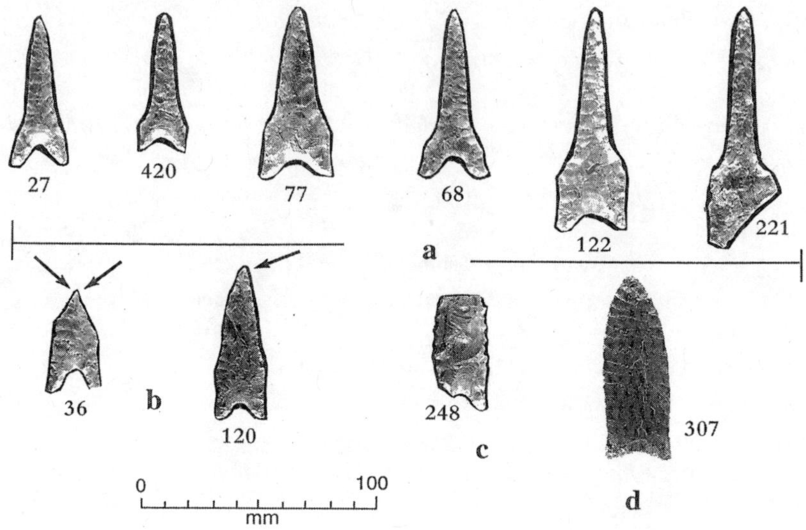

Figure 3.5 Other Dalton points at the Sloan site: *a,* awls; *b,* burins; *c,* scraper; and *d,* preform. Numbers are catalog numbers keyed to tables. Artifacts are approximately one-fourth actual size.

Crowley's Ridge Chert, had a single flake removed from the tip with the result similar to the other specimen. The evident polish is also slight but a little more obvious, with possible striations under high magnification.

BROKEN DALTON SCRAPER (248). Made of Ozark chert (possibly Penters), this Dalton point is missing an ear and tip. The broken distal surface is thinned and exhibits numerous step fractures. The other face exhibits some step fractures but is still a fairly sharp edge (Figure 3.5).

PREFORM (307). Made of Pitkin Chert, this biface is the only accepted Dalton point preform found at Sloan (Figure 3.5). It is what Goodyear termed "completed preform stage" (1974:24–25). It is very well made despite the presence of cortexlike imprints at both ends and on one face.

Table 3.2 is extremely detailed and overwhelming, to say the least. Examples of the kinds of summaries that are possible are presented in Figures 3.6–3.9. It was concluded from these analyses that these points represent a relatively brief temporal span of point manufacture by a single population. A less significant fit such as length versus width at midpoint is probably due to the resharpening process.

The mean maximum length of large Dalton points (not counting the Sloan point) is 111.5 millimeters with a standard deviation of 19 millimeters. The range is 81.2 to 147.4 millimeters. Mean maximum width is 34 millimeters and maximum thickness 8.4 millimeters.

The sizes of beveled and unbeveled points are very similar. Mean maximum lengths are 61.8 and 63.7 millimeters, respectively, with standard deviations of 11.6 and 11.9 millimeters. The range of beveled points is 41.8 to 99.9 millimeters, and of unbeveled points 44.5 to 93.8 millimeters. Mean maximum widths are 22.7 and 23 millimeters, respectively, and mean maximum thickness is 6.4 millimeters for both categories.

Figures 3.6–3.8 clearly demonstrate that the points cluster by length. An overwhelming majority of the values derived from David Anderson's Pearson's Correlation Analysis are high. In contrast, the bifaces do not cluster so tightly (Figure 3.9). Size seems more of a correlate of the size of the original raw material. They probably were hand-held so that size was evidently not as important as it was for points that were hafted in foreshafts. Bruce Bradley (chapter 4) emphasizes that the bifaces as a class are not preforms for points. There is a major difference in the technology of production, the raw material is substantially different, and most of the bifaces are simply too narrow to be made into points.

ADZES. There are forty-two adzes and adze preforms in the collection (Figure 3.10). The preforms are so similar to the finished adzes that they were included in Table 3.3. Eight (15, 157, 224, 280, 281, 354, 485, 487) are finished except for lateral grinding and some bit thinning. In fact, one (281) still has a cortexed bit. Three (425, 426, 488) are lightly ground laterally and still need some bit refinement.

Specimen number 427 was not included as a preform because despite being only lightly ground much of the butt is cortexed and may not have needed grinding. In addition, the bit appears to be ready to use. All the other adzes are heavily ground laterally and lightly to heavily ground over the faces of the end that was hafted.

This group is extraordinary. If interpretations are correct, this assemblage represents about a century, or less, of an early portion of the Dalton period. Despite the proliferation of extremely well-crafted Native American wooden objects, including masks with movable parts, archaeologists are reluctant to infer an earlier, prehistoric ability to craft wood with stone tools. Discoveries in the Florida Glades region have demonstrated that wooden art was much more versatile than ceramics, shell, bone, or lithic art (Gilliland 1975).

The lack of formal woodworking tools in Pleistocene deposits may be more a lack of recognition on the part of archaeologists than a lack of native sophistication. Steel tools are better than stone tools in most situations. Not only can they be made to uniform dimensions but mistakes can be recast or reforged. In addition, steel tools are much easier to resharpen and last longer. Hafting is much easier and more secure. But this does not mean stone tools are not adequate woodworking implements. A good craftsman can do wonders with the crudest tools, as an examination of Ozark and Appalachian make-do tools can amply demonstrate.

It was postulated almost thirty years ago that the locally termed "turtle backed scrapers" were probably adzes (Morse and Goodyear 1973). This was not met with universal approval (comments on a paper rejected by *American Antiquity*) presumably because the Dalton adze would represent one of the earliest, if not the earliest formal adzes in the world. It is odd that very few Dalton-period adzes have been recognized outside northeastern Arkansas. This may be due to an apparent climax of the American Paleolithic being limited to this region. The ground-stone grooved ax is coincidental with the beginnings of horticulture and hence land clearing in the eastern United States, whereas the adze was present in the Pleistocene period at a location where the artifact inventory was larger than expected and more stable settlement has been inferred.

There is enough variety in shape to suggest that a variety of woodworking tasks were accomplished with these tools. Some of the adzes are smaller and more oval (53, 223, 227, 427). The other adzes tend to be essentially triangular to almost trapezoidal. All were made on chert cobbles, most or all of which were obtained from the Crowley's Ridge deposits.

The adzes all tend to have a flattened, slightly convex ventral surface and a pronounced convex dorsal surface. In longitudinal cross section, they are plano-convex except for the bit. Bits are gougelike. The dorsal surface is convex and the ventral surface concave. The working edge or bit itself is convex. On some adzes the bit is almost pointed, but in others the bit is rounded with a tendency for pronounced edges.

Selection of a cobble to make into an adze must have been done carefully so that only minimum retouch was necessary. Specimen 281 exhibits cortex at both ends. Most (twenty-seven) of the adzes exhibit cortex on the base, and some (seven) have retained substantial cortex on part of one face. There is an excellent correlation between length and weight (Figure 3.11), but other correlations seem to reflect the irregular size of cobbles available to make into minimally modified edged tools (Figure 3.12).

Based on earlier observations on Dalton adzes, I think that the pointed bits were used to aid penetration into the wood. As the adze wore and/or was resharpened into a more rounded configuration, the corners were utilized to aid penetration of the adze into wood. Striations observed on polished facets on the rounded ventral bit surface are straight, an indication of an adze use rather than an ax function. Axes are swung in an arc, attached to a handle with the blade face parallel with the handle, causing curved striations on both faces. Adzes are swung in an arc, but the blade surfaces are perpendicular to the handle. Penetration striations are straight and occur primarily on one face (Semenov 1964:122–135).

All of the adzes appear to have been made of Crowley's Ridge Chert cobbles. Half of the Pearson's Correlation values determined by David Anderson were higher than 0. 5. Despite a size dependence on the original cobble size, they were carefully selected in terms of length and weight and many other physical attributes.

As a group the adzes range from eleven unfinished examples to four that are evidently exhausted (177, 204, 223, 341). The latter four are small, crude, and exhibit a damaged bit. The remaining twenty-seven adzes have sharp bits. Some bits are lightly ground. All exhibit some bit step fractures on the dorsal surface. Most also exhibit light wear and/or polish on the ventral surface. One (99)

Table 3.2
Measurements of points

Catalog No.	Maximum Length (mm)	Maximum Length of Stem (mm)	Maximum Length of Body (mm)	Maximum Width at Base (mm)	Maximum Width of Stem (mm)	Distance from Base to Maximum Width of Stem (mm)	Maximum Width at Shoulder (mm)
1	75.8	16.1	59.7	22.3	19.3	13.1	21.4
2	71.9	20.6	51.3	23.7	19.9	11.5	25.7
3	52.2	13.7	38.5	22.3	18.2	9.2	20.4
4	57.4	19.0	39.5	—*	20.5	8.0	21.7
5	80.1	20.2	59.9	25.5	19.5	17.3	22.5
6	89.9	18.4	71.5	31.9	30.5	7.0	33.4
8	80.5	18.9	61.6	26.3	25.1	9.2	28.9
16	69.9	19.5	50.4	21.4	20.2	4.4	21.3
23	92.1	23.6	68.5	32.8	31.6	14.7	33.6
24	45.5	11.3	34.2	21.7	19.3	6.6	20.3
25	48.0+*	14.2+*	33.8	—*	18.9	9.6	19.7
27	60.6	12.7	47.9	23.1	—	—	17.1
30	46.4	13.2	33.2	22.0	19.1	9.5	21.2
36	44.5	15.7	28.8	22.9	—	—	20.9
37	54.3	21.1	33.2	24.5	22.2	9.8	23.1
42	62.7	17.5	45.2	27.7	20.4	8.7	23.0
43	60.7	17.6	43.4	26.0	20.9	12.2	23.3
45	66.8	16.5	50.3	20.6	18.5	8.8	19.5
46	66.4	19.8	46.6	20.3	19.1	14.4	20.2
50	41.8	14.4	26.4	19.6	18.9	8.2	20.4
51	45.7	13.8	31.9	24.6	21.3	11.7	22.2
56	60.7	19.6	46.4	—*	21.4	7.3	23.1
58	59.7	16.3	43.4	21.0	20.7	6.2	21.3
59	74.1	22.4	51.7	22.8	21.9	11.2	23.3
60	67.6	22.1	45.5	22.2	22.1	7.7	23.4
68	69.6	13.6	56.0	29.4	—	—	25.0
73	75.4	19.9	55.5	25.3	22.3	12.9	25.5
74	67.1	19.9	47.2	23.4	21.3	8.8	24.5
77	70.7	20.1	50.6	30.0	27.1	15.8	27.4
81	76.6	19.2	57.4	24.3	21.6	11.1	26.7
85	78.2	23.3	54.9	23.2	22.4	15.6	24.7
89	55.0	14.9	40.1	23.4	20.7	10.7	23.7
93	70.8	22.0	48.8	24.0	21.2	12.5	22.9
94	60.9	18.8	42.1	24.2	21.5	8.7	26.6
95	55.6	14.7	40.9	23.4	21.5	9.4	22.5
96	49.8	13.8	36.0	23.3	21.0	10.1	21.7
101	58.9	18.1	40.8	23.0	19.9	10.8	22.9
102	79.1	16.6	62.5	23.6	21.0	8.6	28.2
107	73.3	20.6	52.7	26.3	25.5	7.0	27.9
108	114.7	20.0	94.7	36.7	32.5	9.9	35.5
109	56.5	16.7	39.8	21.7	19.3	9.8	22.6
111	52.0	13.8	38.2	22.0	19.3	7.1	20.0
113	106.5	21.7	84.8	31.0	26.4	15.3	27.5
116	63.6	16.7	46.9	21.4	20.3	16.9	21.4
118	114.6	28.8	85.8	32.3	26.7	19.4	31.0
120	62.1	19.9	42.2	20.0	19.0	10.8	19.9
122	93.4	24.3	69.1	29.4	27.7	14.8	28.7
128	84.3	20.2	64.1	32.3	27.1	15.2	30.5

Maximum Width of Body (mm)	Distance from Base to Maximum Width of Body (mm)	Width at Midpoint of Body (mm)	Basal Depth (mm)	Maximum Thickness of Stem (mm)	Distance from Base to Maximum Thickness of Stem (mm)	Maximum Thickness of Body (mm)	Distance from Base to Maximum Thickness of Body (mm)	Artifact Weight (g)
22.8	17.3	15.4	5.7	4.9	16.1	6.3	27.9	8.4
25.9	26.7	21.6	6.8	6.0	14.8	6.0	23.9	10.4
18.0	16.4	14.1	4.4	4.9	13.7	6.7	23.7	5.0
20.8	22.5	16.6	8.8	4.0	17.7	4.5	33.2	5.4
21.5	25.1	17.1	9.6	6.0	20.2	6.2	22.2	9.2
32.8	22.7	26.1	6.6	7.2	18.4	7.7	25.8	21.8
28.4	25.3	21.0	5.9	5.6	18.9	7.6	48.6	15.7
19.8	21.1	13.9	7.5	4.6	19.5	5.6	31.5	7.2
33.1	26.8	24.9	8.3	7.6	23.6	8.0	39.1	22.7
20.4	15.2	15.2	4.2	4.5	11.3	6.5	22.0	4.4
21.0	22.2	17.8	—*	5.4	14.2	5.5	15.4	5.7
14.2	17.6	8.4	8.5	6.3	12.7	6.8	18.4	5.8
23.7	16.8	17.4	6.7	5.4	13.2	6.8	14.9	5.4
19.7	21.6	15.0	8.4	4.2	15.7	5.4	20.7	4.2
20.3	24.2	15.2	10.8	5.8	15.7	6.9	22.9	6.3
23.9	21.5	19.3	8.1	4.2	15.5	6.3	26.3	7.1
22.8	21.1	18.1	7.4	4.5	12.7	6.7	24.2	8.2
19.5	17.4	13.1	6.4	4.8	16.5	6.1	30.3	6.7
20.8	23.1	15.1	5.7	4.8	19.8	5.7	23.5	6.4
19.3	18.6	10.8	5.6	4.4	12.7	5.2	29.5	3.9
22.6	14.8	12.2	5.9	4.9	13.0	5.0	25.3	4.3
24.1	22.7	22.5	7.2	5.0	14.3	5.8	27.6	7.8
20.1	16.9	15.6	6.5	4.8	21.3	5.4	31.7	5.8
23.9	31.1	17.9	7.8	5.3	23.3	6.8	36.1	10.4
25.0	28.1	20.5	8.9	6.2	16.2	6.9	32.4	10.2
22.0	16.3	9.0	8.8	4.3	13.6	5.9	25.2	6.1
25.2	29.1	18.7	10.9	4.5	18.4	6.1	39.5	9.8
22.5	23.5	16.5	7.6	5.4	19.9	5.4	20.1	8.4
24.8	21.3	13.3	8.0	7.1	18.1	7.0	24.5	11.2
22.3	23.8	22.1	10.2	5.3	15.9	6.3	46.1	11.9
25.0	23.2	22.2	5.3	6.8	23.3	7.0	35.0	13.2
23.3	17.7	16.9	6.2	6.0	14.9	7.5	17.4	6.6
22.8	25.3	17.8	9.3	6.8	17.5	7.5	22.7	10.2
27.4	26.5	21.4	7.4	5.3	18.8	5.8	37.3	8.8
22.3	21.2	19.0	7.1	5.5	14.7	6.3	27.0	7.1
20.6	14.5	10.7	6.3	5.3	13.8	6.2	24.0	5.0
23.5	20.4	18.9	5.2	5.5	17.9	6.0	18.9	6.8
29.4	28.5	24.9	6.0	5.6	16.6	6.8	32.8	14.1
29.8	31.9	25.3	7.2	5.6	16.4	6.4	26.9	14.5
38.9	33.4	34.8	6.6	7.5	20.0	9.9	31.5	39.1
24.1	18.4	15.6	6.1	5.1	16.7	5.6	31.4	6.2
19.3	16.2	16.7	5.4	4.3	13.8	5.1	28.8	5.3
28.1	38.8	24.8	8.3	6.1	20.3	7.0	40.1	22.7
19.5	18.1	11.1	10.1	4.6	16.7	5.7	25.4	5.6
29.3	29.3	21.8	9.7	7.6	28.8	7.9	43.2	26.1
18.6	22.5	12.0	6.8	5.5	19.9	5.8	29.3	6.9
24.4	25.6	10.3	7.4	6.4	20.9	6.2	33.7	11.3
30.9	29.4	25.3	7.0	7.6	20.2	8.4	36.2	21.2

Continued on next page

Table 3.2 Continued

Catalog No.	Maximum Length (mm)	Maximum Length of Stem (mm)	Maximum Length of Body (mm)	Maximum Width at Base (mm)	Maximum Width of Stem (mm)	Distance from Base to Maximum Width of Stem (mm)	Maximum Width at Shoulder (mm)
131	67.3+★	17.3	50.0+★	24.2	—	—	23.4
133	189.2	—	—	59.1	—	—	—
134	63.8	19.6	44.2	20.1	18.6	11.3	19.4
138	85.7	20.4	65.3	34.1	27.4	9.5	31.8
141	54.6	18.6	36.0	21.9	19.7	16.9	21.0
147	52.4	13.9	38.5	25.5	22.7	13.9	22.7
148	50.7	16.5	34.2	25.1	22.6	12.5	22.9
151	46.5	14.6	31.9	26.0	21.9	12.5	22.0
160	78.3	21.5	56.8	33.7	25.5	14.6	28.3
164	67.7	20.6	47.1	29.2	24.5	9.8	23.5
165	113.2	25.4	87.8	31.6	29.2	9.3	30.2
173	50.5+★	15.0	35.5+★	24.5	21.1	11.2	22.3
174	137.4	26.2	111.2	37.1	32.4	14.7	36.7
179	57.4	16.2	41.2	18.1	16.9	4.5	19.7
181	147.4	28.8	118.6	38.4	36.1	13.6	49.2
183	69.5+★	—★	—★	—★	—★	—★	—★
184	68.5	16.4	52.1	26.3	24.4	9.3	25.3
185	45.1	14.3	31.2	—★	19.0	8.2	19.8
186	46.3	14.6	31.7	24.2	21.1	13.2	21.2
187	60.5	15.1	45.4	25.8	22.1	11.2	22.7
188	53.9	12.8	41.1	22.3	20.1	12.4	22.6
193	55.4	5.7	39.7	23.2	20.0	10.8	21.0
195	50.6	14.5	36.1	22.6	20.3	9.9	20.7
207	80.5	19.6	60.9	22.2	21.3	11.3	23.8
208	78.8	19.6	59.2	22.1	20.7	13.0	23.0
212	75.7	18.1	57.6	22.2	19.7	8.4	22.7
213	80.3	22.9	57.4	22.7	21.7	16.2	24.1
216	130.0	31.8	98.2	35.3	35.4	9.2	37.2
221	100.0+★	31.9+★	68.1	—★	—★	—★	24.8
228	55.0	13.3	41.7	22.3	20.6	7.6	21.7
237	48.6	19.6	29.0	23.7	22.3	11.4	22.6
244	52.9	13.5	39.4	24.7	23.0	9.9	23.2
248	48.7+★	17.6	31.1+★	—★	20.0	14.6	21.5
249	46.7+★	16.9	29.8+★	24.7	22.2	13.0	22.8
252	47.2+★	13.3	34.1+★	—★	—★	—★	—★
255	57.7	18.4	39.3	24.1	21.9	16.8	23.4
264	31.4+★	12.8	18.6+★	20.8	19.8	5.8	22.3
265	133.4	25.9	107.5	40.9	37.0	15.0	38.6
271	99.9	16.5	83.4	29.6	21.0	12.3	22.4
274	75.3	12.6	62.7	22.4	20.4	9.3	21.9
275	81.2	18.0	63.2	28.7	23.8	10.1	28.4
277	130.3	26.7	103.6	38.2	34.4	24.2	35.2
278	116.6	28.3	88.3	37.3	31.6	15.1	35.8
287	80.3	24.4	55.9	22.5	20.8	11.5	22.3
288	57.9	21.1	36.8	22.6	22.0	2.1	23.7
289	70.4	21.0	49.4	19.4	17.8	15.9	19.2
290	52.9	15.7	37.2	20.9	19.4	12.5	20.0
291	58.1	18.0	40.1	23.0	22.2	11.7	23.0
292	60.6	16.1	44.5	21.6	20.6	6.5	21.2
293	76.8	17.0	59.8	22.5+★	21.6	15.3	22.0
294	182.1	50.2	131.9	42.8	38.8	19.4	41.9

Maximum Width of Body (mm)	Distance from Base to Maximum Width of Body (mm)	Width at Midpoint of Body (mm)	Basal Depth (mm)	Maximum Thickness of Stem (mm)	Distance from Base to Maximum Thickness of Stem (mm)	Maximum Thickness of Body (mm)	Distance from Base to Maximum Thickness of Body (mm)	Artifact Weight (g)
20.4	19.3	14.3	5.5	5.2	13.4	7.2	23.4	8.6
—	—	—	10.7	—	—	11.1	43.8	113
19.0	22.2	15.6	4.2	5.8	19.6	6.6	23.6	8.0
30.8	22.7	17.1	4.8	7.4	20.4	8.6	45.3	17.7
18.6	21.1	13.9	6.0	4.7	14.5	5.1	21.3	4.7
19.3	22.2	13.1	7.8	4.9	13.9	6.8	30.4	5.6
19.4	18.5	10.6	9.5	6.0	16.5	6.4	18.5	5.3
20.2	18.4	12.3	8.8	5.5	14.6	5.8	23.3	4.7
27.4	24.2	20.3	8.6	6.4	21.5	7.4	22.2	13.8
23.3	33.5	19.1	11.4	5.1	23.5	6.4	33.4	9.4
30.7	50.3	28.7	5.7	7.1	25.4	7.4	70.5	28.6
22.2	15.9	14.4	5.6	4.8	15.0	5.7	25.8	6.0
35.6	31.2	24.8	11.6	8.9	26.2	9.5	37.9	40.1
20.5	17.9	15.3	4.9	4.9	16.2	5.4	25.8	5.7
40.4	36.0	34.0	9.6	7.8	26.3	9.3	52.9	53.2
—★	37.2+★	—★	—★	—★	—★	8.3+★	—★	18.2+★
25.7	25.4	20.7	6.0	5.7	16.4	7.2	37.3	12.2
20.5	17.5	13.3	6.7	4.6	13.9	4.8	20.2	3.8
21.4	18.2	14.8	7.5	5.2	14.6	6.3	21.6	5.6
23.5	21.5	18.9	8.9	5.3	15.0	6.0	21.2	7.9
23.0	16.4	18.5	5.7	4.9	12.8	6.9	33.8	7.6
20.2	17.3	12.8	4.5	6.0	15.7	5.8	17.0	5.8
18.6	17.8	10.4	8.7	5.2	14.2	5.4	27.7	4.3
24.5	20.3	19.4	6.5	5.4	19.6	7.4	40.8	12.4
23.2	38.9	20.5	6.5	5.9	19.6	6.7	30.0	12.4
22.1	22.2	19.4	4.8	4.8	18.1	6.4	44.2	10.3
24.1	31.7	20.7	6.1	6.1	22.9	6.7	44.4	12.9
36.9	37.3	32.0	6.3	7.3	26.3	7.5	45.1	36.5
17.7	33.1	8.3	—★	8.5	21.6	8.9	35.6	14.2
20.5	15.5	13.5	7.5	4.7	13.3	5.0	13.8	4.8
21.3	21.0	16.7	5.0	5.9	16.8	6.1	23.4	7.0
22.4	14.6	15.3	3.0	5.9	13.5	6.2	17.8	6.6
22.8	22.7	21.6	7.8	6.2	16.4	6.7	34.1	7.8
21.8	18.1	15.1	7.6	6.4	16.9	7.5	19.3	6.8
17.9	21.8	14.0	6.7	4.9	11.6	6.2	21.7	4.9+★
22.2	24.0	17.7	8.7	6.6	17.5	5.8	21.8	7.2
19.8	15.8	16.8	5.9	5.7	12.8	6.3	14.2	4.1
38.3	31.0	31.1	10.2	7.7	25.9	9.4	58.4	40.7
22.6	21.7	15.0	8.4	4.2	16.5	5.6	24.3	9.6
23.0	14.6	16.1	6.8	5.5	12.6	6.2	4.2	7.8
23.6	20.9	22.9	6.8	5.7	18.0	7.2	33.0	16.9
35.9	34.4	28.3	5.0	8.5	26.7	8.4	31.5	40.3
34.2	43.4	27.1	12.5	8.6	28.3	10.0	52.9	38.5
21.3	24.6	13.0	5.0	5.3	4.4	7.3	51.6	9.7
25.3	22.3	16.6	7.2	5.1	21.1	5.3	23.8	7.1
19.9	29.6	16.7	5.3	6.4	21.0	7.9	31.7	9.8
17.0	19.6	11.1	4.0	5.0	15.7	5.3	17.4	4.0
24.0	20.6	18.7	6.8	5.7	18.0	6.6	26.6	7.8
19.9	18.8	13.7	6.0	4.9	16.1	5.4	23.6	5.8
21.4	20.5	16.4	5.0	5.5	17.0	7.3	36.2	9.3
41.6	52.3	32.6	13.3	10.7	36.9	12.4	70.1	85.9

Continued on next page

Table 3.2 Continued

Catalog No.	Maximum Length (mm)	Maximum Length of Stem (mm)	Maximum Length of Body (mm)	Maximum Width at Base (mm)	Maximum Width of Stem (mm)	Distance from Base to Maximum Width of Stem (mm)	Maximum Width at Shoulder (mm)
295	122.2	25.1	97.1	38.9	34.5	14.4	35.9
299	66.9	18.1	48.8	26.3	22.7	13.8	23.6
300	71.4	16.8	59.6	24.3	20.6	10.2	22.8
302	59.8	16.9	42.9	19.3	17.7	11.2	18.0
303	72.5	19.1	53.4	25.8	24.1	9.4	27.4
304	54.8	16.1	38.7	23.8	20.7	15.8	21.0
305	59.0+*	17.3	41.7+*	26.1	22.8	10.4	23.8
307	80.6	—	—	28.9	27.2	13.6	—
308	54.5	15.5	39.0	24.9	22.7	9.9	24.8
309	54.0	20.6	33.4	23.9	19.1	11.4	21.3
310	58.0	14.9	43.1	25.0	21.3	11.1	22.2
311	70.5	18.7	51.8	19.9	18.2	14.9	19.3
314	93.8	18.9	74.9	29.6	26.5	10.9	30.2
316	57.2	14.3	42.9	22.2	20.4	10.1	21.3
317	47.3+*	13.1	34.2+*	22.2	19.4	6.5	20.9
324	58.8	15.5	43.3	22.7	20.0	12.7	21.0
325	62.1	15.9	46.2	22.6	20.3	7.5	20.8
331	62.8	20.8	42.0	26.2	21.7	11.9	23.4
332	66.5	18.8	47.7	24.6	22.0	7.3	24.9
333	57.4	17.7	39.7	25.6	22.1	10.5	24.7
336	57.4	18.3	39.1	27.1	23.7	10.1	25.9
360	85.2	23.7	61.5	25.3	22.4	15.1	26.4
362	77.8	24.6	53.2	35.8	33.4	12.4	36.0
393	54.9	14.5	40.4	30.1	25.4	11.8	26.4
401	52.8	16.1	36.7	20.2	19.3	5.2	19.9
403	107.9	27.5	80.4	36.9	32.7	15.3	36.9
408	60.3	18.8	41.5	25.3	22.4	12.8	22.8
410	52.1	17.9	34.2	23.9	21.9	8.8	24.4
414	105.8	25.4	80.4	29.5	27.9	5.8	33.9
420	56.2	9.6	46.6	19.0	18.8	5.2	19.2
428	95.7	26.7	69.0	31.4	26.8	13.0	28.3
429	60.4	17.2	43.2	23.0	21.9	6.6	22.9
433	72.2	18.5	53.7	25.4	25.5	7.5	26.3
435	79.6	19.0	60.6	22.2	20.4	11.0	22.4
436 & 453	47.4	12.0	35.4	21.7	18.7	10.0	19.2
442	48.9	16.7	32.5	—	18.9	6.3	20.3
445	103.4	31.9	71.5	30.7	29.7	7.9	32.4
448	61.8	17.0	44.8	21.7	19.8	8.6	20.9
452	57.0	15.8	41.2	21.2	20.4	10.5	20.9
459	72.0	16.1	55.9	24.5	23.4	7.9	23.3
462	130.1	23.6	106.5	32.5	32.1	13.8	32.2
467	53.9	14.8	39.1	21.5	19.3	7.4	19.9
471	81.2	26.5	54.7	23.3	26.6	11.2	28.1
473	78.7	25.4	53.3	21.5	19.8	8.6	21.4
474	70.8	18.6	52.2	22.9	21.1	9.5	22.2
491	26.8+*	13.2	—*	—*	—*	—*	19.7
1414	67.4	18.7	48.7	23.5	21.6	14.1	23.9
Mean	73.0	18.8	53.1	25.8	22.8	11.1	24.5
Standard Deviation	25.8	5.0	19.8	5.8	4.6	3.4	5.2
Count	134	141	134	135	137	137	142

*Broken.

Maximum Width of Body (mm)	Distance from Base to Maximum Width of Body (mm)	Width at Midpoint of Body (mm)	Basal Depth (mm)	Maximum Thickness of Stem (mm)	Distance from Base to Maximum Thickness of Stem (mm)	Maximum Thickness of Body (mm)	Distance from Base to Maximum Thickness of Body (mm)	Artifact Weight (g)
32.5	28.6	18.6	15.1	8.1	25.1	9.3	36.2	31.3
23.7	21.7	16.5	8.2	6.0	18.1	7.1	38.0	9.4
22.5	18.5	13.7	10.5	5.4	16.8	5.9	22.5	6.8
18.2	17.9	13.6	5.6	5.7	16.9	6.6	27.7	6.0
28.0	22.7	19.8	6.3	7.0	19.1	7.2	33.3	14.2
20.7	18.2	13.8	4.1	5.5	16.1	6.6	18.2	5.7
24.8	19.2	18.3	7.2	5.0	17.3	6.6	26.0	8.5
29.6	35.3	—	4.9	—	—	7.1	37.3	17.9
25.3	18.4	20.2	5.8	5.1	15.5	6.1	19.1	7.4
21.9	22.3	15.8	7.4	6.2	20.6	6.0	23.1	6.2
23.8	18.2	16.3	6.4	5.0	14.9	6.0	18.8	7.6
19.4	23.0	16.5	6.0	6.9	18.7	6.6	30.3	8.3
30.9	31.7	23.9	7.8	7.3	18.9	8.1	62.4	23.6
19.7	19.2	11.7	5.1	5.4	14.3	5.8	18.4	6.1
20.7	14.6	15.8	6.4	4.6	20.9	5.7	21.3	5.2
20.9	19.5	19.4	9.3	5.3	15.5	6.3	26.6	7.0
21.3	16.9	17.3	5.3	5.1	15.9	5.8	22.8	7.3
22.5	23.6	18.3	6.1	6.7	17.5	6.6	21.8	9.5
25.2	26.2	17.9	10.5	5.4	18.8	6.8	32.7	10.2
24.1	22.6	18.4	5.5	5.4	17.7	6.1	24.8	8.0
21.2	20.6	18.6	8.2	6.3	18.3	6.8	22.6	9.6
25.1	27.9	17.0	8.1	6.2	23.7	7.9	50.5	14.8
35.5	31.2	24.7	5.8	7.4	24.6	8.0	40.9	23.6
23.5	16.2	12.1	8.4	5.9	14.5	7.1	25.8	7.5
19.0	16.8	11.4	5.4	4.3	10.8	4.7	23.3	3.9
37.0	28.1	30.1	11.1	6.9	27.5	8.4	53.5	32.3
25.5	23.0	20.9	8.1	6.9	18.8	7.1	22.7	9.0
21.6	23.1	17.0	6.8	5.8	17.9	6.4	23.5	6.7
34.9	41.3	30.6	10.8	7.3	25.4	8.4	48.3	29.3
15.7	11.5	7.9	5.4	4.2	9.6	5.9	32.7	4.2
28.0	32.9	25.2	7.4	7.3	26.7	7.7	43.4	19.5
22.6	18.1	14.3	7.1	6.3	17.2	6.2	17.8	7.8
26.0	19.9	22.2	6.7	5.8	18.5	7.1	42.7	13.5
23.3	26.4	18.9	5.7	6.1	19.0	7.1	26.1	12.1
18.8	17.2	12.5	5.3	4.6	12.0	5.7	21.1	4.1
17.1	17.8	8.2	5.7	6.1	16.4	6.6	18.3	4.1
32.9	36.0	28.2	4.8	7.3	31.9	7.9	31.3	25.7
20.5	21.0	15.6	7.0	5.2	17.0	5.2	17.6	6.7
17.9	19.0	10.3	8.4	4.4	15.8	5.5	30.7	4.7
26.6	29.9	22.6	5.7	6.5	16.1	8.2	24.4	14.3
32.8	26.9	27.3	11.7	7.3	23.6	8.9	36.5	36.8
18.3	17.8	12.1	6.0	4.6	14.8	4.8	15.9	4.4
26.8	29.7	21.6	8.0	6.7	21.8	6.8	44.2	16.0
21.4	27.4	16.8	4.9	6.0	25.4	6.3	37.3	10.8
25.3	26.3	20.8	8.0	5.4	18.6	6.1	27.7	10.9
21.6	15.7	—*	—*	5.0	13.2	5.8	22.2	2.6+*
24.2	20.0	17.0	9.4	4.7	18.7	6.1	37.2	8.2
24.0	29.4	18.0	7.2	5.8	18.2	5.8	29.9	13.2
5.3	7.0	5.6	2.0	1.1	4.5	1.5	11.2	14.3
144	144	142	142	143	143	145	145	143

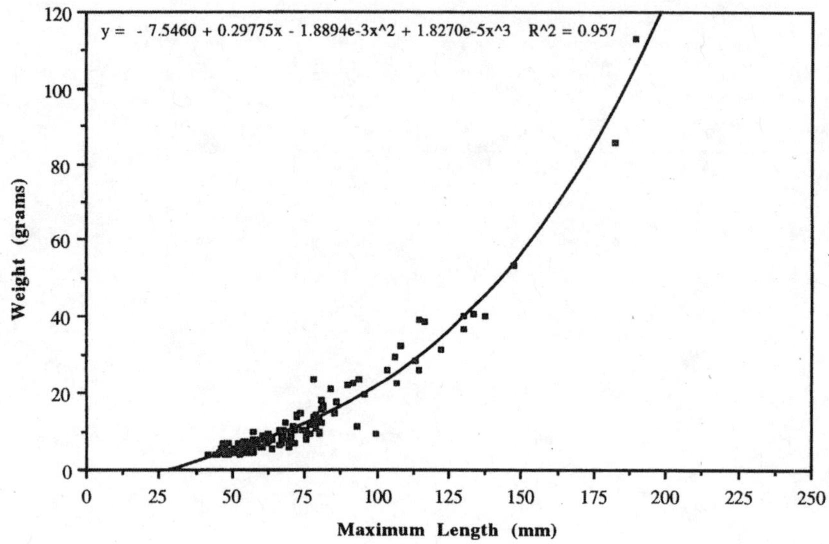

Figure 3.6 Sloan-site Dalton points: maximum length versus weight.

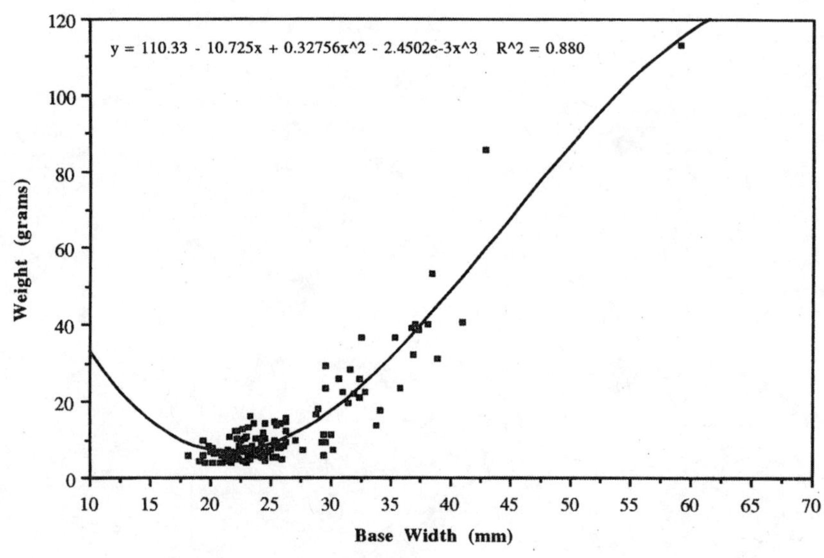

Figure 3.7 Sloan-site Dalton points: maximum width at base versus weight.

exhibits a very heavy polish over much of the ventral face, but only striations at the very edge of the bit. Another (315) has been almost completely rechipped on its bit, leaving a small, heavily polished remnant.

BIFACES. In total, ninety-two complete bifaces were recovered (Figure 3.13; Table 3.4). Many were in two caches. Obviously this category is an important one in Dalton culture, but it has not been recognized until the excavation of the Sloan site. At Brand, we assumed that the few recognized Dalton bifaces collected were preforms. It has become increasingly obvious since about 1974 that not all bifaces are necessarily preforms (Daniel and Wisenbaker 1987:57). At Sloan almost all of the recovered bifaces could not be preforms for Dalton points based on size alone. There are two Pitkin Chert bifaces (67, 152), one of Crescent Quarry Chert (106), and a possible Cotter Chert biface (20). The bifaces mostly appear to be made from Crowley's Ridge Chert. Only twenty-six do not exhibit cortex, and most of those (nineteen) probably are Ozark chert. Shapes vary from oval to lanceolate to triangular. Some may have been meant to be tools but most are roughly percussion-flaked, and as a group they may be more symbolic than potentially useful.

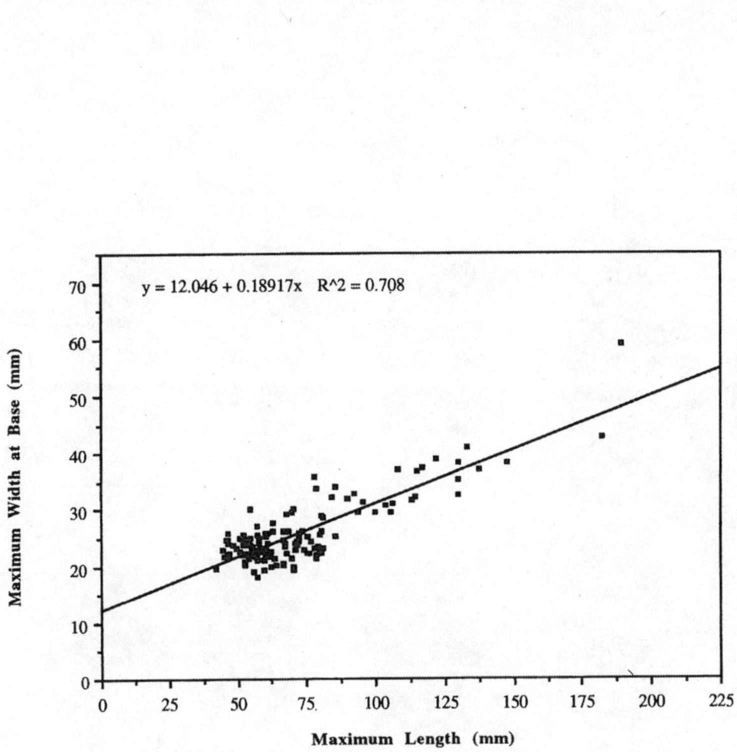

Figure 3.8 Sloan-site Dalton points: maximum length versus maximum width at base.

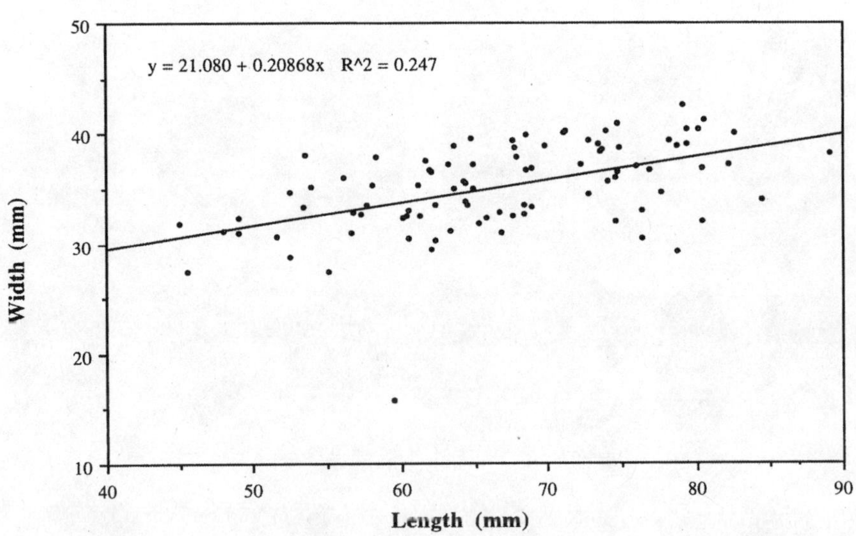

Figure 3.9 Sloan-site bifaces: maximum length versus maximum width.

Biface caches are well known from terminal Archaic and especially Hopewell sites as grave lots similar to those at the Sloan site.

The biface made of Crescent Quarry Chert is different from the others. It is a slender, drill-like, pointed biface with a convex base. It has a knifelike shape. The tip is sharp. The base is laterally battered for 29 millimeters as if prepared for hafting.

BROKEN BIFACE TOOLS. Three biface fragments were recovered that had been used as scrapers and/or gravers after their breakage (Table 3.5). Specimen 75 is a cortexed tip with a 15-millimeter-long, slightly concave steeply retouched end-worn edge extending back from a broken corner. The corner itself was lightly retouched and could have functioned as a graver. Specimen 284 is also a cortexed tip that has a 15-millimeter-long, slightly convex edge of the break lightly retouched and worn. Specimen 286 is a biface base with a worn broken corner that was prepared by the removal of a single small flake.

END SCRAPERS. Fan-shaped transverse-edged unifaces are part of the normal Paleoindian tool kit (Hester 1972:102, 125; Frison and Stanford 1982:46, 121) and part of the unifacial inheritance from the Upper Paleolithic of the Old World. They constitute a substantial part of the Sloan site inventory. At Brand these tools were classified as "hafted end scraper with steep retouch" (Good-

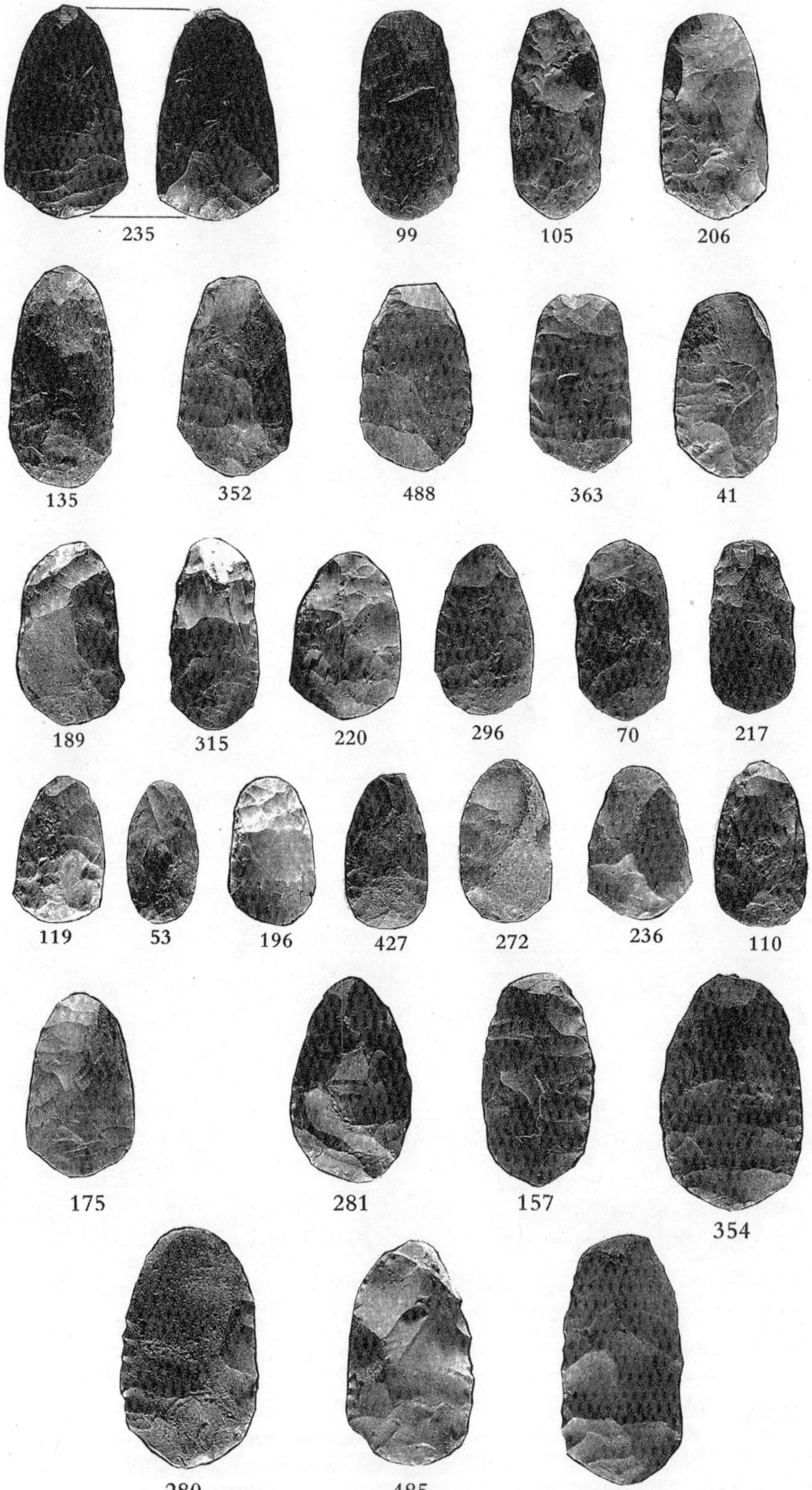

Figure 3.10 Adzes and adze preforms at the Sloan site. Numbers are catalog numbers keyed to tables. Artifacts are approximately one-fourth actual size.

Table 3.3
Measurements of adzes

Catalog No.	Maximum Length (mm)	Width at Bit (mm)	Distance to Base (mm)	Maximum Width (mm)	Distance to Maximum Width (mm)	Width at ½ Distance to Base (mm)	Width at 10 mm from Base (mm)	Maximum Thickness (mm)	Thickness Distance from Base (mm)	Weight (g)
15	91.8	44.5	76.5	49.4	63.9	46.0	26.4	16.8	60.9	80.4
41	82.5	42.0	69.7	44.9	55.3	43.0	31.8	17.0	43.4	76.0
53	62.8	21.4	52.1	32.7	35.7	31.1	20.7	14.1	23.1	27.6
70	81.7	37.5	70.6	40.5	50.2	38.8	29.4	16.6	20.5	60.8
90	64.7	40.4	54.3	40.4	54.3	39.6	31.8	16.9	36.6	49.0
99	95.3	42.1	83.1	44.1	65.6	42.6	33.3	16.7	37.8	88.1
105	92.1	37.8	77.7	40.5	49.7	39.6	29.2	18.4	43.0	74.4
110	72.6	39.8	63.5	40.9	48.8	37.3	27.1	15.7	46.3	53.7
119	65.4	38.1	56.4	38.1	56.4	36.2	24.0	16.7	27.2	45.3
135	97.1	46.2	81.7	46.3	71.2	43.4	27.3	19.0	40.3	96.7
157	86.1	35.8	72.1	42.8	45.7	41.0	27.9	15.4	58.6	64.7
175	74.9	42.2	59.9	42.2	59.9	37.4	26.3	19.7	47.2	64.3
177	64.5	44.1	47.8	44.1	47.8	36.5	29.5	16.6	44.1	48.4
189	82.8	42.5	69.5	45.1	60.6	40.9	27.6	18.8	31.3	73.1
191	61.4	33.5	51.5	35.6	44.7	31.9	23.0	14.0	18.1	34.9
196	65.5	38.9	49.4	38.9	49.4	35.1	27.2	15.5	25.3	45.0
204	63.0	36.7	52.6	38.8	47.3	34.5	26.7	15.6	26.6	41.4
206	83.9	39.9	73.5	41.8	56.6	39.3	28.4	16.9	55.9	66.1
217	78.4	34.5	66.5	36.2	47.8	36.1	26.2	18.4	30.8	56.0
220	67.6	40.5	58.1	42.1	43.9	39.7	25.6	18.1	33.6	51.4
223	65.8	32.4	53.8	33.3	32.7	32.4	23.9	18.5	41.4	38.8
224	78.1	40.4	68.5	44.7	52.6	40.0	19.8	16.2	32.4	54.6
227	73.4	32.9	64.1	33.4	42.4	32.2	22.5	13.7	36.8	34.5
235	95.0	52.8	79.4	52.8	79.4	43.3	27.5	20.7	36.2	106.2
236	67.5	45.3	56.7	45.3	56.7	37.7	25.8	17.8	38.2	53.9
272	73.4	37.6	64.8	40.1	45.0	39.2	27.3	16.5	36.8	53.7
280	94.6	44.2	86.3	49.4	29.3	53.1	55.9	15.1	47.3	85.5
281	82.7	41.9	67.5	46.2	41.1	45.0	22.1	17.8	27.8	63.8
296	76.6	42.7	67.1	42.7	67.1	38.8	23.5	15.1	27.9	53.6
315	85.2	36.3	74.2	38.4	58.6	36.3	27.7	16.8	38.8	65.5
341	52.3	37.9	37.8	37.9	37.8	35.0	31.3	16.5	15.4	33.3
348	74.6	37.0	63.6	40.9	43.2	38.5	28.9	15.7	47.9	51.6
352	88.6	48.4	77.4	48.4	77.4	43.4	26.1	18.5	27.9	87.7
354	95.3	45.7	84.4	53.5	54.8	50.9	31.4	18.9	45.9	108.1
363	78.3	44.7	67.0	44.7	67.0	41.9	32.8	15.5	49.1	66.6
425	76.1	39.6	66.4	41.4	38.3	40.2	25.9	14.5	39.9	55.3
426	76.4	35.9	65.8	39.4	43.9	38.8	28.3	17.4	38.6	52.3
427	70.5	32.3	63.8	35.6	36.4	34.4	24.5	14.1	13.6	41.3
460	62.4	41.9	55.4	42.3	36.3	40.8	33.3	14.4	25.9	44.0
485	89.8	46.9	74.1	49.0	65.1	46.1	30.3	18.8	50.5	84.9
487	100.7	43.9	87.8	46.9	78.9	43.9	31.0	20.6	36.6	100.6
488	83.2	44.9	72.1	49.2	53.7	45.2	31.8	18.8	42.5	86.4
Mean	78.0	40.3	66.3	42.4	52.2	39.7	28.1	16.9	36.9	62.4
Standard Deviation	11.9	5.0	11.4	5.0	12.5	4.8	5.5	1.8	11.1	20.7
Count	42	42	42	42	42	42	42	42	42	42

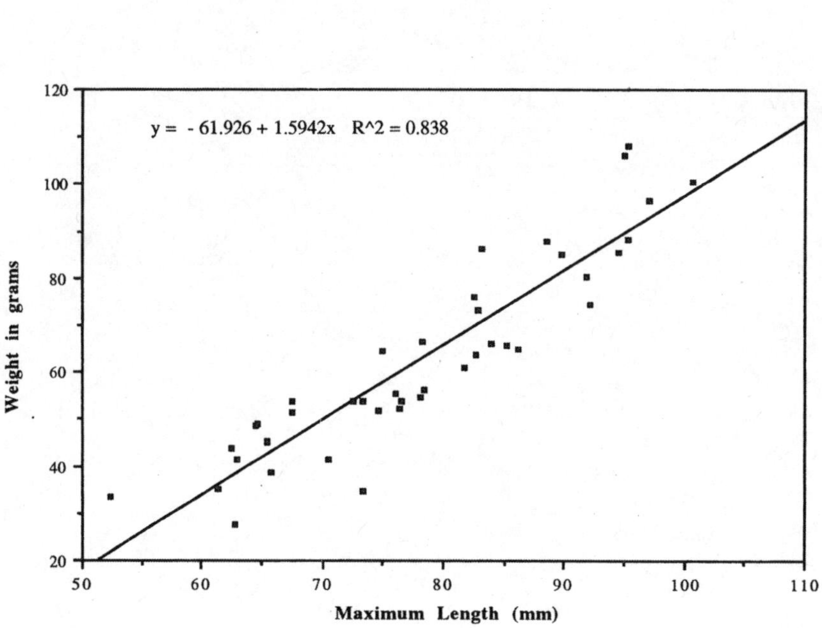

Figure 3.11 Sloan-site Dalton adzes: maximum length versus weight.

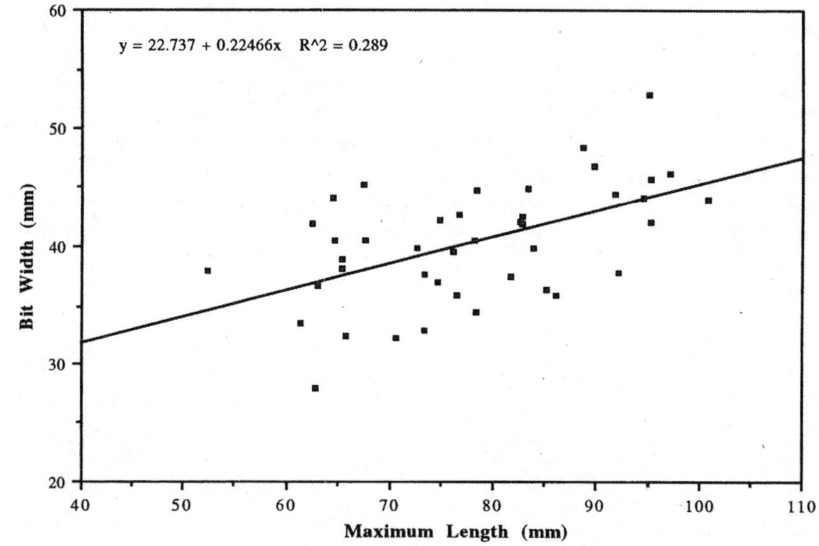

Figure 3.12 Sloan-site Dalton adzes: maximum length versus width at bit.

year 1974:44f). At that site, nineteen were recovered; at Sloan, there were thirty-three (Figure 3.14). End scrapers are characteristic of the Paleoindian Period, and it is not known how long they continued in use as an artifact type into the Holocene in the East. Evidently the basic Paleoindian uniface assemblage dates exclusively or primarily in the Pleistocene. The Hardin complex, however, in Wisconsin is associated with end scrapers (Behm 1985:65–67).

End scrapers made on flakes of bifacial retouch number seventeen. Of the remaining scrapers, twelve were made on core flakes, and four seem to have had the bulbar ends detached during the retouch stage. It is obvious that as a cobble was reduced to a tool through a bifaced preform stage, appropriate flakes were selected to be made into end scrapers. There evidently is no specific flake or blade technology present that involved the manufacture of cores to produce end scraper blank flakes (see chapter 4).

Specimen numbers 180 and 330 are made of Pitkin Chert. Fifteen scrapers are probably Crowley's Ridge Chert, and fifteen are made of Ozark cherts. One (492) is made of quartzite, probably obtained from Crowley's Ridge gravels. For the most part scrapers match the points and other bifaces in color and texture.

There is variety in the end scraper class. All are made on flakes that have a distinct dorsal downcurve opposite

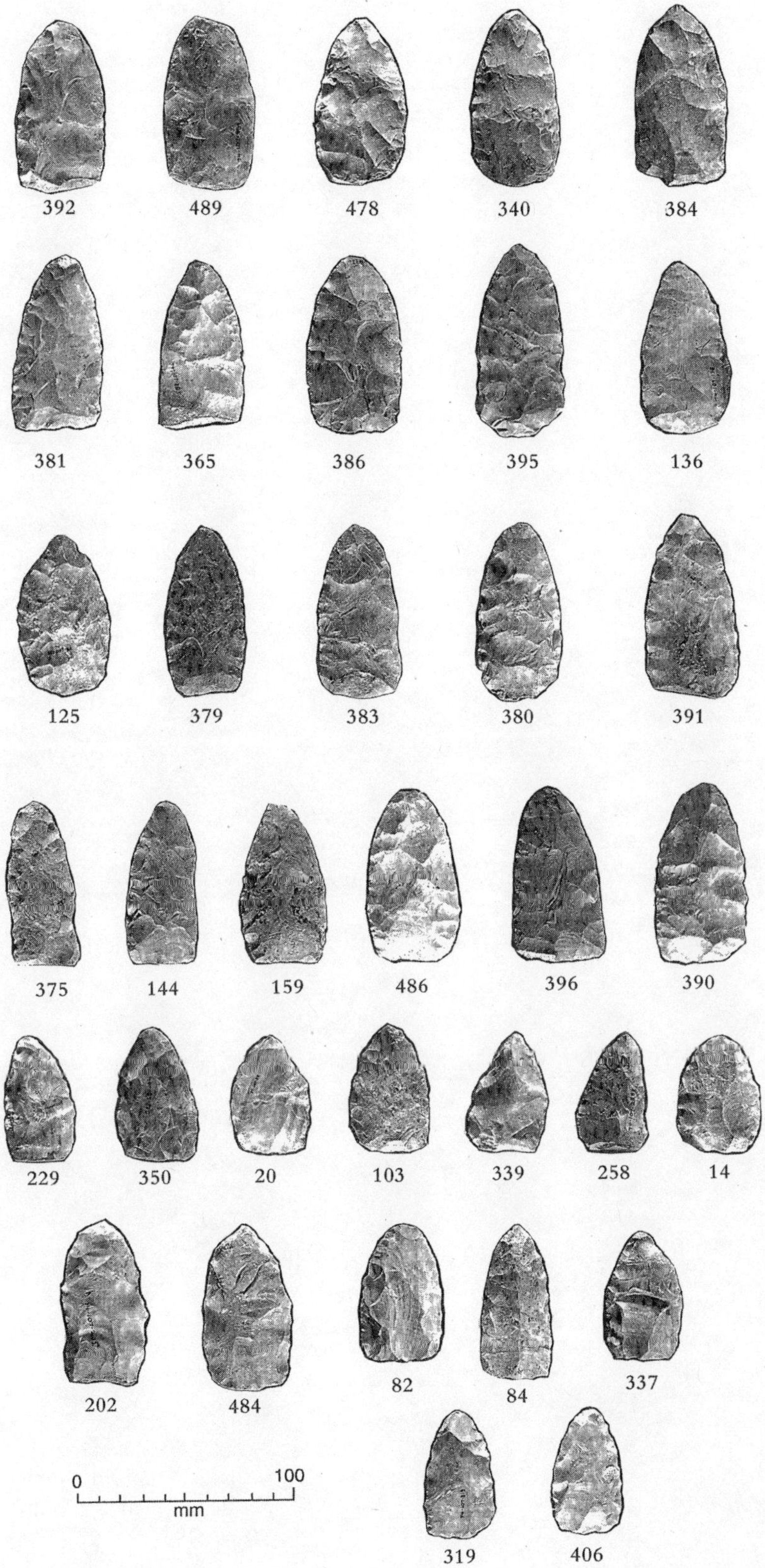

Figure 3.13 Bifaces at the Sloan site. Numbers are catalog numbers keyed to tables. Artifacts are approximately one-fourth actual size.

Table 3.4
Measurements of bifaces

Catalog No.	Maximum Length (mm)	Maximum Width (mm)	Width Distance from Base (mm)	Maximum Thickness (mm)	Thickness Distance from Base (mm)	Weight (g)
14	53.6	38.1	18.2	7.2	13.9	18.7
20	52.5	34.6	21.5	10.3	12.2	19.4
57	61.3	32.5	14.4	9.1	17.3	21.3
61	45.0	31.8	15.8	8.8	15.3	14.2
65	64.4	35.5	20.9	19.4	27.4	38.1
67	74.6	31.9	18.9	10.6	32.6	24.8
82	61.7	37.5	21.1	9.3	22.0	27.5
84	68.4	32.6	16.8	11.9	22.6	26.1
97	68.4	33.4	22.7	9.3	23.0	23.6
103	56.2	36.0	20.6	8.3	34.3	18.0
106	59.5	15.8	13.8	9.0	16.8	7.7
123	71.3	40.2	25.9	11.4	34.9	35.2
124	49.0	30.9	22.6	10.1	26.9	15.4
125	74.7	40.9	26.2	11.4	33.9	31.7
126	74.1	35.7	24.6	11.6	26.8	28.2
130	64.4	33.8	18.8	8.6	12.1	18.7
136	79.4	39.0	26.7	10.8	15.2	35.0
144	76.4	32.9	19.0	10.4	20.3	25.4
152	62.4	33.4	21.8	9.7	24.3	24.2
153	64.3	35.7	21.0	10.9	32.6	27.5
155	78.8	29.2	14.5	8.5	45.8	17.6
159	73.5	39.0	25.2	12.6	58.5	34.3
201	67.7	32.4	20.5	8.0	28.3	20.7
202	72.8	39.4	30.1	11.9	15.5	36.8
203	84.4	33.9	25.4	11.5	21.4	33.7
229	56.8	32.8	16.1	8.9	17.0	19.8
257	69.9	38.9	23.1	11.1	18.3	36.0
258	53.4	33.3	13.7	10.8	22.8	17.8
276	55.1	27.3	19.4	8.5	15.4	14.6
279	61.9	36.7	25.9	9.8	18.5	24.8
318	60.6	33.0	18.5	10.7	26.8	23.6
319	57.3	32.7	14.9	10.9	21.7	21.0
320	65.3	31.8	19.1	9.9	27.8	21.8
321	64.9	34.9	14.4	11.6	25.4	26.4
328	64.8	39.6	23.3	10.1	19.8	29.2
329	62.3	30.3	18.0	11.1	19.5	24.8
337	58.1	35.4	26.9	8.8	20.1	19.7
339	53.9	35.1	16.6	9.5	11.8	18.8
340	74.6	36.0	27.8	9.1	25.6	28.6
342	64.5	33.4	24.1	8.9	44.1	22.6
349	60.4	32.4	21.8	8.6	26.5	20.4
350	60.2	32.2	20.6	10.4	14.3	23.8
351	66.7	32.8	19.8	10.5	30.4	20.8
355	57.7	33.5	17.3	8.8	31.2	16.6
356	66.9	30.9	21.3	10.5	38.0	19.7
357	63.4	31.1	37.9	11.6	25.9	23.8
358	64.9	37.2	20.5	10.1	30.2	21.9
359	62.1	29.4	30.5	9.9	38.9	19.2

Table 3.4
Continued

Catalog No.	Maximum Length (mm)	Maximum Width (mm)	Width Distance from Base (mm)	Maximum Thickness (mm)	Thickness Distance from Base (mm)	Weight (g)
365	76.9	36.7	13.1	9.9	16.4	32.4
366	69.0	36.8	19.8	11.5	50.5	27.0
367	67.9	37.8	14.6	10.9	15.5	29.3
371	68.5	39.8	25.9	10.3	14.2	32.0
374	60.5	30.5	11.4	10.6	23.1	16.4
375	76.4	30.4	33.7	9.7	12.6	25.6
376	65.8	32.3	20.4	9.9	11.3	22.2
378	61.2	35.3	31.4	10.9	20.3	25.1
379	77.7	34.6	25.6	10.2	56.6	29.3
380	82.2	37.1	30.7	9.9	44.2	32.9
381	74.8	36.5	10.5	9.3	45.0	29.2
383	80.4	36.8	12.0	10.2	26.6	33.3
384	76.0	37.0	39.4	11.0	19.0	32.1
385	67.8	38.7	33.5	8.4	44.4	32.4
386	74.9	38.7	36.6	10.2	28.7	35.5
387	72.8	34.4	24.4	9.4	37.3	29.1
388	73.6	38.3	23.7	10.8	46.7	33.1
389	68.5	36.6	31.1	8.6	8.4	25.0
390	82.7	40.1	28.5	9.7	57.2	38.9
391	80.6	41.3	11.1	9.9	19.3	38.6
392	78.7	38.8	19.9	9.9	35.7	36.9
394	68.9	33.3	24.2	8.8	27.1	23.9
395	89.1	38.2	23.8	9.9	16.1	40.4
396	80.2	40.4	7.8	9.9	51.6	34.9
402	58.4	37.9	19.3	10.5	26.3	23.1
404	51.6	30.6	19.3	8.7	12.5	15.1
405	49.1	32.3	31.6	9.4	20.6	18.0
406	56.7	31.0	25.2	8.3	30.0	16.2
407	45.5	27.3	21.1	7.0	24.2	9.9
409	52.5	28.7	3.1	9.11	6.9	11.7
411	63.6	38.8	30.1	11.4	34.6	29.4
412	63.2	37.1	22.1	12.4	6.6	25.7
439	63.7	34.9	26.6	15.7	30.4	29.4
465	48.0	31.1	11.7	8.9	10.8	15.8
468	80.5	32.0	17.4	12.5	43.8	32.0
478	71.1	40.0	34.8	11.1	17.5	37.0
479	62.1	36.5	21.2	9.8	39.5	24.4
480	67.7	39.3	25.1	9.9	48.2	28.3
481	72.3	37.2	41.6	9.7	12.3	32.5
482	73.7	38.5	16.3	12.5	43.1	34.8
483	78.2	39.3	28.7	9.7	42.0	31.6
484	74.0	40.2	39.7	10.1	35.9	35.1
486	79.1	42.5	22.8	10.9	36.2	37.4
489	79.4	40.4	37.4	9.8	62.1	38.5
Mean	66.8	35.0	22.5	10.2	27.4	26.1
Standard Deviation	9.7	4.1	7.4	1.6	12.7	7.5
Count	92	92	92	92	92	92

Table 3.5
Measurements of broken biface tools

Catalog No.	Maximum Length (mm)	Maximum Width (mm)	Thickness (mm)	Weight (g)
75	24.0	37.0	8.0	7.9
284	26.0	33.3	9.2	6.8
286	32.0	36.0	12.7	15.6
Mean	27.3	35.4	6.6	n/a
Standard Deviation	4.2	1.9	3.5	n/a
Count	3	3	3	n/a

the bulbar end. This distal end in all cases was the working edge. Almost all are triangular with a working edge that matches about a 30–40° sweep on a standard desk protractor. All working edges are convex. Maximum width, with the exception of number 267, in Table 3.6 is the distal measurement. The distal measurement of number 267 is 19.3 millimeters. The narrowest measurement of the scrapers is at the bulbar end, with the exception of number 267. Most scrapers are thickest at the working edge.

With one exception, all have a very carefully steeply retouched working edge. The exception is specimen 180, which has a roughly chipped steep distal edge that exhibits

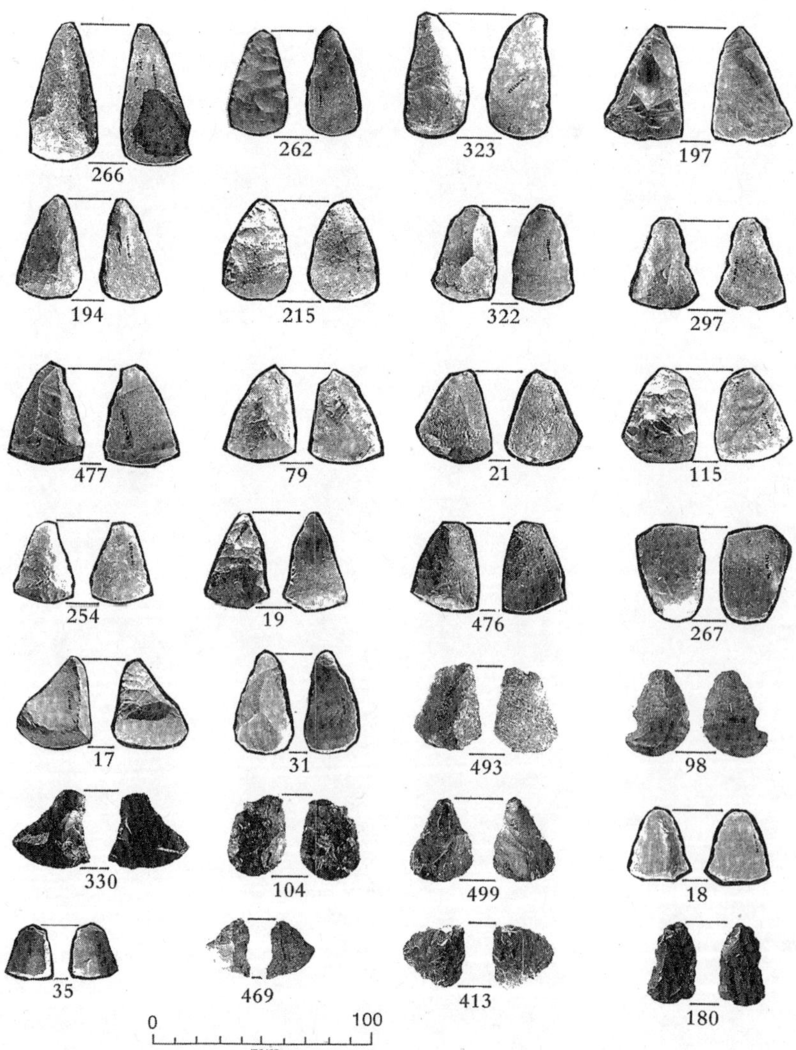

Figure 3.14 End scrapers at the Sloan site. Numbers are catalog numbers keyed to tables. Artifacts are approximately one-fourth actual size.

Table 3.6
Measurements of end scrapers

Catalog No.	Maximum Length (mm)	Maximum Width (mm)	Maximum Thickness (mm)	Working Edge Depth (mm)	Edge Angle	Weight (g)
17	40.3	34.0	10.0	11.6	73.3°	12.2
18	31.2	26.4	8.8	9.3	87.0°	7.8
19	41.7	27.6	8.4	6.4	95.0°	9.3
21	41.2	32.9	9.4	7.5	77.0°	11.9
31	46.4	25.4	6.0	5.6	94.0°	7.6
34	34.2	24.4	7.1	3.1	84.3°	5.9
35	23.6	20.2	4.0	4.4	70.0°	2.4
78	59.0	34.3	11.1	6.7	73.2°	16.3
79	42.2	29.7	9.1	9.0	67.0°	11.2
98	26.2	40.6	7.4	4.3	54.0°	9.8
104	37.1	27.2	8.0	7.2	76.1°	8.3
115	40.2	32.8	7.7	6.0	63.5°	10.9
180	38.2	21.6	7.4	3.7	92.0°	7.0
194	45.7	27.7	11.0	9.5	69.4°	13.9
197	50.2	34.2	7.6	7.1	68.0°	11.7
215	45.2	28.8	8.4	6.7	62.8°	9.8
254	35.1	25.8	6.9	8.2	65.0°	7.3
262	45.4	25.0	10.8	8.3	56.2°	12.2
266	63.3	29.6	8.6	7.8	62.1°	16.7
267	45.2	28.3	8.4	5.5	76.0°	12.7
297	40.7	28.6	8.6	8.5	66.0°	9.6
322	42.0	25.0	7.5	8.1	71.5°	9.9
323	55.0	26.3	7.4	6.4	66.7°	12.3
330	37.2	37.1	11.9	10.9	62.8°	13.8
413	28.2	30.4	8.7	5.1	81.0°	7.7
418	33.7	36.6	9.2	7.9	80.5°	15.3
469	24.7	25.0	8.2	6.0	70.5°	4.3
476	40.2	29.0	7.8	7.3	53.5°	9.7
477	44.0	32.2	8.3	6.5	59.3°	12.7
492	48.4	26.1	8.8	6.5	60.0°	11.5
493	40.0	31.4	11.4	8.5	51.0°	14.5
499	39.5	28.7	7.1	6.5	80.0°	9.1
1416	34.0	30.0	7.0	7.0	75.0°	7.2
Mean	40.6	29.2	8.4	7.1	71.0	10.4
Standard Deviation	8.9	4.5	1.6	1.9	11.5	3.3
Count	33	33	33	33	33	33

considerable wear. All the scrapers exhibit apparent wear in the form of minute chips at the edge (step fractures). Six exhibit distinct polish and striations perpendicular to the edge (18, 215, 262, 322, 323, 477). Wear is confined within an area that extends about 2–4 millimeters from the edge.

All scrapers are retouched laterally. Specimen 492 (not illustrated) has a broken side and a retouched side. All the others were retouched on both sides. Retouch is usually toward the ventral surface. Specimen 17 is retouched toward the dorsal face, probably because of the nature of the flake. It is steeply cortexed on one side, very thin on the

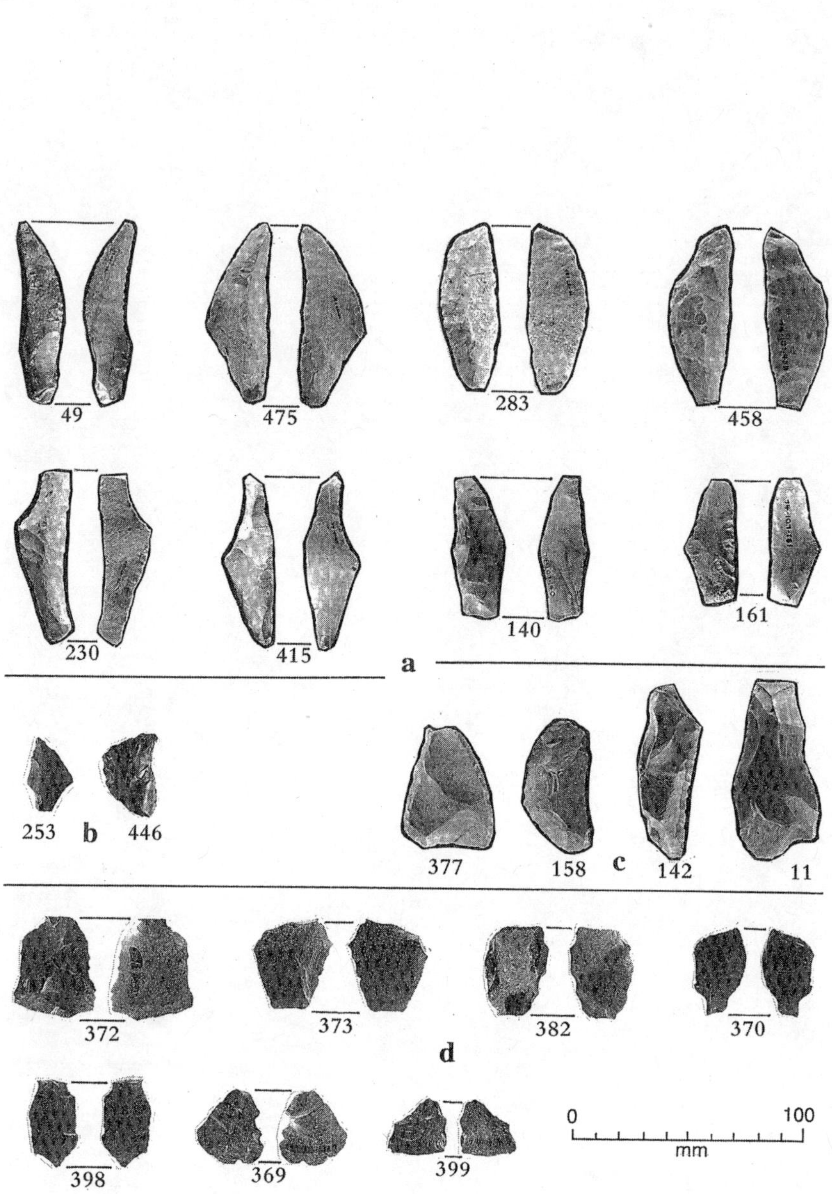

Figure 3.15 Other unifaces at the Sloan site: *a,* backed unifaces; *b,* perforators; *c,* retouched flakes; *d,* utilized Pitkin Chert flakes. Numbers are catalog numbers keyed to tables. Artifacts are approximately one-fourth actual size.

other, and has a very prominent bulbar surface. On some scrapers, retouch covers the entire ventral surface (78, 79, 194, 215, 254, 262, 323, 330, 476). The tendency was to allow for a prominent central ridge, possibly for strength. The scrapers at Sloan are mostly triangular and secondarily trapezoidal in cross section. Eight scrapers were retouched on the bulbar surface. Twenty-eight, which also were the basic triangular scrapers, were lightly ground laterally. Presumably, lateral retouch and grinding were done to allow the scraper to be easily hafted into a socketed handle of antler or wood. The other five scrapers (34, 104, 267, 418, and 1416) may not have been hafted. Three have flatter and wider bases, one has a wider and thicker base, and one (34) is pointed with an adjacent retouched concavity at the end opposite the transverse working edge. Specimen 469 also has a lateral graver tip and number 98 has a concavity 8 millimeters wide and 4 millimeters deep near the working edge.

BACKED UNIFACES. This constitutes a category that generally has been recognized as Dalton in the past but that was not proved to be so until the Sloan site excavation. In total, eight complete and one broken "backed unifaces" were recovered (Figure 3.15*a;* Table 3.7). The broken uniface (285), a tip segment, appears to be broken similar to one of the end scrapers but it was collected considerably below the cultivation zone. Close examination of the break revealed small flake scars that could be the result of the artifact being crushed or could indicate use after breakage. Next to this specimen was one of the very few broken biface tools.

"Backed Uniface" as defined here is a long bladelike

Table 3.7
Measurements of backed unifaces

Catalog No.	Maximum Length (mm)	Width at Shoulder (mm)	Width at ½ Length (mm)	Distance to Shoulder from Base (mm)	Maximum Thickness (mm)	Weight (g)	Edge Angle (degrees)
49	78.7	16.7	16.7	28.0	11.6	14.6	66°
140	61.5	21.2	21.2	31.0	9.0	10.3	62°
161	52.6	21.0	17.2	25.7	8.7	8.3	65°
230	73.9	20.8	18.4	27.0	9.3	12.5	68°
283	71.2	23.6	23.6	31.0	8.7	14.0	56°
285*	42.6	20.1	—	—	6.0	5.4	—
415	74.0	21.7	21.7	40.0	10.6	12.0	68°
458	78.0	24.8	24.6	54.0	7.4	15.8	66°
475	77.0	24.6	24.0	34.0	11.6	19.9	64°
Mean	70.9	21.8	20.9	33.8	9.6	13.4	64.4
Standard Deviation	9.2	2.6	3.1	9.3	1.5	3.5	3.9
Count	8	8	8	8	8	8	8

*Broken.

flake modified in the following manner. The bulbar end is the base. It is thinned in most cases, rarely truncated. The basal segment is retouched and laterally ground to a shoulder. The body exhibits a convex or straight edge op posite a concave working edge. The straight or convex edge is lightly to heavily ground, as if backed—hence its name. The concave end often is lightly ground (from use?) but often is sharp and slightly serrated with a steep edge angle. This artifact probably was hafted like an end scraper and used as a spokeshave scraper.

The closest analogy is the Edgefield/Albany scraper on the Coastal Plain, which dates to the early Holocene (note Webb et al. 1971:fig. 10*d, f*). The tool type is very rare yet persistent at some Dalton sites. The group from Sloan may have almost doubled the entire sample. Not a single one was recovered at the Brand site.

Average length is 70.9 millimeters, average width at the shoulder is 21.8 millimeters, and the average length of the hafted base is 33.8 millimeters. Average thickness and weight are 9.61 millimeters and 14.1 grams, respectively. It is hoped that this artifact class will be recognized elsewhere and a functional analysis attempted in the near future. Edge angles of these specimens are remarkably similar. The average angle is about 65°.

Table 3.8
Measurements of perforators

Catalog No.	Maximum Length (mm)	Maximum Width (mm)	Width at ½ Length (mm)	Maximum Thickness (mm)	Weight (g)
253	33.0	19.9	17.4	7.4	3.8
446	37.1	25.8	21.4	7.4	7.4
Mean	35.1	22.9	19.4	7.4	5.6
Standard Deviation	2.9	4.2	2.8	0.0	2.5
Count	2	2	2	2	2

Specimen 161 is made of Crescent Quarry Chert. Most of the rest are definitely or probably made of Crowley's Ridge Chert. Two (230, 283) may be made of cherts from the Ozarks.

PERFORATORS. Specimen numbers 253 and 446 represent the recognition of a new artifact type for the Dalton period. The perforators at Sloan (Figure 3.15*b;* Table 3.8) are similar in shape to those associated with Poverty Point (Webb 1982:fig. 25), but the tip was not manufactured at the bulbar end as the "Jaketown perforators" were, nor are the Sloan tips chisel-like (Webb 1982:52). Perforators are also found in early Mississippian complexes and however they functioned, obviously there was also a need for similar-shaped tools in the Paleoindian. Specimen 253 was in a disturbed position and not definitely associated with a Dalton cluster. Number 446 was undisturbed and associated with several definite Dalton artifacts.

Specimen 253 is made of a flake of secondary decortication with a tip opposite the bulbar end that has been chipped into a bifacial rounded nib measuring 6.0 by 4.6 by 3.4 millimeters. Number 446 is made of a core flake that has been retouched laterally on both sides. The tip is also opposite the cortexed bulbar end. The bifacially chipped tip has been made at one corner of the broken flake end. It measures 6.0 by 6.0 by 4.0 millimeters. The tip is emphasized by a spokeshavelike treatment of the lateral edge of the flake that measures 16 millimeters long. Both tips exhibit wear and possible polish, but no striations are apparent. Specimen 253 is made of Crowley's Ridge Chert and specimen 446 is probably of Ozark chert.

RETOUCHED FLAKES. In total, twenty-two flakes were retouched, but fit none of the formal Dalton tool categories and probably were not hafted (Figure 3.15*c;* Table 3.9). Most are made of Crowley's Ridge gravel. One (504) is made of gray quartzite, also probably from the ridge gravels. One (167) is Pitkin Chert, and one (437) is Everton Chert. Two others (39, 168) are made of probable Ozark chert (Boone?). Fifteen are flakes of secondary cortex; in many cases, the cortex provided a backed surface. Only two (121, 167) are made on flakes of bifacial retouch.

MINIMALLY RETOUCHED FLAKES. Seven flakes were roughly retouched for apparent use as spokeshaves (39, 121, 143, 282, 437, 470, 504). Concavities range from 16 to 31 millimeters long and average 25 millimeters. Another six flakes (11, 69, 112, 142, 463, 497) exhibit light retouch along almost the entire lateral edge that ranges in shape from slightly concave to straight. Two (268, 327) are lightly retouched along part of one lateral edge to produce a slightly convex working edge. A single flake (430) has a convex working edge 13 millimeters long exhibiting steep retouch on an edge just under 2 millimeters thick.

Table 3.9
Measurements of retouched flakes

Catalog No.	Maximum Length (mm)	Maximum Width (mm)	Width at ½ Length (mm)	Maximum Thickness (mm)	Weight (g)
11	77.2	34.4	30.0	10.2	20.4
29	71.6	28.8	26.8	11.5	24.4
39	26.2	23.0	17.2	9.0	4.6
69	55.4	30.4	26.7	7.1	12.9
112	44.4	33.0	29.9	8.0	12.1
121	47.1	34.4	20.6	9.4	10.7
142	75.6	22.6	22.0	7.7	14.1
143	101.8	39.0	37.3	18.9	65.5
158	58.0	26.4	25.3	9.6	15.6
167	40.2	29.4	27.3	6.2	7.5
168	43.2	39.4	33.2	10.1	16.2
268	45.6	28.1	25.7	8.3	10.0
282	68.6	41.2	41.2	10.8	25.4
327	43.8	36.2	36.0	10.4	13.2
377	52.9	38.4	33.2	5.9	13.1
421	68.5	26.2	25.2	7.0	15.5
430	36.6	27.4	24.9	4.8	13.8
437	59.9	36.6	33.2	9.0	19.5
463	39.9	19.6	19.0	6.2	4.8
470	67.2	34.8	30.0	9.2	17.9
497	50.6	32.3	28.7	7.4	12.0
504	43.0	24.8	19.1	9.7	10.0
Mean	55.3	31.2	27.8	8.9	16.3
Standard Deviation	17.2	6.1	6.2	2.8	12.2
Count	22	22	22	22	22

MORE EXTENSIVELY RETOUCHED FLAKES. Specimen 377 is a classic steeply retouched scraper. It is retouched on all edges and the bulb of percussions is absent, having been removed by the knapper. Edge angle varies from 57° to 64° on the two steeply retouched sides. Two flakes (167, 168) are retouched on all edges and appear to have been useful for a variety of tasks.

Three bladelike flakes have been retouched fairly extensively. Two (29, 158) are similar in shape to those artifacts included in the backed uniface category. They are lunate in basic shape and have been retouched on all edges. There has been no attempt to remove the bulb of percussion. The third bladelike flake is a flake of secondary decortication with an edge 25 millimeters long carefully manufactured laterally near the distal end of the flake.

Table 3.10
Measurements of other unifaces (utilized flakes)

Catalog No.	Maximum Length (mm)	Maximum Width (mm)	Width at ½ Length (mm)	Maximum Thickness (mm)	Weight (g)
12	45.0	27.8	27.8	6.0	5.2
44	37.8	30.2	30.2	7.4	9.7
52	47.4	24.2	24.2	8.4	7.1
63	42.4	28.7	28.7	7.4	5.7
64	50.6	45.9	41.9	13.8	28.7
66	57.6	49.2	38.8	10.8	27.0
72	36.4	25.1	20.4	6.8	5.2
92	54.8	35.7	23.9	9.9	16.6
100	53.0	35.7	35.7	12.0	20.3
114	53.0	24.4	24.4	13.6	11.7
117	73.1	24.3	24.3	7.4	12.3
127	44.1	20.6	18.2	5.0	4.2
137	72.8	47.2	38.8	11.3	28.6
145	34.3	26.0	26.0	4.3	4.5
162	44.0	15.6	14.3	3.4	2.2
166	59.3	20.5	16.4	4.8	5.4
199	66.2	41.2	36.1	10.2	25.8
243	42.8	29.3	26.2	10.2	13.2
245	41.2	37.3	37.3	8.9	10.8
256	76.4	26.2	22.8	12.4	25.3
260	45.1	23.3	18.6	6.5	4.8
326	56.1	20.5	20.5	5.0	6.2
369	32.6	29.2	29.2	3.7	3.0
370	40.0	21.8	20.2	2.9	2.3
372	45.1	36.1	30.0	4.0	5.4
373	40.6	34.0	28.8	4.8	5.5
382	39.3	27.2	27.2	3.6	4.5
398	38.9	20.9	20.6	4.8	2.5
399	25.5	24.6	22.4	4.6	2.3
422	56.2	25.6	25.4	7.8	10.3
432	56.8	33.2	28.6	20.2	31.2
438	[illegible] 4	27.0	26.9	10.6	12.7
444	39.3	29.8	18.0	7.4	6.6
447	52.5	24.1	20.2	6.4	6.3
472	21.0	21.2	17.5	3.5	1.6
Mean	47.5	29.0	26.0	7.7	10.7
Standard Deviation	12.6	8.0	7.0	3.8	9.0
Count	35	35	35	35	35

UTILIZED FLAKES. In total, thirty-five flakes that exhibit evidence of use were recovered in apparent Dalton deposits (Figure 3.15*d;* Table 3.10). Seven flakes are made of Pitkin Chert; all appear to have originated from a single Dalton deposit and probably constituted a single grave lot. The other twenty-eight utilized flakes fit the definition of Crowley's Ridge Chert and were probably all locally quarried.

PITKIN CHERT FLAKES (369, 370, 372, 373, 382, 398, 399). All seven are flakes of bifacial retouch that may have been removed from the same core or biface. No matches could be made, however. One (382) is cortexed over much of one surface. All seem to have been used slightly on a lateral edge.

BLADELIKE FLAKES (117, 127, 162, 166, 326, 447). Six bladelike flakes include two that are flakes of bifacial retouch. Four are flakes of secondary decortication. Only very slight lateral wear is present.

GRAVERS. A total of three crude flakes was possibly retouched and/or used as scrapers and/or gravers. They are not at all similar to the gravers described from Brand (Goodyear 1974:fig. 18) or that exist in substantial numbers in our other Dalton site collections. These tools are examples of what we usually classify as expedient tools, similar to the three broken bifaces that were used as scrapers and/or gravers.

Specimen numbers 44, 114, and 245 are crude flakes (two core and one thick flake of bifacial retouch) each with a natural spur that has been used with no, or very minimal, retouch. They probably would not have been identified as gravers if recovered from a site with notable debitage.

OTHER FLAKES. The remaining nineteen flakes include four that are flakes of bifacial retouch, one primary decortication flake, and twelve secondary decortication flakes. All exhibit very minor lateral wear; some of the observed wear may not be due to use as a tool.

CHERT DISCOID HAMMERS. Three Dalton discoid hammers made from chert cobbles are represented (Figure 3.16*a;* Table 3.11). All three are bifaces with little or no cortex extant. All three are extensively battered and worn,

Figure 3.16 Other artifacts at the Sloan site: *a*, chert discoid hammers; *b*, *pièce esquillée*; *c*, chert chopper/core; *d*, grooved sandstone abrader; *e*, notched sandstone abrader; *f*, edge-abraded cobble. Numbers are catalog numbers keyed to tables. Artifacts are approximately one-fourth actual size except for *e*, which is one-half.

even to the extent of exhibiting edge polish with finc striations perpendicular to the edge. The first recognition that these hammers were probably unique to Dalton was the Sloan site excavation. A search of the Arkansas Archeological Survey collections indicated that these hammers are present at other Dalton sites in northeastern Arkansas but are extremely rare.

PIÈCE ESQUILLÉE. A single example is made of Pitkin Chert (443). It is a classic example, being rectangular and measuring 31.2 by 20.4 by 7.6 millimeters thick (Figure 3.16*b*). All four edges are battered, particularly the two lateral edges and one end. *Pièces esquillées* are thought to be either exhausted bipolar cores and/or wedges to split bone. The Sloan example may have been recycled into a transverse-edged cutting tool with the lateral edges backed because those two sides are very dull.

CHERT CHOPPER/CORE. The apparent chopper (163) is a Pitkin Chert cobble with flakes crudely removed from two ends. The wider end with the most flakes removed exhibits minute flake scars at the chipped and sharp edge. The narrow end also exhibits minute flake scars. Most of the cortexed surface exhibits minute striations that probably are natural from battering within a gravel deposit. If a core, as thought in 1974, it certainly is a very crude one. But a chopper, if indeed it is one, would be difficult to use without a piece of hide to protect one's hand when

Table 3.11
Measurements of discoid hammers

Catalog No.	Maximum Length (mm)	Maximum Width (mm)	Maximum Thickness (mm)	Weight (g)
91	52.3	48.3	18.7	43.4
182	54.7	40.8	17.2	35.9
343	47.0	39.2	16.0	35.1
Mean	51.3	42.8	17.3	38.1
Standard Deviation	3.9	4.9	1.4	4.6
Count	3	3	3	3

Table 3.12
Measurements of pebble cores

Catalog No.	Maximum Length (mm)	Maximum Width (mm)	Maximum Thickness (mm)	Weight (g)
32	3.8	3.7	2.3	31.6
261	4.4	2.9	2.0	20.9
273	3.5	2.1	1.4	14.8
306	3.3	3.0	1.7	13.7
Mean	3.8	2.9	1.9	20.3
Standard Deviation	0.5	0.7	0.4	8.2
Count	4	4	4	4

chopping. Our impression is that Pitkin Chert is rare and hence probably exotic. A crude chopper or core is not an expectation, which means we may not be interpreting this artifact correctly. It measures 57.4 by 64.4 by 41.3 millimeters thick and weighs 176.1 grams (Figure 3.16*c*).

PEBBLE CORES. In total, four pebble cores that seem to be part of the Dalton deposit were recovered (Table 3.12). Three (32, 261, 306) are typical exhausted pebble cores with a cortex back. Two (261, 306) exhibit minute flake scars that may be due to either platform preparation or use as a small chopper or scraper. The fourth core (273) has a cortex end and also exhibits minute flake scars on its sharp edges. All are made of Crowley's Ridge Chert. All are similar to pebble cores recovered at the Brand site (Goodyear 1974:fig. 24). But they also occur throughout the subsequent prehistoric sequence. Specimen 306 does not seem to be associated with other Dalton-period artifacts and may not be part of the original deposits.

SANDSTONE ABRADERS. In total, thirty-five sandstone abraders were recovered. These are classified as: sixteen grooved, nine notched, three grooved and notched, one disintegrated, and six other. An additional twenty fragmentary and disintegrated possible abrader remnants were omitted from the final tally. They consisted mainly of fragments of ironstone and probably were not abraders. A group of five (149, 169, 170, 171, and 172) had been identified as abraders but now are classified as unknown ironstone objects. Four abrader fragments (129/132, 424/434) were portions of two abraders.

Sandstones are relatively common in the Arkansas Ozarks, as is ironstone in Crowley's Ridge. But these have not been extensively studied except for the Ordovician St. Peter sandstone, readily available almost directly west of Jonesboro in Izard, Sharp, and Independence Counties at the edge of the Ozarks (Giles 1930). This is the major area where most of the Ozark cherts were also most available to people living near the Sloan site.

Abrasion is accomplished by the cutting action of microscopic edged particles. The basic shape of the abrader should be of prime importance for categorization. This statement is based on abrading tools in our culture being categorized on the basis of shape. Examples are hand and bench stones, strop, grinding wheels, sandpaper, and files such as the taper file and the 10-inch mill bastard file. Important attributes of abrader particles are size, hardness, angularity, and spacing. The important characteristic of the bonding agent is strength. About all we could measure was particle size. "Their toughness, degree of angularity, and durability make the . . . [Ordovician sandstones] . . . very satisfactory for friction and abrasive purposes." (Giles 1930:XV) The "coherence of the [St. Peter] sandstone is variable" (Giles 1930:21). Without grinding the abraders up and passing them through sieves, we cannot tell if the usually fine-grained St. Peter sandstone is actually represented here or not. The Dalton people, however, were not randomly selecting their stone; they presumably needed certain-sized grains.

Sand abrasive was not used on wood until relatively recently in our society (Mercer 1975:135). Sand grains would have dulled the edges of the tools used to shape wood. An exception is the use of paired sandstone grooved abraders to smooth arrowshafts in the Plains. A logical reason for the existence of sandstone abraders would be to use on chert during tool processing (Crabtree 1972:8). One major function was to abrade sharp lateral edges for strength and/or to allow the item to be bound to a haft (Titmus and Woods 1991). A second major function was to prepare a potential striking platform (Crabtree 1972). In addition, abraders were employed to sharpen antler tools used in chipping chert tools (Crabtree 1972). Another logical function for abraders obviously would be the sharpening of bone and antler awls and needles. Eyed needles were needed for the manufacture of tailored clothing, necessary to the original inhabitants of the continental United States as they passed through the Arctic. Needles and awls have been found in Paleoindian and Dalton context (Logan 1952:55, plate XXII, *J, K*). Antler tools such as the baton for percussion knapping and the antler tip for pressure chipping can be inferred based on our knowledge of lithic technology. Based on the Old World Paleolithic bone and antler assemblages and the similarity of mutual types of lithic tools thought to have been prominent in their manufacture, there must have been a rich bone and antler industry for Dalton culture as well.

Because so many of the other artifacts found at Sloan are pristine or at least serviceable tools instead of discarded exhausted and fragmented specimens, we can expect that the abrader category is the same. Therefore these Sloan site data present us with a unique chance to identify the initial manufacture, use, and recycling processes involved. Comparisons with site assemblages such as that from Brand may indicate the extent of reworking involved before the abrader was discarded. Until now we have only seen the final step.

GROOVED ABRADERS. In total, sixteen grooved abraders were found (Figure 3.16*d*). Seven (233, 234, 13, 364, 368, 129/132, 62) are larger oval, prominently centrally grooved examples. An eighth is broken and only two fragments were recovered (424/434) The grooved surface is flat, and the ungrooved surface and lateral edges are convex. Four (55, 150, 219, 250) are ends of what were larger abraders. One (48) seems to be a recycled side. The remaining three are or were (28, 154, 156) smaller, more disklike abraders with a groove that is deeper at one lateral end and does not extend completely across the stone before it fades away. Variations in abrader size and in the size and shape of the groove involved indicate that these tools functioned to abrade different items. Just how specialized each abrader is, or how multipurpose one is, of course is not known. All we now know is that each probably began its existence essentially the same size and shape and that other physical attributes are similar (Table 3.13). Recycled abrader fragments were usually shorter than 73 millimeters long, whereas pristine abraders were more than about 73 millimeters long. Only the possible recycled side fragment was substantially narrower than pristine abraders. Thickness and weight depend upon the nature of suspected recycling.

Grooves measured at the center range in width from 10.1 to 26.6 millimeters. The two nicest abraders have grooves measuring 14.5 and 13.1 millimeters wide. The mean of all grooves (including two grooves on specimens 156 and 219) is 15.9 millimeters. Twelve of the grooves taper slightly, from 0.4 to 4.6 millimeters with an average of 1.7 millimeters. Average maximum depth of all seventeen grooves is 3.7 millimeters, and average minimum depth is 2.5 millimeters. The overall range of depth is 1.1 to 8.4 millimeters.

Particle size as it was measured is somewhat subjective. A series of microscope slides was made based upon the Wentworth grade scale in millimeters, which in turn is tied into the U.S. standard American Society for Testing Materials (A.S.T.M.) sieve numbers. These slides were compared with each abrader on the grooved surface under a microscope until a match with what appeared to the most common grain size was made. In addition, the maximum observed grain size was similarly noted. The grooved abrader range is 0.21–0.71 millimeters with an approximate mean of 0.52 millimeters. This range encompasses 45 to 25 on the U.S. standard A.S.T.M. sieve number scale with a mean at about 35. This mean is just beyond the border between medium and coarse sand; the range extends through part of the coarse sand bracket and slightly into the medium sand bracket. The range of maximum grain size extends up into the granule gravel bracket, with the mean just beyond the border between coarse and very coarse sand with a normal range only about halfway through the very coarse sand bracket. Ten of the abraders are mainly coarse textured and seven are mainly medium textured, but all seventeen essentially overlap with each other across the border between medium and coarse.

The particles on all grooved abraders are mostly quartz, with a hardness of 7 on the Mohs scale of 1–10. This is the same hardness as modern sandpaper particles but less

Table 3.13
Measurements of grooved abraders

Catalog No.	Maximum Length (mm)	Maximum Width (mm)	Maximum Thickness (mm)	Weight (g)	Usual Range of Grain Size (mm)	Maximum Range of Grain Size (mm)
13	87.0	51.8	22.4	116.1	0.500–0.590	1.00–1.19
28	59.9	49.9	14.9	41.5	0.420–0.570	1.00–1.19
48	60.4	25.5	26.7	34.7	0.210–0.250	0.350–0.420
55	61.8	52.2	22.5	74.3	0.420–0.500	0.590–0.710
62	72.8	42.1	28.0	84.1	0.420–0.500	0.590–0.710
129/132	120.0	57.0	24.4	219.3	0.59–0.710	1.41–1.68
150	50.6	50.0	20.5	59.7	0.590–0.710	2.00–2.38
154	43.8	27.8	14.9	20.5	0.420–0.500	0.590–0.710
156	44.4	29.5	12.8	20.8	0.350–0.420	0.840–1.00
219	54.9	52.8	17.7	64.5	0.420–0.500	0.840–1.00
233	102.0	53.3	25.3	172.1	0.500–0.590	0.840–1.00
234	110.5	50.6	26.3	168.0	0.500–0.590	0.590–0.710
250	64.8	59.3	27.3	118.0	0.500–0.590	1.00–1.19
364	79.8	42.7	21.7	88.5	0.420–0.500	0.590–0.710
368	89.8	52.0	19.7	109.1	0.59–0.500	0.840–1.00
424/434	52+	65.4	23.2	108.4	0.350–0.420	0.840–1.00
Mean	72.2	47.6	21.8	93.7		
Standard Deviation	23.7	11.4	4.7	56.8		
Count	16	16	16	16		

than the 9 of aluminum oxide (corundum, emery), the usual modern grinding wheel grit. Angular grains are necessary for effective abrasion. The angularity of particles on the grooved abraders is difficult to ascertain without a complicated photographic and random counting technique (personal communication, David Vosburg, professor of geology, Arkansas State University), which is beyond our present capabilities. It is informative to note that although many of the grains are rounded, there is more angularity present than would be expected given a random selection of sandstones for abraders. It is difficult to ascertain whether selection was also for sandstone that, so to speak, presented its best points in a consistent direction.

The uniformity of particles on abraders is important. Larger grains tend to cut more and leave scratches that cannot be erased. The grooved abraders appear to be fairly uniform with occasional larger grains of 1 millimeter or so in size on the average. This uniformity in fact rules out the typical Crowley's Ridge "ironstone" as a source as suggested by Goodyear (1974:69) for the abraders recovered at the Brand site. Microscopic examination of ferruginous sandstone collected from Crow Creek, which drains Crowley's Ridge near Forrest City, revealed more clear quartz, considerably more chert, and a much greater variation in grain size than exist in the Sloan site abraders.

Spacing is important in abraders because dust (bone or chert) or dirt can clog the close- spaced abrader surface to the extent that even with proper lubrication it glazes and no longer cuts. Too wide a spacing means that the fewer particles will provide a relatively ineffective abrading surface. To ascertain spacing, the grains would have to be counted by size within a randomly selected known-sized blocked area on the abrader surface. So many variables exist that we hesitated, because of our lack of recommended facilities and time limitation, to begin such a project. Subjectively, the spacing noted on the grooved abraders appears to be almost optimum based on comparison with modern sandpaper.

Bonding is very important, in fact crucial, for abrader effectiveness. The abrader surface has to break down in order for worn quartz particles to be removed to expose fresh, more angular particles. However, if the surface breaks down too fast, the contours will change and the size will diminish to the extent that effectiveness is impaired. Although the sandstone used here is much more consolidated than geologically recent Crowley's Ridge "ironstone" and more consolidated than many sandstones, it is not as consolidated as the other major sandstone abrader category. This may be necessary because many of the sand grains are more rounded and hence not as effective as abrading elements.

Each abrader surface was tested with 10% strength hydrochloric acid, which revealed two things: (1) that there was no bone residue on the working surfaces, and (2) that the binding substance is not calcareous. The sandstone source is probably somewhere in the Ozark uplands. Published descriptions, although brief, of Lamotte and Roubidoux Sandstones (Branson 1944:16, 48) indicate that these should be considered first. Roubidoux is available in Missouri throughout Butler and Stoddard Counties and part of Ripley County along the edge of the highlands and beyond. Lamotte Sandstone is located farther north, in Ste. Genevieve County. Roubidoux appears to be the most logical of the two and would have been easily available via the Cache River, which at that time may have been larger and headwatered in several appropriate Ozark valleys.

The function, if indeed there is supposed to be only a single function involved, of this particular kind of artifact can be guessed at but must be tested by experimentation. Two hypothesized functions that complement each other pertain to chert knapping. The flakes of bifacial retouch recovered at the Sloan site indicate that the purpose in preparing the edges of striking platforms is to grind off the rough parts of the biface edge. Abrasion can be seen at the edge and over the face adjacent to the edge on these flakes. This abrasion would not be as extensive if caused merely by the actual striking of the knapping tool itself. A groove would be beneficial because it would allow the edge of the biface to be ground in the center and the adjacent faces to be ground alternatively on the lateral extents of the groove. Pane glass being cut for windows at the Arkansas State University physical plant involved use of a coarse sandpaper to roughly abrade the edges to straighten the edge for mounting. Ron Carmack, superintendent of the physical plant, explained that whatever sandpaper was handy would be used if roughing were thought to be necessary; there was no concentrated effort to use a particular size to smooth the freshly cut window pane. However, on several occasions at the physical plant during observations spaced over four years it was noticed that coarse sandpaper was being used. But lithic replicators appear to favor a finer abrader (Don Crabtree, personal communication) and the second hypothesized function outlined below may be more logical (Crabtree 1972:8).

Most probably a bone, antler, or wood punch was being used to knap. This punch would have had to be resharpened periodically. Although the abraders being discussed here are coarser than I would expect for such a function, it is a possibility and should be tested experimentally. The grooves themselves lend some credence to this hypothesis because they taper from one end to another on many of the specimens. However, this could be due to consistent use of the abrader by the same individual for biface platform preparation as well as for resharpening the knapping punch. The tapering on many of the abraders does not indicate foreshaft or haft abrading; however, motor habits would have to be observed during actual experimental abrading to test this notion.

NOTCHED ABRADERS. A total of nine abraders cluster according to a number of attributes. The most prominent and universal attributes are the finer particle size, tighter bonding, and notches on one or more edges (Figure 3.16*e;* Table 3.14). The stock consisted of tabular, relatively thin plates with little if any subsequent modification expect for use. Usually a flat surface was utilized; occasionally a V-shaped groove on the surface was distinct enough to be followed to a notch on one edge.

Particle size is medium. The range of the most common particles is 0.21 to 0.59 millimeters and of maximum particles from 0.35 to 0.71 millimeters (actual largest particle observed was 2.39 millimeters). The respective means are 0.31 and 0.50 millimeters (0.77 if the large exceptional particle is included). However, it is a mistake to view the particle size as indicating about a 45-grit abrader because these particles do not represent the actual abrading elements. A secondary quartz overgrowth is present. The secondary crystallization is apparent in the silica binding as well as over the rounded particles. The secondary overgrowth is euhedral over the original particles. Although autormorphic, it provides a new, more finely textured surface with which to abrade. Two abraders are classified as orthoquartzite because the overgrowth is so intense. The actual grit size is 80 to 120.

A hypothesized function for the notched abrader pre-

Table 3.14
Measurements of notched abraders

Catalog No.	Maximum Length (mm)	Maximum Width (mm)	Maximum Thickness (mm)	Weight (g)	Usual Range of Grain Size (mm)	Maximum Range of Grain Size (mm)
54	54.8	47.0	14.0	51.4	0.250–0.297	0.350–0.420
71	53.5	50.4	18.7	56.9	0.420–0.570	02.00–02.38
76	55.9	41.5	23.8	66.9	0.210–0.250	0.350–0.420
259	87.3	50.9	16.0	73.1	0.210–0.250	0.500–0.590
269	58.8	35.8	16.5	39.2	0.297–0.350	0.570–0.710
298	58.0	30.6	17.1	41.2	0.250–0.297	0.500–0.590
431	61.4	49.9	15.7	43.3	0.350–0.420	0.590–0.710
490	70.2	52.3	12.6	45.5	0.250–0.297	0.350–0.420
500	31.5	29.8	15.5	16.2	0.500–0.590	0.590–0.710
Mean	59.0	43.1	16.7	48.2		
Standard Deviation	14.8	9.0	3.2	16.7		
Count	9	9	9	9		

sented elsewhere (Morse 1973) is to grind the hafting portions of points. This could be expanded to include adzes and other stone tools in need of having edges and faces ground for hafting purposes. The reason for such grinding would be to prevent cutting of the haft and bindings during use of the object concerned. In addition grinding strengthens the tool (Titmus and Woods 1991).

The ground edges observed on points and adzes are smooth. The general lack of striations indicates flat abraders and/or some flexibility in the process so that exactly the same grinding surface was not used throughout the activity. Adzes tend to be ground over their faces as well as along their edges, understandable in view of the hypothesized hafting of Dalton adzes (Figure 3.10). Again, a flat abrader is indicated. The V-shaped grooves and notches are not overly prominent but would accommodate the edges of lithic bifaces such as points and possibly adzes initially. The closest analogy in our society, perhaps, is the grinding of plate glass after being cut, for instance to place on top of a desk. These edges are usually ground with 80- and 120-grit abrading belts (Ronnie Roberts, president, Interstate Glass and Supply, Inc., Jonesboro, personal communication). In this later case, grit values as coarse as 60 and as fine as 220 are used, but the 80- and 120-grit abraders are preferred and mostly used.

A second hypothesis for the function of the edge-notched abrader is to finish and keep sharp the small-eyed needles and fine-tipped awls known and expected in Dalton culture. Other hypotheses can be envisioned but little can be accomplished further until experimentation is conducted on them. Again, we should not feel we must think in terms of monofunctions; an expectation is multiple-functional tools, especially abraders.

GROOVED AND NOTCHED ABRADERS. Three abraders are grooved and notched. They are most similar to the notched category, particularly in shape and particle size (Table 3.15).

OTHER ABRADERS. Specimen number 139 is a flat stone that may be a blank for a notched abrader. The other five are irregular; two of these (417, 501) are eroded small corner fragments. Only the possible blank exhibits workmanship and this seems to be limited to squaring off edges and surfaces (Table 3.16).

In summary, there appear to be two basic kinds of abraders. One type is a coarse oval-shaped stone with a long and wide central groove on one flattened surface. As this type of abrader was used, it fragmented, and ends, sides, and midsections continued to be used as single-grooved abraders. The other major category of abrader is fine, tabular, and fairly irregular in shape with notched edges. Obvious functions are related to the preparation of biface edges both for knapping and for hafting. This is

Table 3.15
Measurements of grooved and notched abraders

Catalog No.	Maximum Length (mm)	Maximum Width (mm)	Maximum Thickness (mm)	Weight (g)	Usual Range of Grain Size (mm)	Maximum Range of Grain Size (mm)
361	100.8	55.9	28.1	139.6	0.177–0.250	0.350–0.420
416	54.7	33.8	20.9	39.5	0.297–0.420	0.420–0.500
461	66.7	52.8	22.2	56.9	0.250–0.297	0.420–0.500
Mean	74.1	47.5	23.7	78.7		
Standard Deviation	23.9	12.0	3.8	53.5		
Count	3	3	3	3		

Table 3.16
Measurements of other abraders

Catalog No.	Maximum Length (mm)	Maximum Width (mm)	Maximum Thickness (mm)	Weight (g)	Usual Range of Grain Size (mm)	Maximum Range of Grain Size (mm)
7	105.7	62.0	37.5	246.8	0.250–0.297	1.19–1.41
9	59.6	52.6	16.7	40.2	0.420–0.500	1.19–1.41
139	75.0	70.4	17.2	110.0	0.210–0.250	0.350–0.420
270	73.5	58.0	22.7	87.6	0.590–0.710	1.41–1.68
417	45.4	34.0	18.3	23.3	0.297–0.420	0.840–1.00
501	34.0	28.2	18.0	13.4	0.297–0.420	0.350–0.420
Mean	65.5	50.9	21.7	86.9		
Standard Deviation	25.3	16.5	8.0	86.9		
Count	6	6	6	6		

particularly valid for notched abraders. Bone awl finishing could have been accomplished as well, particularly with many of the grooved examples.

EDGE-ABRADED COBBLE (441). A heavy (714.4 grams) quartzite cobble exhibits a 60 by 75 millimeter slight depression on each flat face and two areas of prominent edge abrasion on its edges. The cobble measures 121 by 104 by 36 millimeters thick. It is oval except for a battered skewed end. The battering looks natural. The generally smoothed shallow depressions are centrally lightly pecked. The edge abrasions are obvious with no apparent striations (Figure 3.16*f*). Other quartzite edge-abraded cobbles from northeastern Arkansas do exhibit slight and short striations that are parallel with the edge.

Besides northeastern Arkansas, the only similar "edge-abraded cobbles" found reported in the literature are from the Northwest (Crabtree and Swanson 1968) and Panama (McGimsey 1956:155–156). Butler (1966:95) suggested that edge-abraded cobbles in the Northwest were vegetable-grinding tools. Crabtree (personal communication, 1975) on the other hand interpreted the Idaho tools as hammerstones used to detach blades. Dalton did not seem to include a true blade technology, so this latter function does not appear to be valid for the northeastern Arkansas artifacts. The absence of a stone mortar with the cobble tool means that we cannot be absolutely certain it was used to grind vegetable matter. However, the edge-abraded cobble would have also made an excellent mortar for grinding by a similar stone (see Butler 1962:fig.

Table 3.17
Measurements of cobble abraders

Catalog No.	Maximum Length (mm)	Maximum Width (mm)	Maximum Thickness (mm)	Weight (g)
83	11.7	7.1	3.0	353.9
178	10.1	5.1	3.4	229.8
344	7.5	5.5	2.6	165.7
345	6.3	6.2	5.0	270.9
Mean	8.9	6.0	3.5	255.1
Standard Deviation	2.4	0.9	1.1	78.8
Count	4	4	4	4

13*h, i*). Butler (1962:45) reviewed the occurrence of "edge-ground cobbles" in the New World and the associated radiocarbon dates, which indicate that the earliest examples date back to circa 10,000–11,000 B.P.

COBBLE ABRADERS. Four quartzite cobbles exhibiting at least light abrasion and/or battering at one end were recovered (Table 3.17). Two (344, 345) found together were thought to be unmodified cobbles until very careful scrutiny with a hand lens revealed striations. The major function of all four appears to be the preparation of biface platform edges for knapping with an antler baton. On two, consistent end abrasion has resulted in small but distinct notching.

Specimen 83 is an oval, flat cobble that exhibits light battering on both ends, one edge, and upon both surfaces. Striations are perpendicular to the long axis and two notches are obvious. Specimen 178 is lightly battered and abraded mostly on the narrower end where two notches spaced close together exist. Both surfaces near that end appear worn, and on one surface very slight striations parallel with the stone axis are just visible. Specimen 344 is a flat, oval cobble that has had one end removed. On one face at the end opposite the break are very fine striations that are perpendicular to the long axis of the stone tool. Specimen 345, which was found immediately beside number 344, is roughly spheroid in basic shape. There are very fine striations on part of an edge that are perpendicular to that edge.

OCHER. Five stains representing ocher were recorded (226, 313, 494, 495, 496). The latter three were found near each other and included the only "yellow ocher" stain. The other stains were of red ocher. Red ocher (hematite) occurs in a relatively pure state within ironstone concretions on Crowley's Ridge. Limonite, if that indeed was the "yellow ocher" observed, does occur as a primary deposit at least as close as southeastern Missouri (Branson 1944:399). Red ocher was associated with Folsom points at the Hanson site (Frison and Bradley 1980:9, 90). It is surprising that more red ocher was not present at Sloan, but even the little that was observed was impossible to collect.

IRONSTONE OBJECT. Specimen number 149 (which includes 169, 171, 172, and probably 170, which was lost in the field) is fragments of an ironstone object that must have disintegrated in the ground. Two (149, 171) exhibit a convex smoothed surface. It is too fragmentary to identify.

HOLOCENE ARTIFACTS FOUND AT THE SLOAN SITE

Artifacts dating from about the entire period of the Holocene are present on this and neighboring sand dunes. At Sloan were found Archaic, Woodland, and Mississippian points and even a few potsherds. Most of the artifacts were in the cultivation zone. However some were found beneath the cultivation zone.

Three early Holocene points were found at the Sloan site. All were excavated. At a depth of 42 centimeters was found a Palmer point (circa 9800 B.P.). It was lying flat and about 7 centimeters from a corner-notched unifacial point with an unground base. Both artifacts were found

28–30 centimeters "beneath" a level containing three Dalton-period artifacts (195–197). The Palmer artifacts were located 10 centimeters and 17 centimeters south of the Dalton artifacts, which were very near the cultivation zone. Because of the age difference we assume that the two Palmer artifacts were intrusive through the Dalton "level." All subcultivation-zone artifacts at Sloan, of course, were intrusive into the sand dunes. The Palmer was simply a deeper intrusion.

A Cache River point (circa 9800 B.P.) with a chip off its base was found at point 46.62 R 48.00 at a depth of 18 centimeters. The point was on edge and at an angle and obviously disturbed. A Hardin point (circa 8500 B.P.) was found also on edge and at an angle, hence obviously disturbed. It was at point 52.4 R 51.55 at a depth of 25 centimeters. The point had been resharpened, without beveling, as if remade from a broken point.

At point 51.74 R 45.08, in an area measuring about 6 by 14 centimeters, were six artifacts (two pebble cores, two flakes, one crude biface, one fire-cracked rock fragment) that were found just beneath the cultivation zone to a depth of at least 7 centimeters. These were in a disturbance rather than in an Archaic pit feature. We did not get good evidence of a more permanent Archaic occupation, possibly just centuries of foraging activities.

A variety of twenty-four points that are Woodland and Late Archaic in date were found. An Archaic encampment of some sort is also a logical expectation. Another seven points were excavated. All but one was immediately below the cultivation zone. That one is a possible Big Creek point (circa 2000–3000 B.C.) found at an angle at point 46.15 R 45.00 and at a depth of 27 centimeters. Archaic hunters seem to have frequented these dunes.

The most spectacular non-Dalton discovery was a burial. The adult skeleton was flexed on its left side, mostly in the 1 by 1 meter square 52 R 55. Bone preservation was very poor. Because no artifacts were present, and in the absence of radiocarbon dating, the skeleton can only be generally dated to the Archaic or Woodland periods, somewhere about 1000 B.C.–A.D. 700. The burial allowed us to gather soil samples to compare with those found elsewhere in the dune (Akridge 1994a,b). This skeleton was just at the northeastern edge of the Sloan Dalton cemetery.

There must have been a small, seasonal, late-Woodland house here at one time about A.D. 500–700. Two sherds were excavated. One was in a disturbance at point 49.20 R 52.28 about 10 centimeters below the cultivation zone. The other was found at point 49.09 R 52.62 at a depth of 24 centimeters. Both were Barnes Cordmarked and probably date circa A.D. 500–700.

Several small fragments of Mississippi Plain and Barnes Plain and Barnes paste eroded-surface sherds were also found on the surface. The Mississippian sherds are reinforced by the presence of five Shugtown side-notched and two Scallorn points as well as three aborted preforms. Possibly a Mississippian farmstead dating about the twelfth century once existed here. A Nodena point indicates that a protohistoric hunter in the fifteenth or sixteenth century hunted here at least once. Occasional finds of Nodena points are made in this area but no base camps or villages have been found, nor are villages expected to be found. This area was abandoned to permanent occupation during Late Mississippian (Morse and Morse 1983). The latest sherd found on the surface was a mid-nineteenth-century stick spatter decorated fragment.

4
Sloan Site Biface and Projectile Point Technology

BRUCE A. BRADLEY

The Sloan site artifact assemblage is extraordinary because of the large numbers of whole artifacts that are available for study. The following discussion is a technological reconstruction of the objects classified as Dalton points and bifaces. A near total lack of debitage has meant that interpretations are based on observations of the implements.

A production sequence for Dalton points was presented by Morse (1971b:13), but it is so generalized that the same sequence may be used to describe almost all projectile points of Paleoindian and Archaic age. The Sloan site assemblage allows a more detailed technological reconstruction. Similar reconstructions (e.g., Bradley 1974:191–197; Flenniken 1978:473–480), especially of Paleoindian technologies, have allowed better comparisons and led to more refined inferences of relationships between archaeological cultures. These include recognition of regional and/or chronological variations, as well as similarities over wide areas. Morphological variations of Dalton points, especially related to resharpening sequences, have been the focus of previous technological discussions (Goodyear 1974:24–32; Morse 1971b:10–12). The main reason is that the majority of Dalton assemblages have consisted primarily of used-up, discarded artifacts and it was resharpening that made the final forms so distinctive. The Sloan site assemblage is unusual because it consists mostly of either original unused forms or at least freshly resharpened artifacts. Most of the items were also deposited intentionally (see chapter 6) rather than being discarded.

There is a wide range of morphological variation in the Sloan-site Dalton point assemblage. This includes outline, size, margin form, basal treatment, and finish. There is, however, a single production technology present. It is possible to identify various stages and steps of a manufacturing process, and to classify each of the pieces into specific stages and steps of manufacture. Although this is possible, I view the technology as a continuous process, with different pieces representing different points of manufacture termination along a continuum.

Manufacture of Dalton points has been discussed, with examples of different stages described and illustrated (Morse 1971b; Goodyear 1974:21–25; Morse and Morse 1983:fig. 4.2*a–b*). Overall, I believe that this interpretation is correct for the smaller points, but the regularity and thinness of the larger points would have demanded a more refined percussion thinning process.

A curious aspect of the Sloan-site point assemblage is

the general lack of evidence of the early stages of manufacture. There are only a few minor remnants of percussion flaking on a few of the artifacts. The great majority of remaining flake scars resulted from pressure flaking, even on large specimens. One of the largest points (133) retains evidence of the original raw material exteriors on both sides (Figure 3.2). In this case, the artifact was made from a single, probably tabular or lenticular, piece of chert. The lack of manufacturing debitage in the assemblage also makes raw material form and initial manufacture difficult to reconstruct.

Early or preform stages have been recovered from other Dalton sites (Morse 1971b:fig. 2*a–c;* Goodyear 1974:fig. 11*a–c*), but they are rare and very few of them are of a size or form that could have produced many of the Sloan-site Dalton points.

Lack of this early stage evidence at the Sloan site does not preclude a detailed look at the later stages of manufacture technology. Sloan Dalton-point technology exhibits several distinct traits: (1) substantial preliminary pressure shaping/thinning; (2) alternate serial pressure flaking in preparation for systematic margin serration; (3) pressure fluting (throughout the sequence); and (4) distinctive margin serration.

Whatever the initial processes were, preform preparation must have included fairly well controlled percussion thinning (Figures 4.1*a,* 4.2) followed by selective pressure shaping and thinning (Figure 4.1*b*) to produce regular faces and margins. It is very likely that preforms were fluted at this stage (Figure 4.1*b*), but clear evidence is lacking in the Sloan-site assemblage. Many of the finished points exhibit basal thinning flake scars that have been greatly altered by subsequent lateral flake removals. Frequently, the remnant is wide and has a substantial negative bulb. This probably indicates that the flake scars were originally also substantial. The next stage was abrupt, continuous margin beveling, on opposing faces on opposite margins (Figure 4.1*c*). This produced a small but evident bibeveling. These abrupt margins served as continuous platforms for carefully spaced and executed serial pressure flake removals (Figure 4.1*d*). These sequences usually originated at the base of the preform and progressed toward the tip. The serial pressure flakes are commonly perpendicular to the margins and extend past the midline. This produced a preform that had one side of each face (usually the left side if viewed with the tip up) with serial flaking, while the other side of the same face exhibits selective, nonpatterned flaking. When serial flaking was completed, the preforms (see Morse and Morse 1983:fig. 4.2*b*) resembled Goshen/Plainview points of the High Plains (Frison 1991:fig. 2.17*a;* Bradley and Frison 1996).

Generally in other technologies, for bifacial points that exhibit serial pressure flaking of this sort, the next step was the removal of the small triangular areas between the flake scars and regularization of the edges. This is true of the Sloan Dalton points as well; however, there is a basic difference. Most other technologies remove these areas by fine selective flaking on the same face as the serial flaking, but the Dalton point technology achieves the same effect by continuous edge beveling on the same face as the continuous edge platform bevel (Figure 4.1*e*). The edge is literally moved inward until the triangular areas are removed. This again accentuates the alternate beveling. Because the serial pressure flakes were removed from steep platforms, and they ran past the midline, the negative bulbs were quite pronounced. The centers of these negative bulbs were used to produce the distinctive serrations of the Dalton points (original points).

At each place where there was a negative bulb scar adjacent to the edge, a shallow notch was produced by abrupt edge retouch (Figure 4.1*f*) on the same face as all previous edge beveling. Once a notch was made, a large single flake was removed on the same face as the beveling (Figure 4.1*f*). Occasionally this was done with two or more flake removals. This focused pressure flaking accentuated the notch, leaving the inside edge sharp. Overlapping of these notching flake scars produced protruding points along the edges, with most formed by a single ridge between the serial flake scar remnants. A general edge bevel was retained because of the direction of the notch preparation.

After serration was accomplished on both edges, the hafting area was finished by selective pressure flaking and grinding (Figure 4.1*g*). Basal preparation included both simple retouch followed by grinding and basal thinning/fluting followed by grinding (Figure 4.1*h*).

Fluting has two expressions: (1) technological, and (2) morphological. Technological fluting is where basal thinning is done by the removal of one or more flakes that proportionally reduce the longitudinal thickness of the biface. This involves the removal of flakes that travel past the point of maximum longitudinal thickness. It makes no difference whatsoever if the resulting flake scars are retained in subsequent flaking. Morphological flutes, on the other hand, are simply basal flake scars that extend past

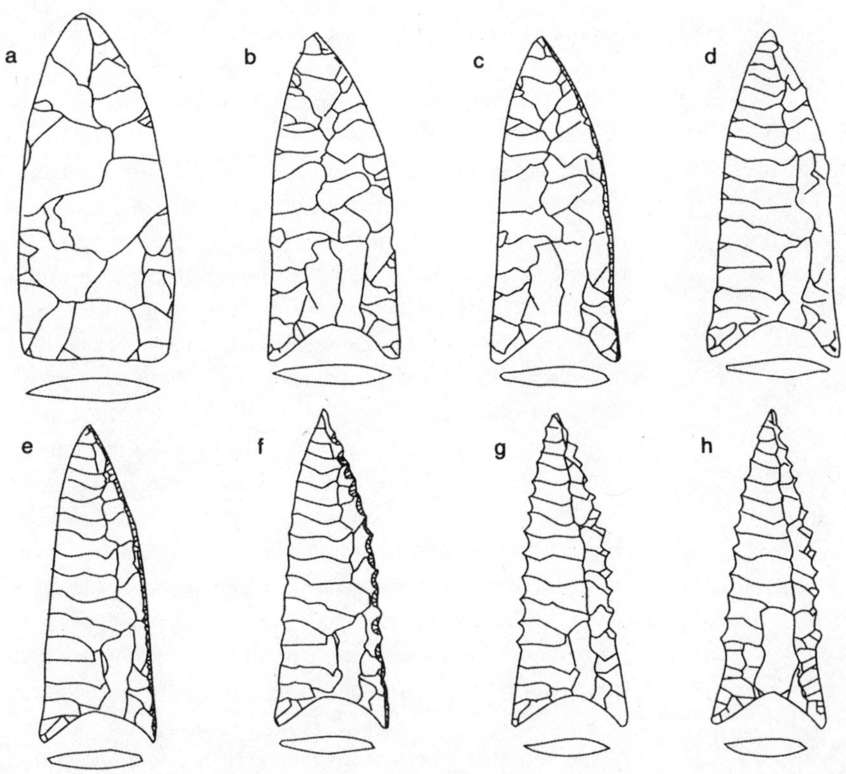

Figure 4.1 Idealized Sloan Dalton-point manufacture sequence: *a,* percussion biface; *b,* selective pressure biface; *c,* alternate margin beveling; *d,* alternate serial pressure flaking; *e,* alternate margin beveling; *f,* notch preparation; *g,* final notching/serration; and *h,* basal/stem preparation.

the point of the hafting element and are visible on the finished object.

With these definitions, it is possible to have points that were technologically fluted but are not morphologically fluted, if the channel scars are removed by subsequent flaking. It is also possible to have points that are morphologically fluted but whose basal flakes did not extend past the point of maximum longitudinal thickness. These did not technically thin the preform.

Most Sloan Dalton points, and probably most other Dalton points, are not morphologically fluted. I suspect, however, that the majority were technologically fluted at some stage in their manufacture and probably more than once. A detailed study of an assemblage of Dalton-point manufacturing debitage should show this. I expect that channel flakes, probably highly fragmented, would be a common component. I believe that it is a correct conclusion that Dalton-point technology includes systematic technological fluting and should be considered a fluted-point technology.

What is clear is that there was no real attempt to retain the channel scars on the finished points. Basal thinning was still achieved, and serial and notching pressure flaking for the most part eliminated the channel scars. Only when basal thinning was applied as one of the last stages of manufacture were morphologically fluted points produced.

These distinctive flaking sequences need not have been applied only in initial point manufacture. It would have been possible to use the same edge-bevel and serial-pressure sequences to resharpen used or damaged Dalton points. Several resharpenings using this process would have produced some of the narrower point forms in the collection (Figure 3.4), but it is difficult to distinguish them from initial manufacture forms.

When resharpening was accomplished in the way described by Morse (1971b:10), the distinctive serrations of the initial forms would not be produced. Beveling would be accentuated and the continuation of the process would eventually produce the highly bibeveled forms (Figure 3.3) usually found on "used-up" Dalton points. Both types of edge beveling are present in the Sloan-site assemblage, which indicates either that both resharpening processes were being employed or that the former type represents initial manufacture.

Although there is no direct evidence of bifacial resharpening in the Sloan-site assemblage, the scarcity of ex-

Figure 4.2 Bruce Bradley manufacturing a Dalton point.

amples with deep serration, originating from negative bulb scars, in most Dalton collections indicates to me that this process was an initial-manufacture technology rather than one used for resharpening. If this is the case, the morphological range of variation of initial Dalton point forms should be considered great, and complicated form analyses will probably be unproductive until additional assemblages of initial forms are available for comparative analyses.

Distinct bibeveling is present on many Dalton points. Morse and Morse (1983:72) concluded that the direction of the bevels (in relation to the faces) indicates the handedness of the knapper. To come to that conclusion it is necessary to assume how the preforms were being held during flaking. There is no archaeological evidence of this presented. Bevels may be produced easily in either direction, regardless of the handedness of the knapper. Where bevel direction does become important is when the points are used as knives. This again depends upon the way in which the tool is held and the direction of the cutting motion. If one assumes that the knife was held with the point away from the body and the cutting motion was in the direction of the other hand, most of the Dalton points were designed for right-handed people. On the other hand, without empirical evidence, one may not easily assume how a tool was held or used. For example, most of us would have no problem in describing how a handsaw is usually held and used. It is held in one hand with the blade extending away from the body. If one assumes that this is the only efficient way to use a handsaw, it would be a mistake. George Frison once described to me an instance in which he had a student from Easter Island working with him. During the course of an activity there was the need to cut the end off of a two-by-four. Dr. Frison asked the student to do it and gave him a standard handsaw. Instead of holding it in the way just described, he held the saw handle in his right hand, right arm extended, with the distal end of the blade nearly touching his right shoulder. The two-by-four was supported between the shoulder and the hand and a few back-and-forth movements served to cut the end neatly from the board.

Such alternative tool use behavior could greatly affect the design of a tool. We should not assume how tools were held and used unless we come to the conclusion based on physical evidence. If, however, the technique illustrated by Morse and Morse (1983:fig. 4.4) accurately represents that used by Dalton people, the edge bevels were designed for right-handed people.

My ability to compare Dalton technology with others of Paleoindian times is restricted to my knowledge of the High Plains of North America. Although I have viewed numbers of individual specimens from the central Mississippi Valley area, I have not studied them in detail. I have also been unable to find such detailed studies in the literature. This is not to say that they do not exist, just that I am not aware of them.

The generally accepted sequence of Paleoindian point types in the High Plains begins with Clovis, followed by Folsom and Goshen/Plainview, and continues with Agate Basin, Hell Gap, Alberta, Alberta/Cody, Cody, and the Frontier Complex (Bradley 1991). The larger Dalton points from the Sloan site closely resemble Clovis points in outline, size, and margin grinding. Where Dalton and Clovis points diverge is in thinning and finishing technologies. Many Clovis points exhibit remnants of percussion flake scars, and where pressure flaking is present it is generally shaping rather than thinning. In addition, Clovis points seldom exhibit consistent serial pressure flaking, and morphological fluting is normal. Large Dalton points, on the other hand, exhibit basal thinning, and morphological fluting is minimal if present. To my knowledge, edge beveling and serration are also not present on Clovis points.

Technological traits of smaller Dalton points are more similar to Folsom and Goshen/Plainview points. Although very different in many respects, Dalton points have an intermediate technology similar to Folsom. Folsom points may exhibit abrupt margin beveling followed by serial pressure flaking. This served to form the surface for the removal of massive channel flakes (resulting in morphological flutes). Alternate beveling is not present, and serration, although rarely present (Margaret Jodry, personal communication), was not accomplished in the same way as Dalton serration.

There is a closer resemblance of smaller intermediate-stage Dalton points to Goshen/Plainview points. This resemblance is superficial, however. What may look like serial pressure-flaking sequences on Goshen/Plainview points are actually well-spaced selective sequences (Bradley and Frison 1996). Margin beveling, serration, and fluting (technological and morphological) are lacking on Goshen/Plainview points. Later Paleoindian styles share even fewer technological traits with Dalton points.

I believe that the data currently point to an in situ technological development of Dalton points directly out of a Clovis technology. Resemblances to post-Clovis Paleoindian styles in the High Plains are superficial and at most represent a common origin out of a Clovis predecessor.

Along with the assemblage of Dalton points, several other artifact forms were recovered at the Sloan site. These included bifaces and adzes. The manufacturing process of the bifaces might be interpreted as representing the early part of point manufacture, but none of them has either the morphological or the technological potential to have been made into the Dalton points recovered from the Sloan site. Generally speaking, these bifaces were unrefined and were produced by direct percussion, probably with a stone hammer, based on the focus, depth, and size of the flake scars. Few if any thinning flakes were removed, and many of the bifaces retain evidence of the original raw material exterior. Crowley's Ridge Chert was the preferred raw material for this artifact form, and the stream cobble origin of the material may have greatly influenced the technology used and the resulting morphology. I do not believe that the technology of the bifaces necessarily reflects early stage technology of the Dalton points in the assemblage. It is also apparent to me that some of the "waste" flakes were carefully selected to make into unifaces, particularly end scrapers.

5
Microwear Analysis of Dalton Artifacts

RICHARD YERKES AND LINDA M. GAERTNER

The chipped-stone tools found at Dalton sites in the central Mississippi Valley are quite distinctive. In fact, several archaeologists have proposed that each distinctive implement in the "Dalton tool kit" was used for a specific task (Michie 1973; Morse 1973; Morse and Goodyear 1973; Goodyear 1974; House 1975; Morse and Morse 1983). However, these functional interpretations are based on morphological considerations, ethnographic analogies (including comparisons with nineteenth-century iron or steel hand tools [Morse and Morse 1983:fig. 4.]), or observation of the patterns of abrasion and striation on the edges of artifacts that were visible under "low-power" magnification (House 1975). Methods of manufacturing, resharpening, and using Dalton points have been reconstructed through experimental replication studies (Goodyear 1974:27–30), and white-tailed deer have been butchered with replicas of serrated Dalton points (Michie 1973), but the functional interpretations that resulted from those studies have not been confirmed by high-power microscopic analyses of the use-wear traces on the tools.

To remedy this situation, Dan F. Morse requested that R.Y. conduct a microwear analysis of "typical" Dalton artifacts that he (Morse) selected from the Sloan site (3GE94) and compare the wear traces on those tools with the microwear observed on the tools in a Dalton "type collection" selected from habitation areas such as the Lace (3PO17) and Brand (3PO139) sites. An incident-light microscope was used to examine twenty-four Dalton tools from the Sloan cemetery for use-wear traces. The microwear patterns on the Sloan tools were compared with the wear traces observed on modern replicas of Dalton chipped-stone implements that were used in a variety of antler-, bone-, hide-, shell-, stone-, and wood-working activities (as well as butchering, grass-cutting, and digging/cultivating experiments). In addition the microwear patterns on thirty-eight Dalton artifacts from base settlements and hunting camps (including the Lace and Brand sites) were examined and compared with the use-wear on the Sloan-site tools. Four research questions were addressed in the microwear study: (1) were Dalton adzes used on wood?; (2) were Dalton points used as butchering tools as well as projectiles?; (3) were Dalton end scrapers used on hide and/or wood or bone?; and (4) were certain tools from the Sloan site unused? The first question was investigated by L.M.G. as part of her senior honors thesis on the function of the Dalton adze (completed at Ohio

State University under R.Y.'s supervision), and R.Y. concentrated on the second and third questions. The fourth question was considered by both analysts.

METHODS OF ANALYSIS

The majority of the artifacts found at Dalton sites were knapped from alluvial chert cobbles found in gravel deposits in the Mississippi Valley (House 1975). Similar alluvial cherts from the Ohio and Mississippi Valleys were used to make the replicas of the Dalton point (made by Bruce Bradley), the Dalton adze (made by Albert M. Pecora III), and other Dalton tools (made by the authors) that were used in experimental activities that had been suggested by Morse, Goodyear, and House (e.g., cutting meat and sawing bone with replicas of Dalton points; gouging charred wood with copies of Dalton adzes).

The experimental implements were cleaned in an ultrasonic cleaner with a detergent (Top Job) and 10% solutions of HCL and KOH, and then examined for use-wear traces with a metallurgical microscope (Olympus) at magnifications of 50, 100, 200, and 500 x (see L. H. Keeley [1980] and Yerkes [1987] for details on cleaning procedures and techniques of microscopic examination).

The distinctive microwear traces that resulted when different activities were performed with the replicas were recorded. Next, the Dalton tools from the Sloan cemetery and the other Dalton sites were cleaned and examined for microwear traces. The functions of the prehistoric tools were determined by matching the microwear on their edges with the use-wear patterns observed on the replicas that were used for specific tasks in the experimental program.

RESULTS OF THE ANALYSIS

The microwear sample included two of the eleven adze preforms (18% of the total), six of the thirty-one adzes (19%), two of the eighty-nine possible Dalton point preforms (2%), ten of the 145 Dalton points (7%), one of the other seven bifaces (14%), two of the thirty-three retouched unifacial tools (6%), and one of the thirty-three end scrapers (3%) from the Sloan cemetery. In addition, nine adzes, fourteen Dalton points and preforms, one biface, three unifacial tools, seven end scrapers, two gravers, one microlith, and one *pièce esquillée* from seven Dalton habitation sites were examined microscopically for use-wear traces (Table 5.1). Microscopic examination of these sixty-two Dalton tools provided information on artifact function that can be used to answer the four research questions.

(1) Were Dalton Adzes Used on Wood?

At the Sloan site, thirty-one Dalton adzes and eleven adze preforms were found in clusters that suggest that they were associated with graves (Morse 1982:154, 156, table 7.2; Morse and Morse 1983:75, 90, 93, fig. 4.10, table 4.2; chapter 6). Three adzes, four "rejected adzes," and two adze preforms were also part of the "tool kit" of forty Dalton artifacts that was found in the Hawkins Cache (Morse 1971b). Many preforms and adzes were collected at the Lace (3PO17) base settlement (Redfield and Moselage 1970; Morse and Morse 1983:83), but no adze preforms nor "whole or usable adzes" were found at the nearby Brand site (3PO139). Only adze fragments were found at the Brand hunting camp (Goodyear 1974:39; Morse and Morse 1983:86). Adzes have also been found on the surface of a number of Dalton sites in northeastern Arkansas and southeastern Missouri (Redfield 1971; Morse 1973; Price and Krakker 1975; Morse and Morse 1983).

Dalton adzes have been described as heavy-duty woodworking tools that probably were used to manufacture large wooden objects such as dugout canoes and smaller wooden items such as food bowls. They also may have been used for woodworking tasks associated with house construction (Morse and Goodyear 1973; House 1975:61; Morse and Morse 1983:78). However, none of these wooden items has been preserved at Dalton sites, and no house plans, posthole patterns, or other structural features have been recorded. The hypothetical woodworking activities at Dalton sites and the substantial number of wooden artifacts proposed for the material culture of the Dalton people have been projected from the functional interpretation of the Dalton adze.

The asymmetrical shape of the Dalton adzes and the pattern of striations on the bits of the tools (visible under low-power magnification) led Morse and Goodyear (1973) to conclude that they were "true adzes" (following Semenov 1964). In other words, the Dalton adzes were hafted at an acute angle with the bit oriented across the long axis of the handle, rather than along the axis of the handle like an ax. The different hafting arrangements

Table 5.1
Summary of microwear analyses

Artifact Type	Site	Catalog No.	Shape	Bit Shape	Bevel	Grinding		Abrasion	Method of Use	Material Worked
						Basal	Lateral			
Dalton Adze										
Preform	Sloan	74-107-354	Oval	Slight convex	None			None	Not used[a]	Wrapped in hide?
	Sloan	74-107-485	Pear[b]	Slight convex	Slight		Weak	None	Not used	None
Dalton Adze										
	3P053	68-144	Pear	Very concave	Steep	X	X	Light	Adzing	Wood/Charred wood
	3P081	69-645A	Bell/Oval	Very concave	Moderate	X	X	Light, Sheen	Adzing	Charred wood
	3P081	69-645B	Rectangular	Straight	Slight	X	X	Light, Sheen	Adzing/Planing	Wood/Charred wood
	3P081	70-329	Pear	Concave	Moderate	X	X	Light, Sheen	Adzing/Planing	Charred wood
		71-412A	Oval	Slight concave	Moderate	X?	X	Light[c]	Adzing	Wood
		71-412B	Oval	Slight concave	Slight	X	X	Light	Adzing	Wood/Charred wood
		72-214	Bell	Slight concave	Moderate			Moderate, Sheen	Adzing[d]	Charred wood
		72-458	Oval	Very concave	Moderate	X	X	Sheen only	Gouging, Wedging[e]	Charred wood
		74-100	Pear	Slight concave	Moderate	X	X	Light[c], Sheen	Adzing/Planing	Wood/Charred wood
	Sloan	74-107-41	Oval	Slight concave	Moderate	X	X	Sheen only	Adzing	Charred wood
	Sloan	74-107-99	Oval	Slight convex	Slight	X	X	Sheen only	Adzing	Wood/Charred wood
	Sloan	74-107-110	Pear	Slight concave	Moderate		X	Light	Adzing	Wood/Charred wood
	Sloan	74-107-196	Pear	Slight convex	Slight	X	X	None	Adzing	Wood/Charred wood
	Sloan	74-107-235	Pear	Slight concave	Moderate	X	X	Sheen only[f]	Adzing	Charred wood
	Sloan	74-107-363	Bell	Slight concave	Slight	X	X	Sheen only	Adzing	Charred wood
Dalton Point			Base	Bevel	Deut.					
Preform Stage	Brand	72-207E	Concave	X				Light	Not used[g]	
	Brand	73-23	Indented	X		X	X	Medium	Not used	
	Sloan	74-107-307	Indented					Light	Not used	
	Sloan	74-107-414	Concave			X	X	Sheen[h]	Not used	
Initial Stage	Lace	71-386	Concave[i]	X		X	X		Not used	
	Brand	72-207B	Concave	X	X	X	X		Not used	
	Brand	75-337	Concave				X		Cutting	Meat
	Sloan	74-107-58	Concave	X	X	X	X		Not used	
	Sloan	74-107-59	Concave	X	X	X	X	Light	Not used	
	Sloan	74-107-74	Concave	X	X	X	X	Light	Not used	
	Sloan	74-107-102	Concave	X	X	X	X		Not used	
	Sloan	74-107-213	Concave		X	X	X	Light	Not used	

Advanced Stage	Brand	71-569A	Concave	X	X	X	X	Light	Cutting/Projectile	Meat/Fresh hide
	Brand	71-569B	Concave	X	X	X	X	Patina	Cutting/Projectile	Meat/Fresh hide
	Brand	72-207A	Concave	X	X	X	X		Cutting	Meat/Fresh hide
	Brand	72-207C	Concave	X	X	X	X	Light	Projectile	Unknown
	Brand	74-89A	Concave	X	X	X	X		Projectile	Unknown
	Brand	74-89B	Concave	X	X	X	X		Boring?	Unknown
	Brand	74-89C	Concave	X	X	X	X		Projectile	Unknown
	Sloan	74-107-116	Concave	X	X	X	X	Light	Not used	
	Sloan	74-107-271	Concave	X	X	X	X		Not used	
	Sloan	74-107-287	Concave	X	X	X	X	Light	Not used	
Final Stage	Sloan	74-107-68	Concave	X		X	X	Light	Awl[j]	Dry hide
Burinated Dalton Point										
	3CG485	74-559	Concave	X		X	X	Light	Not used	
	Brand	78-951	Concave	X	?	X	X	Light[k]	Not used	
	Sloan	74-107-36	Concave	X		X	X		Point[l]	Unknown
Biface										
	3PO27	68-315	Convex						Cutting[j]	Meat
	Sloan	74-107-390	Straight					Light[m]	Not used	
Uniface			Shape	Retouch						
	3GE93	68-197	Large "Blade"	Proximal/Distal				Moderate/Patina	Cut/Scrape	Meat/Fresh hide
	3GE58	68-233	"Blade"	Proximal/Lateral				Moderate	Cut/Scrape	Hide
	3CG71	68-246	Crescent	Extensive	X	X		Heavy patina	Unknown[n]	Unknown
	Sloan	79-107-49	Crescent	Lateral				Heavy[o]	Reamer	Hide?
	Sloan	79-107-377	Flake	Lateral				Moderate	Scraping	Dry hide

Continued on next page

Table 5.1 Continued

Artifact Type	Site	Catalog No.	Shape	Retouch	Hafted	Thermal Alteration	Abrasion	Method of Use	Material Worked
End Scraper									
	Lace	70-231	Pear	Distal	X	X	Moderate	Scraping	Dry hide
	Lace	70-470	Triangular	Distal	X	X	Moderate	Scraping	Dry hide
	Lace	70-701A	Pear	Distal/Lateral	X		Moderate	Scraping	Dry hide
	Lace	70-701B	Broken	Distal		X	Light	Scraping	Dry hide
	Lace	783L3	Triangular	Distal			Light	Scraping	Dry hide
	Brand	72-207X	Pear	Distal			Moderate	Scraping	Dry hide
	3PO161	70-917	Spurred[p]	Distal/Lateral			Light	Scraping	Dry hide
	Sloan	74-107-194	Triangular	Proximal/Distal	X		Moderate	Not used	
Graver									
	Lace	70-386	Flake	Unifacial lateral			X	Light engraving	Bone or antler
	Lace	70-687	Flake	Unifacial lateral			X	Light engraving	Bone or antler
Other			Type						
	Brand	70-355-3145	Microlith	Unifacial			Moderate	Not used	
	Brand	70-355-347	*Pièce esquillée*					Fine cutting	Meat/Fresh hide

[a]This preform is heat-treated and made of exotic raw material.

[b]Cortex covers about 1/4 of the dorsal surface of the implement.

[c]Patina.

[d]May have been used as a hand-held "Adze Knife" for gouging and chiseling charred wood.

[e]May have been used for finer woodworking. Does not have typical adze shape; made of exotic raw material.

[f]Grinding on dorsal side.

[g]A knapping flaw or "knot" may have caused this preform to be discarded.

[h]Some weakly developed surface polish is present on this point. It may have been kept in a leather sheath.

[i]An exceptionally long flute is present on the dorsal surface of this point.

[j]Very lightly used.

[k]Possibly hafting traces.

[l]Burin facets may be the result of impact fracture.

[m]Green and red pigment observed on the surface of the artifact.

[n]Apparently hafted.

[o]Red pigment observed on the surface of the artifact.

[p]Spurred corners seem to be the result of resharpening.

make it necessary to use different motions when wielding the true adze and the ax. Consequently, the adzing motion results in asymmetrical use-wear traces on the dorsal and ventral surfaces of the adze (also see Olausson 1983).

Morse and Goodyear (1973) suggested that the adzes were woodworking tools, because end scrapers were abundant at Dalton sites (hence the adzes were not hide-working tools) and macrowear patterns indicated that the adzes were not used as digging tools. Although ethnographic observations and replication experiments support the interpretation that adzes were used for woodworking (Mitchell 1959; Carneiro 1979; Harding and Young 1979; Olausson 1983; Binneman and Deacon 1986; Gaertner 1990), examination of the working edges under incident light at high magnification was necessary to test these functional hypotheses.

Six of the thirty-one adzes (19% of the total) and two of the eleven adze preforms (18%) from the Sloan site were examined for microwear traces. In addition, Dan Morse selected nine "typical" adzes from other Dalton sites for our study (three are illustrated in Morse and Goodyear [1973:fig. 1]). The adzes ranged from oval or rectangular to pear-shaped in outline. The bits were straight or concave, usually beveled, and wider than the polls. The adzes were asymmetrical in cross section, with concave dorsal surfaces and flat ventral surfaces.

The microwear traces on the prehistoric adzes were compared with the wear that formed on a series of experimental replicas of Dalton adzes that were hafted and used to: (1) adze or gouge charred wood, dry or "seasoned" wood, and "green" wood (Figure 5.1); (2) chop, adze, and gouge antler bone; and (3) dig and cut roots (Gaertner 1990:table 2). The wear traces on seventeen other experimental tools that were hand-held and used for a variety of boring, cutting, scraping, chiseling, gouging, and sawing tasks were also compared with the use-wear on the prehistoric Dalton adzes (Gaertner 1990).

All of the Dalton adzes examined in this study had similar well-developed wear traces that indicated that they had been used to adze or gouge charred wood and dry (seasoned) wood (Table 5.1). The working aspects of the adzes (the bit end and dorsal and ventral surfaces) showed extensive charred-wood micropolish and, to some extent, dry-wood polish (Figure 5.2). All six adzes from the Sloan cemetery and five of the adzes from the other Dalton sites had amorphous, angular black inclusions wedged into or beneath the well-developed charred-wood polish (Figure

Figure 5.1 Experiments with replicas of Dalton adzes and bifaces: *A*, using a hafted adze replica on green wood; *B*, sawing charred wood.

5.3). There were also black stains on the proximal ends of eight of the adzes.

Wear traces like these were observed on the experimental adzes that had been used in the charred wood-working experiments (Gaertner 1990). However, neither of the two unused Dalton adze preforms from the Sloan site had

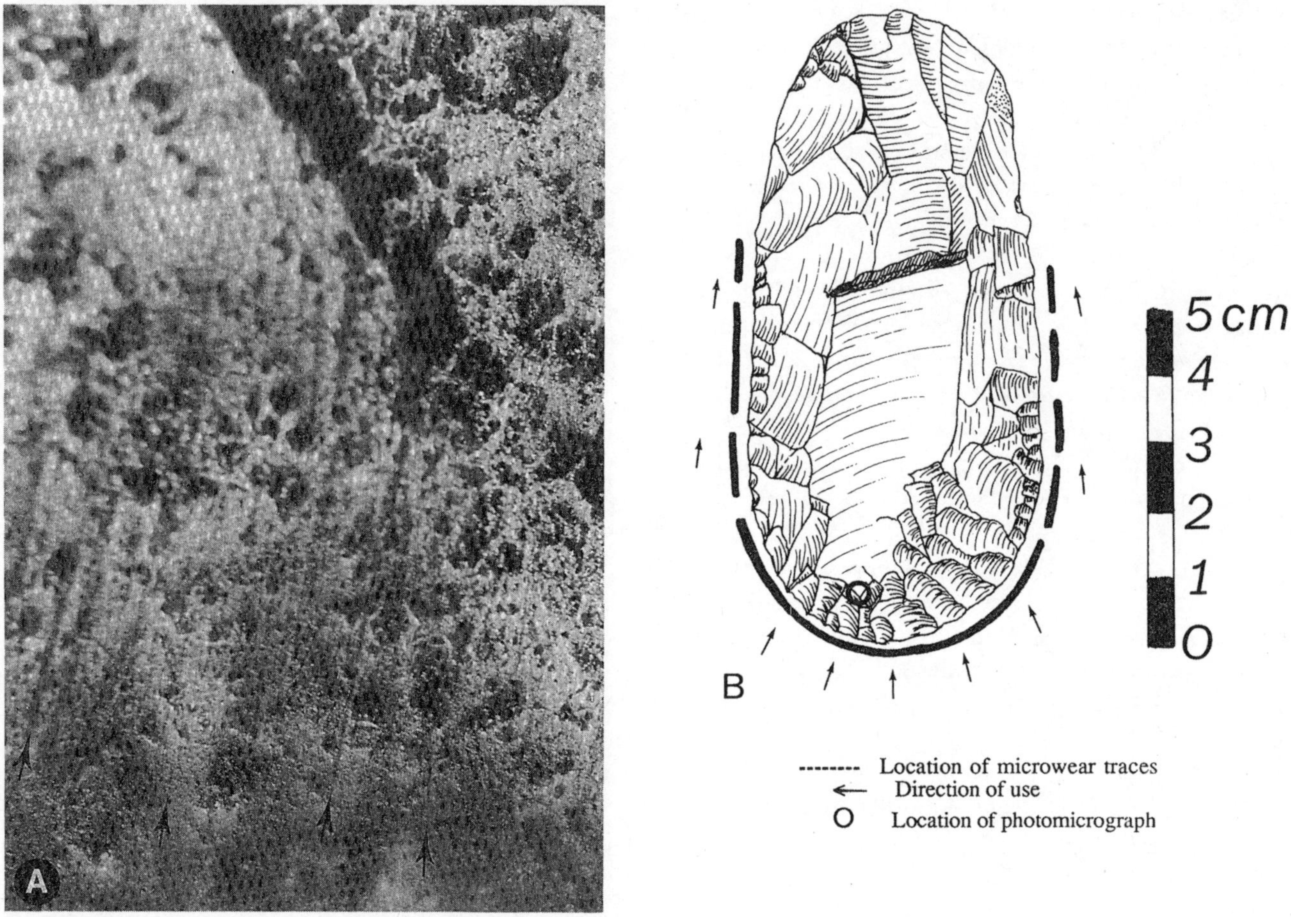

Figure 5.2 Dalton adze from the Sloan site (cat. no. 74-107-99): *A*, photomicrograph, and *B*, sketch. Magnification 80x, width of photomicrograph is about 467 micrometers.

black inclusions on their surfaces, and no black inclusions were observed on any of the points, scrapers, bifaces, or other implements in the microwear sample. Numerous parallel striations were also found running lengthwise along the dorsal and ventral surfaces of the adzes. Morse and Goodyear (1973) and House (1975:61) also observed these wear features and used them to define the functional attributes of the Dalton adzes. The presence of so many striations (along with the charred-wood polish) supports the heavy woodworking functional interpretation of the Dalton adzes. The regular orientation of the striations (parallel to the long axis of the tool) dispels any notion that the sheen or polish on the Dalton adzes is the result of postdepositional surface modification (cf. Levi Sala 1986). These regular striations were not present on the two Dalton preforms from the Sloan site, even though they were found in the same depositional context as the adzes.

Heavy striations are not typically observed on prehistoric woodworking tools (Keeley 1977; Moss 1983). However, our experiments showed that they are attributes of microwear polishes that formed when the adzes were used on charred wood (Gaertner 1990; see also Bettison 1985; Binneman and Deacon 1986). The charred, desiccated surface of the burned wood may have presented a more abrasive surface to the adzes than "fresh" wood (or even dry wood). Consequently, striations are more common on stone tools that were used on charred wood than on tools that had been used in "typical" woodworking activities on fresh (green) or dry (seasoned) wood. In addition, our analysis revealed a strong association between the striations, charred-wood microwear polish, and the macroscopic sheen observed on ten of the fifteen adzes in the sample (Table 5.1). This sheen or luster on the surface of bifacially chipped stone tools is often assumed to be "plant

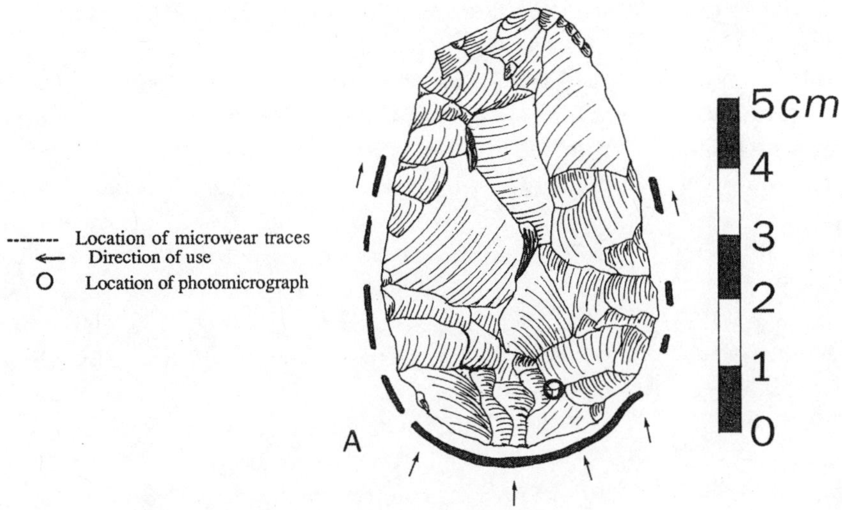

Figure 5.3 Dalton adze from site 3PO81 (cat. no. 70-329), with charred-wood polish and amorphous, angular black inclusions (arrow): *A*, sketch, and *B*, photomicrograph. Magnification 80x, width of photomicrograph is about 467 micrometers.

gloss" or "sickle gloss" that formed on the implements when they were used in some sort of agricultural activity (Gaertner 1990). However, the wear traces on the Dalton adzes do *not* look like the "hoe polish" observed on Woodland or Mississippian hoes. The wear on the Dalton adzes lacks the fluid polish with filled-in striations and comet-shaped pits that is present on those agricultural tools (Keeley 1980:60; Yerkes 1987:plate 5). Under the microscope, the sheen on the adzes does not look like the natural luster that forms on some chert artifacts after they have been abraded by wind or water or have undergone some other "weathering" process. The sheen on the Dalton adzes seems to have formed when the tools were used to work charred wood.

HAFTING TRACES ON THE DALTON ADZE. Hafting traces on chipped-stone tools are often difficult to detect because a well-made haft does not allow the stone tool to "wiggle" or rub against the handle or hafting material (Keeley 1982). However, seasoned wood or antler were probably used as handles for Dalton adzes, because microwear traces were observed that indicated that the poll ends of the tools were in contact with those materials (Gaertner 1990). The analysis also suggested that the adzes were bound to the handles with leather strips or thongs (Gaertner 1990:44). Pitch or mastic also may have been used to bind the adzes to their handles. It is possible that leather pads may have been used to "seat" the flat, ventral surface of the Dalton adzes against their handles. However, once they were hafted, they were not removed, flipped over, and rehafted like the Australian adzes that were examined by Kjel Knuttson (1988).

The hafting traces on the adzes are also probably related to their use on charred wood. Morse, Goodyear, and House (see above) noted that Dalton adzes were hafted for efficient, heavy woodworking activities, and the microwear analysis supports that interpretation. Lateral and basal edge grinding were present on almost all the adzes in our sample (exception: cat. no. 72-214), and there were well-developed hide polishes on the ground edges and distal faces of the adzes. The dorsal surfaces of some of the adzes had been carefully abraded and made smooth with a stone. These locations were also covered with hide polish. Occasionally, black stains and black microinclusions were associated with the hide polish on the haft area of the adzes (Gaertner 1990:44). This probably means that the poll of the adze and its binding also came into contact with charcoal during use.

Red pigments were associated with the dry hide hafting traces on all but three (cat. nos. 72-458, 70-329, and 74-107-235) of the adzes, although the brick-red color of the latter adze from the Sloan site may have camouflaged any red stains. It is interesting that one of the Dalton adze preforms from the Sloan site (cat. no. 72-107-354) also had red stains and globular residues on its surface. These red pigments may have resulted from chemical and physical changes in the stone (and the hide polish) that began when the adzes were ground with the iron-rich sandstone abraders that often are associated with adzes and adze fragments (Morse 1971b, 1982; Goodyear 1974; Morse and Morse 1983). However, we suggest that these red stains were mastic residues, because they were usually found on the dorsal surfaces of the adzes in the area of the haft that would have been in contact with the leather (dry hide) strips that bound the adze to its handle.

These results support the hypothesis that Dalton adzes were heavy woodworking tools and suggest that they may have been used to fell burned trees and hollow out charred logs that could have been made into dugout canoes or wooden containers. However, two of the adzes in the microwear sample may have been used for more generalized woodworking activities (see Gaertner 1990:23, table 3). One of these (cat. no. 72-214) may have been hand-held and used to adze, gouge, and split (wedge) charred wood. A long, thin "adze" in the sample (cat. no. 72 548) seems to have functioned as a gouge or wedge that was used on charred wood.

(2) Were Dalton Points Used as Butchering Tools as Well as Projectiles?

The typical Dalton point has been described as both a serrated knife and a saw, and experiments have shown that it is an efficient tool for butchering deer and sawing bone (Morse and Morse 1983:72). Our microwear study was designed to find if the use-wear traces on Dalton points indicated that they had been used in this fashion or if some other function was suggested. Goodyear (1974:21–32) described five stages in the manufacture, maintenance, and use of Dalton points, and these stages have been used to classify the points examined in this study (although Goodyear's Preform and Completed Preform stages have been combined in our "Preform" stage). Four of the Dalton points that we examined were assigned to the Preform stage (Table 5.1). These were lanceolate or triangular bifaces with concave or indented bases. Two of the preforms exhibit the typical right-hand bevel, but none has serrated edges. Basal and lateral grinding was observed on the haft area of two of the preforms. None of them appears to have been used.

Eight of the Dalton points in our microwear sample had serrated blade edges that were convex or excurvate with little or no indentation at the shoulder. This indicates that they had reached Goodyear's (1974:25) Initial stage of manufacture. Although almost all of these points were beveled and had serrated (or denticulate) edges (as well as basal and lateral grinding), only one of the points had microwear traces on its edges. This point (cat. no. 75-337) from the Brand site had weakly developed polish along both lateral edges that indicated that it had been used to cut meat (Table 5.1).

Ten of the points that were examined were assigned to the Advanced stage of manufacture and use (Goodyear 1974:26). These points had been resharpened at least once and had triangular blades that were indented at the shoulder. Three of these points were from the Sloan site, but they had not been used before being deposited in graves at the cemetery. However, the other seven of the Advanced-stage points were from the Brand site, and they all seem to have been used. Five of the Brand-site points had impact fractures or damage that showed that they had been used as projectiles. Three points (including two with projectile damage) had been used to cut fresh hide or meat (Figure 5.4), and the last of the points from the Brand site had been used as a boring tool (but the material that was drilled could not be identified).

One of the points in our sample from the Sloan site had been resharpened until its blade had taken on a drill-like appearance. Although it was beveled, the edges of the point blade lacked serrations (not denticulate). The ground haft area had also been reduced in size. These characteristics define Goodyear's (1974:30) Final stage of Dalton point manufacture and use. Our analysis revealed that weakly developed dry hide polish was present on both lateral edges of the tip of this point. A few very small stria-

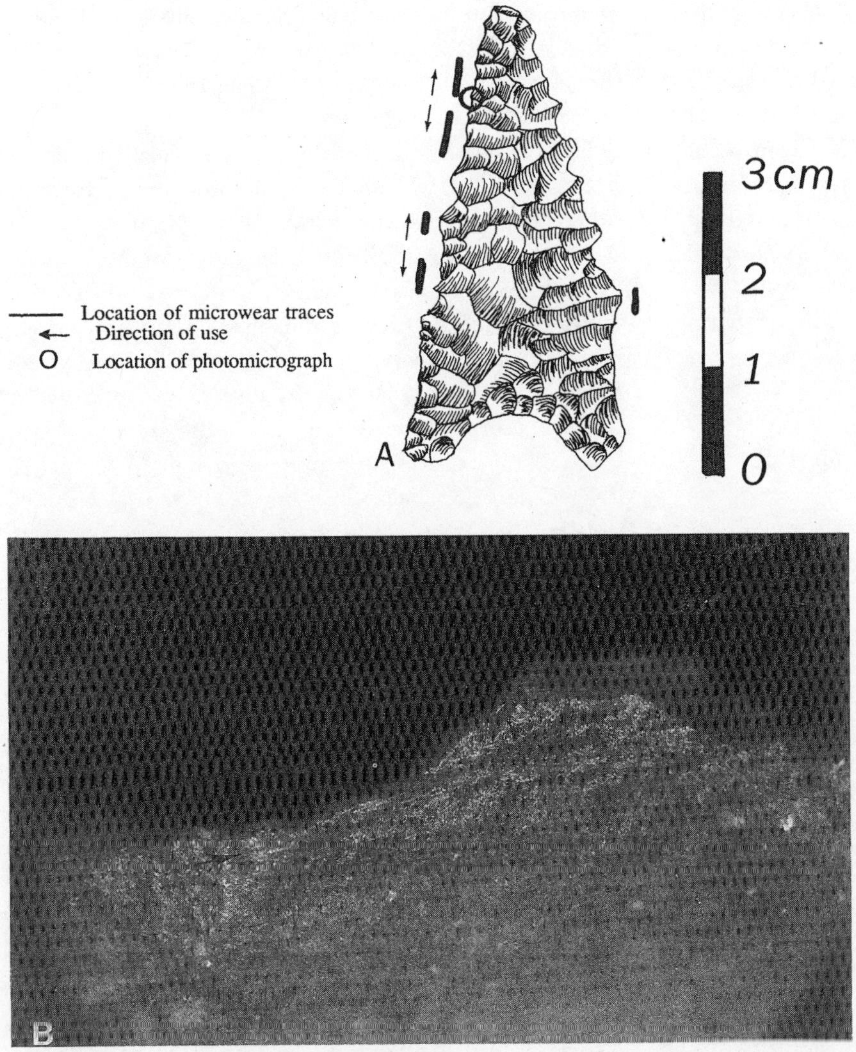

Figure 5.4 Advanced-stage Dalton point from the Brand site (3PO139; cat. no. 71-569B), with fresh hide/meat polish and very light striations running parallel to the edge of the point (arrow): *A*, sketch, and *B*, photomicrograph. Magnification 80x, width of photomicrograph is about 654 micrometers.

tions were oriented parallel to the long axis of the point, and this suggests that the tool was used as a hide awl or reamer. The microwear data support Morse's suggestion that these Final-stage Dalton points were used as awls or gimlets (Morse and Morse 1983:72). However, they appear to have been used on leather, not wood (also see Goodyear 1974:32).

Only one of the eleven Dalton points and preforms that we examined from the Sloan site had been used, and it seems to have functioned as an awl. However, eight of the twelve points from the Lace and Brand sites were used. One Initial-stage point served as a meat knife, while three Advanced-stage points showed projectile damage (including two of the points that had been used as fresh hide/meat knives), and one had been used to drill some unknown material (Table 5.1). The microwear patterns indicate that Dalton points were used as projectiles and butchering tools, but there is no evidence that they functioned as bone saws. Our analysis supports the interpretation that the points were hafted in short foreshafts that could be inserted in mainshafts and used as atlatl darts, or the foreshafts could serve as handles when the points were used as serrated knives during butchering activities. After several resharpening episodes, the points could have been removed from the foreshafts and used as awls (Morse and Morse 1983:72). Morse also suggested that broken Dalton points could be recycled by "burination" of the tip. He noted that several burin blows to the tip of the point would produce an edge that would be suitable for grooving and splitting bone to make awls and needles (Morse and Morse 1983:72).

Our analysis of three "Burinated" Dalton points could not confirm this hypothesis. The burin facet on one point from the Sloan site may be an impact fracture (Table 5.1). "Burination" of the tip of a projectile point can result from impact if the point hits a hard surface (see Odell and Cowan 1986; Yerkes and Pecora 1990). The other two burinated Dalton points that were examined had burin facets that could have resulted from impact fracture or from resharpening.

(3) Were Dalton End Scrapers Used on Hide and/or Wood or Bone?

Morse and Morse recognized that the hafted, unifacially retouched Dalton end scrapers exhibited two types of working edges. They suggested that scrapers with acute edge angles and polish on their bits were hide-working tools and that scrapers with steep edge angles and crushing or "Quina" retouch were probably used on bone or wood (Morse and Morse 1983:78). This distinction was also noted by Goodyear (1974:44–45) and House (1975:62) and is based on Wilmsen's (1970) study of the edge angles on scrapers. Some of the Dalton end scrapers have "graver spurs," but although House (1975:63) suggested that these varieties of scrapers functioned as composite tools used to groove and scrape bone or wood, the Morses argued that the spurs may have resulted from resharpening the scraper bit in a manner that retained a standard width of the working edge (Morse and Morse 1983:78). Eight end scrapers were examined in our study, and all of them were used except the single example from the Sloan site (Table 5.1). The seven end scrapers from Dalton habitation sites were all used to scrape or "curry" dry hide (Figure 5.5), including the "spurred" end scraper from site 3PO161. The variability in the edge angles on these scrapers does not relate to any functional differences (see also Yerkes 1987).

Another (rarer) type of unifacially retouched tool has been identified in the Dalton tool kit. This hafted implement has an asymmetrical concave crescent-shaped blade with a steep working edge (Morse and Morse 1983:78). House (1975:63) suggested that concave-edged side scrapers such as these probably served as spokeshaves that were used to smooth bone or wood handles. However, the microwear traces on one of these unifaces from the Sloan site (also shown in Morse and Morse [1983:fig. 4.2*n*]) indicate that it may have been used as a reamer to enlarge holes in hides. Another of these crescent-bladed unifaces from site 3CG71 was abraded and covered with a patina, so microwear traces were not visible on its edges.

Three other unifacially retouched tools were examined in this study, including a large "bladelike" uniface that does not appear to have been hafted. This tool (from site 3GE93) seems to have been used to cut and scrape fresh hide and/or meat. The microwear patterns on a smaller uniface (also not hafted) from site 3GE58 indicate that it was used to cut and scrape fresh or dry hide. A retouched uniface (or side scraper) from the Sloan site (also shown in Morse and Morse [1983:fig. 4.2*r*]) seems to have been used to scrape dry hide. This implement does not appear to have been hafted during use. None of the unifacially retouched tools that were examined in this study was used to scrape or groove bone or wood. The tools functioned as butchering or hide-working implements, with the end scrapers being used to "curry" dry hide.

USE-WEAR TRACES ON OTHER IMPLEMENTS OF THE DALTON TOOL KIT. In addition to the bifacial and unifacial tools described above, four other types of Dalton implements were examined in this study. Two bifaces were included in the microwear sample. These were large, lanceolate or leaf-shaped implements that do not appear to have been hafted and resemble preforms or "cache blades" (Morse 1971b). The biface from the Sloan site was not utilized (although traces of green and red pigment were observed on its surface). It may have served as a preform. However, the other biface (from site 3PO27) was used as a butchering tool. Microwear analysis was necessary to distinguish between "bifacial knives" and bifacial preforms, because the form of these implements is identical.

Two gravers from the Lace site exhibited microwear traces that indicate that they were used to engrave bone or antler material. The microwear on the graver "spurs" on these small unifacially retouched tools was weakly developed, but it is certainly possible that the graver spurs could have been used to incise the eyes in bone needles, as Morse suggested (Morse and Morse 1983:78).

A microlith and a *pièce esquillée* from the Brand site were also examined. The steep unifacially retouched microlith

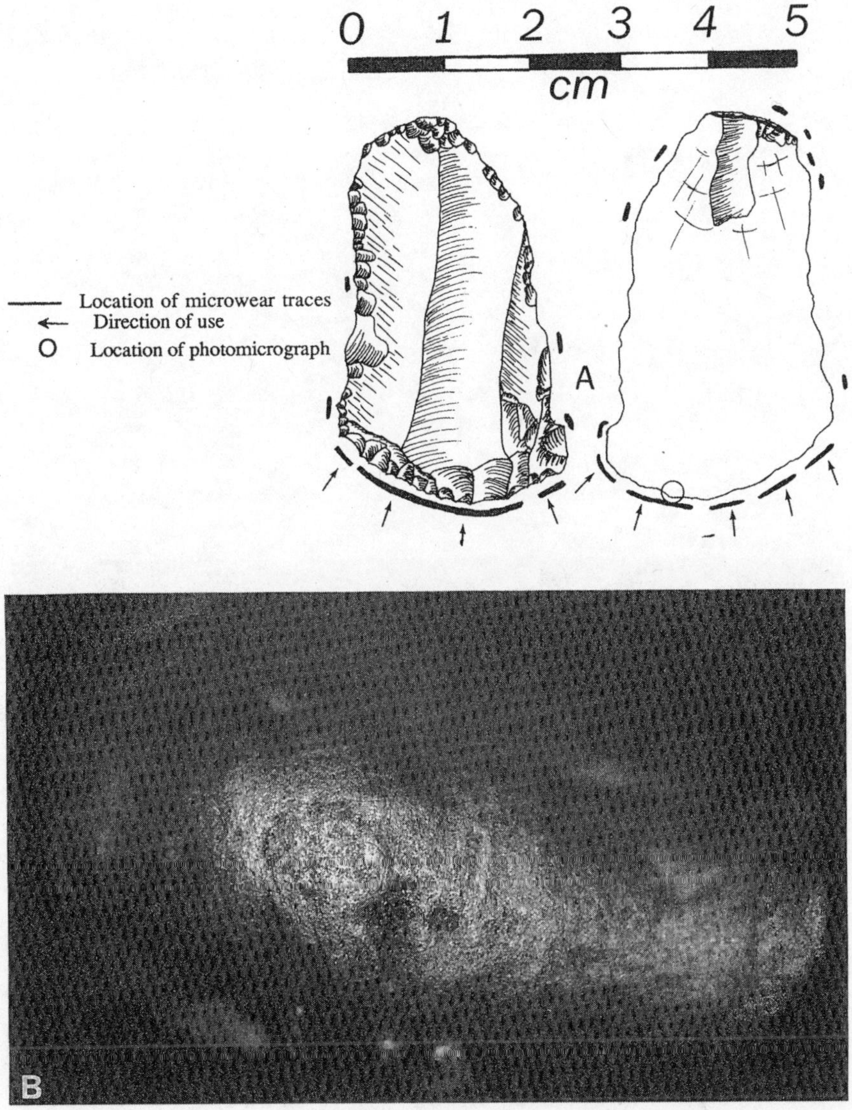

Figure 5.5 End scraper from the Brand site (3PO139; cat. no. 72-207D), with rounded edge and dry hide polish: *A*, sketch, and *B*, photomicrograph. Magnification 80x, width of photomicrograph is about 654 micrometers.

did not appear to have been used, but the *pièce esquillée* was used for fine cutting of meat or fresh hide (Table 5.1; Figure 5.6). There has been some debate about the function of the *pièce esquillée,* with some suggesting that they served as wedges that were used to split antler, bone, wood, or even ivory (Goodyear 1974:61–63; House 1975:64–65). However, others have argued that the *pièce esquillée* is a bipolar core (Morse and Morse 1983:79). The meat/fresh hide-cutting function of the *pièce esquillée* from the Brand site is something of an enigma, and our analysis of this implement sheds very little light on the wedge versus core debate.

(4) Were Certain Tools from the Sloan Site Unused?

All of the Dalton points from the Sloan cemetery that were examined in our study did not have any visible use-wear traces on their edges except the "Final-stage" Dalton point that was resharpened into an awl (which was briefly used on dry hide). By contrast, all of the "Advanced-stage" Dalton points from the Brand site that were examined, and one of the "Initial-stage" points from that site, were used.

In addition, the larger, well-made Dalton points (made

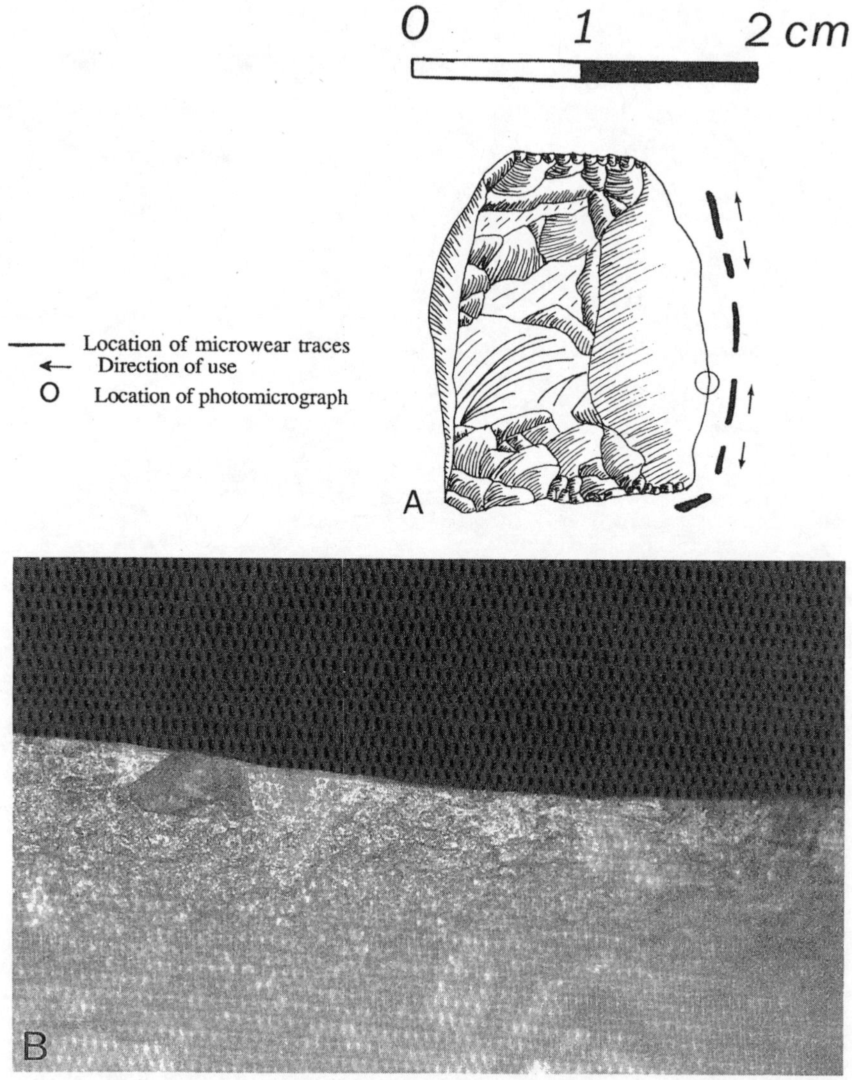

Figure 5.6 *Pièce esquillée* from the Brand site (3PO139; cat. no. 70-355-347), with fresh hide/meat polish: *A,* sketch, and *B,* photomicrograph. Magnification 80x, width of photomicrograph is about 654 micrometers.

of exotic white or black cherts) from the Sloan site seem to have served a ceremonial, rather than a utilitarian, function. These impressive artifacts did not seem to have been made for use in the "real" world. It is more likely that they were grave offerings that had been manufactured (or resharpened) before being placed in the graves at the Sloan site.

The clusters of adzes and adze preforms at the Sloan site may also be grave offerings. Like the Dalton points, the Dalton adze preforms seem to have been manufactured just before being placed in the graves. The adzes from the Sloan site were resharpened, but they were briefly used to work wood before they were buried with the dead. During the analysis of the flake scars on the Dalton adzes from the Sloan site, it was apparent that the woodworking activities that took place after the Dalton adzes were resharpened (and before interment) had not been done as vigorously as during their earlier use lives.

The single end scraper and the lone biface from the Sloan site that were examined in our study did not appear to have been used either. However, the burinated Dalton point and two unifacially retouched tools from the cemetery were utilized. It appears that certain types of tools were manufactured (or resharpened and revitalized) to serve as grave offerings (points, adzes), and other types of tools that had been used were also placed in graves. These tools may have been used in activities that were associated with the construction of the grave site, or they may have been spontaneously placed in the grave by mourners during the burial ritual.

DISCUSSION

In this study we set out to determine the functions of various types of artifacts in the Dalton tool kit and to compare the wear patterns on tools from the Sloan cemetery and from Dalton habitation sites. Our microwear analysis confirmed most of the prior functional interpretations of the Dalton tools and revealed that there is a strong correspondence between the form and function of these implements. Most of the Dalton tools are distinctive and standardized. They were knapped into specific shapes, and each tool was used for a very limited number of tasks. Dalton points served as projectiles (darts) and as meat knives or butchering tools. Dalton adzes functioned as heavy-duty woodworking tools. End scrapers were used to "curry" dry hide, and the curious crescent-shaped unifaces also seem to have been used in hide-working activities. The gravers were used for fine incising of antler or bone—possibly as part of the process of cutting eyes in bone needles.

The function of the burinated Dalton points is less clear. The "burination" may have resulted from impact fractures or it may represent attempts to resharpen broken points. Also, the "graver spurs" on some end scrapers do not seem to be functional gravers, but rather resulted from maintenance of the bits of the hide-scraping tools.

The Dalton points (and possibly the Dalton adzes) that were placed in clusters associated with graves at the Sloan cemetery seem to have been manufactured for interment with the dead or resharpened before being placed in the graves. Some of the other tools from the Sloan site had been used, but the large points were in "mint" condition.

Like some of the Dalton points, the Dalton adzes seem to have been rejuvenated before they were deposited. Unlike the points, however, some of the adzes had been used for a short time as woodworking tools between the resharpening activities and burials. Of the two adze preforms, the one that was heat-treated (cat. no. 74-107-354) wore a coat of fresh-hide polish on most of its surface, but not on the bit. Even though it may seem possible that the straight, nonabraded lateral edges of this biface could have cut meat or fresh hide, the lack of bone polish on the edges and the lack of evidence for cutting motions, as well as the presence of probably mastic residues, better support the idea that it had been wrapped in greasy hide. Other possible reasons why this preform has the "hide/mastic" complex on its surface would be that the biface had a previous (albeit short) use life as a hafted adze, and any microscopic evidence for use had been bifacially flaked off. Or perhaps the biface was hafted as an adze solely for ritual functions. The other adze preform (cat. no. 74-107-485), on which cortex remained covering approximately one-fourth of the dorsal surface, showed no evidence of use.

Because there were at least three tools from the Sloan site, the awl and the two unifaces, that had been used to work hide, and because at least six of the Dalton adzes from the Sloan cemetery had been used to work charred wood and perhaps dry wood, it seems likely that these activities were involved in ceremonial activities at the Sloan site. Hide preparation may have occurred during the manufacture of clothing or body wraps for the deceased, or the creation of hide pouches or bindings to be placed ceremoniously around individual or clusters of stone tools. Wooden objects may also have been fashioned for the burial occasion: items such as grave markers (Morse and Morse 1983), wooden grave gifts, or (in concert with the hide preparation) hafted implements for the dead.

ACKNOWLEDGMENTS

We thank Dan F. Morse for the opportunity to conduct this investigation and for arranging loan of the artifacts that were examined. Bruce Bradley made replicas of the Dalton points that were used in our experiments. Albert M. Pecora III made replicas of the Dalton adzes, helped with the experiments, and provided many useful comments and suggestions. James B. Stoltman reviewed an early draft of this chapter and made many timely comments. This study was partly funded by an Ohio State University Undergraduate Research Scholarship to L.M.G.

6
Provenience of Artifacts

DAN F. MORSE, PHYLLIS A. MORSE,
ROBERT C. MAINFORT JR., JAMI J. LOCKHART,
AND GLEN AKRIDGE

Over the last twenty-five years, an impressive corpus of studies pertaining to the analysis of archaeological mortuary remains has established that there is a relationship between status in life (in the broadest sense) and the treatment received at death (e.g., J. A. Brown 1971, R. Chapman et al. 1981, O'Shea 1984), although the relationship is not as straightforward as suggested by some earlier studies. Not all elements of mortuary ritual are expressed at the time of burial. Moreover, a considerable amount of social information materially expressed at the time of burial may be lost through the vagaries of preservation (e.g., O'Shea 1984). At the Sloan site, not only has an unknown amount of Dalton material culture been lost, but even individual graves are not evident.

Interpretation of the Sloan site as a cemetery has been confirmed by the identification of numerous human bone fragments that were recovered in the immediate vicinity of the artifacts (Figure 6.1; see chapter 2). Bone preservation at the site was poor. No complete, or even partial, skeletons could be identified during fieldwork, so the actual number of individuals represented remains speculative. Although it has been convincingly demonstrated that space—place of burial—is an important dimension of status in the mortuary domain (e.g., Goldstein 1981; Mainfort 1985), the lack of identifiable graves and individuals limits interpretation of the spatial distribution of artifacts at the Sloan site. For example, the statistically derived artifact groups discussed in this chapter cannot be confidently interpreted as objects placed within single graves. But human bone is distributed across the site and occurs within or in close proximity to virtually all of the artifact clusters discussed here. Thus, we are confident that the artifacts represent grave inclusions rather than artifact caches buried for some other purpose.

INDIVIDUAL ARTIFACT PROVENIENCE

Our analysis of spatial patterning utilized the data presented in Table 6.1, which was compiled by P.A.M., based on the site field catalog and field maps. Using detailed information recorded during fieldwork, D.F.M. evaluated the reliability of provenience data for each individual artifact and assigned provenience reliability rank values from 1 to 5 to each object, where 1 represents an undisturbed context and 5 is a highly disturbed context. Items ranked as 1 were found lying flat with no evidence of disturbance,

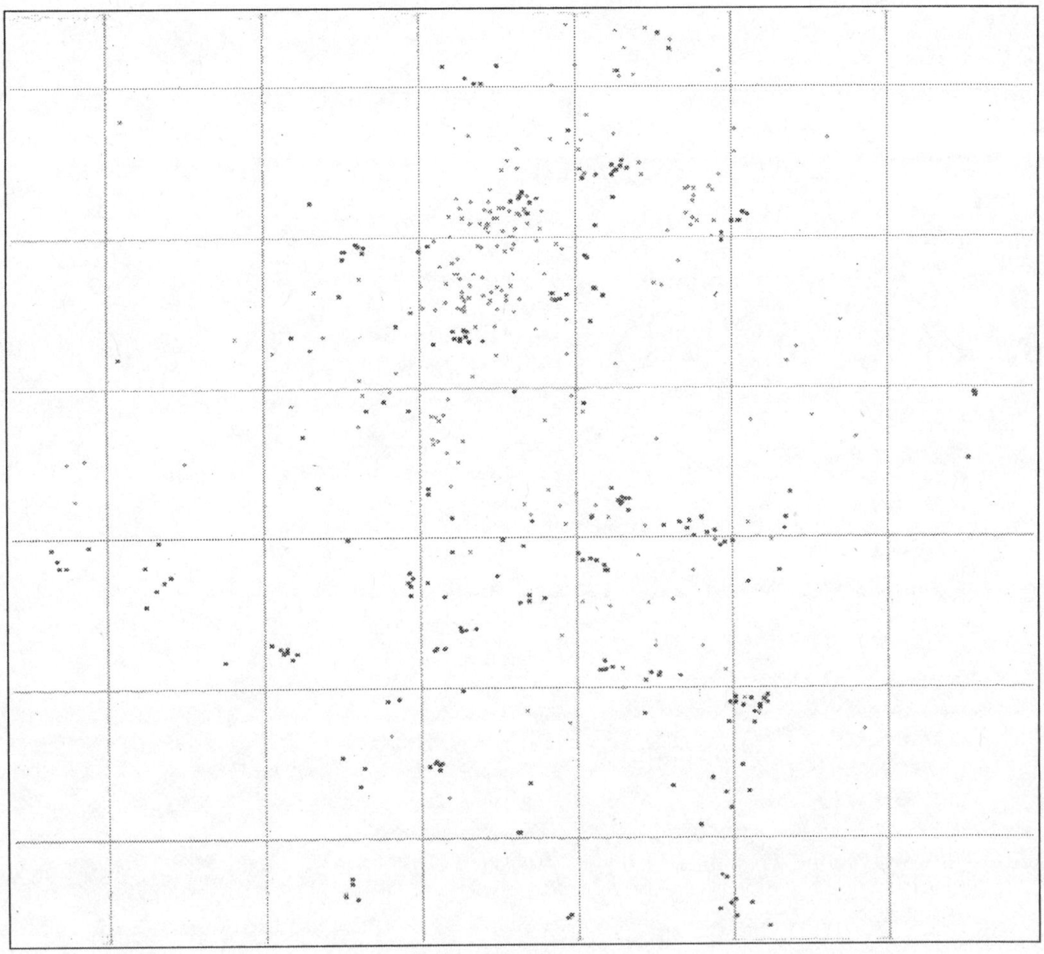

Figure 6.1 Distribution of artifacts used in spatial analysis (in black) and human bone fragments (in gray).

Scale: For distribution maps in this chapter, each unit is 2 meters square.

such as soil discoloration or roots, in close proximity. Objects on edge, but near other evidently undisturbed items received a rank of 2. Specimens without catalog or note comments and that were not photographed were assigned a rank of 3; their recorded provenience is regarded as uncertain. A rank of 4 indicates an artifact found below the cultivation zone, but in an obviously disturbed context. All items in the cultivation zone were given a provenience reliability rank of 5. The distribution of all Sloan-site artifacts found below the cultivation zone is shown in Figure 6.2.

D.F.M.'s assessment of provenience reliability was crucial in our attempts to discern spatial patterning among the artifacts. Because of the uncertainties about the locations and placement of individual graves, it was of critical importance that only those objects of the highest provenience reliability be included in the statistical analyses designed to explicate spatial patterning within the cemetery (Figures 6.3 and 6.4).

It is intuitively obvious that the spatial distribution of artifacts within the cemetery is not random (Figures 6.4 and 6.5). A number of artifacts were recovered as large "caches." Two virtually undisturbed biface caches provide clear indications that the sand dune has been essentially stable since deposition, although in both cases, slight lateral movement of some artifacts was apparent during excavation, indicating that bioturbation had affected the deposits (Figure 6.6). Using all artifacts for which some provenience data was available (i.e., excluding plow-zone specimens), D.F.M. inferred the presence of at least

Table 6.1
Sloan site artifact provenience

Catalog No.	Grid Point	Depth (cm)	Disturbance Code[a]	Specimen
1	48.66 R 48.12	12	2	Dalton point (beveled)
2	48.58 R 48.12	12	2	Dalton point (unbeveled)
3	48.82 R 48.30	15	3	Dalton point (beveled)
4	49.82 R 47.55	16	2	Dalton point (beveled)
5	49.01 R 47.46	0	5	Dalton point (beveled)
6	47.48 R 48.99	18	2	Dalton point (large)
7	49.63 R 49.77	15	3	Sandstone abrader
8	48.67 R 46.71	31	1	Dalton point (unbeveled)
9	48.04 R 49.00	15	3	Sandstone abrader
11	48.66 R 48.45	16	3	Retouched flake
12	48.53 R 48.34	16	3	Utilized flake
13	47.45 R 47.91	14	2	Sandstone abrader (grooved)
14	47.52 R 47.87	13	2	Biface
15	47.40 R 47.86	15	2	Adze
16	49.68 R 47.32	19	2	Dalton point (beveled)
17	47.86 R 49.27	22	3	End scraper
18	47.5 R 47.2	0	5	End scraper
19	47.84 R 49.32	36	3	End scraper
20	47.77 R 49.16	37	3	Biface
21	47.4 R 46.6	0	5	End scraper
23	48.21 R 49.43	18	2	Dalton point (large)
24	46.5 R 46.9	0	5	Dalton point (beveled)
25	47.97 R 49.06	24	2	Dalton point (unbeveled)
27	47.40 R 48.10	18	2	Dalton point (awl)
28	47.35 R 47.89	17	2	Sandstone abrader (grooved)
29	47.23 R 47.89	18	2	Retouched flake
30	46.79 R 48.27	16	3	Dalton point (beveled)
31	47.21 R 48.32	16	2	End scraper
32	46.30 R 48.48	20	3	Pebble core
34	47.83 R 49.23	29	3	End scraper
35	49.37 R 45.30	41	3	End scraper
36	47.88 R 49.32	30	2	Dalton point (burin)
37	47.30 R 49.45	0	5	Dalton point (beveled)
39	47.38 R 48.50	24	3	Retouched flake
41	47.82 R 48.41	32	2	Adze
42	47.18 R 49.58	19	1	Dalton point (beveled)
43	47.23 R 49.38	20	1	Dalton point (beveled)
44	47.80 R 48.68	37	3	Utilized flake
45	49.68 R 47.87	23	2	Dalton point (beveled)
46	49.83 R 47.43	26	4	Dalton point (beveled)
48	46.17 R 48.24	22	4	Sandstone abrader (grooved)
49	46.46 R 48.41	22	3	Backed uniface
50	48.25 R 48.42	30	1	Dalton point (beveled)
51	46.00 R 49.63	20	3	Dalton point (beveled)
52	48.32 R 46.53	28	3	Utilized flake
53	46.52 R 48.32	24	1	Adze
54	46.50 R 48.19	24	1	Sandstone abrader (notched)
55	46.53 R 48.22	24	1	Sandstone abrader (grooved)
56	46.79 R 48.71	19	2	Dalton point (unbeveled)
57	46.61 R 48.39	20	3	Biface

Table 6.1 Continued

Catalog No.	Grid Point	Depth (cm)	Disturbance Code[a]	Specimen
58	46.80 R 48.52	26	1	Dalton point (beveled)
59	46.75 R 48.53	26	1	Dalton point (unbeveled)
60	46.77 R 48.58	26	2	Dalton point (unbeveled)
61	47.30 R 47.92	23	3	Biface
62	49.57 R 47.98	24	4	Sandstone abrader (grooved)
63	46.50 R 47.51	17	3	Utilized flake
64	48.68 R 48.48	30	3	Utilized flake
65	48.72 R 47.95	37	4	Biface
66	46.49 R 48.25	25	1	Utilized flake
67	46.46 R 48.26	28	1	Biface
68	46.52 R 48.29	25	1	Dalton point (awl)
69	46.52 R 48.21	26	1	Retouched flake
70	46.38 R 48.37	26	1	Adze
71	46.46 R 48.43	24	2	Sandstone abrader (notched)
72	46.58 R 48.10	28	2	Utilized flake
73	47.15 R 49.39	21	1	Dalton point (unbeveled)
74	47.13 R 49.27	25	2	Dalton point (beveled)
75	46.77 R 48.58	26	3	Broken biface tool
76	46.49 R 48.30	24	1	Sandstone abrader (notched)
77	48.00 R 51.35	0	5	Dalton point (awl)
78	49.0 R 50.0	0	5	End scraper
79	49.87 R 50.08	0	5	End scraper
81	47.06 R 49.20	26	3	Dalton point (unbeveled)
82	48.20 R 51.31	14	2	Biface
83	48.22 R 51.44	14	2	Cobble abrader
84	48.22 R 51.44	14	2	Biface
85	48.02 R 51.50	12	1	Dalton point (unbeveled)
89	48.06 R 51.67	12	1	Dalton point (beveled)
90	46.50 R 50.20	0	5	Adze
91	46.80 R 50.53	13	3	Chert discoid hammer
92	48.08 R 51.94	12	3	Utilized flake
93	47.93 R 51.91	14	2	Dalton point (beveled)
94	48.85 R 51.93	12	3	Dalton point (unbeveled)
95	46.60 R 51.64	17	3	Dalton point (beveled)
96	48.15 R 51.11	14	1	Dalton point (beveled)
97	49.19 R 50.00	14	3	Biface
98	49.72 R 51.86	13	4	End scraper
99	47.66 R 51.27	15	3	Adze
100	50.31 R 47.81	22	3	Utilized flake
101	50.37 R 47.46	23	3	Dalton point (beveled)
102	49.39 R 51.83	19	3	Dalton point (unbeveled)
103	46.09 R 50.89	18	3	Biface
104	46.05 R 50.89	20	3	End scraper
105	49.34 R 51.84	22	3	Adze
106	48.85 R 51.25	20	4	Biface
107	49.50 R 51.01	20	3	Dalton point (unbeveled)
108	50.82 R 47.71	46	1	Dalton point (large)
109	50.50 R 46.61	10	1	Dalton point (beveled)
110	49.94 R 49.21	17	2	Adze

Continued on next page

Table 6.1 Continued

Catalog No.	Grid Point	Depth (cm)	Disturbance Code[a]	Specimen
111	50.25 R 46.26	22	3	Dalton point (beveled)
112	46.11 R 51.59	21	3	Retouched flake
113	47.08 R 47.97	25	1	Dalton point (large)
114	50.67 R 46.59	22	3	Utilized flake
115	50.61 R 50.39	0	5	End scraper
116	50.67 R 46.37	29	1	Dalton point (beveled)
117	50.35 R 50.44	15	3	Utilized flake
118	50.87 R 50.18	12	1	Dalton point (large)
119	46.03 R 49.14	39	3	Adze
120	46.0 R 49.23	36	3	Dalton point (burin)
121	45.98 R 48.99	36	3	Retouched flake
122	46.23 R 50.31	28	2	Dalton point (awl)
123	46.24 R 50.36	24	2	Biface
124	46.23 R 50.28	28	2	Biface
125	46.27 R 50.45	29	2	Biface
126	46.35 R 50.35	21	2	Biface
127	46.41 R 50.61	26	4	Utilized flake
128	50.61 R 48.82	14	1	Dalton point (large)
129	46.19 R 50.95	23	2	Sandstone abrader (grooved, 132)
130	46.15 R 51.04	27	1	Biface
131	46.16 R 51.31	26	1	Dalton point (beveled)
132	46.10 R 50.88	27	2	Sandstone abrader (grooved, 129)
133	50.57 R 48.18	16	1	Dalton point (Sloan)
134	46.08 R 51.84	21	3	Dalton point (beveled)
135	50.80 R 49.55	13	3	Adze
136	50.65 R 48.46	18	1	Biface
137	50.74 R 48.43	18	1	Utilized flake
138	50.76 R 48.57	21	1	Dalton point (large)
139	50.65 R 48.53	18	1	Sandstone abrader
140	50.62 R 48.53	18	1	Backed uniface
141	50.60 R 48.64	19	1	Dalton point (beveled)
142	50.74 R 48.61	22	1	Backed uniface
143	50.68 R 48.60	18	1	Retouched flake
144	46.20 R 51.06	31	1	Biface
145	46.98 R 49.91	21	4	Utilized flake
146	47.78 R 50.02	17	2	Sandstone abrader
147	47.70 R 50.07	22	1	Dalton point (beveled)
148	47.71 R 50.17	22	1	Dalton point (beveled)
149	47.69 R 50.25	18	2	Ironstone object
150	47.63 R 50.35	18	1	Sandstone abrader (grooved)
151	47.56 R 50.36	16	2	Dalton point (beveled)
152	47.55 R 50.38	21	1	Biface
153	48.12 R 51.42	18	1	Biface
154	48.49 R 50.53	17	1	Sandstone abrader (grooved)
155	48.36 R 50.66	19	1	Biface
156	48.53 R 50.57	18	1	Sandstone abrader (grooved)
157	48.51 R 50.61	23	1	Adze
158	48.44 R 50.56	24	1	Retouched flake
159	48.47 R 50.57	24	1	Biface
160	48.66 R 50.45	22	2	Dalton point (unbeveled)

Table 6.1 Continued

Catalog No.	Grid Point	Depth (cm)	Disturbance Code[a]	Specimen
161	48.51 R 50.67	23	2	Backed uniface
162	48.25 R 51.60	23	2	Utilized flake
163	48.08 R 51.78	24	2	Chert chopper/Core
164	47.94 R 52.00	18	1	Dalton point (unbeveled)
165	47.89 R 51.85	31	1	Dalton point (large)
166	50.63 R 50.60	31	3	Utilized flake
167	50.37 R 50.83	34	3	Retouched flake
168	50.36 R 50.37	39	3	Retouched flake
173	48.25 R 50.19	27	2	Dalton point (beveled)
174	49.78 R 50.10	30	1	Dalton point (large)
175	47.37 R 46.24	15	4	Adze
177	46.84 R 46.0	18	4	Adze
178	49.05 R 45.15	14	3	Cobble abrader
179	47.45 R 45.92	23	3	Dalton point (unbeveled)
180	46.75 R 45.35	25	3	End scraper
181	46.34 R 45.49	16	1	Dalton point (large)
182	46.50 R 45.88	25	3	Chert discoid hammer
183	48.21 R 52.00	0	5	Dalton point (large)
184	48.28 R 52.17	0	5	Dalton point (unbeveled)
185	46.0 R 45.0	30	3	Dalton point (beveled)
186	47.55 R 52.60	16	1	Dalton point (beveled)
187	49.85 R 52.39	17	3	Dalton point (beveled)
188	49.91 R 52.45	17	3	Dalton point (beveled)
189	48.12 R 52.68	15	2	Adze
191	51.87 R 48.12	20	1	Adze
193	49.48 R 52.50	15	3	Dalton point (beveled)
194	49.17 R 52.48	18	3	End scraper
195	51.38 R 48.24	12	3	Dalton point (beveled)
196	51.38 R 48.11	14	3	Adze
197	51.47 R 48.13	14	3	End scraper
199	47.38 R 53.65	21	3	Utilized flake
201	51.95 R 51.87	14	1	Biface
202	52.05 R 51.88	14	1	Biface
203	51.90 R 47.20	20	2	Biface
204	51.70 R 47.03	12	2	Adze
206	51.80 R 48.00	18	2	Adze
207	51.23 R 49.88	18	2	Dalton point (unbeveled)
208	51.25 R 49.70	25	2	Dalton point (unbeveled)
212	51.16 R 49.74	26	1	Dalton point (unbeveled)
213	51.17 R 49.80	26	1	Dalton point (unbeveled)
215	51.05 R 50.55	0	5	End scraper
216	51.22 R 46.98	32	1	Dalton point (large)
217	51.82 R 51.39	28	3	Adze
219	51.80 R 47.03	12	1	Sandstone abrader (grooved)
220	51.88 R 47.23	9	1	Adze
221	51.86 R 47.30	10	2	Dalton point (awl)
223	51.32 R 50.23	10	1	Adze
224	51.22 R 50.35	14	1	Adze
226	51.76 R 50.20	10	3	Ocher

Continued on next page

Table 6.1 Continued

Catalog No.	Grid Point	Depth (cm)	Disturbance Code[a]	Specimen
227	51.31 R 50.25	12	1	Adze
228	51.07 R 51.15	16	4	Dalton point (beveled)
229	51.80 R 47.05	16	1	Biface
230	51.79 R 47.29	14	2	Backed uniface
233	51.72 R 50.15	24	1	Sandstone abrader (grooved)
234	51.75 R 50.12	24	1	Sandstone abrader (grooved)
235	46.07 R 53.02	23	3	Adze
236	51.00 R 47.90	42	2	Adze
237	46.80 R 51.90	26	3	Dalton point (unbeveled)
243	47.93 R 52.10	20	3	Utilized flake
244	47.40 R 52.20	18	2	Dalton point (beveled)
245	47.45 R 53.35	21	4	Utilized flake
248	49.91 R 52.59	24	3	Dalton point (scraper)
249	49.83 R 52.80	24	3	Dalton point (beveled)
250	49.50 R 52.73	18	3	Sandstone abrader (grooved)
252	50.35 R 52.74	17	4	Dalton point (beveled)
253	48.46 R 52.25	24	3	Perforator
254	48.30 R 51.61	26	3	End scraper
255	49.81 R 52.62	26	3	Dalton point (beveled)
256	49.07 R 52.40	22	3	Utilized flake
257	49.12 R 52.65	25	3	Biface
258	49.18 R 52.60	22	3	Biface
259	49.20 R 52.59	23	3	Sandstone abrader (notched)
260	49.19 R 52.62	24	3	Utilized flake
261	49.18 R 52.32	26	3	Pebble core
262	49.05 R 52.96	27	3	End scraper
264	50.10 R 52.63	24	4	Dalton point (beveled)
265	48.26 R 52.69	36	1	Dalton point (large)
266	48.60 R 52.75	37	2	End scraper
267	48.75 R 52.90	38	3	End scraper
268	45.4 R 48.3	0	5	Retouched flake
269	45.16 R 49.81	14	3	Sandstone abrader (notched)
270	45.87 R 52.03	14	1	Sandstone abrader
271	45.95 R 48.54	16	2	Dalton point (beveled)
272	45.86 R 52.23	15	1	Adze
273	45.90 R 48.70	16	3	Pebble core
274	45.95 R 46.86	24	3	Dalton point (beveled)
275	45.65 R 50.86	18	2	Dalton point (large)
276	45.09 R 49.91	30	4	Biface
277	45.85 R 47.73	28	1	Dalton point (large)
278	45.82 R 47.59	24	1	Dalton point (large)
279	45.79 R 52.45	22	2	Biface
280	45.76 R 52.13	20	1	Adze
281	45.79 R 52.03	18	2	Adze
282	45.54 R 51.94	18	2	Retouched flake
283	45.92 R 45.58	34	4	Backed uniface
284	46.01 R 45.64	42	3	Broken biface tool
285	45.79 R 51.96	33	2	Backed uniface
286	45.37 R 51.88	33	3	Broken biface tool
287	45.02 R 48.20	27	1	Dalton point (beveled)

Table 6.1 Continued

Catalog No.	Grid Point	Depth (cm)	Disturbance Code[a]	Specimen
288	45.00 R 48.18	27	1	Dalton point (beveled)
289	44.98 R 48.24	29	1	Dalton point (unbeveled)
290	44.99 R 48.27	28	1	Dalton point (beveled)
291	44.95 R 48.11	32	2	Dalton point (unbeveled)
292	44.91 R 48.24	31	2	Dalton point (beveled)
293	45.65 R 45.25	21	3	Dalton point (beveled)
294	45.52 R 52.28	24	1	Dalton point (large)
295	44.72 R 49.38	10	1	Dalton point (large)
296	44.17 R 51.57	12	2	Adze
297	44.80 R 51.73	8	2	End scraper
298	44.69 R 51.21	9	2	Sandstone abrader (notched)
299	44.39 R 51.97	10	2	Dalton point (beveled)
300	44.59 R 51.91	12	2	Dalton point (beveled)
302	44.65 R 46.95	0	5	Dalton point (beveled)
303	44.06 R 49.23	13	1	Dalton point (beveled)
304	44.06 R 49.25	13	1	Dalton point (beveled)
305	44.57 R 47.47	0	5	Dalton point (beveled)
306	44.03 R 45.58	30	3	Pebble core
307	44.96 R 52.12	11	2	Dalton point (preform)
308	44.61 R 52.20	15	2	Dalton point (unbeveled)
309	45.08 R 47.0	14	2	Dalton point (beveled)
310	44.70 R 47.22	14	1	Dalton point (beveled)
311	44.94 R 47.28	14	1	Dalton point (unbeveled)
313	44.66 R 48.12	33	3	Ocher
314	44.02 R 47.44	27	3	Dalton point (large)
315	44.36 R 50.52	17	3	Adze
316	44.81 R 47.83	20	3	Dalton point (beveled)
317	44.25 R 50.62	24	3	Dalton point (unbeveled)
318	45.73 R 52.35	17	1	Biface
319	45.77 R 52.35	18	2	Biface
320	45.89 R 52.45	21	2	Biface
321	45.67 R 52.28	28	2	Biface
322	45.84 R 52.40	28	2	End scraper
323	44.75 R 53.80	0	5	End scraper
324	43.05 R 47.14	0	5	Dalton point (unbeveled)
325	43.15 R 46.90	18	3	Dalton point (beveled)
326	43.88 R 47.93	0	5	Utilized flake
327	44.88 R 53.71	24	3	Retouched flake
328	43.86 R 50.75	14	3	Biface
329	43.04 R 51.81	16	2	Biface
330	43.43 R 48.62	18	3	End scraper
331	43.18 R 47.18	22	2	Dalton point (beveled)
332	43.22 R 47.03	24	2	Dalton point (beveled)
333	43.46 R 47.11	20	2	Dalton point (beveled)
336	43.40 R 47.11	27	2	Dalton point (unbeveled)
337	43.46 R 51.91	20	1	Biface
338	43.50 R 51.85	19	2	Sandstone abrader (disintegrated)
339	43.11 R 51.96	25	2	Biface
340	43.17 R 52.02	14	2	Biface

Continued on next page

Table 6.1 Continued

Catalog No.	Grid Point	Depth (cm)	Disturbance Code[a]	Specimen
341	43.07 R 52.12	0	5	Adze
342	43.12 R 52.23	16	2	Biface
343	43.95 R 53.44	0	5	Chert discoid hammer
344	42.92 R 49.86	19	1	Cobble abrader
345	42.96 R 49.90	18	1	Cobble abrader
348	42.81 R 52.46	18	1	Adze
349	52.65 R 51.98	0	5	Biface
350	42.94 R 52.03	21	1	Biface
351	47.12 R 53.52	0	5	Biface
352	52.60 R 49.76	19	3	Adze
354	45.95 R 45.00	0	5	Adze
355	52.46 R 49.17	21	2	Biface
356	52.50 R 49.27	26	1	Biface
357	52.54 R 49.28	28	1	Biface
358	52.57 R 49.32	26	1	Biface
359	52.59 R 49.31	26	1	Biface
360	52.30 R 49.38	26	1	Dalton point (beveled)
361	52.50 R 49.50	24	1	Sandstone abrader (grooved, notched)
362	52.40 R 48.84	34	4	Dalton point (large)
363	52.77 R 50.08	18	1	Adze
364	52.82 R 50.26	16	1	Sandstone abrader (grooved)
365	52.82 R 50.46	15	2	Biface
366	52.95 R 50.46	12	1	Biface
367	52.86 R 50.49	18	1	Biface
368	52.88 R 50.51	15	1	Sandstone abrader (grooved)
369	52.93 R 50.57	12	1	Utilized flake
370	53.00 R 50.58	12	1	Utilized flake
371	52.90 R 50.66	14	2	Biface
372	53.05 R 50.58	0	5	Utilized flake
373	Area of 363–372	0	5	Utilized flake
374	49.91 R 55.12	24	1	Biface
375	49.90 R 55.13	28	1	Biface
376	49.91 R 55.12	28	1	Biface
377	49.05 R 55.05	29	2	Retouched flake
378	49.92 R 55.12	31	1	Biface
379	52.15 R 50.25	21	1	Biface
380	52.15 R 50.25	21	1	Biface
381	52.15 R 50.25	21	1	Biface
382	52.15 R 50.25	21	1	Utilized flake
383	52.15 R 50.25	21	1	Biface
384	52.15 R 50.25	21	1	Biface
385	52.15 R 50.25	21	1	Biface
386	52.15 R 50.25	21	1	Biface
387	52.15 R 50.25	21	1	Biface
388	52.15 R 50.25	21	1	Biface
389	52.15 R 50.25	21	1	Biface
390	52.15 R 50.25	21	1	Biface
391	52.15 R 50.25	21	1	Biface
392	52.15 R 50.25	21	1	Biface
393	52.15 R 50.25	21	1	Dalton point (beveled)

Table 6.1 Continued

Catalog No.	Grid Point	Depth (cm)	Disturbance Code[a]	Specimen
394	52.15 R 50.25	21	1	Biface
395	52.15 R 50.25	21	1	Biface
396	52.15 R 50.25	21	1	Biface
398	52.52 R 50.47	28	2	Utilized flake
399	52.89 R 50.06	27	2	Utilized flake
401	53.41 R 49.92	16	1	Dalton point (beveled)
402	52.45 R 49.42	38	1	Biface
403	52.21 R 52.00	22	2	Dalton point (large)
404	52.20 R 52.09	13	2	Biface
405	52.20 R 52.11	16	1	Biface
406	52.32 R 52.14	16	1	Biface
407	52.29 R 52.20	19	1	Biface
408	53.95 R 53.19	0	5	Dalton point (unbeveled)
409	53.91 R 53.31	19	3	Biface
410	53.39 R 52.01	14	3	Dalton point (beveled)
411	49.87 R 55.14	35	2	Biface
412	49.90 R 55.14	35	2	Biface
413	54.30 R 50.60	0	5	End scraper
414	54.21 R 50.53	16	1	Dalton point (large)
415	54.49 R 51.20	16	1	Backed uniface
416	54.71 R 51.06	20	1	Sandstone abrader (grooved, notched)
417	54.69 R 51.06	20	1	Sandstone abrader
418	50.96 R 54.35	15	3	End scraper
420	56.0 R 50.50	0	5	Dalton point (awl)
421	51.02 R 54.47	27	3	Retouched flake
422	51.12 R 54.43	24	3	Utilized flake
424	54.27 R 48.32	10	2	Sandstone abrader (grooved, 434)
425	54.10 R 48.60	12	2	Adze
426	54.04 R 48.71	11	2	Adze
427	54.04 R 48.80	11	2	Adze
428	54.28 R 49.0	10	2	Dalton point (large)
429	52.45 R 46.61	0	5	Dalton point (beveled)
430	53.88 R 46.50	33	3	Retouched flake
431	53.45 R 45.56	33	3	Sandstone abrader (notched)
432	53.46 R 45.40	33	3	Utilized flake
433	52.22 R 46.24	45	3	Dalton point (unbeveled)
434	54.84 R 47.75	0	5	Sandstone abrader (grooved, 424)
435	54.81 R 45.27	0	5	Dalton point (unbeveled)
436	44.92 R 44.66	0	5	Dalton point (beveled, 453)
437	44.15 R 44.67	0	5	Retouched flake
438	43.16 R 44.88	23	5	Utilized flake
439	42.48 R 45.81	22	5	Biface
441	47.31 R 44.62	30	1	Edge-abraded cobble
442	47.49 R 44.81	29	1	Dalton point (beveled)
443	47.41 R 44.72	30	2	*Pièce esquillée*
444	47.94 R 44.65	22	2	Utilized flake
445	50.39 R 44.15	42	2	Dalton point (large)
446	47.10 R 44.49	31	1	Perforator
447	47.62 R 44.48	37	1	Utilized flake

Continued on next page

Table 6.1 Continued

Catalog No.	Grid Point	Depth (cm)	Disturbance Code[a]	Specimen
448	49.78 R 44.10	44	3	Dalton point (beveled)
452	43.24 R 43.87	0	5	Dalton point (beveled)
453	43.19 R 43.80	0	5	Dalton point (beveled, 436)
458	47.85 R 43.29	38	2	Backed uniface
459	47.62 R 43.39	41	2	Dalton point (unbeveled)
460	47.72 R 43.36	42	1	Adze
461	47.62 R 43.48	42	2	Sandstone abrader (grooved, notched)
462	47.88 R 43.77	38	1	Dalton point (large)
463	50.07 R 43.83	0	5	Retouched flake
465	50.04 R 43.60	0	5	Biface
467	49.65 R 43.86	44	3	Dalton point (beveled)
468	51.35 R 43.66	44	3	Biface
469	51.35 R 43.48	56	3	End scraper
470	51.0 R 42.5	0	5	Retouched flake
471	48.9 R 51.0	60	3	Dalton point (unbeveled)
472	47.4 R 47.9	14	3	Utilized flake
473	46 R 48	0	5	Dalton point (unbeveled)
474	46 R 54	0	5	Dalton point (unbeveled)
475	48.08 R 47.0	0	5	Backed uniface
476	46.20 R 53.60	0	5	End scraper
477	c.43.6 R 43.2	0	5	End scraper
478	49.34 R 46.51	35	1	Biface
479	49.34 R 46.51	35	1	Biface
480	49.34 R 46.51	35	1	Biface
481	49.34 R 46.51	35	1	Biface
482	49.34 R 46.51	35	1	Biface
483	49.34 R 46.51	35	1	Biface
484	49.34 R 46.51	35	1	Biface
485	49.34 R 46.51	35	1	Adze
486	49.34 R 46.51	35	1	Biface
487	49.34 R 46.51	35	1	Adze
488	49.34 R 46.51	35	1	Adze
489	49.34 R 46.51	35	1	Biface
490	49.34 R 46.51	35	1	Sandstone abrader (notched)
491	N/A	0	5	Dalton point (beveled)
492	N/A	0	5	End scraper
493	ca. 53 R 51	0	5	End scraper
494	53.45 R 49.90	18	3	Ocher
495	53.21 R 49.72	24	3	Ocher
496	53.38 R 48.49	38	3	Ocher
497	42.30 R 42.50	0	5	Retouched flake
499	ca. 47 R 48	0	5	End scraper
500	42.08 R 45.86	26	3	Sandstone abrader (notched)
501	47.07 R 51.67	34	3	Sandstone abrader
504	52.3 R 47.15	25	3	Retouched flake
1414	N/A	0	5	Dalton point (beveled)
1416	N/A	0	5	End scraper

[a]Disturbance code: 1, undisturbed; 2, slightly disturbed; 3, unknown; 4, considerably disturbed; 5, cultivation zone.

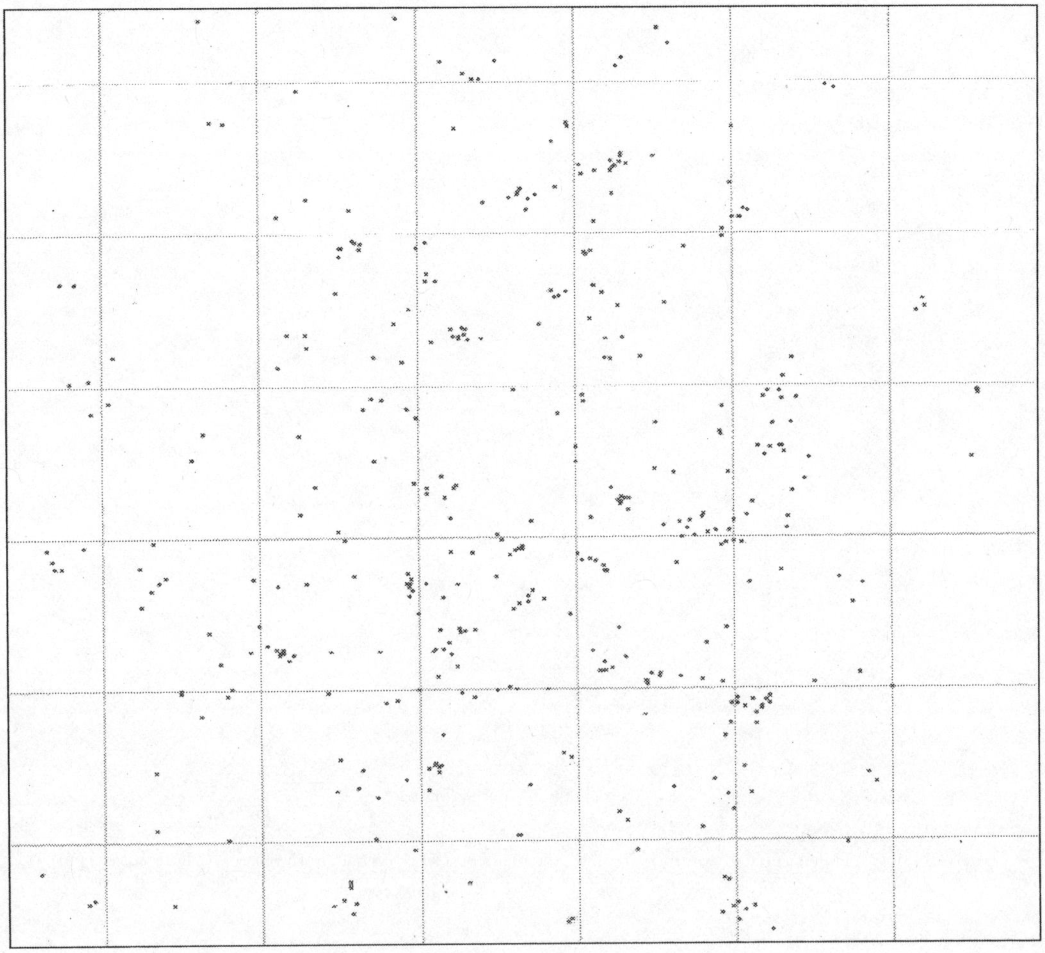

Figure 6.2 Distribution of artifacts at the Sloan site (provenience reliability 1–4).

twenty-seven discrete groups of artifacts (possible grave lots), which was used as a baseline for our statistical study. Only the results of the latter are presented here.

Spatial Analysis

Analysis of the spatial distribution of artifacts in the Sloan cemetery had two primary goals. The first was to determine the number of statistically valid (or at least, objectively defined using statistical methods) spatial clusters of artifacts. Although not providing a direct measure of the number of individuals interred in the cemetery, the resulting figure does provide an objective parameter upon which a reasonable estimate can be made. A second goal, which we did not successfully accomplish, was to identify spatial distributions of specific artifact types that could potentially be related to differential status within the cemetery. As a corollary, we sought to identify Dalton tool kits among the artifact clusters.

We chose a purely locational approach to spatial analysis using *K*-means clustering, as first proposed by Kintigh and Ammerman (1982) and subsequently employed by a number of other researchers in analyzing activity areas within archaeological sites (e.g., Gregg et al. 1991; Rigaud and Simek 1991). In contrast to materials found in habitation deposits, however, the Sloan-site artifacts were intentionally placed in specific locations where they remained essentially undisturbed for thousands of years until the time of their discovery.

Determining the "true" number of clusters in a data set

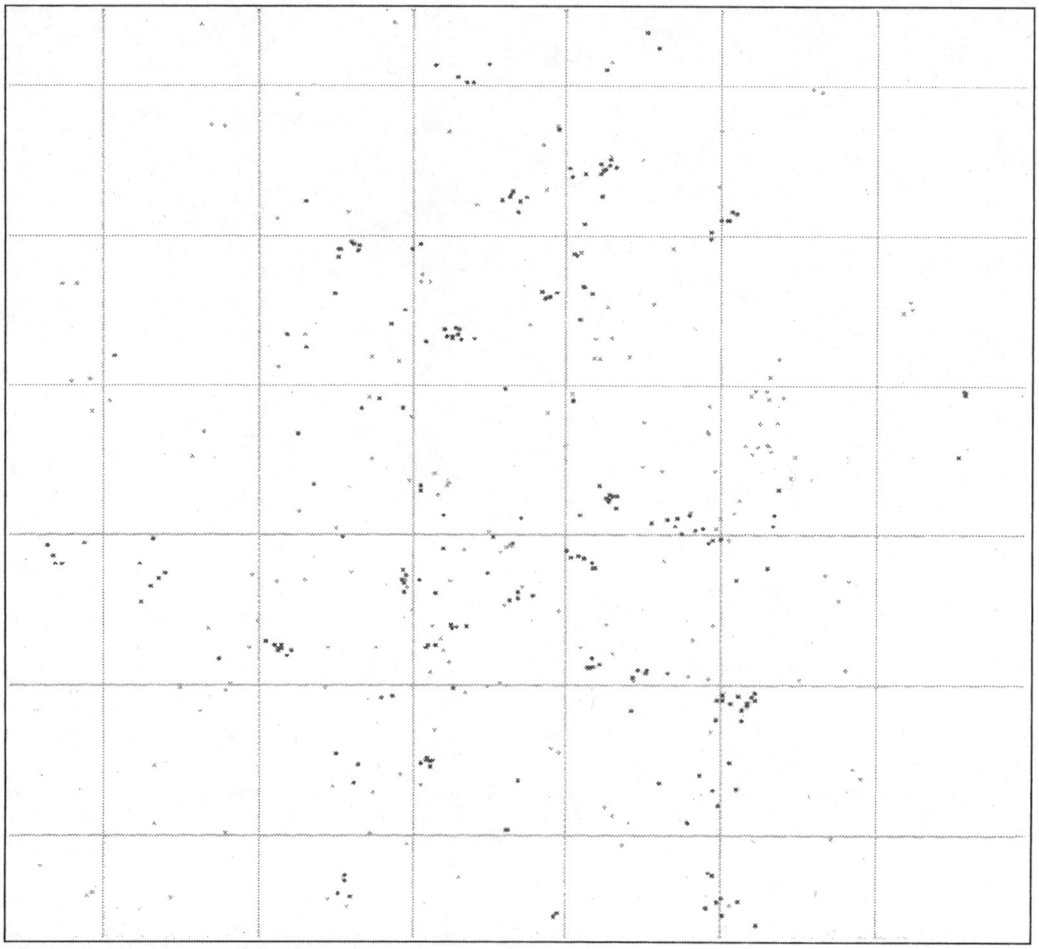

Figure 6.3 Distribution of artifacts at the Sloan site. Provenience reliability less than 3 shown in black; provenience reliability more than 2 shown in gray.

is perhaps the fundamental problem of cluster validity (e.g., Dubes 1993). This is of critical concern in examining the Sloan site because the number of isolatable artifact clusters provides our best window, albeit an indirect one, on the actual number of interred individuals. Kintigh and Ammerman (1982) proposed plotting $\log_{10}$ SSE (square error) for multiple clusterings and examining the resulting plot for a prominent point of inflection as a guide to determining the actual number of clusters present. This measure obviously is a direct function of square-error, which decreases as the number of clusters is increased, and is not among the measures routinely employed in the cluster analysis literature (e.g., Jain and Dubes 1988). Milligan and Cooper (1985) tested thirty proposed indices by applying them to a generated data set. Of these, the Calinski-Harabasz index performed best, and we employed it in our analysis of the Sloan cemetery data.

The Calinski-Harabasz index (*CH*) is calculated as follows:

$$CH(K) = \frac{n - K}{K - 1}\left[\frac{E_1^2}{E_K^2} - 1\right]$$

where *n* is the number of patterns (artifacts), *K* is the number of clusters in the clustering being evaluated, and *E* is the square-error of the clustering. The index is always positive and is 0 for $K = 0$; its upper limit depends on the specific problem. An estimate of the number of clusters is

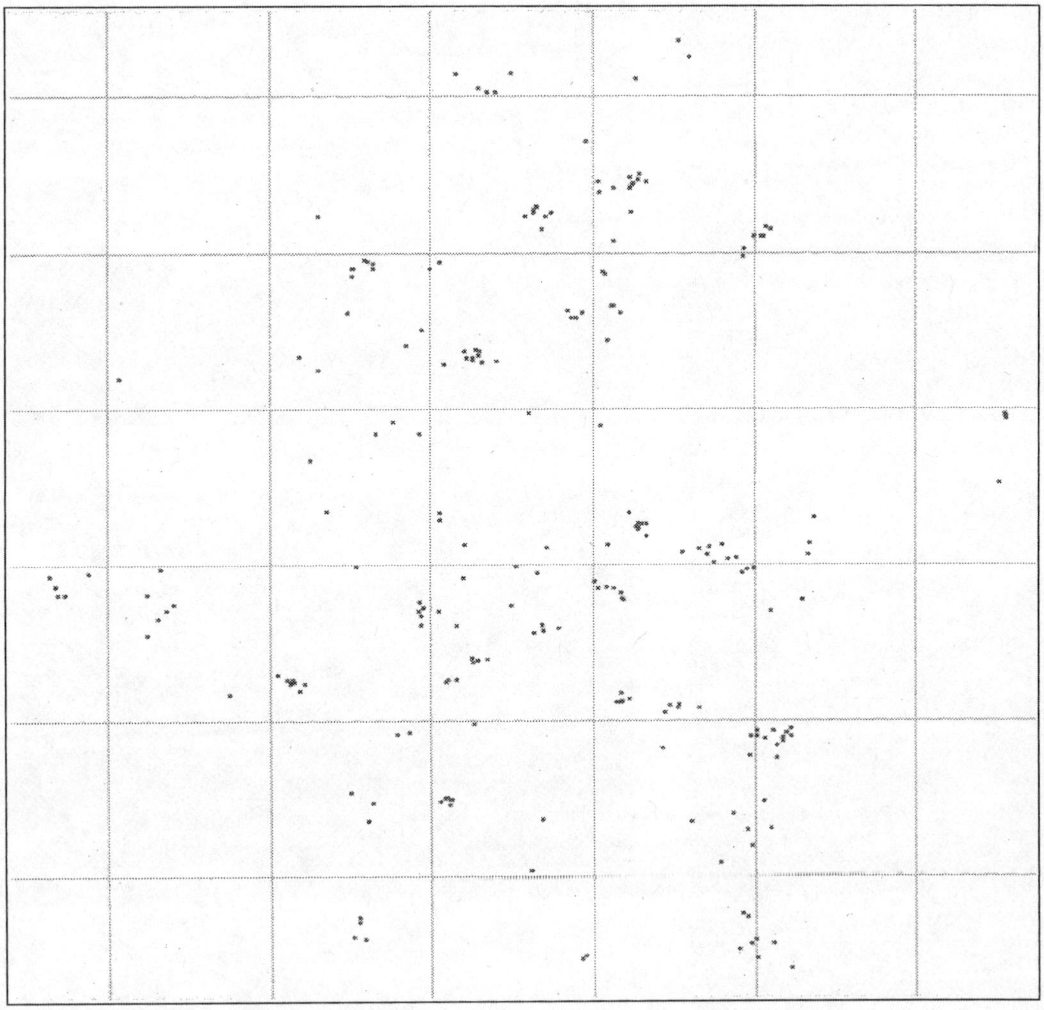

Figure 6.4 Distribution of artifacts used in spatial analysis (provenience reliability less than 3).

obtained by plotting the index as *K* varies and searching for a maximum, minimum, or inflection in the curve. Thus, there is an element of subjectivity in interpreting the results, as is the case with all other proposed indices (e.g., Kintigh and Ammerman 1982). It must also be stressed that even though the *CH* index proved superior in tests with generated data, the behavior and performance of this and other indices with real data are poorly known (Dubes 1993; Jain and Dubes 1988).

Two other guidelines were considered in determining the number of clusters present. The first was D.F.M.'s visual observation that approximately thirty spatially discrete groups of artifacts seem to be present. Second, we performed several average-linkage hierarchical clusterings on the Sloan data, all of which we interpret as implying the existence of approximately thirty clusters. The resulting clusters are listed below and are summarized in Table 6.2. Figure 6.7 illustrates the clusters.

CLUSTER 1 (355–361, 363–371, 379–396, 398–399, 401–402). This cluster, numerically the largest identified by *K*-means analysis, combines what intuitively seems to represent two spatially distinct groups of artifacts; these may have been associated with two or more individuals. Among the artifacts is one of two intact biface caches recorded at the site (379–396), represented by sixteen bifaces, a Dalton point, and a utilized flake within an area measuring approximately 20 by 25 centimeters. An additional twenty artifacts are scattered within a 200 by 50 centimeter area.

Figure 6.5 Artifact concentrations indicative of possible graves: *a,* cluster 1 (AAS neg. 742622); *b,* cluster 21(AAS neg. 742480); *c,* cluster 7 (AAS neg. 742400); and *d,* cluster 1 (AAS neg. 742700).

a

b

c

d

Figure 6.6 Artifacts indicative of insignificant disturbance at the Sloan site: *a,* specimens 102, 105, and *b,* specimen 294 are artifacts lying flat and relatively undisturbed; *c,* specimens 379–396 in a cache with minimum disturbance; *d,* specimens 154–161 in a very slightly disturbed condition. Photo negative numbers: *a,* AAS 742492; *b,* AAS 742685; *c,* AAS 742703; and *d,* AAS 742621.

Table 6.2
Artifact clusters at the Sloan site

Cluster	Large Dalton	Beveled Dalton	Unbeveled Dalton	Biface	Adze	Abrader	Backed Uniface	Retouched Flake	Utilized Flake	End Scraper	Dalton Awl	Other	No. of Classes	No. of Items
1	0	3	0	26	1	3	0	0	5	0	0		5	38
2	0	4	1	3	1	4	1	1	0	0	0	Ironstone object	8	16
3	0	2	3	0	1	2	0	0	0	0	0		4	8
4	0	0	0	6	0	0	0	1	0	0	0		2	7
5	0	0	1	9	3	1	0	0	0	0	0		4	14
6	1	0	0	5	3	1	1	1	0	1	0		7	13
7	4	1	0	1	1	1	2	1	0	0	0	Sloan Dalton	8	12
8	2	6	3	0	0	0	0	0	0	0	0		3	11
9	1	0	0	0	3	1	0	0	0	0	0		3	5
10	1	0	0	0	0	0	0	0	0	0	0		1	1
11	1	1	1	0	1	1	1	0	2	0	0	Abraded cobble, *pièce esquillée*, perforator	10	11
12	1	0	4	0	3	2	0	0	0	0	0		4	10
13	1	2	0	0	0	0	0	0	0	0	0	2 cobble abraders	3	5
14	1	4	2	3	0	0	0	0	1	0	0	Cobble abrader, Chopper/Core	7	13
15	0	0	0	6	1	1	0	0	0	0	0		3	8
16	1	0	0	6	0	0	0	0	0	0	0		2	7
17	1	0	0	1	1	2	0	1	2	0	1		7	9
18	1	1	0	2	4	1	1	0	0	0	1		7	11
19	0	2	1	1	2	2	0	1	0	1	1		8	11
20	1	0	0	0	0	2	1	0	0	0	0		3	4
21	1	1	0	6	0	2	0	0	0	0	1		5	11
22	1	0	0	0	1	0	0	0	0	0	0		2	2
23	0	3	1	0	0	0	0	0	0	0	0		2	4
24	0	2	0	0	0	0	0	0	0	0	0		1	2
25	0	2	1	0	1	1	0	0	0	1	0	Dalton preform	6	7
26	0	3	0	0	0	0	0	0	0	0	0		1	3
27	1	1	0	0	1	0	0	0	0	1	0		4	4
28	1	0	0	0	0	0	0	0	0	0	0		1	1
29	2	3	2	0	0	0	0	0	0	0	0	Dalton burin	4	8

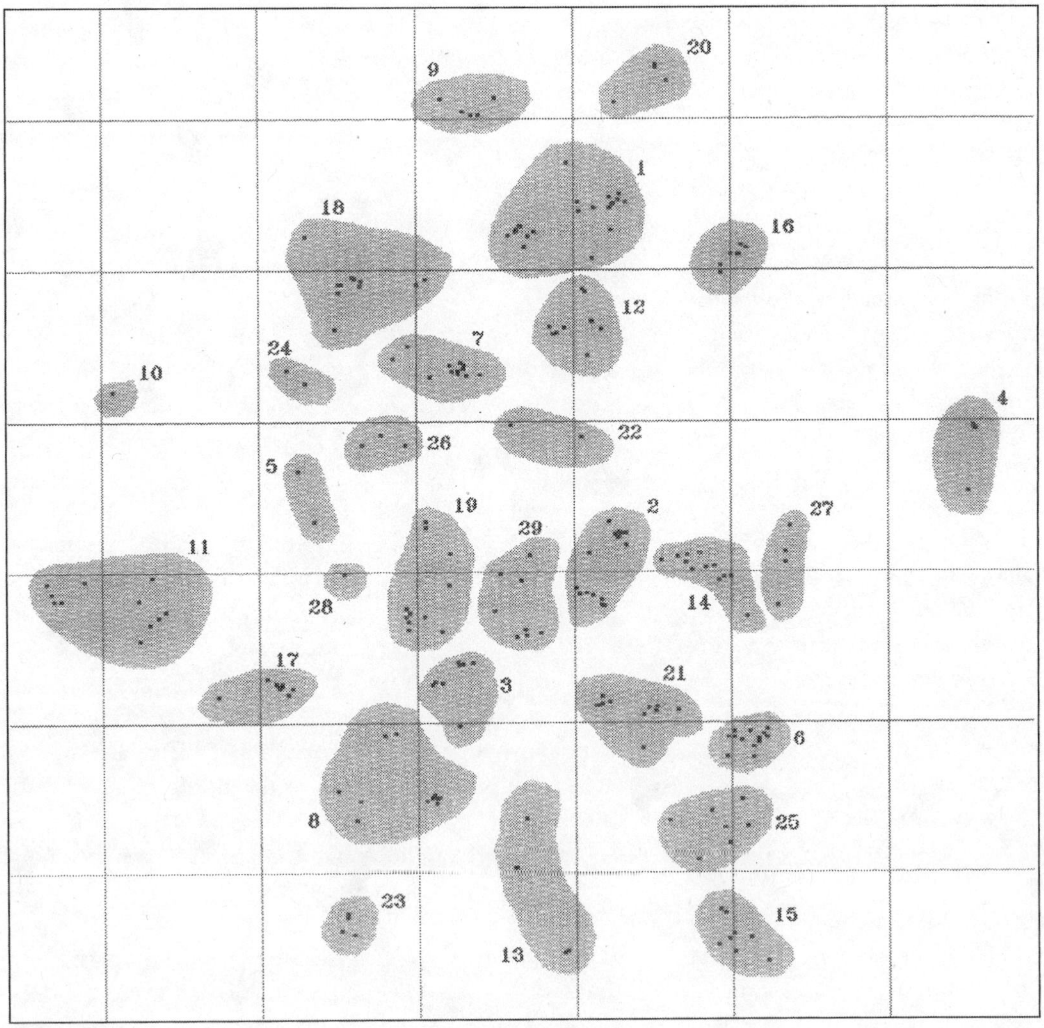

Figure 6.7 Artifact clusters at the Sloan site.

CLUSTER 2 (146–152, 154–161, 173). Two intuitive groups are also included in cluster 2. Among the associated artifacts are four beveled Daltons, an unbeveled Dalton, three bifaces, an adze, four abraders, a backed uniface, a retouched flake, and a fragmentary ironstone object of uncertain function.

CLUSTER 3 (53–56, 58–60, 271). Two beveled Daltons (one of Burlington Chert), three unbeveled Daltons, an adze, and two abraders compose this cluster.

CLUSTER 4 (374–378, 411–412). The most intuitively obvious cluster includes six bifaces and a retouched flake. Five of the bifaces evidently were essentially stacked on top of each other.

CLUSTER 5 (8, 478–490). A second biface cache included nine bifaces, three adzes, and an abrader. An unbeveled Dalton point was nearby.

CLUSTER 6 (270, 272, 279–282, 285, 294, 318–322). These thirteen artifacts were found within an area measuring about 50 centimeters in diameter and 17 centimeters deep. These include a large Dalton of Crescent Quarry Chert, five bifaces, three adzes, an abrader, a backed uniface, a retouched flake, and an end scraper.

CLUSTER 7 (108, 128, 133, 136–143, 236). Two grave lots may be combined in this cluster, which is distinguished by the presence of five large Dalton points (including the Sloan Dalton of Burlington Chert). A beveled Dalton point, a biface, an adze, an abrader, two backed unifaces, and a retouched flake compose the other associated artifacts.

CLUSTER 8 (277–278, 287–292, 309–311). Two large Daltons were side by side facing in opposite directions. Four Daltons were abutting pairs, lying on their edges. These points undoubtedly were hafted onto foreshafts only slightly longer than the largest point and rolled up into a bundle. Two other Daltons were lying flat. Three Daltons were in a group nearby.

CLUSTER 9 (424–428). A large Dalton, three adzes, and a broken abrader were found within an area measuring about 75 by 35 centimeters. The other half of the abrader (434) is associated with cluster 11. Immediately to the south of this cluster was a dark, roughly circular stain, approximately 1.1 meter in diameter, probably representing a root or animal disturbance.

CLUSTER 10 (445). This "cluster" consists of an isolated large Dalton point.

CLUSTER 11 (441–444, 446–447, 458–462). The most diverse group of artifacts, cluster 11 includes a large Dalton of Burlington Chert, a beveled Dalton, an unbeveled Dalton, an adze, an abrader, a backed uniface, two utilized flakes, an edge-abraded cobble, a *pièce esquillée,* and a perforator.

CLUSTER 12 (118, 207–208, 212–213, 223–224, 227, 233–234). The four unbeveled Dalton points were a slightly disturbed cache within an area measuring about 20 by 25 centimeters. Three adzes (223, 224, 227) were located to the east. A large Dalton and two abraders are the remaining items in this cluster.

CLUSTER 13 (295, 303–304, 344–345). This small, somewhat dispersed cluster consists of a large Dalton point, two beveled Daltons, and two cobble abraders.

CLUSTER 14 (82–85, 89, 93, 96, 153, 162–165, 244). Some artifacts in this cluster were found at the base of the plow zone and may have been disturbed by cultivation; these include three beveled Daltons, an unbeveled Dalton, two bifaces, and a cobble abrader. To the southeast, undisturbed by plowing, a large Dalton, an unbeveled Dalton, a biface, a utilized flake of Pitkin Chert, and a chert chopper/core were found. A beveled Dalton point was found nearby.

CLUSTER 15 (329, 337–340, 342, 348, 350). Six bifaces, an adze, and an abrader compose this distinct cluster.

CLUSTER 16 (201–202, 403–407). Possibly representing a slightly disturbed cache, the large Dalton (403) and four bifaces were found within a 20 by 25 centimeter area. Two bifaces were located about 60 centimeters to the west.

CLUSTER 17 (66–72, 76, 181). A biface, an adze, two abraders, a retouched flake, two utilized flakes, and a Dalton awl were located in close proximity to each other; the large Dalton (181) was found nearby.

CLUSTER 18 (191, 203–204, 206, 216, 219–221, 229–230, 429). Some plow-zone artifacts, including debitage and an Archaic point, were observed near this in situ group of Dalton artifacts. A large Dalton, a beveled Dalton, a Dalton awl, two bifaces, four adzes, an abrader, and a backed uniface compose this cluster.

CLUSTER 19 (1–2, 13–15, 27–29, 31, 41, 50). This cluster includes two beveled Daltons, an unbeveled Dalton, a Dalton awl of Burlington Chert, a biface, two adzes, two abraders, a retouched flake, and an end scraper.

CLUSTER 20 (414–417). The four specimens in this cluster are a large Dalton of Burlington Chert, two abraders, and a backed uniface.

CLUSTER 21 (122–126, 129–132, 144, 275). Associated with this cluster are a large Dalton point, a beveled Dalton, a Dalton awl, six bifaces, and two abraders.

CLUSTER 22 (110, 174). A large Dalton point and an adze compose this small cluster.

CLUSTER 23 (331–333, 336). These four Dalton points (three beveled, one unbeveled) were found within a slightly disturbed area measuring about 40 centimeters in diameter.

CLUSTER 24 (109, 116). Located about 2 meters east of an isolated large Dalton (445) was this pair of beveled Dalton points.

CLUSTER 25 (296–300, 307–308). Included are two beveled Daltons, an unbeveled Dalton, a Dalton preform, an adze, an abrader, and an end scraper.

CLUSTER 26 (4, 16, 45). This is a group of three beveled Dalton points.

CLUSTER 27 (186, 189, 265–266). The large Burlington Chert Dalton (265) and the adze (189) were located adjacent to each other, with the beveled Dalton and end scraper nearby.

CLUSTER 28 (113). This specimen is one of two spatially isolated large Dalton points.

CLUSTER 29 (6, 23, 25, 36, 42–43, 73–74). One of three clusters with more than one large Dalton (6, 23), this cluster also includes three beveled Daltons, two unbeveled Daltons, and a Dalton point reworked into a burin.

Spatial Analysis Results and Conclusions

Assessing the composition of the inferred clusters as grave lots is complicated by several factors, the most obvious of which is the lack of observed graves. Thus, although it seems likely that many of the artifact clusters represent materials interred with single individuals, this is far from certain. Further, we have no way of knowing the kinds and numbers of possible burial artifacts that were not preserved (see comments in O'Shea [1984]). Nor will it ever be known if any individuals were buried without associated artifacts. Finally, in defining artifact clusters we included only those artifacts from the least-disturbed contexts. Over half of the recovered artifacts were located in deposits exhibiting clear evidence of disturbance; had these remained in situ, the composition of our inferred clusters might have been quite different. Given these caveats, a few pertinent comments can be made about the artifact clusters and the spatial distribution of the artifacts.

Cluster composition is summarized in Table 6.2. Numerically, cluster size ranges from one to thirty-eight artifacts. The latter (cluster 1) represents an extreme outlier; the next largest cluster (cluster 6) includes fifteen artifacts. Excluding cluster 1, the mean number of artifacts per cluster is 7.9, with a standard deviation of 4.1. The mean number of artifact classes per cluster is 4.2, with a standard deviation of 2.4. A simple regression of number of artifacts versus number of artifact classes produced an R^2 value of .655, indicating a moderately strong relationship between these two variables. The spatial extent of the generated clusters ranges from approximately 20 by 20 centimeters to 100 by 80 centimeters.

Impressionistically, there appear to be a number of roughly linear groups of artifacts (Figures 6.2 and 6.4); linear arrangements of artifacts would suggest extended burials. Some of the intuitive, linear groups appear among the clusters generated by *K*-means analysis (e.g., cluster 27), but most are subsumed within more ovoid clusters (Figure 6.7). There is no necessary contradiction between subjective impressions of linearity and the *K*-means clusters. *K*-means analysis defines clusters based on statistical (and in this case, spatial, as well) proximity; the algorithm does not specifically seek linear data structures. Thus, it can be said that although *K*-means analysis does not support the presence of linear clusters of artifacts, such a possibility is by no means disproven.

Several co-occurrence trends are apparent between specific artifact types, although none of these provides strong evidence for either tool kits or differential distribution of artifacts by sex (assuming both females and males were present in the Sloan cemetery). The numbers that follow refer to the number of clusters in which an artifact class is present, not the total number of artifacts in that class. Large Dalton points are the most ubiquitous artifacts, occurring in eighteen of the twenty-nine clusters (two of which are isolated points). As illustrated in Figure 6.8, large Daltons are distributed across the entire cemetery; that is, they are not confined to a specific area within the site. This is an important point because the occurrence of these distinctive sociotechnic objects within only a portion of the site would be suggestive of some degree of social ranking within the social group responsible for the cemetery (e.g., Mainfort 1985).

Dalton awls ($n = 4$) occur only in clusters that also include abraders and bifaces; three awls are associated with large Dalton points. Adzes and abraders often co-occur (14/16 in both cases); each artifact class is present in sixteen clusters. Neither adzes nor abraders exhibit distinctive spatial patterning; the distribution of the former is shown in Figure 6.9.

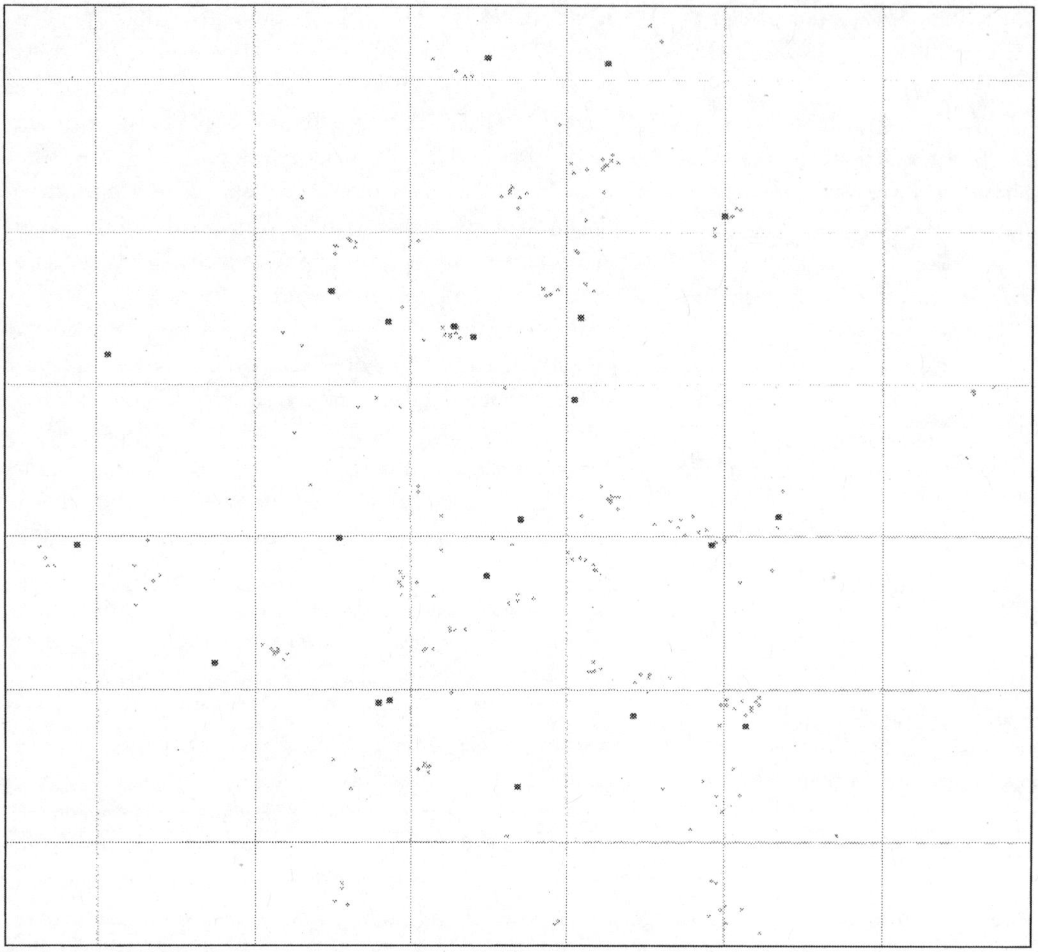

Figure 6.8 Distribution of large Dalton points (shown in black; other artifacts shown in gray).

All of the backed unifaces (n = 6) are in clusters that also include abraders and nonlocal chert artifacts; most (5/6) are also associated with large Daltons or adzes. Retouched flakes (n = 6) occur only in clusters with bifaces as members; most (5/6) co-occur with adzes or abraders. The utilized flakes (n = 4) are all associated with bifaces, and most (3/4) are in clusters that also include adzes and abraders. All end scrapers (n = 4) are associated with adzes, and most (3/4) occur with beveled Dalton points or abraders.

Nonlocal cherts from the St. Louis, Missouri, area (Burlington and Crescent Quarry) tend to be associated with clusters of higher artifact class diversity and greater numbers of artifacts, but this is by no means a straightforward relationship. Of the ten occurrences of these cherts, five are associated with clusters 2, 6, 7, 11, and 19, all of which include at least seven artifact classes and at least twelve individual artifacts. Other clusters with Burlington/Crescent Quarry Chert are 3, 5, 18, 20, 21, and 27. These cherts are distributed throughout the cemetery and are not limited to a specific area.

In conclusion, spatial analysis of the Sloan-site artifacts indicates that at least twenty-nine discrete artifact clusters are present. This implies the existence of approximately thirty individual graves within the cemetery. Because of poor bone preservation, no demographic data could be obtained, thus greatly limiting interpretations of mortuary behavior. The composition of the inferred artifact clusters does not suggest the presence of functionally differentiated tool kits. This is unfortunate because such infor-

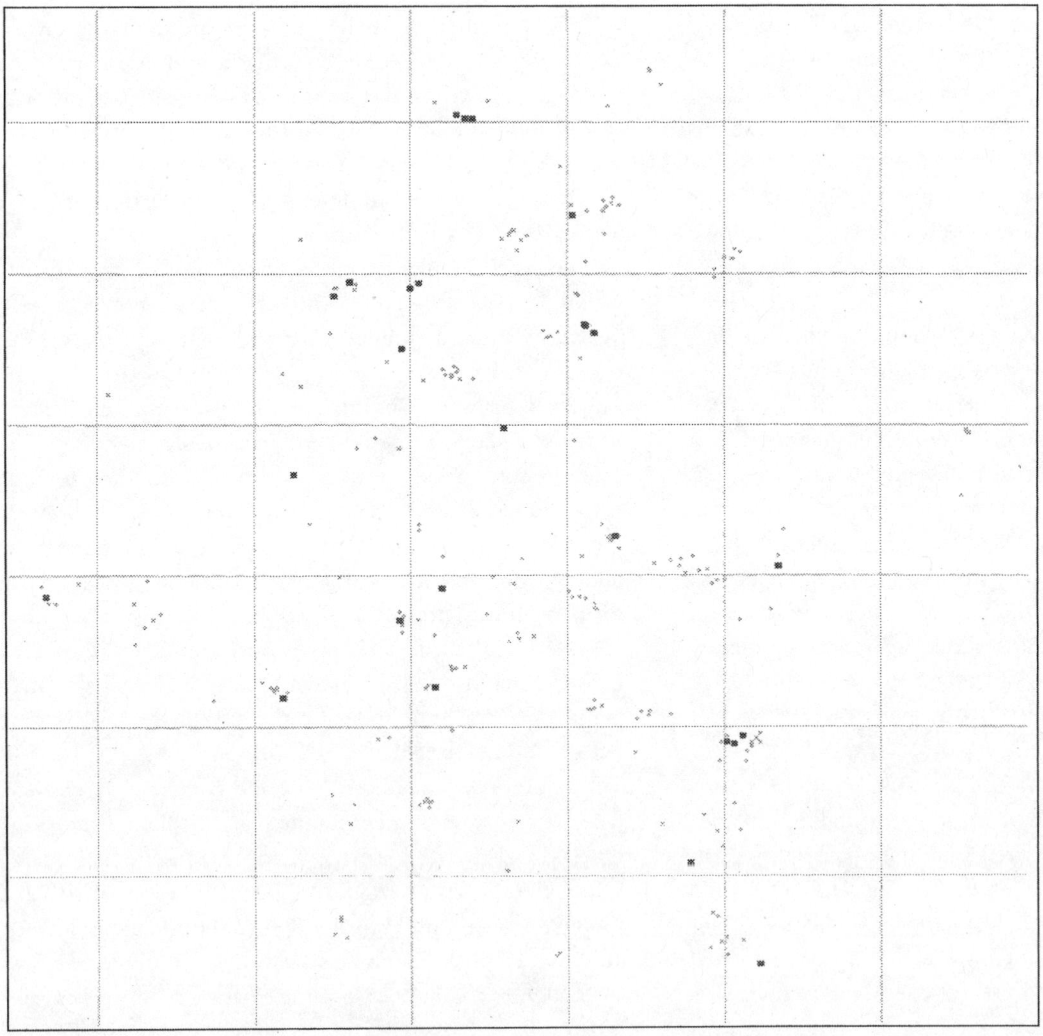

Figure 6.9 Distribution of adzes (shown in black; other artifacts shown in gray).

mation might potentially permit insights about the demography of the cemetery. The spatial distribution of certain individual artifact types and nonlocal materials appears to reflect relatively uniform occurrences throughout the site. The absence of spatially discrete concentrations of distinctive artifacts (particularly large Dalton points, which intuitively seem likely candidates for "high status" markers) supports an interpretation of Dalton society as one in which minimal social differentiation was present. Such a situation would be expected in a relatively mobile foraging group, as the Dalton inhabitants of northeastern Arkansas are believed to represent. On the other hand, the presence of formal cemeteries and possible base camps during Dalton times (Morse and Morse 1983) suggests that the rise of formalized territories may have occurred thousands of year earlier in northeastern Arkansas than is suggested by current interpretations in other parts of eastern North America (e.g., Charles and Buikstra 1983; J. A. Brown 1985).

SOIL SAMPLES

During the excavation, 602 soil samples were collected for later chemical analysis. Of these, 415 were recovered from 50- to 100-centimeter intervals across the base of the excavation. It was hypothesized that disintegration of Dalton skeletons would alter the chemistry of the surrounding soil. Two laboratory tests of this hypothesis were performed. Carol Spears (Morse and Morse 1983) performed the first test, which focused on the calcium and phosphorus abundance in eight selected samples. Her semiquantitative analysis was inconclusive for phosphorus, but results for calcium were positive and support the cemetery hypothesis. The second test, performed by G. A. (Akridge 1994a), used fifty-four soil samples. It focused on two trace elements (zinc and copper) rather than the major components of human bone.

There have been very few previous studies that employed soil chemistry analysis to locate human remains after their decay. However, Keeley et al. (1977) showed that this was possible after discovering the "silhouette" of a fifth-century Saxon burial in Essex, England. Analysis of the soil samples revealed dramatic increases in several elements at burial depth. Most studies of soil associated with human bone focus on bone diagenesis (e.g., Lambert et al. 1984). Diagenesis (the flux of metals into or out of bone) is an important consideration in attempting dietary reconstruction. This type of study, however, is impossible for the Sloan site because of the poor preservation of bone fragments.

The Sloan site provides a unique opportunity for examining the effects burials have on the surrounding soil. Because Sloan can be considered a unifunctional site, we can disregard the effects that other human activities would have on the soil chemistry. Habitation sites have constant soil disturbances that may considerably change elemental distributions in localized areas. Pit digging, post insertion, hearths, and other activities constantly require earthmoving. These processes disguise previous events, making it difficult to determine the chemical effects of any single event. Because the recovered artifacts indicate that Sloan was not a habitation site, we can assume that the only anthropogenic use of the site was for burial of individuals. It was postulated on this basis that an analysis of the soil would reveal chemical differences in spatial patterning resulting from burial locations.

The eight samples tested by Spears showed that spatial differences among certain chemical species could be revealed by the soil samples. Calcium composes about 33% of bone weight (Lambert et al. 1979) and would be ideal for a soil analysis, assuming that the background calcium in the soil was low enough. At Sloan, regions where high calcium concentrations were expected (around suspected grave goods, bone fragments, and burial no. 1) showed increases of up to 200% in calcium levels over samples taken from outside the cemetery. The inconclusive results for phosphorus, present as phosphate in the soil, are probably caused by its high reactivity and abundance. Organic matter contains considerable amounts of phosphate, and plant roots alone could disturb the phosphate distribution left behind by burials.

In a more expanded test, zinc and copper were chosen for study because of their potential as reliable indicators in determining burial locations. Zinc is present in human bone at 160 parts per million (ppm) (Brätter et al. 1977). Copper levels in prehistoric bone are considerably lower, at about 10 ppm (Lambert et al. 1979). In Table 6.3, we see that zinc and copper levels are naturally present in the Sloan soils at 13.4 ppm and 6.8 ppm, respectively. Therefore, we expected soil samples taken near or in grave loca-

Table 6.3
Results of selected soil samples

Catalog No.	Description	Zinc (ppm)	Copper (ppm)	Zn/Cu
	Mean background concentrations in the Sloan soils	13.4 ± 2.5	6.8 ± 1.6	2.0
74-107-1233	Burial no. 1: lower back region	27.6	6.4	4.3
74-107-1239	Burial no. 1: opposite side of pit	14.0	10.2	1.4
Dalton related samples				
74-107-1217	Beneath Dalton point	26.2	6.6	4.0
74-107-1205	Beneath abrader and two Dalton points	26.8	8.0	3.4
74-107-1225	Beneath bone fragment	33.1	7.6	4.4
	Mean concentrations in soil associated with artifacts or bone	31.8 ± 10.6	7.7 ± 1.5	4.1
	Range for soil associated with artifacts or bone	23.3–67.0	6.6–11.7	

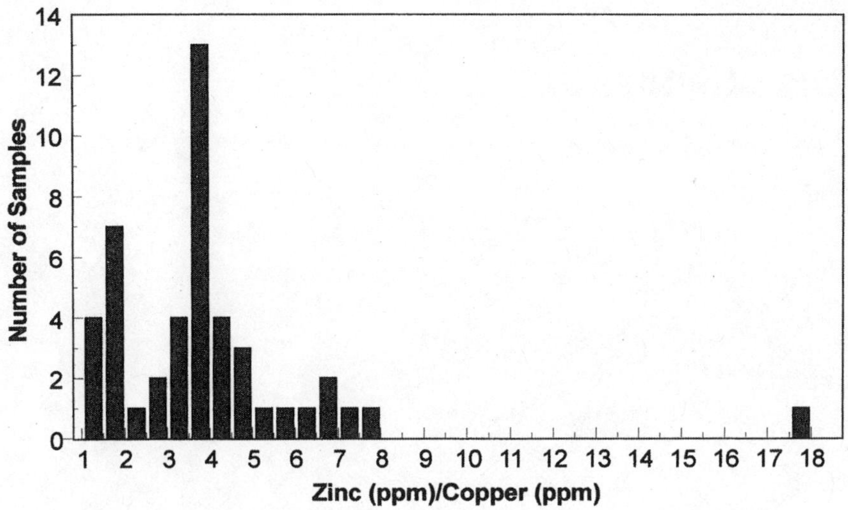

Figure 6.10 Distribution of normalized zinc/copper concentrations for the Sloan-site soil samples.

tions to show higher concentrations of zinc but little or no change in copper levels.

By analyzing the data in terms of zinc/copper ratios we can identify the changing concentration of one element in terms of the other. At Sloan, the copper values of all samples were nearly identical. Thus, changing Zn/Cu ratios identify a special process (human burial) occurring in the soil that alters the concentration of zinc but not copper. Because precipitation of zinc and copper as minerals (Akridge 1994b; Akridge and Morse 1994) is likely to be occurring in the slightly acidic soil (Morse 1975), acid digestion of the samples was required to extract the total zinc and copper.

For a control sample, the discovery of burial no. 1 was quite fortunate. This allowed for comparison between soil samples surrounding a known burial and samples suspected of being near or inside Dalton graves. Soil samples in direct association with burial no. 1 revealed very high Zn/Cu ratios, whereas samples taken from the opposite side of the burial pit (see Figure 6.10) had Zn/Cu ratios similar to the background ratio. Using this knowledge, fourteen samples taken from around or beneath Dalton artifacts and samples located near three bone fragments were analyzed. These results were quite similar to those of the head and body region of burial no. 1 (Table 6.3).

Finally, samples from the base of a randomly chosen square were analyzed. The nine samples were centered around 48R51 and extend in 50-centimeter intervals in each direction. The results show both high and low Zn/Cu ratios, similar to other samples thought to be located near and away from graves. One sample resulted in an extraordinarily large Zn/Cu value of nearly 18. This is probably a contaminated sample resulting from a small overlooked bone fragment, a zinc mineral, or possibly laboratory contamination.

It appears that chemical alteration of the soil from human graves can still be detected in the soil samples collected from the Sloan site. From the histogram in Figure 6.10, it is apparent that two peaks in the data exist, with a near absence of samples in between. This suggests that Sloan-site samples with Zn/Cu ratios below 2.5 are representative of the background Zn/Cu in the soil. Values above this number may be burial locations that exhibit higher levels of zinc. The success of the soil chemical tests suggests that an analysis of all the samples is likely to reveal a more complete picture of grave locations.

7
Late Quaternary Geologic History of the Western Lowlands

ROGER T. SAUCIER

To understand the importance of the Sloan site and indeed the spatial aspects of the Dalton culture in the alluvial valley of the lower Mississippi River, it is necessary to understand the region's geologic origin and development. This includes not only the sequence of events in the region's history (i.e., landscape evolution) but also the geomorphic processes at work. Such information and knowledge are critical because Paleoindian human adaptation occurred in context with a dynamic natural environment that witnessed dramatic changes in landforms as well as in flora and fauna. I will explore certain key events of the region's Late Quaternary history, such as cessation of glacial outwash deposition, and certain natural processes, such as wind deflation and sand dune formation, that had direct influences on where and how the early inhabitants of the Western Lowlands adapted to and utilized the landscape. The adaptation was the exercise of choice within a range of opportunities and limitations in topography, soils, drainage, and other environmental attributes.

REGIONAL PHYSIOGRAPHIC SETTING

As defined on the basis of the extent of Quaternary alluvial deposits of the Mississippi and Ohio Rivers, the Mississippi Alluvial Valley north of the latitude of Memphis, Tennessee, consists of the Western Lowlands and the St. Francis Basin (Figure 7.1). These two alluvial plains are separated by Crowley's Ridge, an upland remnant of mostly Tertiary and older formations, and are bordered on the west and east by dissected uplands of similar age. Both lowlands were created in early Quaternary times when the ancestral Mississippi and Ohio Rivers began discharging copious quantities of glacial meltwater and outwash southward to the Gulf of Mexico, scouring and widening the existing local drainage systems into continuous, broad alluvial plains.

Physiographically, the Western Lowlands is characterized by a valley train (outwash plain) that is manifest by a series of broad, low, sandy terraces. These have flat to gently rolling surfaces interrupted only by several southward-flowing rivers and their narrow, very flat valleys (F. L. Smith and Saucier 1971). Three distinct terrace levels, separated by scarps up to several meters high, have been mapped, the oldest and highest of which lies immediately west of and adjacent to Crowley's Ridge (Figure 7.1). Local relief, up to several meters, is greatest on the older valley train terrace levels and near the scarps, and is a reflection of both and the original patterns and types of de-

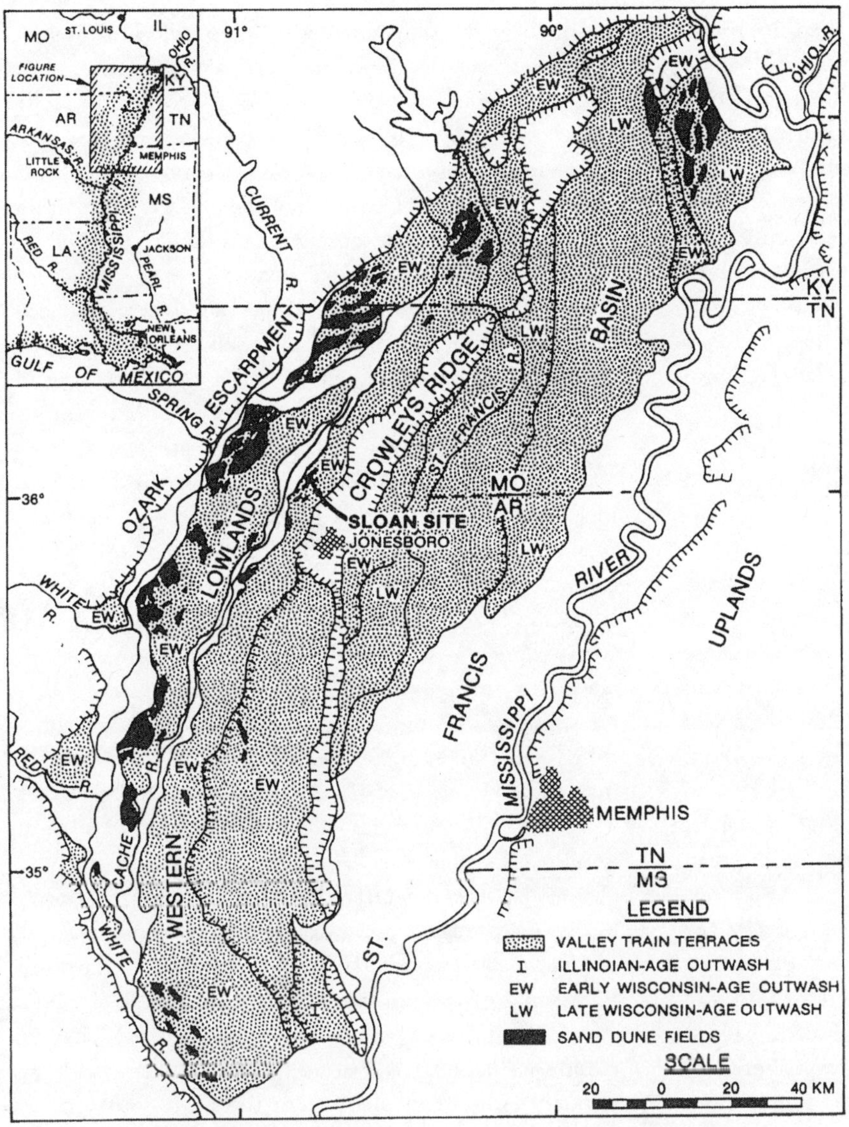

7.1 Major physiographic elements and depositional units of the Western Lowlands and the St. Francis Basin, lower Mississippi Valley.

position of the alluvium of postdepositional erosion and dissection. Because deposition by shallow, anastomosing, braided streams was the primary mode of origin of the majority of the sediments, the current local drainage and relief that are controlled by the relict drainage exhibit a poorly integrated, deranged network with numerous small basins and swales. Despite the inefficient drainage, low regional slope (less than 0.2 meters per kilometer), and occasional backwater flooding of the lower, westernmost terrace levels by the White, Black, and St. Francis Rivers (Figure 7.1), there has been essentially complete clearing of the region for intensive agriculture (Saucier 1978).

An east-west profile across the Western Lowlands through the Sloan site reveals elevations that range from about 77 to 84 meters above mean sea level. This excludes a several-kilometer-wide alluvial apron flanking Crowley's Ridge where elevations are up to 8 meters higher. Because of the slight decline in elevation westward across the terrace levels, the major drainage feature of this part of the lowlands, the Black River (Figure 7.1), hugs the base of the uplands (Ozark Escarpment). However, in the recent geologic past (the early Holocene Epoch), this river combined its flow with that of the St. Francis River and flowed farther eastward down the center of the lowland along the route of the present Cache River. This was an important occurrence that is discussed more fully later in this chapter.

Nearly all of the higher elevations in the Western Lowlands, such as those above an elevation of 82 meters at the latitude of the Sloan site, occur on discontinuous ridges that trend northeast-southwest. Serving as local drainage divides that separate the Cache River valley from Crowley's Ridge and the Black River valley from the Cache River valley, these ridges are relict sand dune fields (Saucier 1978). It is in one of these dune fields that the Sloan site is situated; I will discuss this critical human/landform relationship more fully later in this chapter.

LANDFORMS AND GEOGRAPHIC PROCESSES

The scouring by the glacial outwash-fed ancestral Mississippi River to form the Western Lowlands was an episodic event in this area's history. With the waning of each of the several major Pleistocene continental glaciations, there was an initial period of rapid sedimentation and floodplain buildup (aggradation) followed by much slower rates of sediment accumulation. As the sedimentation tapered off, associated increases in stream competence to carry its load caused progressive downcutting (degradation) and, hence, the formation of the several valley train terrace levels in the outwash deposits.

Each terrace level still exhibits distinctive traces of the braided Mississippi River channels that introduced the sediments that built up the floodplain (F. L. Smith and Saucier 1971; Autin et al. 1991). These are broad, shallow, linear depressions up to 1 to 2 meters deep and a few tens of meters to several kilometers wide. Frequent branching and bifurcation are characteristic. The relict channels survive apparently as a result of periodic major shifts in channel position (dominantly westward) that accompanied the downcutting of the lowland during the late waning glacial stages. As indicated above, the relict channels control the current local drainage pattern and often are characterized by swamp forests or ponds.

It is highly probable that the topographic depressions of the larger and more continuous abandoned braided channels were the impetus for the Black, St. Francis, and White Rivers to establish their later meander belts where they did, including the one along the route of the Cache River (Figure 7.1). Once they occupied these depressions, their meandering initiated the destruction and obscuration of much of the older braided channel fill. This includes the areas cut out by the lateral migration of the river channels and replaced by point bar (meander scroll) deposits and topography, cutoffs or abandoned channels, and natural levee development. Abandoned channels of the later streams are quite unlike those of the braided rivers in that they are much smaller, more regular in width, deeper, and exhibit much smaller radii of curvature.

Once the above-mentioned meandering rivers occupied the abandoned braided channels, the deposition of mostly fine-grained sediments (clays and silts) became dominant, causing a slow, progressive buildup of the floodplains in and adjacent to the meander belts. However, before the abandoned braided channels were reoccupied and the infilling and buildup of fine-grained sediments began, the floors of the abandoned channels were characterized by broad, sandy flats with numerous low islands and bars. This would have especially been the case while there was still some minor amount of glacial outwash being moved in the channels, perhaps during the latter stages of waxing (advancing) glaciation. Such conditions were the impetus for the formation of extensive hummocky tracts of sand dunes (Figure 7.1). During seasonal dry episodes with strong northerly and westerly winds, large quantities of sand were deflated from the channel floors and deposited as dunes on adjacent bars and banks. Deflated silts and clays were carried much farther distances and deposited mostly as loess on Crowley's Ridge and in the uplands east of the Mississippi alluvial valley. A thin loess veneer also occurs on the higher and older outwash terrace levels in the Western Lowlands, but is not an important element in the morphology of the landscape. Deposition of silts continued until the end of the Pleistocene; the Brand-site Dalton level was within and beneath a wind-blown silt deposit (Goodyear 1974). Based on the well-established chronology of glacial outwash deposition and loess formation in the region, this silt veneer must represent only minor, local eolian activity and/or redistribution of older deposits.

Hence, there are three major components of the landscape in the Western Lowlands. On an areal basis, the somewhat poorly drained, terraced valley train is predominant. The next most widespread component consists of the topographically low and flat Holocene meander belts of the current major streams, both active and recently abandoned. Sand dune fields in the form of isolated, prominent ridges compose the third component. All three components are present within several kilometers of the Sloan site and unquestionably were major factors in prehistoric landscape utilization.

A chronological reconstruction of landscape development is presented later in this chapter, but it is important to consider at this point what natural processes were active during the Paleoindian period. No major relief changes (i.e., aggradation or degradation) were occurring on the valley train terraces or in the dune fields; however, there was some subaerial erosion of higher elevations and slight filling of local topographically low areas. Some flooding was intermittent and discontinuous and caused by local precipitation, but within and adjacent to the meander belts of the larger streams, flooding was more regular (spring season) and extensive. The latter was the mechanism responsible for a slow but progressive buildup of the floodplain by vertical sediment accumulation.

PALEOGEOGRAPHIC RECONSTRUCTION

The oldest outwash deposits with surficial expression in the Western Lowlands are probably attributable to waning of the Illinoian glaciation more than 120,000 years ago (Saucier 1974; Autin et al. 1991) (Figure 7.1). During the subsequent interglacial (Sangamonian Stage), the once much more continuous valley train was dissected and entrenched by local and regional drainage, a process that continued into the waxing (i.e., advancing) Early Wisconsin glaciation (Altonian Substage).

Perhaps about 75,000 years ago, the Early Wisconsin glaciation began to wane (i.e., retreat), initiating the deposition of the valley train that characterizes the majority of the Western Lowlands landscape (Figure 7.1). In an episodic manner, this deposition continued through the succeeding Farmdalian Substage, a brief interval of glacial retreat about 35,000 to 25,000 years ago, and into the stage of waxing Late Wisconsin glaciation. Apparently the Farmdalian Substage was so brief that the regime of the ancestral Mississippi River did not change from braided to meandering; hence, no meander belts developed. Regional streams such as the Black and St. Francis Rivers apparently became tributary to the braided Mississippi River.

Onset of the Late Wisconsin glaciation is estimated at about 25,000 years ago. Between that date and the time of maximum glaciation about 18,000 years ago, the discharge of the Mississippi River would have been greatly reduced but not without some seasonal flooding. Climatic conditions during waxing glaciation were characterized by cooler and much moister springs and summers, but cooler and possibly drier falls and winters. Although regional streams increased in size because of net increases in discharges (Saucier 1974), that was also the time of sand dune formation because of the deflation of sand from the barren sand flats of the largely inactive braided channels by strong northerly and westerly winds. Various forms of evidence suggest that the most active phase of dune formation (and loess deposition) was coincident with maximum glacial advance about 18,000 years ago (Saucier 1978). Two sand dune trends became especially well developed. The larger one is along the eastern side of the braided channel that hugged the base of the Ozark Escarpment, and the smaller one flanks the eastern side of the braided channel that is now occupied by the Cache River. The Sloan site is situated on a dune in the latter trend (Figure 7.1).

Between 75,000 and 35,000 years ago, when the Western Lowlands were experiencing rapid alluviation and aggradation, the alluvial fill attained elevations approximating those of several low areas or gaps in Crowley's Ridge. As a consequence, very early in the waning stage of the Late Wisconsin glaciation, probably no later than 16,000 years ago, the ancestral Mississippi River diverted its then voluminous discharge and copious outwash load through such a gap in the ridge into the St. Francis Basin (Figure 7.1). This event marked the sudden and complete termination of all outwash deposition in the Western Lowlands.

At about 16,000 years ago, the two principal abandoned braided channels were shallow, lengthy sandy depressions from which appreciable sand had been deflated. It is logical that these would become the routes of the rivers that entered the Western Lowlands from the Ozark uplands once the Mississippi River flow ceased. Therefore, the Current, Spring, and White Rivers followed the channel along the Ozark Escarpment, and the Black and St. Francis Rivers occupied the channel along the present Cache River (Figure 7.1).

Combined flow of the latter streams in a single channel was of sufficient duration for enough meandering to take place to form cutoffs; however, archaeological evidence indicates that the rivers had diverted from this route along the Cache River to their current separate locations by no later than 12,000 years ago. The cause of this diversion was probably a very slight gradient advantage resulting from minor meander belt alluviation in the relict braided channel. The consequence of the diversion was that only local runoff (i.e., the Cache River) remained thereafter and this drainage system began degrading to a slightly lower level. The Black/St. Francis River meander belt thus became inactive, and surviving portions of this relict floodplain are designated the Cache River terrace. Attainment of the lower level by the local drainage and formation of the modern Cache River floodplain took place no later than 10,000 years ago, thus establishing essentially current conditions. Some meandering by the Cache River has created cutoffs that, with their associated natural levees and accretion topography, postdate that time, however.

Since 10,000 years ago, or for most of the Holocene Epoch, there have been no substantial landscape changes in the Western Lowlands. There have been no additional diversions of streams to new courses and no appreciable regional-scale erosion or deposition. However, during the middle Holocene, there was some response of the landscape to a several-thousand-year-long period of relative warmth and aridity. Variously designated the Hypsithermal, Altithermal, Climatic Optimum, and other terms, this episode of reduced effective precipitation from about 8,000 to 4,000 years ago in the midwestern United States noticeably affected vegetative communities and presumably also stream flow. In the Mississippi Valley, grassland expanded somewhat at the expense of forest, swampy tracts were reduced in size (P. A. Delcourt et al. 1980), and no doubt many small permanent streams and ponds became ephemeral. Since about 5,000 years ago, essentially modern hydrographic conditions have prevailed.

During the glacial maximum and extending until about 16,500 years ago, the lower Mississippi Valley was characterized by cool-temperate coniferous-deciduous forests with boreal species like spruce, fir, and larch present (P. A. Delcourt et al. 1980; chapter 8). However, by 12,500 years ago, climatic amelioration resulted in a change to warm-temperate mixed deciduous hardwood forests and cypress-gum communities with species composition similar to that of today. The mid-Holocene period of relative aridity and warmth was the only notable episode of climatically induced vegetation change that prehistoric inhabitants of the region would have experienced. Indeed, even those changes would not have been perceived within periods as long as several generations.

THE SLOAN SITE SETTING

Major landscape elements in the vicinity of the Sloan site are shown in Figure 7.2. The site lies near the eastern edge of a sharply defined 3.4-square-kilometer, undulating field of sand dunes at an elevation of about 82 meters. This is about 4 meters above the level of the adjacent Buffalo Head Slough, a flat and poorly drained formerly swampy tract several hundred meters wide and several kilometers long with its exit to the southwest. More specifically, the site lies near the south end of a prominent north-south trending dune that is about 1.5 kilometers long and that averages about 120 meters wide. This dune forms the eastern edge of the 3.4-square-kilometer tract; to the west and south of it, the landscape of the interior of the tract is one of irregular, undulating, less-prominent dunes separated by shallow, flat depressions.

On a regional basis, the Sloan site lies nearly midway along a steep environmental gradient between the 150-meters-high, deeply dissected uplands of Crowley's Ridge on the east and the flat, poorly drained floodplain of the Cache River at an elevation of about 76 meters on the west. The Cache River is now and would have been in prehistoric times the only permanent stream along this transect. Otherwise, potable water would have been available year-round only in isolated, shallow depressions and sloughs such as Buffalo Head Slough. On the other hand, seasonal flooding of substantial duration would have occurred only along the Cache River and the adjacent lower parts of the Cache River terrace (Figure 7.2).

In a generally north-south direction, there is no steep environmental gradient. Landscape element distribution and the general physiographic setting are relatively the same as at the Sloan site for tens of kilometers in both directions (see Figure 7.1).

Soils within the area of Figure 7.2 are predominantly deep silty or sandy loams. Only small, isolated areas of clays or silty clays occur in the deeper sloughs or depressions, such as the abandoned channels on the Cache River terrace. All soils are considered poorly drained except those on Crowley's Ridge and in the sand dune fields. Throughout the entire period of human occupation, all soils would have supported forest communities. Grasslands would have occurred only in areas disturbed by fire or on especially sandy, prominent ridges during episodes of unusual moisture stress.

Except during periods of up to a few months along the

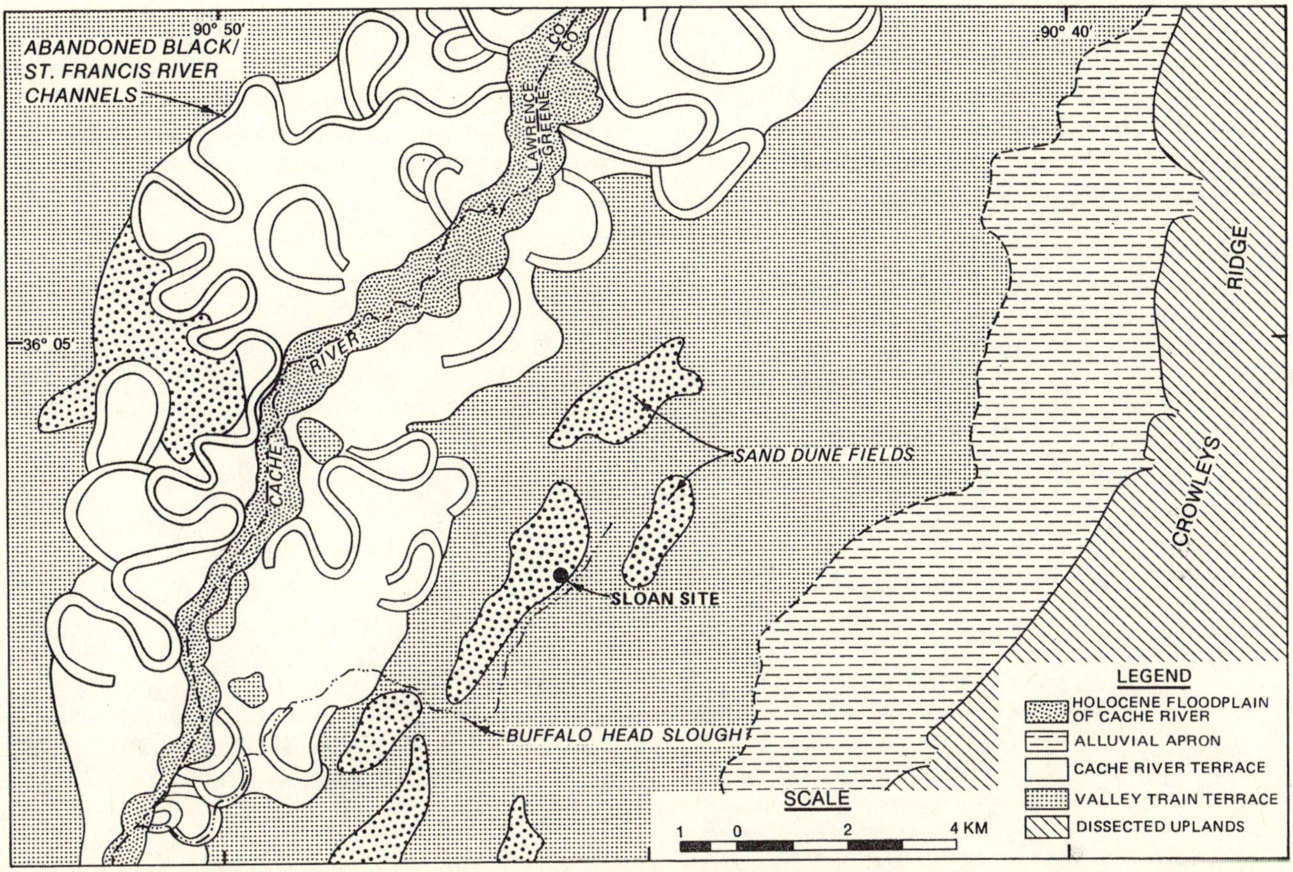

Figure 7.2 Major landscape elements (landforms) in the vicinity of the Sloan site.

major rivers when seasonal flooding may have occurred, the overland movement of humans, game, and wildlife would have been essentially uninhibited in prehistoric times anywhere between Crowley's Ridge and the Ozark Escarpment. Aquatic or paludal areas that could not be crossed could easily be skirted with only a minor detour.

In terms of its physical environmental setting, the Sloan site is in a very favorable and logical location. Even simple archeological site predictive models would rate this an area of high probability for prehistoric habitation/utilization, and indeed many sites, including many of Archaic-period age, have been found in similar settings. However, the site location is far from unique in that many others in this general area offer the same apparent advantages. No doubt many of the other locations do contain sites with Dalton components; however, it is unlikely that they are of the same extraordinary character and importance as the Sloan site. Perhaps the location was strategic in terms of cultural rather than natural environment considerations.

ADDENDUM

In addition to the relationship between the Sloan site (as an entity) and the natural environment, there is the matter of the artifacts within the site and their relationship to natural processes. Indeed, there are some important implications of the remarkable stability of artifact clusters and even individual artifacts that suggest little or no disturbance after placement.

Appreciable disturbance in the form of lateral and/or vertical shifting and even breakage is typical of artifacts originally deposited (or discarded) on the surface or at a very shallow depth. This results primarily from bioturbation by burrowing or digging animals and by plant roots and tree uprooting.

Lack of disturbance of Sloan-site artifacts suggests that they were deliberately buried in caches at an appreciable depth, probably in excess of one-half meter. Such a depth of burial would have been necessary to result in the lack of disturbance from tree roots, especially in view of the probable unusual depth of root penetration one would expect because of the sandy nature of the soils and the probable episode of regionally reduced precipitation during the middle Holocene. Taking into consideration a probable minor amount of surface erosion since burial, the depth of interment may have been even greater than one-half meter. Such depth of burial is also suggested if the artifacts accompanied human burials (as is hypothesized) because it would have been necessary to isolate the remains from detection by scavenging animals.

8
Late Quaternary Vegetational History of the Western Lowlands

HAZEL R. DELCOURT, PAUL A. DELCOURT,
AND P. DANIEL ROYALL

The time interval of cultural transition from Paleoindian to Archaic, from approximately 12,000 radiocarbon years Before Present (^{14}C yr B.P.) to 8,000 yr B.P. (Morse and Morse 1983), was also a time of rapid change from late Pleistocene to Holocene climates (Kutzbach and Wright 1985; Kutzbach 1987), fauna (Graham et al. 1987), and vegetation (P. A. Delcourt and Delcourt 1987; Jacobson et al. 1987). In the Western Lowlands of the central Mississippi Alluvial Valley, changes in the biota during this time interval occurred within a dynamically changing geomorphic context (Saucier 1974 and chapter 7; Royall et al. 1991).

VEGETATIONAL HISTORY

Most paleoecological sites in the vicinity of the central Mississippi Valley Alluvial Valley (Figure 8.1) yield only an indirect view of its vegetational history; either the sites span only a part of the late Quaternary time interval or they are located outside the Western Lowlands Physiographic Province (P. A. Delcourt and Delcourt 1996). For example, spring sites located in the Pomme de Terre River Valley of the western Ozark Plateaus (King 1973) contain sediments that date from more than 40,000 yr B.P. to about 13,500 yr B.P. Pollen records from those Missouri sites show that during the Late Wisconsin glacial maximum, from about 21,000 yr B.P. to 16,500 yr B.P. (King 1973), the upland vegetation of the western Ozarks was a closed forest dominated by spruce (*Picea*) and jack pine (*Pinus banksiana*), with minor populations of fir (*Abies*) and tamarack (*Larix laricina*). Between 16,500 yr B.P. and 13,500 yr B.P., deciduous forest taxa including oak (*Quercus*), ash (*Fraxinus*), elm (*Ulmus*), and hornbeam (*Carpinus/Ostrya* type) began to increase as populations of boreal conifers diminished in response to late-glacial climatic amelioration (H. R. Delcourt and Delcourt 1994).

Farther east, Cupola Pond, located in the southeastern Missouri Ozarks 85 kilometers northwest of the Sloan site (Figure 8.1; E. N. Smith 1984; H. R. Delcourt et al. 1986), has a continuous record of vegetation change that extends from 17,100 yr B.P. to the present. At Cupola Pond, full-glacial forests occurring from 17,100 yr B.P. to 15,700 yr B.P. were dominated by spruce and jack pine, with minor populations of fir and tamarack. Initial response of boreal taxa to late-glacial climatic amelioration was reflected in the collapse of jack pine populations be-

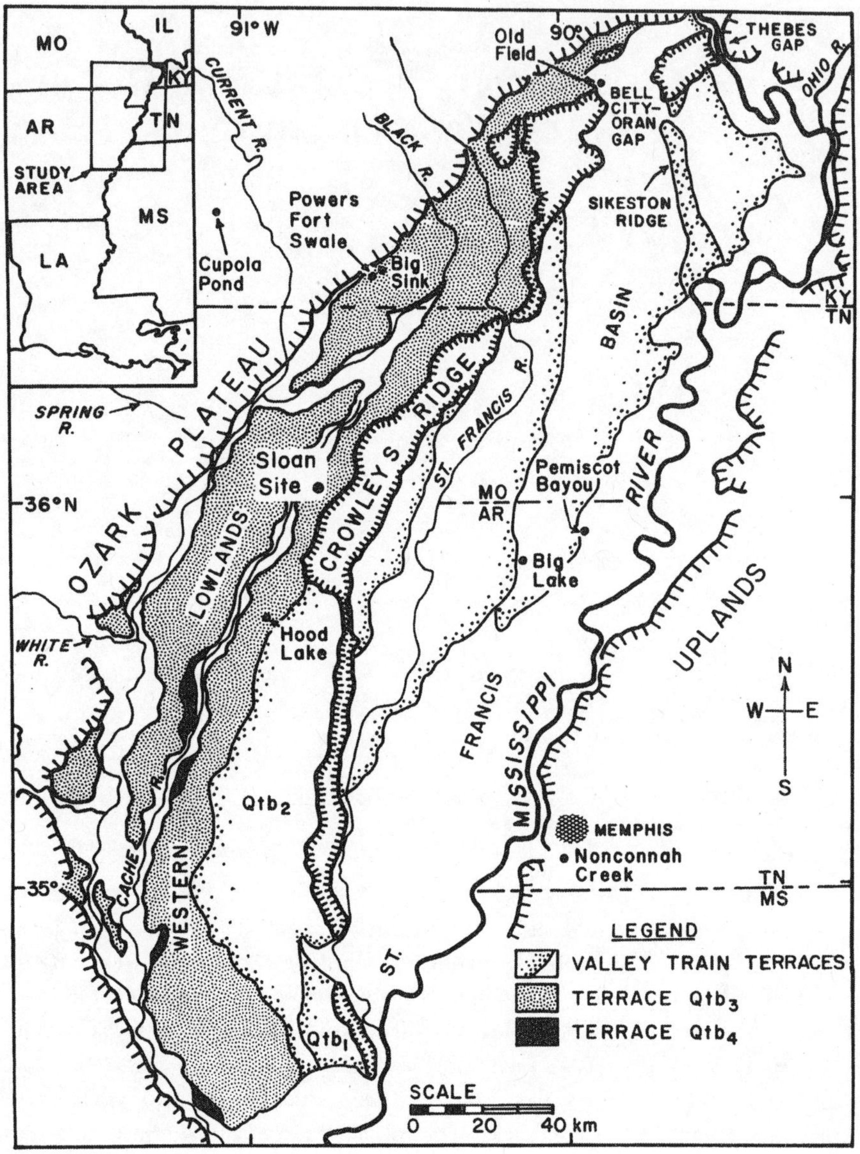

Figure 8.1 Location map of late Quaternary paleoecological sites and landforms in the central Mississippi Alluvial Valley and adjacent uplands (base map modified from Saucier, chapter 7).

tween 15,700 and 15,350 yr B.P. During late-glacial times, temperate, deciduous forest taxa immigrated into the southeastern Ozarks. From 15,300 yr B.P. to 12,300 yr B.P., as spruce gradually declined in importance within the Ozark forest, ash and oak increased. Between 12,300 yr B.P. and 9,100 yr B.P., the vegetation near Cupola Pond was an oak-hickory savanna with forest openings occupied by ragweed (*Ambrosia* type). The vegetation changed to an oak-dominated savanna in which ragweed was replaced by grass (family Gramineae) between 9,100 yr B.P. and 4,550 yr B.P. After 4,550 yr B.P., increases in importance of warm-temperate taxa including the bottomland tree tupelogum (*Nyssa aquatica*), the wetland shrub buttonbush (*Cephalanthus occidentalis*), and the upland shortleaf pine (*Pinus echinata*) resulted in the establishment of the plant communities observable on the watershed of Cupola Pond today. The late Holocene vegetation of Ozark uplands, located directly west of the Western Lowlands, included closed oak-hickory-pine forest on upland ridges and tupelogum-buttonbush swamps locally along the margins of ponds and streams.

Nonconnah Creek, located in southwestern Tennessee

125 kilometers southeast of the Sloan site (Figure 8.1), provides a paleoecological record for uplands east of the central Mississippi Alluvial Valley that dates from full-glacial and late-glacial times (P. A. Delcourt et al. 1980). From 23,000 to 16,500 yr B.P., the full-glacial vegetation growing on the rich, silt-loam soils of these eastern loess-mantled uplands was dominated by spruce, with both fir and tamarack but no jack pine; this forest also included a species-rich admixture of cool-temperate hardwood trees including sugar maple (*Acer saccharum*), beech (*Fagus grandifolia*), tuliptree (*Liriodendron tulipifera*), and black walnut (*Juglans nigra*), in addition to oak, hickory, hornbeam, and ash. Between 16,500 and about 13,000 yr B.P., deciduous trees, including oak, ash, and hornbeam, increased in importance. No record of the vegetation composition during the late-glacial/Holocene transition is available from Nonconnah Creek (P. A. Delcourt et al. 1980).

Within the central Mississippi Alluvial Valley, several published plant-fossil sites date from approximately 9,000 yr B.P. to the late Holocene. Old Field (Figure 8.1), located in the Bell City/Oran Gap through Crowley's Ridge in southeastern Missouri, 140 kilometers northeast of the Sloan site, has a basal date of 8,810 ± 90 yr B.P. (King and Allen 1977). The early to middle Holocene vegetation record from Old Field indicates that the local peatland was dominated by marsh grasses (Gramineae), possibly cane (*Arundinaria gigantea*), and other wet-meadow herbs. The remainder of the pollen assemblage was representative of nearby upland oak-hickory forest and of local bottomland swamp forest including bald cypress (*Taxodium distichum*), willow (*Salix*), ash, and sweetgum (*Liquidambar styraciflua*). The upper portion of the Old Field sedimentary record (after 3,500 yr B.P.) has been truncated by disturbance associated with historic truck farming of the peatland (King and Allen 1977).

Two plant-fossil sites, Pemiscot Bayou and Big Lake (Figure 8.1), are located in the Eastern Lowlands (St. Francis Basin) of northeastern Arkansas, about 65 kilometers east of the Sloan site; these two plant-fossil sites have Holocene pollen sequences, with basal radiocarbon dates of 8,530 ± 300 yr B.P. and 9,050 ± 150 yr B.P., respectively (Scott and Aasen 1987). In the Eastern Lowlands, vegetation of early to middle Holocene times was closed bottomland forest of oak, hickory, and sweetgum. A late Holocene rise in water table after 3,500 yr B.P. favored development of a mosaic including open swamp forest, wet-meadow marshes occupied by herbs in the families Compositae, Chenopodiaceae, and Amaranthaceae, as well as open pools dominated by aquatic plants such as quillwort (*Isoetes*) (Scott and Aasen 1987).

PALEOECOLOGICAL SETTING OF HOOD LAKE AND POWERS FORT SWALE

In this chapter, we present the results of paleoecological analysis of two new sites in the Western Lowlands of southeastern Missouri and northeastern Arkansas that are critical for interpretation of the paleovegetational and paleoenvironmental setting of the Sloan archaeological site because their records span the time interval of the Dalton cultural period, between 10,500 yr B.P. and 9,500 yr B.P. (Morse and Morse 1983). This is the key portion of time that corresponds with the Paleoindian/Archaic transition, a time interval previously represented in only one plant-fossil site located near the central Mississippi Alluvial Valley, Cupola Pond (E. H. Smith 1984; H. R. Delcourt et al. 1986). One of the new sites, Hood Lake, is located in northeastern Arkansas 40 kilometers south of the Sloan site (Figure 8.1) (Anderson et al. 1989). Hood Lake has a paleoecological record that continuously spans the time interval from 11,250 yr B.P. to the present (H. R. Delcourt and Delcourt 1988). The second new site, Powers Fort Swale, is located in southeastern Missouri 60 kilometers north of the Sloan site (Figure 8.1). The sediment record from Powers Fort Swale spans the time interval from 18,300 yr B.P. to the present (Royall 1988; Royall et al. 1991). In this chapter, we present the full pollen and plant macrofossil diagrams from Hood Lake, as well as a summary pollen diagram from Powers Fort Swale. Detailed pollen diagrams for Powers Fort Swale are available in Royall (1988) and are published in Royall et al. (1991).

Environmental Setting of Hood Lake

Hood Lake is located at an elevation of 71 meters in Poinsett County, Arkansas (35°42′N, 90°55′W, Sect. 6, T. 12 N, R 2 E, Risher, Arkansas, 1980 7.5′ U.S.G.S. Topographic Quadrangle). Hood Lake is a basin of permanently standing water (750 meters long by 150 meters wide) on the braided stream terrace Qtb_3 (F. L. Smith and Saucier 1971; Figure 8.2), a fluvial surface abandoned by Mississippi River flow of glacial meltwater during the late-

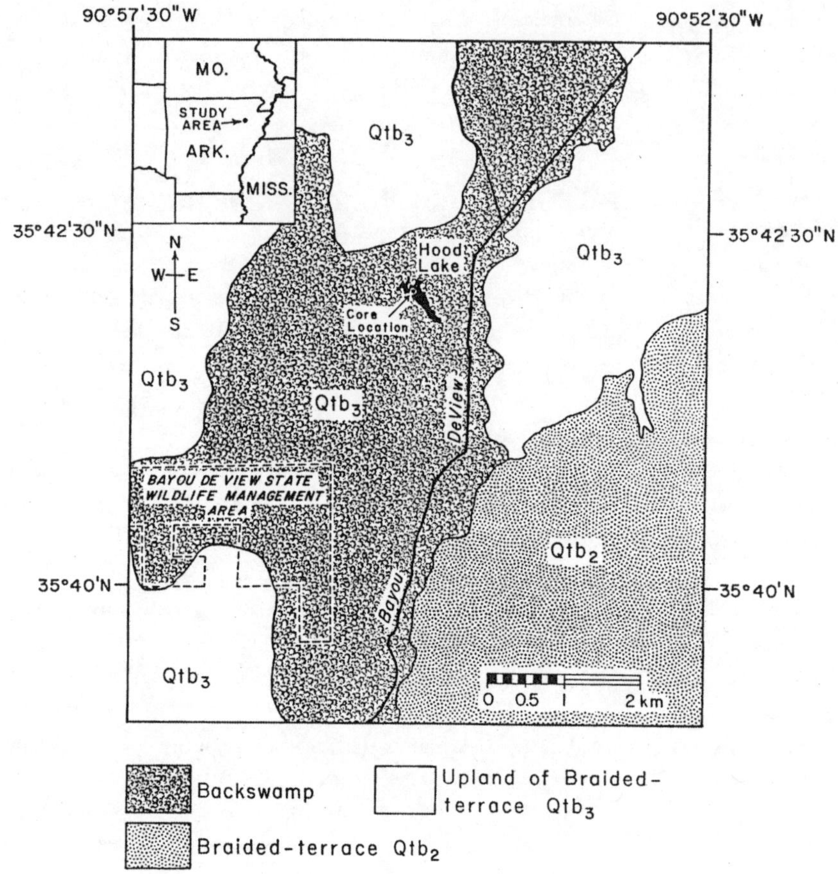

Figure 8.2 Detailed location map for Hood Lake, Poinsett County, Arkansas (Quaternary landforms modified from F. L. Smith and Saucier [1971]).

glacial interval (Royall 1988). Hood Lake is fed today both by overflow water from Bayou De View, which drains the Qtb_3 terrace surface, and by seepage from springs along the 3- or 4-meter-high scarp of the topographically higher, older braided-stream terrace Qtb_2 (F. L. Smith and Saucier 1971) situated 2.2 kilometers southeast of Hood Lake.

Plat maps dating from the General Land Office Surveys of the early A.D. 1800s show that the presettlement vegetation surrounding Hood Lake was a mosaic of wet-meadows and bottomland hardwoods forest, with oak-hickory forest and prairie openings on the nearby terrace uplands (P. and D. Morse, personal communication, 1987). The local vegetation at the margin of Hood Lake today includes a swamp fringe of mature tupelogum trees and an understory thicket of buttonbush shrubs. The water mark on the tupelogum trees indicates that the late-winter/spring flood level is about 60 centimeters higher than the summer level. Although the area of open water in Hood Lake is extensive (11 hectares), the maximum water depth at the time of coring was only 93 centimeters, restricted to a deep basin 50 meters wide in the center of the lake. Wood snags and buttonbush shrubs extended out from the swamp edge to the outer margin of this deep central basin.

Environmental Setting of Powers Fort Swale

Powers Fort Swale is located at an elevation of 91 meters in the Western Lowlands of Butler County, Missouri, approximately 2 kilometers southeast of the Ozark Plateau Escarpment (36°36′N, 90°35′W, Naylor, Missouri, 7.5′ U.S.G.S. Topographic Quadrangle) (Figure 8.3). The site is occupied by a 1.4-hectare slough on the alluvial surface of the braided-stream terrace Qtb_3 (F. L. Smith and Saucier 1971). This portion of the Qtb_3 terrace surface is characterized by a number of large (up to 16 kilometers long by 6 kilometers wide), low (topographic relief of 3.6 meters), and elongate sand ridges oriented parallel to the northeast-southwest trend of the Western Lowlands.

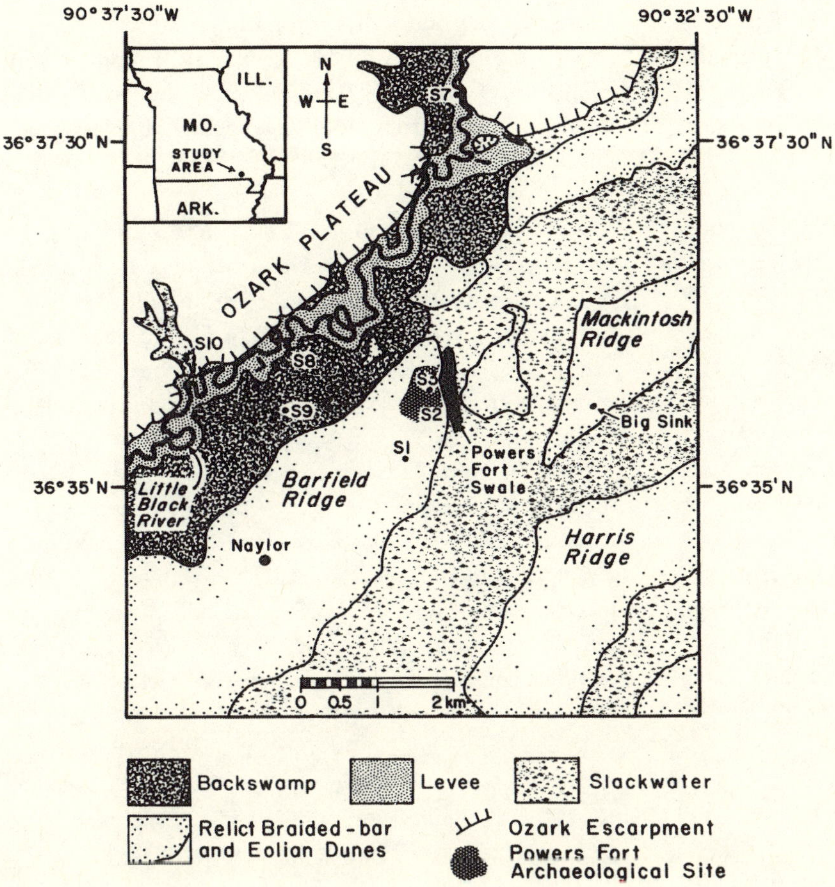

Figure 8.3 Detailed location map for Powers Fort Swale, Butler County, Missouri (after Royall 1988).

These sand ridges are capped by eolian sand dunes and represent midchannel bars and islands similar to those of modern braided streams that are fed by glacial meltwater. The last episode of sand dune formation has been radiocarbon-dated between 17,800 and 11,600 yr B.P. (Saucier 1978 and chapter 7; Royall et al. 1991).

Ponded water of the Powers Fort Swale is maintained by precipitation, groundwater recharged in the adjacent braided-stream bars of Barfield Ridge and Mackintosh Ridge, and seasonal input of floodwaters from the Little Black River, which has a floodplain situated between the Ozark Plateau Escarpment and the western border of Barfield Ridge. Low, poorly drained swales surrounding Barfield Ridge are inundated annually by floodwaters resulting from snowmelt during late winter and early spring. In addition, Powers Fort Swale receives sediment-laden floodwaters of the Little Black River during the spring and summer months of increased precipitation (J. and C. Price, personal communication, 1988). Before construction of drainage ditches across the Western Lowlands in the early A.D. 1900s, water levels at Powers Fort Swale were approximately 50 centimeters higher than at present, promoting sluggish, seasonal streamflow through the Powers Fort swamp.

Vegetation surrounding Powers Fort Swale is a patchwork of upland and bottomland forest in a matrix of cropland and pasture. The swale is occupied by a closed-canopy swamp forest of large bald cypress trees (1–1.5 meters diameter at 1.37 meters height above ground surface; 30 to 35 meters tall). The 15-meter-high forest understory contains hackberry (*Celtis*), red maple (*Acer rubrum*), elm, ash, sweetgum, and locust (*Gleditsia*) along with 3-meter-tall shrubs of buttonbush.

A major archaeological site, Powers Fort, is located on the northeastern tip of Barfield Ridge (Figure 8.3) approximately 100 meters west of the Powers Fort Swale (Price 1978). Powers Fort was a 4.6-hectare civic-ceremonial center occupied during the Powers Phase (circa A.D. 1275 to 1320) of the Middle Mississippian cultural period (A.D. 1000 to 1350) (Price 1978; Morse and Morse 1983).

Field Sampling Method

Sediment cores were obtained from the geographic center of Hood Lake in July 1987; Powers Fort Swale was cored in September 1985 at the geographic center of its deepest pool of permanently standing water. At each site, a square-rod piston corer 5 centimeters in diameter and 1 meter long (Wright 1967) was used to collect sediment cores. Hood Lake was cored from a floating raft to a depth of 330 centimeters below the sediment-water interface. Powers Fort Swale was cored from the swamp-sediment surface to 380 centimeters depth. The sediment was described in terms of texture, color (Munsell Color 1975), and macroscopic presence of plant debris. The core segments were wrapped in plastic and aluminum foil and labeled, and stored at 4°C in the cold room at the Center for Quaternary Studies at the University of Tennessee, Knoxville.

Laboratory Analysis Method

Sediment samples were taken from the sediment-core sequences with a 1-cubic-centimeter calibrated brass sampler (Birks 1976) for loss-on-ignition (LOI) analysis (Dean 1974). Based upon the LOI data and upon preliminary pollen analyses, samples of sediment, each containing 5 grams of organic carbon, were selected for radiocarbon dating. At Hood Lake, eleven core segments were dated; at Powers Fort Swale, ten sediment intervals were radiocarbon-dated. All radiocarbon dates were corrected for isotope fractionation using comparison with ^{13}C measurements. Sediment accumulation rates were calculated by centering radiocarbon dates on the sample midpoints of their respective depth intervals and assuming a uniform rate of sediment accumulation between successive pairs of radiocarbon dates.

From the Hood Lake sediment sequence, pollen samples were selected at depth intervals that represented a resolution of approximately 250-year intervals from 11,250 yr B.P. to 250 yr B.P. and about 25-year intervals to the present. Sediment samples were collected from Powers Fort Swale for pollen analysis at sampling depths representing 500 years or less. Pollen grains and spores were concentrated from each sample using standard chemical extraction techniques for lake sediments (modified from Faegri and Iversen 1975). Completed counts of pollen grains and spores from Hood Lake pollen samples, which ranged from 387 to 631 grains tallied per sample, are tabulated in H. R. Delcourt and Delcourt (1988). A pollen/spore percentage diagram and a plant-macrofossil diagram for Hood Lake show curves for the plant-fossil assemblages plotted on a time scale of radiocarbon age. For Powers Fort Swale, all detailed plant-fossil data are available in Royall (1988). Selected curves for principal types of pollen grains and spores are plotted on a time scale of radiocarbon age.

Each macrofossil sample consisted of a cylinder of sediment core 5 centimeters long (100 cubic centimeters of sediment) and were selected at depth intervals representing approximately 500- to 1,000-year intervals. Plant macrofossils were sieved using 212-, 150-, and 90-micrometer Standard Sieves, picked, and stored in a preservative consisting of 50% glycerine, 35% water, and 15% formaldehyde. Identification was made to the lowest possible taxonomic level using our extensive modern reference collection as well as literature cited in P. A. Delcourt et al. (1979). Complete counts of plant macrofossils are given in H. R. Delcourt and Delcourt (1988).

Results for Hood Lake: Lithology and Chronology

The depositional sequence at Hood Lake (Table 8.1) reflects a progressive shift in sediment particle size (from bottom to top of the core) from sand to silt, then fibrous peat, to organic-rich clay and gelatinous algal mud (gyttja). The dark gray and olive gray colors indicate that permanently standing water persisted in the Hood Lake basin throughout the entire time interval over which these sediments were deposited. The absence of color mottling (particularly the absence of yellow or orange colors in the sediment) indicates that no substantial oxidation or loss of organic material has occurred that might be associated with times of lowered water levels in Hood Lake.

Sedimentation in Hood Lake has been continuous since approximately 11,250 yr B.P.; however, the rate of sediment accumulation has not been constant (Figure 8.4; Table 8.1). The plot of radiocarbon dates portrays a continuous, linear rate of sediment accumulation from 330 to 90 centimeters depth. A dramatic increase in sediment accumulation rate in the upper 90 centimeters, and a change

Table 8.1
Lithologic description of the Hood Lake sediment core

Depth Below Sediment-Water Interface (cm)	Sediment Description
0 to 5	Organic-rich, clayey algal gyttja, dark olive gray (Munsell Sediment Color 5Y 3/2)
5 to 91	Clay, olive gray (5Y 4/2)
91 to 148	Organic-rich, slightly silty clay, dark gray (5Y 4/1)
148 to 160	Clay, dark gray (5Y 4/1)
160 to 254	Fibrous peaty clay, very dark gray (5Y 3/1)
254 to 260	Clayey silt, very dark gray (5Y 3/1)
260 to 276	Slightly clayey, fine-grained sandy silt with common organic fragments dispersed throughout, dark gray (5Y 4/1)
276 to 309	Organic-rich, clayey, medium-grained quartz sand, olive gray (5Y 4/2)
309 to 330	Clayey, fine-grained quartz sand, dark gray (5Y 4/1)

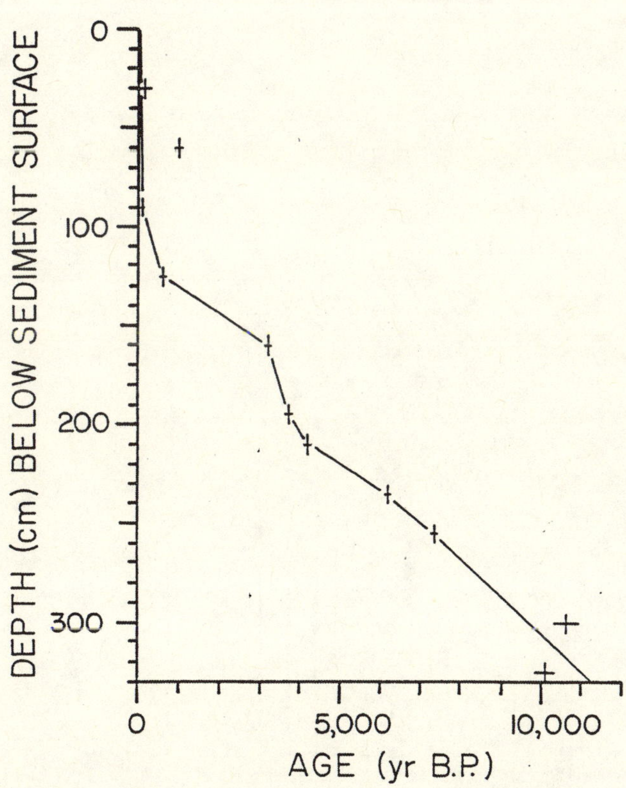

Figure 8.4 Curve of net sediment accumulation rates at Hood Lake (after H. R. Delcourt and Delcourt 1988). The plus symbols represent the corresponding sediment-depth level and radiocarbon age range (^{14}C ± 1 standard deviation) for each radiocarbon date.

in sediment type to olive gray clay and highly organic, gelatinous algal mud, corresponds with Historic land clearance, accelerated erosion of upland soils, and construction of major drainage ditches in the Western Lowlands in the early A.D. 1900s.

Results for Hood Lake: Pollen Assemblage Zones

The percentage pollen diagram (Figure 8.5*a,b*) for Hood Lake has been subdivided into five informal pollen assemblage zones for convenience in characterizing the long-term changes in both the local and regional vegetation. Each plant-fossil zone represents a specific interval of time and sediment depth for the core recovered from Hood Lake; each zone contains diagnostic microfossils of plant species that reflect past changes in the structure and composition of nearby vegetation. The name of each fossil zone is designated by the scientific names of the tree genus and the herbaceous plant genus or family that are key dominants for the zone. The plant-macrofossil diagram (Figure 8.6) also has been subdivided to correspond with the five pollen assemblage zones. Ecologic information concerning the habitat preferences and climatic tolerances of plants are based upon data in Steyermark (1963) and Fowells (1965).

QUERCUS-GRAMINEAE POLLEN ASSEMBLAGE ZONE (AGE 11,250 TO 9,500 YR B.P.; CORE DEPTH 330 TO 297 centimeters). Pollen grains produced by tree species (arboreal pollen, AP) constituted only a minor component of the total pollen assemblage of this zone. The total AP composed between 15% and 33% of the sum of AP plus nonarboreal pollen (NAP) (Figure 8.5*a*). With values of 6% to 15% of the upland pollen-spore sum, oak (*Quercus*) was the major arboreal contributor. Additional trees represented in this zone included hickory (*Carya,* 1% to 9%), ash (*Fraxinus,* 2% to 5%), elm (*Ulmus,* up to 2%), and birch (*Betula,* 1% to 4%). Temperate-climate swamp trees were present within the watershed, as documented by low pollen percentages (usually less than 1%) for bald cypress (*Taxodium distichum*), sycamore (*Platanus occidentalis*), willow (*Salix*), boxelder (*Acer negundo*), red maple (*Acer rubrum*), silver maple (*Acer saccharinum*), and hackberry (*Celtis/Maclura* type). Mesic trees were represented by sugar maple (*Acer saccharum*), beech (*Fagus grandifolia*), hornbeam (*Carpinus/Ostrya* type), tuliptree (*Liriodendron tu-*

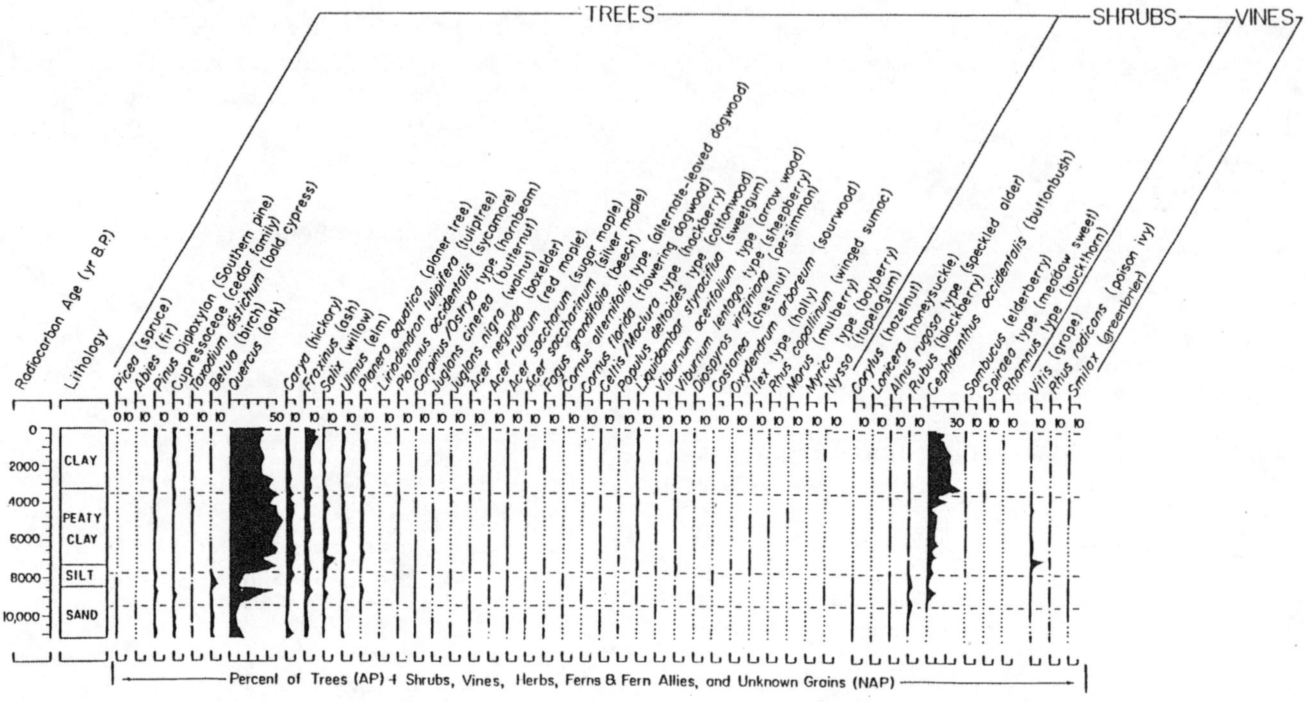

a

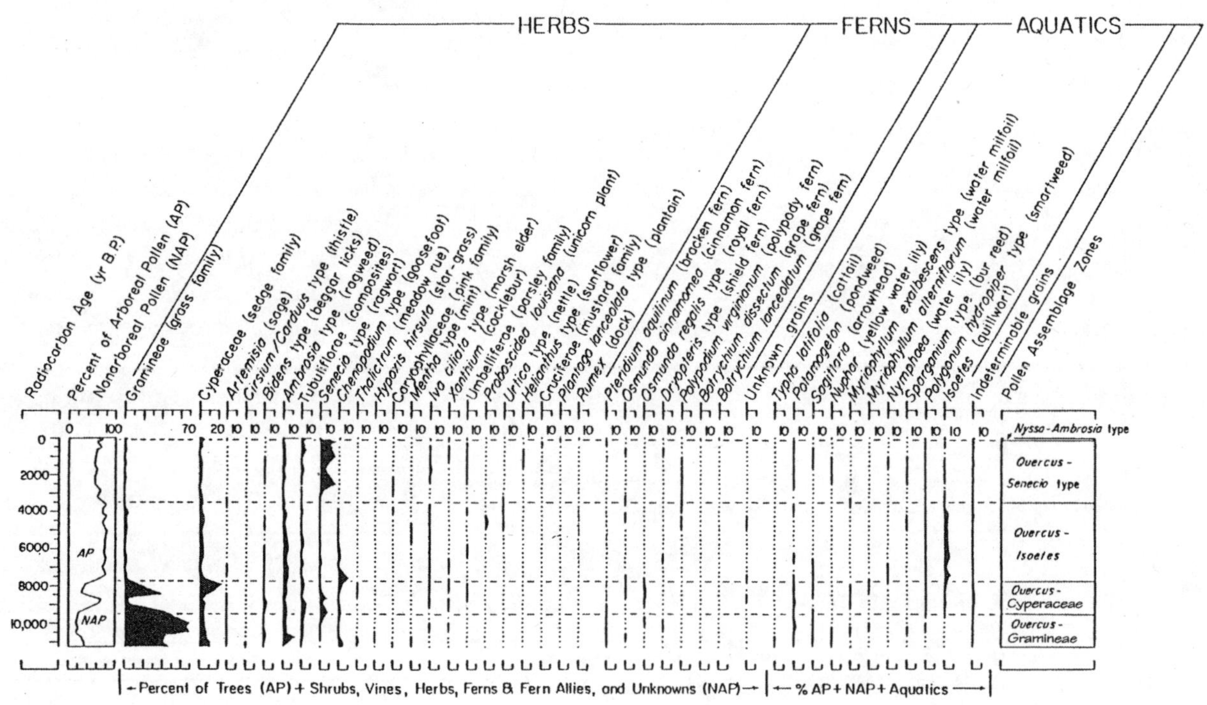

b

Figure 8.5 Percentage diagram for assemblages of pollen grains and spores from Hood Lake (after H. R. Delcourt and Delcourt 1988): *a*, arboreal pollen (AP); *b*, nonarboreal pollen (NAP).

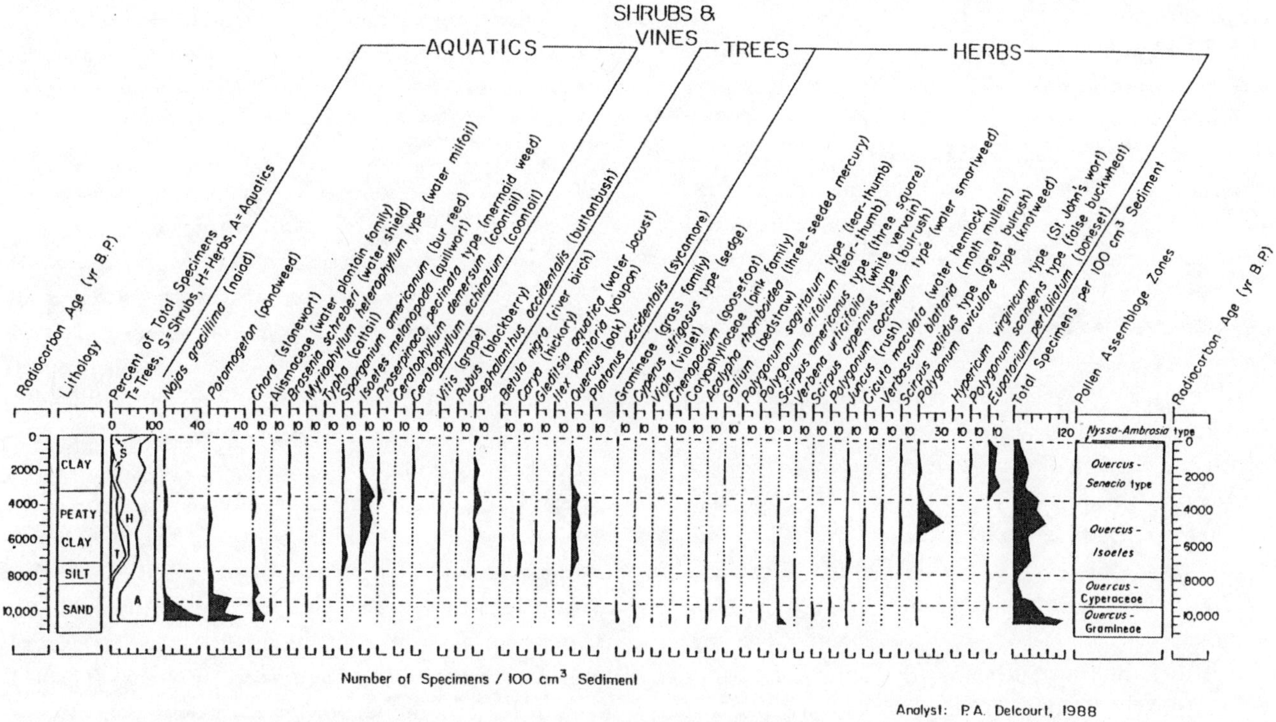

Figure 8.6 Plant-macrofossil diagram for Hood Lake (after H. R. Delcourt and Delcourt 1988).

lipifera), butternut (*Juglans cinerea*), and black walnut (*Juglans nigra*). Trace percentages of pollen grains of boreal species included pollen grains of both spruce (*Picea*) and fir (*Abies*).

Pollen grains produced by native species of wild grass (plant family Gramineae) were the predominant NAP pollen type, with values ranging between 41% and 70% of the AP plus NAP sum (Figure 8.5*b*). In this zone, other nonwoody plants with substantial percentages of microfossils included sedges (family Cyperaceae, from 5% up to 11%), goosefoot (*Chenopodium* pollen type, 1% to 5%), and several members of the family Compositae (ragweed [*Ambrosia* type], 1% to 15%; beggar ticks [*Bidens* type], 1% to 2%). Low percentages of pollen grains were recorded for a number of plants that today grow only in permanent lakes or streams or in seasonally flooded marshes, including pondweeds (with both subgenera *Coleogeton* and *Eupotamogeton* of the genus *Potamogeton*), water milfoil (*Myriophyllum alterniflorum* and *Myriophyllum exalbescens* type), yellow water lily (*Nuphar*), arrowhead (*Sagittaria*), smartweed (*Polygonum hydropiper* type), bur reed (*Sparganium* type), and cattail (*Typha latifolia*).

The plant-macrofossil assemblage recovered from sediments of this zone (Figure 8.6) consisted primarily of plants found today growing exclusively within aquatic environments. The number of macrofossil specimens recovered was relatively high, ranging from seventy-seven to 118 fossils per 100 cubic centimeters of sediment. Between 76% and 84% of the plant macrofossils represented aquatic plant species today found only in habitats with permanently standing or flowing water. For the remainder of the plant-macrofossil assemblage, the herbaceous plants preserved as fossils are species that occupy modern environments such as lakeshore marshes, alluvial wet meadows that are seasonally flooded, and the margins of streams such as Bayou De View. The macrofossil assemblage was composed primarily of four groups of strictly aquatic plants: naiads (*Najas gracillima*), pondweed (*Potamogeton*), stonewort (*Chara*), and water shield (*Brasenia schreberi*). Fossil seeds and fruits were identified as marsh herbs such as grasses (family Gramineae), sedges (*Cyperus strigosus* type), goosefoot (*Chenopodium*), several bulrushes (*Scirpus americanus* type and *Scirpus cyperinus* type), tear-thumb (*Polygonum sagittatum* type), and rush (*Juncus*). Two fossil seeds of three-seeded mercury (*Acalypha rhomboidea*) were found consistently in each 100-cubic-centimeter sample of sediment in this zone; although today this plant species is widely distributed across eastern North America, within the central Mississippi Alluvial Valley this plant is characteristically found growing in prairies, on moist alluvial soils and gravel bars along streams, and in open wet-to-dry woodlands (Steyermark 1963). No macroscopic remains of tree or shrub species were recovered from this sedimentary interval of the Hood Lake core.

QUERCUS-CYPERACEAE POLLEN ASSEMBLAGE ZONE (AGE 9,500 TO 7,750 YR B.P.; CORE DEPTH 297 TO 263 CENTIMETERS). AP and NAP shared dominance in this pollen assemblage zone. Total AP increased from 22% to 70% (Figure 8.5*a*). Oak varied from 12% to 46% of the AP. Other trees included hickory (3% to 10%), ash (2% to 9%), birch (generally 2% to 8%), willow (1% to 5%), elm (1% to 4%), and members of the cedar family (Cupressaceae, 1% to 4%). Intact papillate pollen grains of bald cypress (*Taxodium distichum*) occur in the zone. The undifferentiated pollen category of Cupressaceae may represent pollen of juniper (*Juniperus*) and may also include broken *Taxodium* grains. First occurrences of fossil pollen grains were detected for planer tree (*Planera aquatica,* up to 4%), chestnut (*Castanea,* 1%), flowering dogwood (*Cornus florida,* 1%), sheepberry (*Viburnum lentago* type, 1%), persimmon (*Diospyros virginiana,* 1%), sweetgum (*Liquidambar styraciflua,* 1%), and tupelogum (*Nyssa,* 1%). Scattered pollen grains of spruce persisted until the middle portion of this zone.

The NAP (Figure 8.5*b*) consisted of herbs and shrubs, as well as low percentages of vines (lianas), ferns, and fern allies. Among the herbs, sedge pollen rose from 5% to 25%, and grass dropped from 70% to between 4% and 40%. The composites generally increased in both number of taxa and their abundance (for example, ragwort [*Senecio*], up to 9%; ragweed, 5%; beggar ticks, 3%; marsh elder [*Iva ciliata* type], 1%; and cocklebur [*Xanthium*], 1%). Shrubs included blackberry (*Rubus,* up to 6%) and buttonbush (1% to 11%), with minor values for speckled alder (*Alnus rugosa* type, 1%), hazelnut (*Corylus*), and honeysuckle (*Lonicera*). Continuous pollen curves with consistently low percentages are illustrated (Figure 8.5*b*) for poison ivy (*Rhus radicans*), greenbrier (*Smilax*), and grape (*Vitis*).

The total number of macrofossils per 100 cubic centimeters of sediment decreased from forty-eight to ten specimens throughout this zone, considerably fewer than the peak of 118 specimens per sample obtained in the *Quercus*-Gramineae zone (Figure 8.6). Aquatic plants decreased from 79% to 50% of the assemblage, and both herbs and vines (lianas) increased (from 21% to 40% and from 0% to 10%, respectively). Grape vines were represented by fossil *Vitis* seeds. No macrofossil specimens of shrubs or trees were recovered from this zone.

Aquatic plants included more species but a substantially lower number of plant macrofossil specimens than in the previous pollen assemblage zone. The numbers of specimens per 100 cubic centimeters of sediment declined to two seeds of naiads, seven fruits of pondweeds, and nine reproductive oogonia of stoneworts. Water shield, water milfoil (*Myriophyllum heterophyllum* type), and cattail (*Typha*) were each present at one specimen per plant-macrofossil sample. The assemblage of herbs consisted of plants that today typically grow around lake margins and in open alluvial marshes, including three-seeded mercury, boneset (*Eupatorium perfoliatum*), bedstraw (*Galium*), smartweeds (tear-thumb, *Polygonum arifolium;* knotweed, *P. aviculare* type; and water smartweed, *P. coccineum*), and three square bulrush (*Scirpus americanus* type). White vervain (*Verbena urticifolia*) was found only in this zone. It is diagnostic of frequently disturbed habitats such as alluvial thickets along streams in the Western Lowlands (Steyermark 1963).

QUERCUS-ISOETES POLLEN ASSEMBLAGE ZONE (AGE 7,750 TO 3,500 YR B.P.; CORE DEPTH 297 TO 177 CENTIMETERS). AP composed 70% to 81% of the pollen assemblage in this zone (Figure 8.5*a*). Oak ranged from 42% to 57%, hickory was 8% to 11%, willow was 5% to 14%, and elm was 3% to 5%. Additional trees included ash (4% to 9%), planer tree (2% to 5%), and sweetgum (1% to 2%), with trace amounts of bald cypress, sycamore, hornbeam, butternut, red and sugar maple, hackberry, sheepberry, and holly (*Ilex* type). Sporadic occurrences of pollen were noted for arrow wood (*Viburnum acerifolium* type), box-elder, cottonwood (*Populus deltoides* type), persimmon, mulberry (*Morus*), silver maple, and winged sumac (*Rhus copallinum*). Shrubs included buttonbush (4% to 21%), blackberry, elderberry (*Sambucus*), meadow sweet (*Spiraea* type), and speckled alder. Poison ivy and greenbrier were present, with grape reaching 15% in this zone.

NAP were present in minor amounts throughout this

pollen assemblage zone (Figure 8.5*b*). Those NAP with continuous pollen curves included goosefoot (1% to 12%), grass (1% to 5%), marsh elder, ragweed (1% to 7%), ragwort (about 1%), and sedge (1% to 5%). Only unicorn plant (*Proboscidea louisiana,* 4%) and nettle (*Urtica,* 1%) were restricted exclusively in their microfossil occurrence to this zone at Hood Lake. Unicorn plant grows today across the eastern United States on naturally disturbed sand-and-gravel bars of streams and on cultivated land and pastures. Nettle is also widely distributed within low alluvial bottoms of river valleys and in cultivated and disturbed areas (Steyermark 1963). The microfossil evidence for obligate aquatic plants in this zone includes microspores of quillwort (*Isoetes,* generally 4% to 8%) and pollen grains of smartweed (*Polygonum hydropiper* type, 1%), arrowhead, bur reed (*Sparganium* type), pondweed, and water milfoil.

The plant-macrofossil assemblage increased to between thirty-five and sixty-one specimens per sample (Figure 8.6). Fossil fruits and seeds included a diverse combination of tree species (13% to 35%), shrubs and vines (3% to 17%), herbs (16% to 52%), and aquatic plants (31% to 54%). Five to ten fragments of acorn nuts and caps were found in every sample. Additional fossils were recovered for hickory, river birch (*Betula nigra*), sycamore, water locust (*Gleditsia aquatica*), and yaupon (*Ilex vomitoria*). Shrubs included buttonbush (one to eight seeds) and blackberry (one seed per sample), and vines were represented by grape (one seed at each of three depth levels). Macrofossils of herbs common in alluvial marshes included knotweed (*Polygonum aviculare* type, up to thirty-two specimens per sample), several bulrushes (*Scirpus americanus* type, *S. cyperinus* type, and *S. validus* type), moth mullein (*Verbascum blattaria*), rush (*Juncus*), three-seeded mercury, and water hemlock (*Cicuta maculata*).

Megaspores of quillwort (*Isoetes melanopoda* [identified according to morphological criteria in Boom (1979)], typically ten to eighteen specimens per sample) were most numerous among the macrofossils of aquatic plants. Today, *Isoetes melanopoda* lives in wet swales and on open ground; it is distributed within the central Mississippi Alluvial Valley of Missouri, Arkansas (Steyermark 1963), and Louisiana, as well in temporary shallow ponds north to Minnesota, east to New Jersey, and west to South Dakota, Oklahoma, and Texas (Gleason and Cronquist 1963). Other aquatic macrophytes were represented by specimens of bur reed (*Sparganium americanum*), two species of coontail (*Ceratophyllum demersum* and *Ceratophyllum echinatum*), mermaid weed (*Proserpinaca pectinata* type), naiad, pondweed, stonewort, and water shield.

QUERCUS-SENECIO TYPE POLLEN ASSEMBLAGE ZONE (AGE 3,500 TO 100 YR B.P.; CORE DEPTH 177 TO 90 CENTIMETERS). Total AP constituted 55% to 69% of this pollen assemblage, with shrubs typically 20% to 36% and with lower values for herbs. Oak remained at 32% to 47% (Figure 8.5*a*). Other trees included ash (5% to 15%), hickory (3% to 6%), planer tree (1% to 6%), sweetgum (1% to 4%), elm (1% to 4%), members of the cedar family (1% to 4%), willow (1% to 2%), sheepberry (1% to 2%), sugar maple (1% to 2%), red maple (1%), and butternut (1%). Buttonbush achieved high values of 12% to 35%. Other shrubs included blackberry, buckthorn (*Rhamnus* type), elderberry, hazelnut, and speckled alder. Grape, greenbrier, and poison ivy were represented as discontinuous occurrences in their pollen curves.

In the NAP, members of the Compositae family were conspicuous elements of this assemblage zone (Figure 8.5*b*). Ragwort (*Senecio* type) expanded from 1% to 18% at the top of the *Quercus-Senecio* type assemblage zone. Both the undifferentiated subfamily of Tubuliflorae and ragweed oscillated in abundance, between 0% and 5% and between 1% and 3%, respectively. In addition, trace values occurred for sunflower (*Helianthus* type), beggar ticks, cocklebur, and marsh elder. Sunflower pollen grains occurred at 130 and 135 centimeters depth, with interpolated ages of 980 and 1,350 yr B.P. Grass and sedge were each 2% of the sum of AP plus NAP. The aquatic flora exhibited 1% values for arrowhead, bur reed, pondweed, quillwort, smartweed, yellow water lily, and water lily.

Total plant macrofossils decreased to thirty specimens per sample in this zone (Figure 8.6). Trees were generally represented by only 4% to 7% of the total specimens and were absent in two of the four samples analyzed. Macrofossils of trees and shrubs consisted of oak (up to two acorn fragments), buttonbush (up to six seeds), and blackberry (one seed). Totals for shrubs dropped from 8% at the base of this zone to zero in younger-age sediments. Macrofossils of aquatic plants were 22% to 37% of the total assemblage. The relative contribution of herbs increased to between 54% and 67%. The herb group was composed primarily of seeds of boneset (eight to fourteen specimens of *Eupatorium perfoliatum*) and knotweed (up to six seeds of *Polygonum aviculare* type) and secondary numbers of bedstraw, false buckwheat (*Polygonum scandens* type), great bulrush (*Scirpus validus* type), rush, and St. John's wort (*Hypericum virginicum*). Aquatic macrophytes included quillwort (up to nine megaspores), bur reed, coontail (*Ceratophyllum echinatum*), ditch witch (*Ruppia maritima,* four fruits), mermaid weed, naiad, pondweed, stonewort, and water shield.

NYSSA-AMBROSIA TYPE POLLEN ASSEMBLAGE ZONE (AGE 100 YR B.P. TO PRESENT; CORE DEPTH 90 TO 0 CENTIMETERS). In the uppermost four pollen samples (depths 5, 30, 60, and 90 centimeters) that compose this zone, total AP increased to between 59% and 79% of the total AP plus NAP (Figure 8.5*a*). Tupelogum (*Nyssa*) increased from 0% to 6%. Oak fluctuated between 24 and 44%, and hickory varied from 1% to 5%. Willow rose from 1% in early Historic time to its present 14%. Ash dropped from 8% to 5%. Other trees included bald cypress (1%), birch (1%), elm (3%), hackberry (1%), planer tree (about 2%), sheepberry (1%), sycamore (1%), sweetgum (1%), and southern pine (Diploxylon *Pinus,* 2%). Pollen of southern pine was probably dispersed by wind to this site from the Ozark Plateaus to the west (P. A. Delcourt et al. 1983; E. N. Smith 1984). In the past 100 years, buttonbush declined from 18% to 5%. Other shrubs, including blackberry, elderberry, and speckled alder, decreased from 1% to 0% in modern lake sediments.

Pollen percentages of ragweed rose from 1% to 16% (Figure 8.5*b*). Undifferentiated grains of Tubuliflorae rose from 1% to 10%, goosefoot increased from 0% to 2%, and grass increased from 1% to 4%. Introduced plant taxa represented in Historic sediments include plantain (*Plantago lanceolata*) and dock (*Rumex*). The microfossil record of aquatic plants (Figure 8.5*b*) reflects the substantial reduction of formerly common species. Only isolated pollen grains or spores are recorded in superficial modern sediments of Hood Lake for arrowhead, quillwort, smartweed, and yellow water lily. Bur reed, pondweed, and water lily have been eliminated from the lake. The one sample for the modern suite of macroscopic fruits and seeds contains nine specimens per 100 cubic centimeters of sediment: one megaspore of quillwort, six seeds of buttonbush, one seed of knotweed, and one grass seed (Figure 8.6). No large plant remains of trees were recovered from the lake sediment.

Results for Powers Fort Swale: Lithology and Chronology

The series of radiocarbon dates from the Powers Fort Swale sediment core forms a curve for sediment accumulation in Figure 8.7, with three distinct linear trends during the last 18,300 years (the dashed line from 18,300 to 16,300 yr B.P., the solid line segment from 16,300 to 570 yr B.P., and the solid line segment from 570 yr B.P. to the present). Net rates of sediment accumulation were generally highest in the lower half of the core, reaching about 0.08 centimeter per year between 18,300 and 16,300 yr B.P. (between 380 and 195 centimeters depth). From about 16,300 to about 6,600 yr B.P. (195 to 82 centimeters depth), net sediment accumulation rate decreased to 0.01 centimeter per year. It then diminished to 0.004 centimeter per year between 6,600 and 570 yr B.P. (82 to 60 centimeters depth). Sediment accumulation in the Powers Fort core reached a peak of 0.10 centimeter per year from 570 yr B.P. to the present (the uppermost centimeter of sediment, Table 8.2).

The percentage of organic carbon by dry sediment weight ranged from 0.20% at the base of the sediment core from Powers Fort Swale to 10.95% at the top. Percentage by weight of dry sediment calculated for carbonate (plus water of hydration in clays) ranged from almost 2% at lower depths to trace values in the uppermost LOI sample.

Detailed sedimentological analyses of particle-size distribution, sediment characteristics of grain shape and grain-surface features, and mineralogical composition provide evidence that the full-glacial Mississippi River transported glacial meltwater and outwash from the southern margin of the Laurentide Ice Sheet and deposited outwash in braided-stream channels on the Qtb_3 terrace surface in the Western Lowlands (Royall 1988; Royall et al. 1991). Continuous deposition of medium sands by braided streams infilled Powers Fort Swale from 18,300 to about 16,300 yr B.P. Partial diversion of Mississippi River flow through the Bell City/Oran Gap resulted in progressive funneling of glacial meltwater through this northern gap in Crowley's Ridge and into the Eastern Lowlands. This eastward shift in location of Mississippi River flow resulted in only intermittent braided-stream flow through the Powers Fort Swale, depositing interbedded fine sands and silts between 16,300 and 14,500 yr B.P., and possibly as late as 11,500 yr B.P. (Royall et al. 1991). Eolian reworking of sand grains produced sand dunes on the chan-

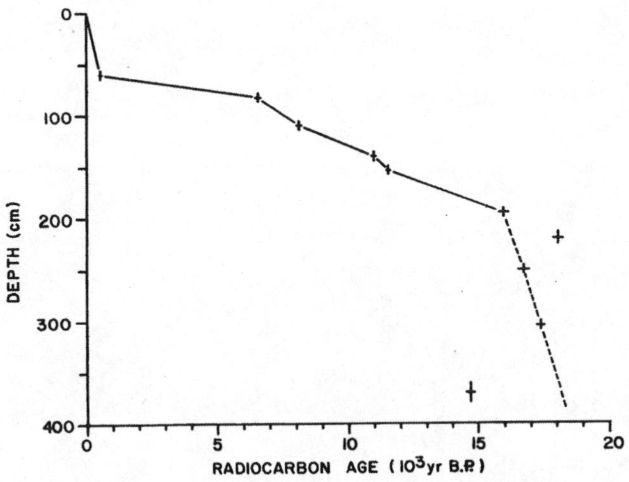

Figure 8.7 Curve of net sediment accumulation rates at Powers Fort Swale (after Royall 1988). The plus symbols represent the corresponding sediment-depth level and radiocarbon age range ($^{14}C \pm 1$ standard deviation) for each radiocarbon date.

nel knolls of the Qtb_3 braided-stream surface from 17,800 until about 11,500 yr B.P. The silts and clays accumulated in the last 11,500 years reflect slackwater deposition of fine-grained deposits in the swale during annual flooding from the nearby meandering Little Black River.

The first linear trend (Figure 8.7) of relatively rapid accumulation of medium sand represents full-glacial conditions of a full braided-stream regime, which lasted until about 16,300 years ago. The second linear trend of sediment accumulation, from 16,300 to 570 yr B.P., reflects the transition to limited braided-stream activity in the late-glacial interval and the Holocene changeover to a meandering stream and slackwater depositional environment. This corresponded with the lithologic shift in the Powers Fort Swale core from interbedded fine sands and silts to silts and clays. The third linear trend in sedimentation, occurring over the last 570 years, was a rapid increase in the rate of deposition of organic-rich silty clays and silts in the Powers Fort Swale. This increase in sedimentation rate reflected forest clearance and crop cultivation on the nearby Qtb_3 braided-stream terrace both by prehistoric Mississippian people and by historic EuroAmericans (Royall 1988; Royall et al. 1991).

Table 8.2
Lithologic description of the Powers Fort Swale sediment core

Depth Below Sediment-Water Interface (cm)	Sediment Description
0 to 46	Water-saturated organic clayey silt, dark grayish brown (Munsell Sediment Color 10YR 4/2)
46 to 78	Organic silty clay, dark grayish brown (10YR 4/2); mottled dark yellowish brown (10YR 4/6)
78 to 89	Silty clay, very dark gray (10YR 3/1)
89 to 145	Organic silty clay, black (10YR 2/1)
145 to 166	Clayey fine sand, very dark grayish brown (10YR 3/2)
166 to 177	Clayey fine sand, dark grayish brown (10YR 4/2)
177 to 201	Organic fine sandy silt, very dark gray (10YR 3/1)
201 to 218	Fine sand, dark grayish brown (10YR 4/2)
218 to 227	Organic clayey silt, very dark grayish brown (10YR 3/2)
227 to 243	Medium to fine sand, very dark gray (10YR 3/1)
243 to 274	Sandy, silty clay, very dark gray (10YR 3/1)
274 to 289	Sandy, clayey silt, dark gray (10YR 4/1)
289 to 301	Medium sand, very dark gray (10YR 3/1)
301 to 323	Silty fine sand, black (10YR 2/1)
323 to 355	Clayey medium sand with granules, dark gray (10YR 4/1)
355 to 360	Coarse sandy, silty clay, dark gray (10YR 4/1)
360 to 380	Clayey medium sand, grading toward base to very coarse sand with granules, dark gray (10YR 4/1)

Results for Powers Fort Swale: Pollen Assemblage Zones

The pollen percentage diagram for the Powers Fort Swale site (Figure 8.8) illustrates selected curves for important taxa of trees, shrubs, and herbs plotted against radiocarbon age for the last 16,000 years, the span of time with continuous sediment accumulation within the swale. From 18,300 to about 16,000 yr B.P., active stream erosion and sediment deposition occurred at Powers Fort Swale within a high-flow regime (circa 70 centimeters per second) of the braided stream. Although pollen spectra were counted for organic lenses dating from before 16,000 yr B.P. (Royall 1988), they are not plotted on the pollen diagram (Figure 8.8).

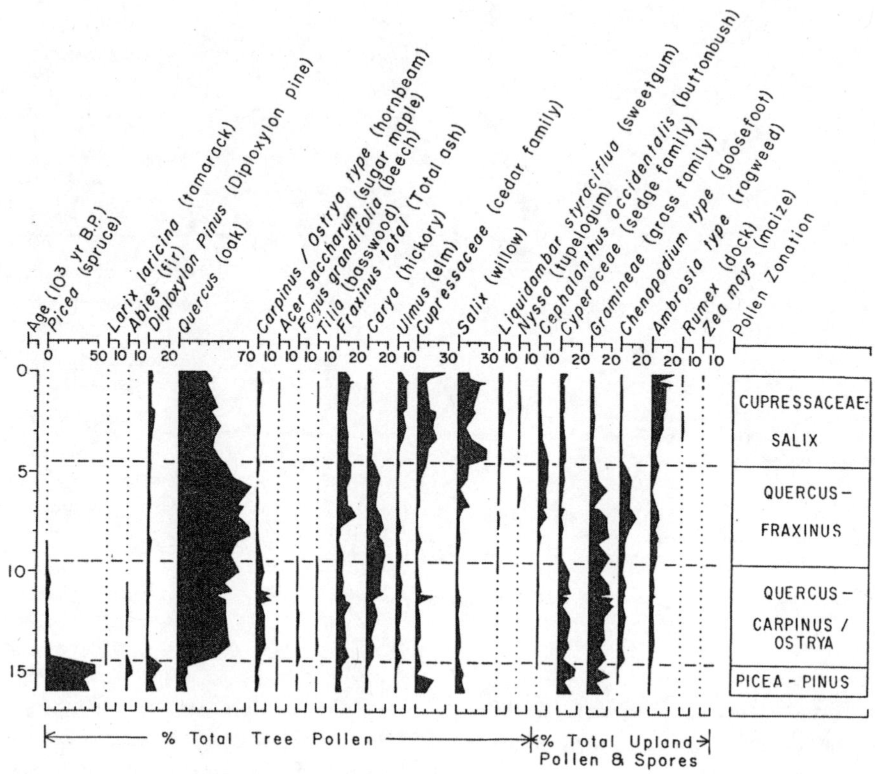

Figure 8.8 Percentage diagram for pollen grains of selected taxa from Powers Fort Swale (after Royall 1988).

PICEA-PINUS ZONE (AGE 18,300 TO 14,500 YR B.P.; CORE DEPTH 380 TO 180 CENTIMETERS). The *Picea-Pinus* zone was dominated by spruce, with 40% to 75% of the AP sum (Figure 8.8). Jack pine (northern Diploxylon *Pinus*) composed up to 18% of the AP. Fir (*Abies*) occurred throughout the zone, with up to 7% of the AP, and tamarack (*Larix laricina*) occurred discontinuously, representing less than 1% of the AP. Pollen grains of broad-leaved deciduous trees included oak (5% to 10%), willow (7% to 28%), and cedar (Cupressaceae, up to 15%). Other trees included hornbeam, ash, elm, hickory, and sugar maple, each ≤2%. Sedge (Cyperaceae) and native grass (Gramineae) were the dominant NAP types within this zone (up to 12% and 18% of the AP plus the NAP sum, respectively, Figure 8.8).

QUERCUS-CARPINUS/OSTRYA ZONE (AGE 14,500 TO 9,500 YR B.P.; CORE DEPTH 180 TO 125 CENTIMETERS). In the *Quercus-Carpinus/Ostrya* zone, total AP decreased from 80% to 50% as NAP percentages increased. The boundary between the *Picea-Pinus* zone and the *Quercus-Carpinus/Ostrya* zone was characterized by major decreases in pollen values for spruce, jack pine, and fir, by the last occurrence of tamarack, and by a major increase in oak (Figure 8.8). Between 15,000 and 14,000 yr B.P., spruce declined from 50% to less than 5% of the AP sum, whereas oak increased from 10% to around 50%. Hornbeam increased to 10%, hickory increased to 15%, elm increased to 4%, and ash increased to 5% of the AP. Sugar maple, beech, and basswood (*Tilia*) were represented throughout the zone. Cupressaceae composed up to 18% of the AP in two samples, but otherwise remained less than 2%. The continuous pollen curve of buttonbush (*Cephalanthus occidentalis*) began at the lower boundary of this pollen zone. Cyperaceae and Gramineae were the dominant NAP types, representing 10% and up to 20%, respectively, of the AP plus NAP sum (Figure 8.8). Goosefoot increased from less than 1% to 6%, and ragweed increased from less than 1% to 3%.

QUERCUS-FRAXINUS ZONE (AGE 9,500 TO 4,500 YR B.P.; CORE DEPTH 125 TO 75 CENTIMETERS). The *Quercus-Fraxinus* zone was characterized by the lowest percentages of total AP. Shrubs composed only 2% to 7%, whereas herb pollen composed up to 65% of the sum of AP plus NAP. The beginning of the *Quercus-Fraxinus* zone was distinguished by the last occurrence of the spruce pollen (absent after 8,500 yr B.P.), an increase in oak pollen from 55% to 75% of the AP sum, and a decrease in hornbeam (from 5% to 1%) and beech (from 1% to 0%), as well as loss of basswood and sugar maple (Figure 8.8). Ash increased from 2% to 10%. Hickory declined from 17% to 3%, and elm declined from 4% to 2%. Willow rose from 1% to 10% late in the zone. Cupressaceae remained less than 1%, and the first papillate pollen of bald cypress was identified. Buttonbush increased from 1% to 7%. Grass (up to 18%), ragweed (8%), and goosefoot (up to 16%) remained high throughout the zone, whereas sedge fell to 2% (Figure 8.8).

CUPRESSACEAE-*SALIX* ZONE (AGE 4,500 YR B.P. TO PRESENT; CORE DEPTH 75 TO 0 CENTIMETERS). The beginning of the Cupressaceae-*Salix* zone was characterized by major increases of total AP (up to 70%), with lowered percentages of herbs; total shrub pollen remained at around 4% throughout this pollen zone. In this zone (Figure 8.8), oak decreased from 70% to 30%, and major increases occurred for bald cypress (from 1% to 18%, including both papillate *Taxodium* grains and broken, undifferentiatable Cupressaceae/Taxodiaceae grains) and willow (from 10% to 28%). Elm increased from 2% to 10%. Sweetgum and tupelogum, which had occurred rarely in the two preceding zones, were represented by continuous pollen profiles at about 2% (Figure 8.8). Buttonbush decreased from 7% to 1%. Ragweed increased from 6% to over 20% early in the zone (by about 600 yr B.P.), decreased to 8% in the middle of the zone, and again rose to above 20% at the end of the zone (Figure 8.8). Sedge and grass remained low (1% to 5%). Goosefoot decreased from 10% to 1%. Maize (*Zea mays*) first appeared at 50 centimeters depth (about 600 yr B.P.), but became continuously represented only in the last 100 years.

DISCUSSION: LATE QUATERNARY VEGETATIONAL HISTORY AT HOOD LAKE

The percentage pollen diagram (Figure 8.5*a,b*) and the plant-macrofossil diagram (Figure 8.6) illustrate that the plant-fossil record from Hood Lake is rich in plant taxa, and that substantial changes in the composition and proportions of trees, upland herbs, and aquatic plants have occurred over the past 11,250 years of the Holocene. The early Holocene time interval includes the lowermost two pollen zones from Hood Lake: the *Quercus*-Gramineae pollen assemblage zone and the *Quercus*-Cyperaceae pollen assemblage zone. The middle Holocene time interval is represented at Hood Lake by the *Quercus-Isoetes* pollen assemblage zone. The late Holocene time interval includes the prehistoric *Quercus-Senecio* type pollen assemblage zone and the Historic *Nyssa-Ambrosia* type pollen assemblage zone.

By 11,250 yr B.P., the beginning of the Hood Lake pollen record, the forests in the central Mississippi Alluvial Valley were predominantly warm-temperate and deciduous. However, boreal conifers persisted until at least 9,500 yr B.P., as reflected by the trace percentages of spruce and fir pollen in basal sediments of Hood Lake. Diminishment of cool-temperate and boreal elements by 9,500 yr B.P. at Hood Lake is consistent with data from other paleoecological sites at comparable latitudes east of the Mississippi River (e.g., Anderson Pond in Middle Tennessee [H. R. Delcourt 1979; P. A. Delcourt and Delcourt 1987]). The abundance of plant macrofossils of submersed aquatic plants, such as naiads and pondweeds, indicates that between 11,250 and 9,500 yr B.P., the central basin of Hood Lake represented a permanent lake of at least 3 meters water depth, subject to seasonal waterflow through the watershed. We interpret the high representation of grass pollen in early Holocene sediments of Hood Lake as local marsh grasses growing at the margins of Hood Lake. Beyond the marsh, bottomland swamp forests with ash, bald cypress, planer tree, and other temperate hardwoods were established. On sandy, braided-stream terraces, upland xeric forests were dominated by oak and hickory. On rich, loess-covered slopes on nearby Crowley's Ridge, mesic forests included sugar maple, beech, hornbeam, and walnut.

By 9,500 yr B.P., changes in the assemblages of obligate aquatic plants and marsh herbs reflect an environmental change toward an overall decrease in water depth and an increase in seasonal stream flow through Hood Lake. This environmental change in nearby Bayou De View triggered a decrease in the lake-pool size and a corresponding expansion of alluvial marsh habitats, dominated by sedges, along the margin of Hood Lake. This environmental change may have resulted from the early Holocene climatic change toward increased seasonality of precipitation and temperature extremes that culminated between

10,000 and 9,000 yr B.P. (Kutzbach 1987; H. R. Delcourt and Delcourt 1994). Alternatively, this local environmental change may have resulted from a hydrologic change. Because of headward growth of the stream drainage system, streams such as Bayou De View in the Western Lowlands may have increased their effective competence for transporting sediment and generated both downstream incision of their floodplains and a local drop in groundwater table (R. Saucier, personal communication; P. A. Delcourt and Delcourt 1996).

During the early Holocene interval, the substrates of both pool and marsh habitats were represented in the sedimentary record by mineral-rich sands and silts. At approximately 254 centimeters depth (about 7,300 yr B.P.), the lithologic changeover from silt to fibrous, peaty clays represented a change in depositional environment that followed a regional climatic and vegetational shift dated at Hood Lake at 7,750 yr B.P. The continued drop in the level of the local water table through the early and middle Holocene reached an extreme low between 7,750 and 3,500 yr B.P. Within the Western Lowlands, the hydrologic regime of streams changed from one of permanently flowing water to one of ephemeral, intermittent flow, with pools of water becoming isolated and persisting throughout the year only in remnant basins such as at Hood Lake.

Our data from Hood Lake indicate that maximum expansion of oak-hickory forest occurred between about 7,750 and 3,500 yr B.P., and that during that time interval the representation of bottomland trees such as river birch, sycamore and planer tree, elm, willow, and ash increased. Although Compositae were represented consistently throughout the interval, grasses were not important, and we interpret the local vegetation surrounding Hood Lake as closed swamp forest, establishing into areas previously occupied by marsh. Peaks in goosefoot pollen and seeds, buttonbush seeds, and quillwort megaspores and microspores indicate that Hood Lake was shallow, with seasonally fluctuating water levels that would have exposed the lake margins for colonization by these plants.

In the Upper Midwest region of Minnesota and Wisconsin, the classic time interval for the eastward expansion of the prairie/forest border and, consequently, for interpretation of a warm/dry middle Holocene "Hypsithermal Interval" is from about 8,500 to 4,500 yr B.P. (Wright 1968). At Hood Lake, middle Holocene warming and drying was reflected in the change from lake and marsh to extensive bottomland forest. The diversity of vegetational responses to middle Holocene climatic change and regionally lowered water tables reflects the differences of paleoecological sites with respect to topographic setting along the regional environmental gradient from Ozark uplands to Mississippi Alluvial Valley.

Between 4,500 and 3,500 yr B.P., a regional change in climate resulted in an increase in effective precipitation that lasted throughout the late Holocene (H. R. Delcourt et al. 1986). The transition from middle to late Holocene represented a shift from zonal to meridional climatic regime (P. A. Delcourt and Delcourt 1984). As a result of this climatic change, water tables rose in the Mississippi Alluvial Valley as well as the nearby Ozark Plateaus and Interior Low Plateaus (H. R. Delcourt et al. 1986). Within the Western Lowlands, the sedimentary record from Hood Lake records a time lag of several hundred years for the subsequent change in depositional environment (the transition from fibrous, peaty clay to massive clay at 160 centimeters depth, dated about 3,200 yr B.P.).

From 3,500 to 100 yr B.P., expansion of herbs indicative of alluvial marshes and swamps, as well as of buttonbush, occurred in response to reestablishment of flowing water in fluvial habitats subject to seasonal flooding. The diagnostic types of composites, represented by *Senecio* type pollen grains and by *Eupatorium perfoliatum* seeds, occur today characteristically within moist swamp woods and at the margins of sloughs and ponds (Steyermark 1963). Pollen of sunflower occurred between 1,350 and 980 yr B.P., possibly reflecting local aboriginal cultivation in Woodland and Mississippian cultural periods.

During the last 100 years, clay and algal mud have accumulated at extremely high rates (Figure 8.4). These rates of accumulation are a result of accelerated soil erosion from the uplands into Hood Lake following ditching, clearance of bottomland forests, and conversion of the landscape to agriculture in the last century. Historic landscape modification is reflected by increases in pollen of weedy plants such as ragweed, dock, and plantain. The algae-rich muds are the result of increased nutrient transport to the lake and its increased productivity. Tupelogum, now forming a conspicuous vegetation zone of swamp forest locally around the margin of Hood Lake, has invaded only in Historic times, as the hydroperiod of flooding was changed with construction of drainage ditches and as Hood Lake filled in with sediment eroded from surrounding agricultural land.

DISCUSSION: LATE QUATERNARY VEGETATIONAL HISTORY AT POWERS FORT SWALE

During full-glacial times, dated at Powers Fort Swale from 18,300 to 14,500 yr B.P., a swamp forest composed of boreal conifers and dominated by spruce occupied the margins of active braided-stream channels of the Western Lowlands (Royall 1988; Royall et al. 1991; P. A. Delcourt and Delcourt 1996). Spruce grows today on alluvial soils as well as on other soil types primarily within the boreal forest region of Canada (Fowells 1965; Ritchie 1987). Boreal jack pine grew nearby in the uplands of the Ozark Plateau (E. N. Smith 1984), but its pollen percentages are too low in the Powers Fort Swale record to indicate the local presence of jack pine within the lowlands of the central Mississippi River Valley. Tamarack, aspen (not shown in Figure 8.8), and fir occurred in minor populations, and several species of boreal shrubs and herbs were also locally present, including soapberry and bunchberry (not shown in Figure 8.8). Cool-temperate deciduous trees, including oak, ash, hornbeam, hickory, and sugar maple, may have grown along the escarpment of the Ozark Plateau west of Powers Fort Swale. High percentages of alder pollen reflect the local presence of alder thickets, which typically occur today in moist valley bottoms and along water bodies, on disturbed alluvial ground and other moist environments (Ritchie 1987). Fluvial disturbance created open area around the swale for establishment of willow as well as sedges and grasses. Cattail, water milfoil, and bur reed grew in shallow ponds.

In the late-glacial/early Holocene interval, from 14,500 to 9,500 yr B.P., the vegetation of the Western Lowlands was characterized by plant taxa typically found today within the midwestern mixed conifer-northern hardwoods region (Braun 1950; P. A. Delcourt and Delcourt 1987). The population of spruce, which had been dominant throughout the full-glacial interval, declined rapidly between 15,000 and 14,000 yr B.P. and was replaced by oak, beech, sugar maple, and other cool-temperate deciduous hardwoods. The decline of spruce at Powers Fort Swale lagged some 800 years behind the initial decline of spruce at Cupola Pond in the Ozark uplands 45 kilometers to the west (E. N. Smith 1984). We suggest that the continuous flow of cool meltwaters through the Western Lowlands during the late-glacial interval (Kennett and Shackleton 1975; Leventer et al. 1982; Broecker et al. 1988) provided cold-air drainage and a fluvial disturbance regime that favored persistence of spruce and other boreal conifers up to 800 years after regional climatic amelioration. We hypothesize that eastward diversion of the Mississippi River through the Bell City/Oran Gap effectively after 14,500 yr B.P. cut off the Western Lowlands from receiving glacial meltwater and altered the fluvial disturbance regime, resulting in local extinction of boreal species (Royall et al. 1991; P. A. Delcourt and Delcourt 1996).

Cool-temperate species of oak and hickory probably dominated crests of sand ridges in the Western Lowlands after 14,500 yr B.P. Cool-temperate deciduous taxa, including beech, sugar maple, and basswood, would have occupied mesic slopes along sand ridges, with ash becoming more prevalent in more frequently flooded bottomlands (Robertson et al. 1978). The late-glacial increase in hornbeam, which probably grew in moist bottomlands and sand-bar margins surrounding the Powers Fort Swale, occurred about 2,000 years before similar increases occurred in paleoecological sites distributed from Missouri to Kentucky and Tennessee (H. R. Delcourt and Delcourt 1994) and may have been favored by a local decrease in the magnitude of fluvial disturbance at Powers Fort Swale.

Buttonbush, today typical of stream and lake margins from the Gulf of Mexico to the Great Lakes and New England (Fernald 1950), first established in the littoral zone of Powers Fort Swale 14,500 yr B.P., indicates local climatic amelioration. Changes in the composition of aquatic plants, including increases in bur reed, spatter dock, and water lily, indicate an increase in extent of shallow-water littoral environment at Powers Fort Swale through the late-glacial interval. This evidence is consistent with an interpretation of the onset of a long-term drop in groundwater level in the Western Lowlands after diversion of higher-energy Mississippi River floodwaters east of Crowley's Ridge.

Between 9,500 and 4,500 yr B.P., cool-temperate deciduous taxa either decreased in representation or were eliminated from the pollen record. Conversely, taxa today restricted in range primarily south of 40°N latitude, such as bald cypress and sweetgum (Fowells 1965), increased during the early and middle Holocene intervals. Oak, ash, and hickory increased in representation in the pollen record from Powers Fort Swale. Ash, sweetgum, and buttonbush grew in a seasonally inundated habitat at the margin of Powers Fort Swale.

During the middle Holocene, an increase occurred in

pollen values for goosefoot and ragweed, taxa adapted to invasion of open mudflats exposed by seasonably lowered water table. High and variable representation of grass in the early and middle Holocene is interpreted as evidence for local cane thickets inhabiting open areas marginal to the swale, similar to those occurring in southeastern Missouri today (Steyermark 1963). The aquatic assemblage, with increased representation of spatter dock and knotweed (not shown in Figure 8.8), reflects the occurrence of more extensive shallow-water environment around the swale.

After 4,500 yr B.P., pollen assemblages from Powers Fort Swale were similar in both species composition and relative abundance of each taxon to the modern pollen spectrum from Powers Fort Swale. Oak decreased by nearly 40%, whereas mesic and hydric taxa such as bald cypress, willow, ash, elm, planer tree, sycamore, and locust (the latter three not shown in Figure 8.8) all increased. Late Holocene climates were characterized by increased precipitation (H. R. Delcourt et al. 1986), which would have resulted in a rise in groundwater level and increased overbank flood frequency of the Little Black River. Higher available moisture permitted the reestablishment of mesic tree species. Increased areal extent of standing water favored populations of hydric trees in bottomland swamps. Increased frequency of overbank flooding of the Little Black River produced fluvially disturbed, open area suitable for reexpansion of willow.

Ragweed reached a peak of 20% around 600 yr B.P., then decreased to about 7%, and finally increased in the Historic period to its present value of 20%. The peak in ragweed at 600 yr B.P. coincides with the first, isolated, stratigraphic occurrence of maize pollen and the radiocarbon-dated Mississippian Powers Phase occupation (Price 1978). Ragweed and maize pollen are thus indicators of prehistoric anthropogenic disturbance, including land clearance and cultivation of terrace uplands located several hundred meters west of the Powers Fort Swale.

CONCLUSIONS

As a basis for interpreting the paleovegetational context of the Sloan site, we have prepared a vegetation map (Figure 8.9) for 10,000 yr B.P. for the central Mississippi Alluvial Valley and adjacent upland areas of the Ozark Plateaus and the Blufflands (the loess-mantled uplands located directly east of the central Mississippi Alluvial Valley). This map is based upon pollen spectra available from three paleoecological sites that directly date from 10,000 yr B.P. (Hood Lake, Powers Fort Swale, and Cupola Pond). Because these three sites with continuous sedimentations indicate minimal vegetational change between 10,000 and 9,000 yr B.P., we also make paleovegetational inferences using the oldest pollen spectra from three additional sites with basal radiocarbon dates of about 8,500 to 9,000 yr B.P. (Old Field, Big Lake, and Pemiscot Bayou). For 10,000 yr B.P., the geographic mapping of the several vegetation types is generalized to correspond with the major landforms and the distribution of soil types across the region.

At 10,000 yr B.P., the Ozark Plateaus were vegetated with oak-hickory savanna; wildfire may have been an important disturbance agent keeping the vegetation relatively open. Along the Ozark border, where the topography was more deeply dissected by river gorges and the upland surface was capped by a thin veneer of loess, wildfire would have been less frequent, and a closed-canopy forest containing an admixture of mesic hardwood trees would have grown. Similar mesic forests dominated for example by beech, maple, and basswood, with an understory of hornbeam, characterized the thick loess regions of both Crowley's Ridge and the Blufflands. Within the central Mississippi Alluvial Valley, the relict, braided-stream terraces of both the Eastern and Western Lowlands were occupied by oak-hickory forest. Species of oak and hickory grew on the braided-stream bars and sand dunes, and lake basins such as Hood Lake occupied abandoned stream channels. Backswamps located in seasonally inundated floodplains of meandering streams were occupied by ash, sweetgum, and bald cypress, along with other riparian species such as willow, elm, and planer tree.

Thus, by 10,000 yr B.P., the last substantial populations of boreal trees had become extinct in the Western Lowlands and adjacent uplands, with only trace pollen percentages of spruce, fir, and tamarack reflecting the persistence of small populations in locally favorable sites until about 8,500 yr B.P. At 10,000 yr B.P., nearly all the warm-temperate plant taxa that characterized the middle and late Holocene had migrated northward and were distributed throughout the region. The combination of relatively high groundwater table and the southwest-to-northeast continuity of riparian corridors maintained by meandering streams facilitated development of an early Holocene

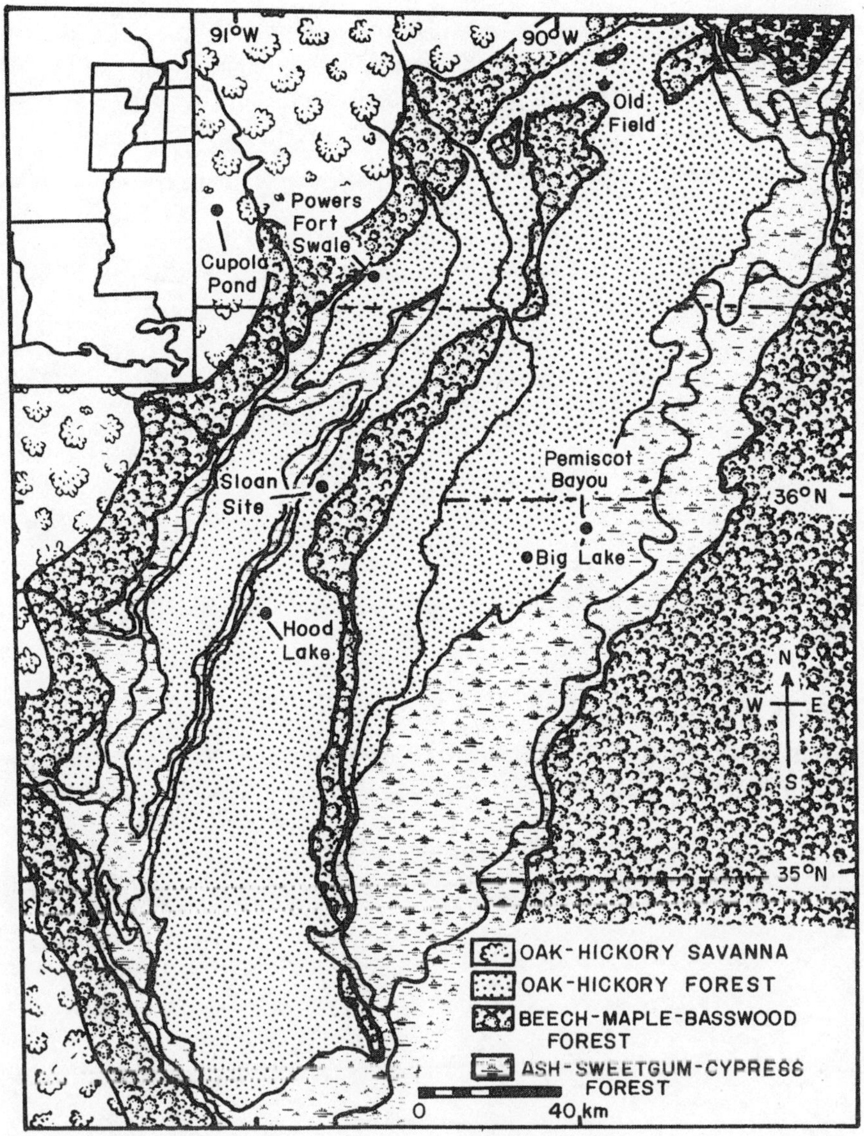

Figure 8.9 Paleovegetation map for the central Mississippi Alluvial Valley and adjacent uplands at 10,000 yr B.P. (base map modified from Saucier, chapter 7).

lowland landscape with areally contiguous wetlands. Bald cypress became established in backswamps and lake margins of the Western Lowlands, reaching Hood Lake before 11,275 yr B.P. and Powers Fort Swale by at least 9,500 yr B.P. Consequently, at the time of the Sloan site occupation, decay-resistant bald cypress wood was locally available for construction of canoes for navigation of riverways in the Western Lowlands. At 10,000 yr B.P., upland forests would have provided both mast trees and other edible plants. The abundance of aquatic habitats would have provided both fish and waterfowl, and the diverse landscape mosaic would have supported a variety of game.

ACKNOWLEDGMENTS

We thank Paul Pickel, of Jonesboro, Arkansas, for permission to core sediments from Hood Lake. Joanne Juchniewicz, Preston Miracle, and David Anderson provided invaluable assistance in the fieldwork and successful recovery of sediment cores from Hood Lake. Fieldwork, radiocarbon dates, and the laboratory analysis of Hood Lake sediments were supported by the Memphis Division, U.S. Army Corps of Engineers, through a contract to David Anderson, Project Director, Garrow & Associates, Inc., Atlanta, Georgia. Sediment cores from Powers Fort Swale were collected by a field crew that included Jolee Pearson Gardner, Donald Rosowitz, and E. Newman Smith, Jr. The Powers Fort Swale study was supported by the National Park Service through a grant to James E. Price. David Anderson, Dan F. Morse, Phyllis Morse, James E. Price, Cynthia Price, and Roger Saucier graciously offered insightful suggestions and advice throughout the analysis of paleoecological data from Hood Lake and Powers Fort Swale and the completion of this chapter.

9
An Overview of the Dalton Period in Northeastern Arkansas and in the Southeastern United States

DAN F. MORSE

The inhabitants of, and visitors to, northeastern Arkansas have always been curious about the mounds, pots, and stone artifacts so evident in the landscape (Morse and Morse 1983:17–30). The post-Archaic prehistoric and Historic periods were emphasized by collectors, treasure seekers, and museums throughout the nineteenth century and during the first half of the twentieth century. Museum-sponsored and private surveys during those periods included those of the Smithsonian, Capt. C. W. Riggs, Putnam Museum (Davenport, Iowa), Peabody Museum of Harvard University, C. B. Moore, University of Arkansas Museum, and the Alabama Museum of Natural History.

Museum collections tend to be heavily biased toward artifacts characteristic of the latest major prehistoric deposits of a region. For instance, the Missouri Historical Society's collection from the central Mississippi Valley consists mostly of whole pots. Artifacts collected and donated from the northeastern Arkansas region are characteristic, with rare exceptions, of the Late Period Mississippian. These late sites are numerous and obvious, being largely fortified towns, and only a very few artifacts representative of the Woodland period are present. Only a single Dalton point (of circa five hundred artifacts) exists in the Missouri Historical Society's collection from the central Mississippi Valley. Modern treasure collectors are equally biased toward the pottery vessels of the latest prominent prehistoric period but today put more emphasis upon stone artifacts, particularly fluted points, largely as a result of local professional reports on early complexes.

The modern archeological era in the central Mississippi Valley was heralded by the publication in 1951 of *Archaeological Survey in the Lower Mississippi Alluvial Valley, 1940–1947* by Phillips et al. In that volume there was the beginning of the recognition of earlier periods: "While there is so far little indication of a pre-ceramic period in the Survey Area, such sites are presumed to exist . . ." (Phillips et al. 1951:429). In 1952, Griffin still lamented "Unfortunately, there is very little evidence for the presence of man in the Central Mississippi Valley during the Archaic Period" (p. 228). It is interesting that in Griffin's fig. 205, "Dalton" was placed just shy of 1000 B.C. within a column including northeastern Arkansas. The potential richness of this region in the Archaic period was already indicated. In 1926 when Calvin Brown illustrated fluted points found in northwestern Mississippi (his figs. 33, 45), he even described one point as "fluted on both faces" (p. 138) and clustered three fluted points, a Dalton and two other lanceolate points, into a type he named "Coldwater." Brown's pioneering work continued to be ignored or forgotten by many investigators: "Poverty Point: an essentially preceramic period, the earliest we have or are likely to have in the geologically recent alluvial valley of the Mississippi River" (Phillips 1970:19). Geological guesses of the age of the alluvial surfaces of the valley were late: "Fisk assumed all meander belts of the Mississippi River to be no older than 2000 years, the oldest sub delta to be no more than 4000 years, and all outwash plains formed by a braided river regime to be no more than 6000 years old" (Saucier 1981:9; also see Williams 1954:35). In other words, in the 1944 chronology of Fisk, still followed as late as 1967, the alluvial valley surface was "created" about the time of Bishop Ussher's world at 4004 B.C. It is no wonder then that fluted points and early lanceolate forms were not recognized here until the late 1960s. In 1936, Wakefield and Dellinger illustrated a typical Dalton point (their fig. 3) as a possible primitive surgical tool used by the "Mound Builders." Saucier (1968, 1974) reconstructed a new chronology in 1968 based on radiocarbon dates and the recognition that Dalton points in the central Mississippi Valley did not necessarily mean a backward people practicing a four-thousand-year-old culture in northeastern Arkansas.

When I arrived in northeastern Arkansas in late 1967 with the beginning of the Arkansas Archeological Survey, I was confronted with early artifacts in a presumably late setting. On 7 October 1967 the second accession number was for a classic fluted point found at site 3PO53, located in the Western Lowlands, in Poinsett County, Arkansas. Without hesitation I assumed that the Fisk chronology was in error and this was later confirmed during conversations with Roger Saucier in 1967 and 1968 (Morse 1969) and by the discovery of a mastodon, tapir, and possible sloth in a single deposit in the Eastern Lowlands (Morse 1970). This attitude allowed us to proceed immediately in the investigation of Dalton so as to develop hypotheses concerning the Dalton tool assemblage and settlement system (Morse 1971a,b, 1973), which were first tested in 1970 by the excavation of the Brand site (Goodyear 1974).

THE CONCEPT OF DALTON

The Sloan site is a "Dalton" site. The term "Dalton" was first used by Carl Chapman, who based it on the surname of S. P. Dalton (1892–1965) of Jefferson City, Missouri, who was a member and later chief justice of the Missouri Supreme Court (C. H. Chapman 1948; Anonymous 1965). Judge Dalton also was an avocational archaeologist and trustee of the Missouri Archaeological Society. He discovered and reported 134 archeological sites to the director of the University of Missouri American Archaeological Division, Carl Chapman (Dalton 1960, 1961). One, known as the "Dalton" site in Cole County, had been exposed, buried five to eight feet deep, by a highway borrow pit (editor's footnote in Logan 1952:69; C. H. Chapman 1975:135–143). The Dalton site is located east of Jefferson City adjacent to the Osage River. Construction of a bridge nearby necessitated the removal of almost two meters of fill, which exposed the Dalton deposits. The region, which became known locally as the "badlands" because nothing grew after the borrow process, is known for its richness in Dalton points. One point found north of Jefferson City is rumored to have measured "ten to twelve inches" in length (personal communication from Jim Duncan, who grew up in the vicinity of the Dalton site). Artifacts recovered by Judge Dalton included several examples of the distinctive lanceolate "Dalton point" and end scrapers but none of the ground stone tools known to be distinctive of a later Archaic time period (C. H. Chapman 1948:138). Confirmation of the 1948 hypothesized primary position of Dalton in the Missouri archaeological sequence was made in 1949 and 1950 at Graham Cave (Logan 1952; C. H. Chapman 1952).

Dalton points and hence a Dalton complex or period is today recognized over almost the entire southeastern United States, the Midwest, and the eastern edge of the Plains. Until about 1960, however, Dalton points were thought to be mostly concentrated within the state of Missouri. Marie Wormington (1957:114) early recognized that Dalton points were widespread outside Missouri. Cambron and Hulse (1960) reported that a substantial number of Dalton points had been recorded from twenty-one sites in the Tennessee Valley of Alabama and Tennessee. They considered Dalton points to be "Paleo-Indian or Transitional Paleo-Indian" (1960:11). The Stanfield-Worley bluff shelter site, overlooking the Tennessee Valley in northwestern Alabama, was first excavated in 1960 and 1961 (DeJarnette et al. 1962). The lowest level contained "Points of the Dalton-Meserve class" and the "Big Sandy I point." Later excavation demonstrated that the "Big Sandy I" points were stratigraphically superior to the basal Dalton level (Craig Sheldon, personal communication, 1975).

The "Meserve" point (Perino 1985:252) is thought to be Dalton in type, or at least part of the Dalton complex. F. G. Meserve was head of the Department of Biology at Grand Island College, Grand Island, Nebraska. He excavated parts of two *Bison occidentalis* skeletons in 1923 (Meserve and Barbour 1932) at a location reported to him by two high-school students. While excavating one of the bison he discovered a lanceolate point beneath a scapula. The point was later donated by Professor Meserve to the Nebraska State Museum. A second point, a resharpened Dalton-like specimen, was found at the same site in 1931 by Nebraska State Museum personnel "amongst a bunch of ribs" (Meserve and Barbour 1932:241; Barbour and Schultz 1932). "Meserve" as a complex may occupy a geographical buffer zone between Folsom and Dalton. Meserve points, like Folsom, were made by Plains-oriented bison hunters. Dalton is thought to be characteristic of deer hunters in the eastern deciduous or mixed deciduous-southern pine forests (see Delcourt and Delcourt 1981). Other fluted point styles were characteristic of the caribou/elk hunters of the northern spruce and jack pine forests of the Great Lakes region (Morse et al. 1996).

The earliest professional recognition in southeastern Missouri was made about 1950–1952 by Stephen Williams (1954:35), who also recognized the presence of fluted points in the same region (Williams and Stoltman 1965). The earliest professional recognition of Dalton points in northeastern Arkansas was probably by Gregory Perino, who visited the Lace site in 1958 (Perino 1967:10–13). Redfield (1971:42) later stated: "This is the most important and impressive Dalton site examined by this project. It was the original site which got Ford interested in the problem of Late Paleo-Indian materials in the valley." Perino showed two Memphis amateurs, Charley Scheel and John Moselage, Dalton sites so that they could collect them and begin to discover other sites.

Williams independently influenced Alden Redfield to do his dissertation at Harvard on the basis of a survey for Dalton sites in Missouri and Arkansas directed by James A. Ford during 1961 and 1962 (Redfield 1971). The field crew consisted of the very two amateurs influenced by Gregory Perino. It was a survey reminiscent of the nineteenth century (Lindsay 1993) but was extremely efficient and successful. This survey recorded 366 sites in six survey areas (one Missouri and five Arkansas) and 769 cataloged collections were made (Redfield 1971). Sixteen sites were tested. In total, 436 Dalton and 269 other early points were collected. There was little doubt by 1961–1962 that the Memphis area was rich in deposits dating no later than the early Holocene (Brain 1970), but for some unknown reason the importance of these discoveries was not immediately understood by many investigators (Williams and Stoltman 1965:675, 678).

Rodgers Shelter in west-central Missouri was excavated from 1963 to 1968 (Wood and McMillan 1976). A major importance of these excavations to Dalton studies is that ^{14}C dates were obtained from wood charcoal associated with Dalton hearths, a unique primary context for this complex (Goodyear 1982; see following). These early dates are now being substantiated by ^{14}C dates on the later Bolen point in Florida (Dunbar et al. 1988; Dunbar et al. 1989) and early side-notched points at Dust Cave in Alabama, located virtually next door to the Stanfield-Worley shelter (Goldman-Finn and Driskell 1994). Dalton as a period is now dated at 10,700 to 10,200 yr B.P. and is recognized to be at least partially if not essentially contemporaneous with Folsom.

NORTHEASTERN ARKANSAS

The beginning of our Arkansas Dalton investigation in 1967 was an attempt to reconstruct a Dalton assemblage and make some interpretations of Dalton behavior. It was a conscious effort to go beyond the "Were Dalton points Archaic or Paleoindian" and "How many point varieties existed" ruts. The first field test took place in 1970 at the Brand site after a year-long review of potential sites. Confirmation of a hypothesized Dalton assemblage based on surface finds and Upper Paleolithic studies by François and Denise Bordes was accomplished (Morse 1971a; Goodyear 1974). In addition, a controversy about basic Dalton behavior in Arkansas and Missouri was initiated (Morse 1971a; Goodyear 1974; Price and Krakker 1975; Schiffer 1975a). Brand was followed by the accidental discovery and subsequent salvage of Sloan in 1974.

The Dalton complex in northeastern Arkansas has emerged as more abundant and sophisticated than the Dalton complexes known elsewhere (Figure 9.1). Hundreds of sites and thousands of points are known to have existed. Because of extensive cultivation involving considerable land modification for rice irrigation (Medford 1972), numerous additional sites and artifacts have been destroyed. Northeastern Arkansas is a relic-hunter's paradise. Unfortunately, almost all of the artifacts found here disappear into the obscure curio shelves of relic collectors, middle-class descendants of the European Renaissance dilettantes.

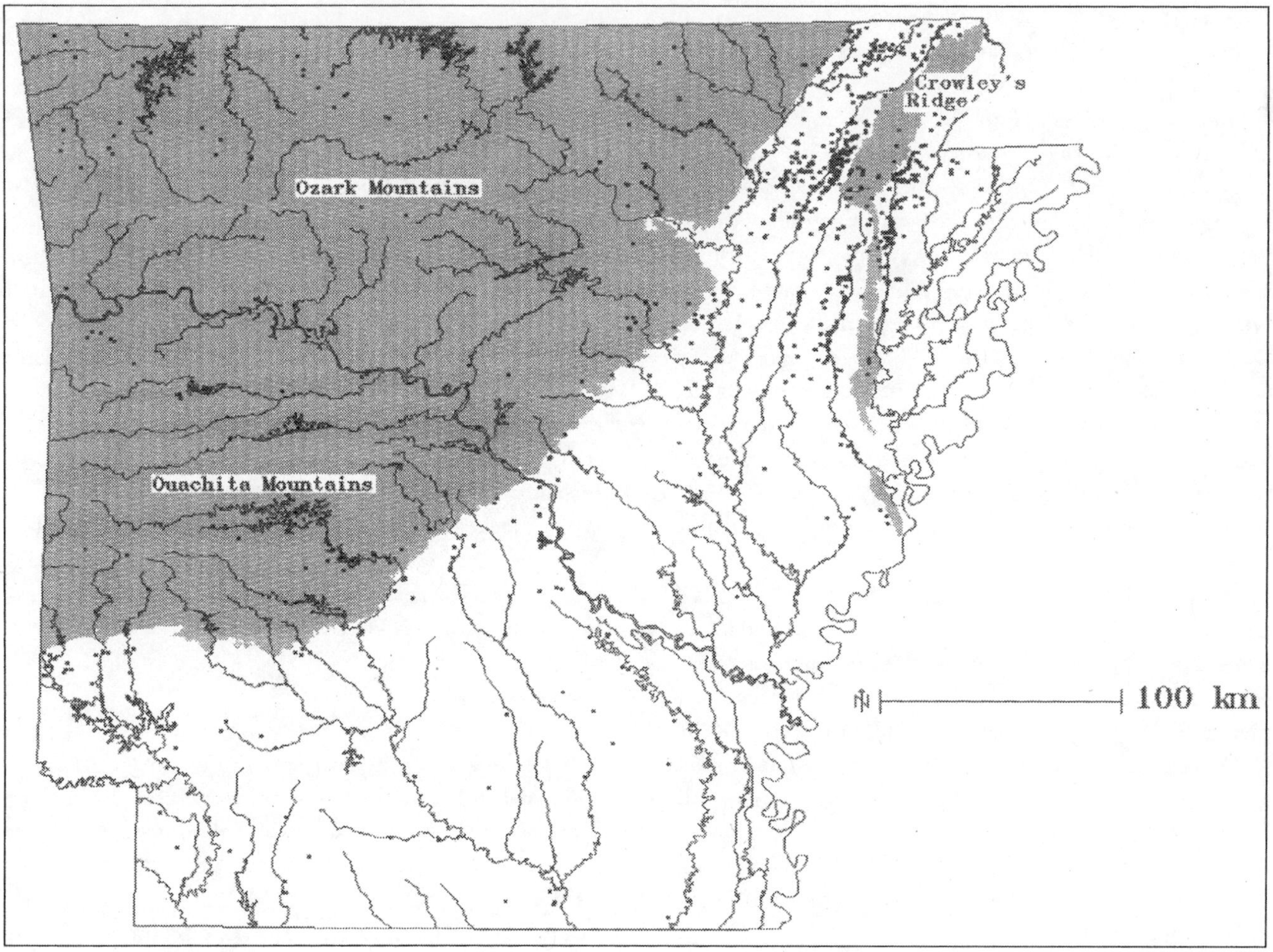

Figure 9.1 Distribution of Dalton-period sites in Arkansas.

Professional sampling is just barely adequate to expose this richness. Over 750 Dalton sites were recorded in northeastern Arkansas during the first twenty-eight years of the existence of the Arkansas Archeological Survey. One important site, Brand, was partially excavated (Goodyear 1974). Unfortunately, the site was vandalized before a second season could be organized. An important cache of Dalton artifacts found by a collector of another site was analyzed (Morse 1971b), but, unfortunately, the actual site location was not divulged by the collector; in fact, a false location was given. It is fortunate we have been able to learn as much as we have. The Sloan site represents an incredible archaeological discovery. Only some fourteen years after the recognition that Dalton remains are early and widespread, a Dalton site was excavated that demonstrates that late (Dalton) Paleoindian behavior included the practice of cemetery burial.

After the actual excavation of the Sloan site, I felt we needed more data from the immediate surrounding locality. An intensive pedestrian survey was started. Money for an assistant to help in the survey was not forthcoming and the project was put off. Today, the region where Sloan is located has been modified so extensively by agribusiness that an intensive pedestrian survey would not provide important additional data. It is difficult to make a case for emergency money when so many projects compete for the same limited funds.

We were able to map several of the sites near Sloan (Figure 9.2). Virtually every sand dune had site debris exposed on its surface. Dalton-period artifacts were scattered

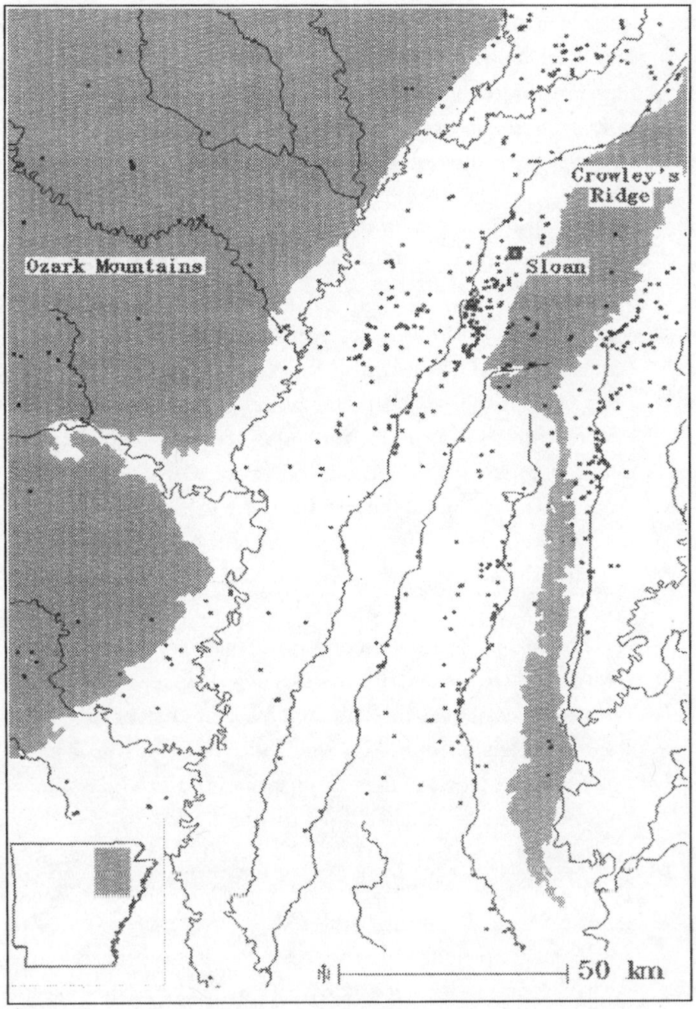

Figure 9.2 Distribution of Dalton-period sites within the Cache River Basin, showing the location of the Sloan site.

and indicative of short-term extraction-camp occupation. One exception was 3GE3, the Forkum site discovered and tested during the 1962 Ford-Redfield Survey (Redfield 1971:41). This site is located about 1-1/2 kilometers northeast of Sloan. It was considered in 1962 to be the richest Dalton site in the area surveyed around the town of Light. The Forkum site is a prime candidate for the base settlement where the people buried at Sloan lived. When we visited the site on 18 February 1975, there were two neighboring 0.1-hectare scatters, each on a sandy knoll connected by a slight ridge. A Dalton adze, a notched abrader, and a Pitkin Chert uniface were collected. These are artifacts reminiscent of the Lace site in Poinsett County, which has been interpreted as a Dalton-period base settlement (Morse and Morse 1983). The Ford-Redfield Survey purchased four Dalton points from the owner and found three during a single visit. The owner would not allow them to finish a test pit that they had excavated to a depth of 55 centimeters under his watchful and suspicious eyes (field notes in the Arkansas Archeological Survey archives).

Probably the most impressive Dalton-period site recorded in the counties north of Lace is located only about 9.5 kilometers to the southwest of Sloan, but on the other side (west) of the Cache River. This is site 3LW13, where early Paleoindian fluted points have also been recovered. It is located on a prominent knoll and was occupied through much of prehistory, but most intensively in the late Pleistocene and early Holocene. It is very similar to the Lace site in size and history of occupation.

The Hawkins Cache (3LW654; Morse 1971b) was probably found about 8 kilometers southwest of site

3LW13 on the west side of the Cache River. A smaller probable Dalton-period base settlement village, which originally had been reported as the location of the Hawkins Cache, is site 3LW89, located about 9 kilometers south of 3LW13 and only about 3 kilometers southeast of the probable Hawkins cache site.

What appears to have been a rather elaborate scam involved site 3GE26. Rumors about the Sloan-site "caches of Dalton points" had leaked out into the relic collection world. So "caches" of Dalton points and even one consisting of five bannerstones and a grooved ax were allegedly found at depths of "eight feet," and upwards of two hundred points were sold to three major buyers in the eastern United States for exorbitant prices. Buyers were reportedly shown the backhoe ditches dug at the site to convince them of the validity of the find. I wrote one of the buyers, but he did not respond. I visited the site with some law-enforcement personnel, and no end scrapers, bifaces, or adzes were present. A "junk box" reportedly filled with site debris was examined at a relic show by a friend and no Dalton-period artifacts were present. Caveat emptor!

The region around 3LW13 (including 3GE3, 3GE94, 3LW89, and 3LW654) may be the center of a Dalton-period Cache River watershed territory similar to what has been interpreted for the Lace site on the L'Anguille River (Morse 1971a, 1976). The Cache River Basin is about 5000 square kilometers in maximum extent (Schiffer and House 1975:11, fig. 2) or about double the size of the L'Anguille Basin. In both cases the major sites are located in a tight cluster near the center of the watershed and sites are less evident at the extremes of the basin (Arkansas Archeological Survey files, Anderson et al. 1989). I have interpreted the bulk of Dalton sites to represent temporary extraction-camp debris. Less than 5% of the recorded sites have been interpreted as (1) long-term base settlements or villages and (2) cemeteries. Figures 9.3 and 9.4 illustrate this interpretation of archaeological site debris in northeastern Arkansas.

Schiffer (1975a,b) interpreted the northeastern Arkansas site debris differently. He suggested seasonal camps of various sizes being moved fairly constantly across drainages and to one or more of the uplands bordering the western valley. However the distribution of sites in northeastern Arkansas clearly indicates major clusters of activity in a *single* portion of each watershed or basin. There are five such clusters in this region. Schiffer's model just does not seem to us to match the recorded site debris. His statement that "the remains of isolated, single occupational hunting-butchering camps fall below the current threshold of archeological visibility" (1975a:111) is also just not valid and cannot be used as an argument to negate our hypothesis. Archaeologists have recorded single-episode hunting camps of the Protohistoric and late-period Mississippian, including a bear skeleton associated with a Nodena point.

Problems with constantly moving populations are numerous. The Dalton tool kit is large. Also, we infer dugout canoes, houses, baskets, wooden bowls, masks, and so forth from the presence of woodworking tools. Older people and young children can be burdens during constant moving unless they can be left in a campsite to be reoccupied soon. We have resorted to a Schiffer-like model for Archaic and some late Woodland expressions, and even some non-Valley Dalton groups.

The resources are varied in northeastern Arkansas. Each watershed, however, originates with springs in an upland where chert is available and the associated river flows toward the Mississippi via a lowland rich in seasonal plant and animal life. Moving a camp site in the late Pleistocene might not make much sense. In the Archaic of the early to middle Holocene, movement over larger regions may have made greater sense because of the environmental disruption from less water and a warmer climate. With the advent of horticulture, increased population, and more water, winter base settlements in smaller watersheds seem to have become characteristic. The Protohistoric provinces noted by De Soto are interpreted as watershed political territories (Morse and Morse 1990). Watershed association seems to have been the norm, not the exception, in northeastern Arkansas.

The primary association of a Dalton-period settlement, whatever its nature, is an ecotone consisting of an upland-lowland border. This is evident in Arkansas (Figure 9.1), in Mississippi (Sam Brookes, personal communication), and in North Carolina (Coe 1964). A primary question is why are there so many more remains in northeastern Arkansas than in the rest of Arkansas. Obviously, we have concentrated on this prehistoric period, and extensive farming practices have exposed most of the late Pleistocene surfaces. We also think that the presence of Crowley's Ridge as an upland apart from the Ozark Escarpment has essentially tripled the number of ecotones in northeastern Arkansas, and we should expect triple the number

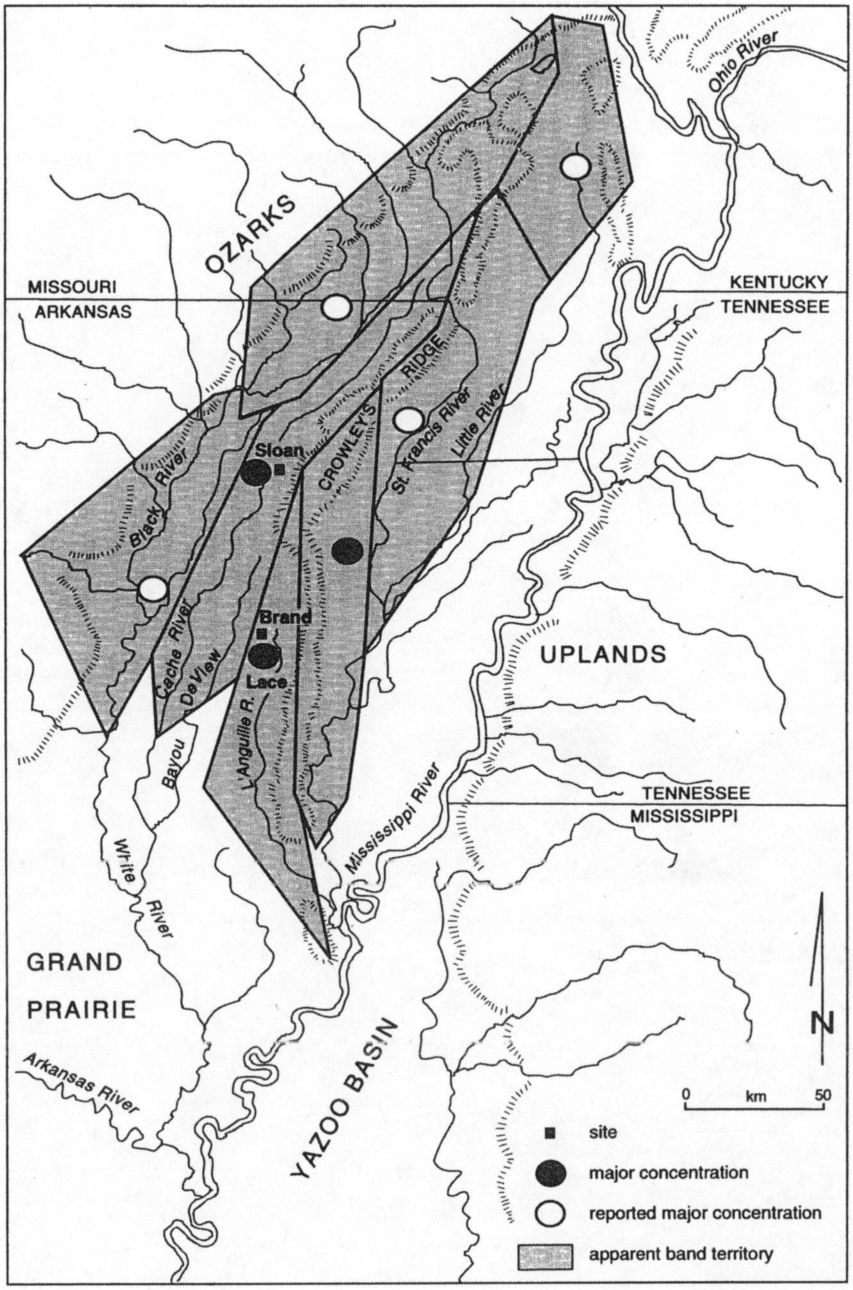

Figure 9.3 Distribution of hypothesized Dalton local groups in northeastern Arkansas (after Morse and Morse 1983:fig. 4.1).

of sites. This region is unique and environmentally rich. Exotic stone such as Pitkin Chert only occurs in the Ozarks, and Crescent Quarry Chert, suitable for large bifaces, occurs just south of St. Louis. Raw materials most suitable for adzes and red ocher are unique to Crowley's Ridge. Trade in stone and red ocher would have reinforced a network of bands in the valley. If we assume that a band or local group population was around twenty-five to fifty and that about a half dozen bands were present in northeastern Arkansas, the population of the band network would have been around 150–300. Band size is based on the supposed "optimal" number of four active mature males to conduct a drive ambush for deer (Martin 1973). A group of two to three active mature females is thought to be the optimal unit for gathering wild plants (Martin 1973). An average hunting-gathering local group

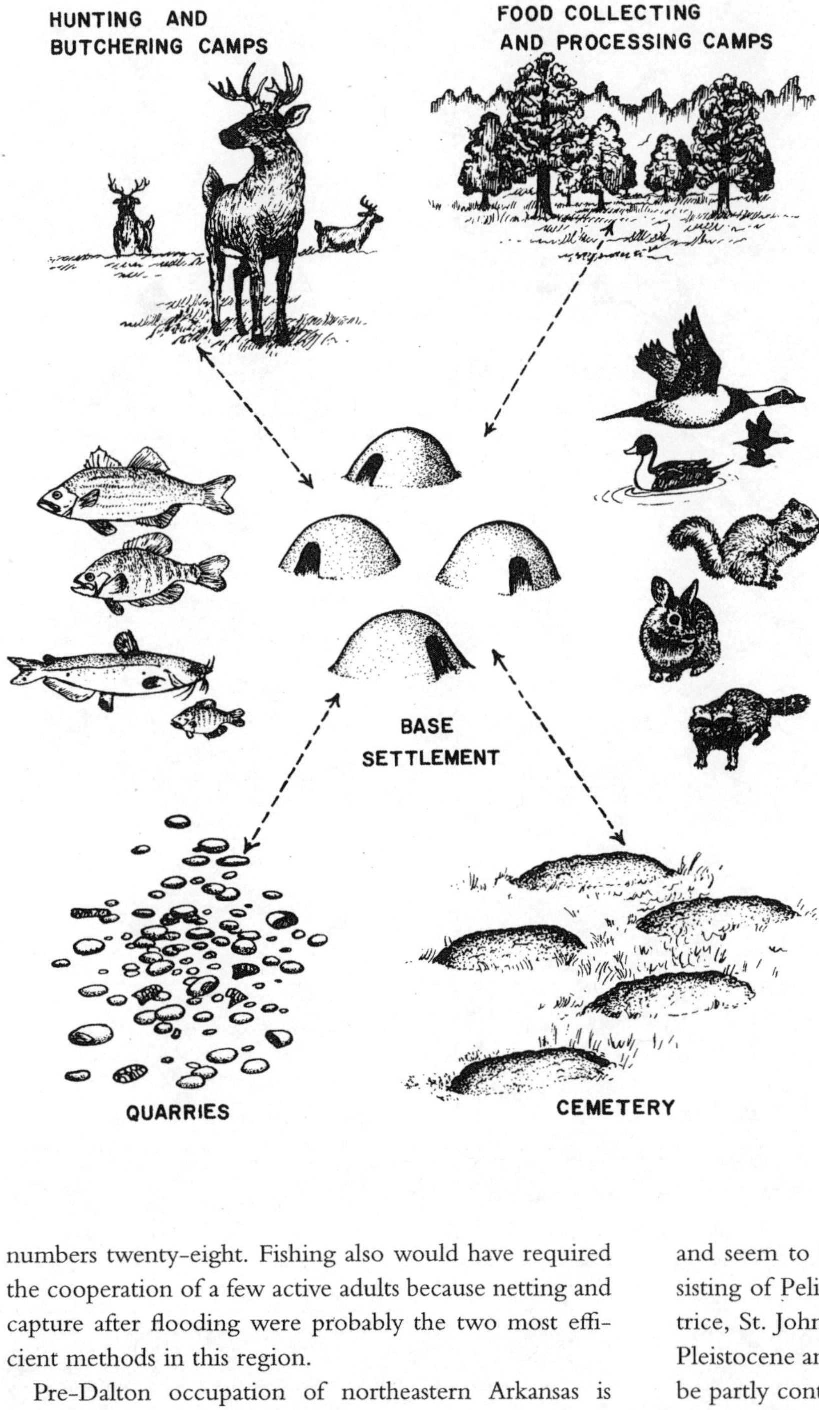

Figure 9.4 Distribution of hypothesized northeastern Arkansas settlements during the Dalton period (after Morse and Morse 1983:fig. 4.6).

numbers twenty-eight. Fishing also would have required the cooperation of a few active adults because netting and capture after flooding were probably the two most efficient methods in this region.

Pre-Dalton occupation of northeastern Arkansas is thought to be represented by discoveries of more traditional fluted points. There are at least three varieties: (1) Crowley's Ridge, thought to be typical of a basic Clovis type; (2) Sedgwick, thought to be more Folsom-like; and (3) Pelican, with a very wide body and a relatively narrow base. Pelican points are very rare in northeastern Arkansas and seem to be peripheral to a Louisiana tradition consisting of Pelican, San Patrice, Hope variety, and San Patrice, St. Johns variety (Webb et al. 1971) during the late Pleistocene and early Holocene. Pelican points could well be partly contemporaneous with Dalton.

Figure 9.5 is a GIS map of the distribution of probable pre-Dalton fluted point localities in northeastern Arkansas. Note that the distribution is a more central one than that for Dalton as shown in Figure 9.1. It is possible that the distribution would look more like the Dalton one given a larger sample. However, the pre-Dalton distribu-

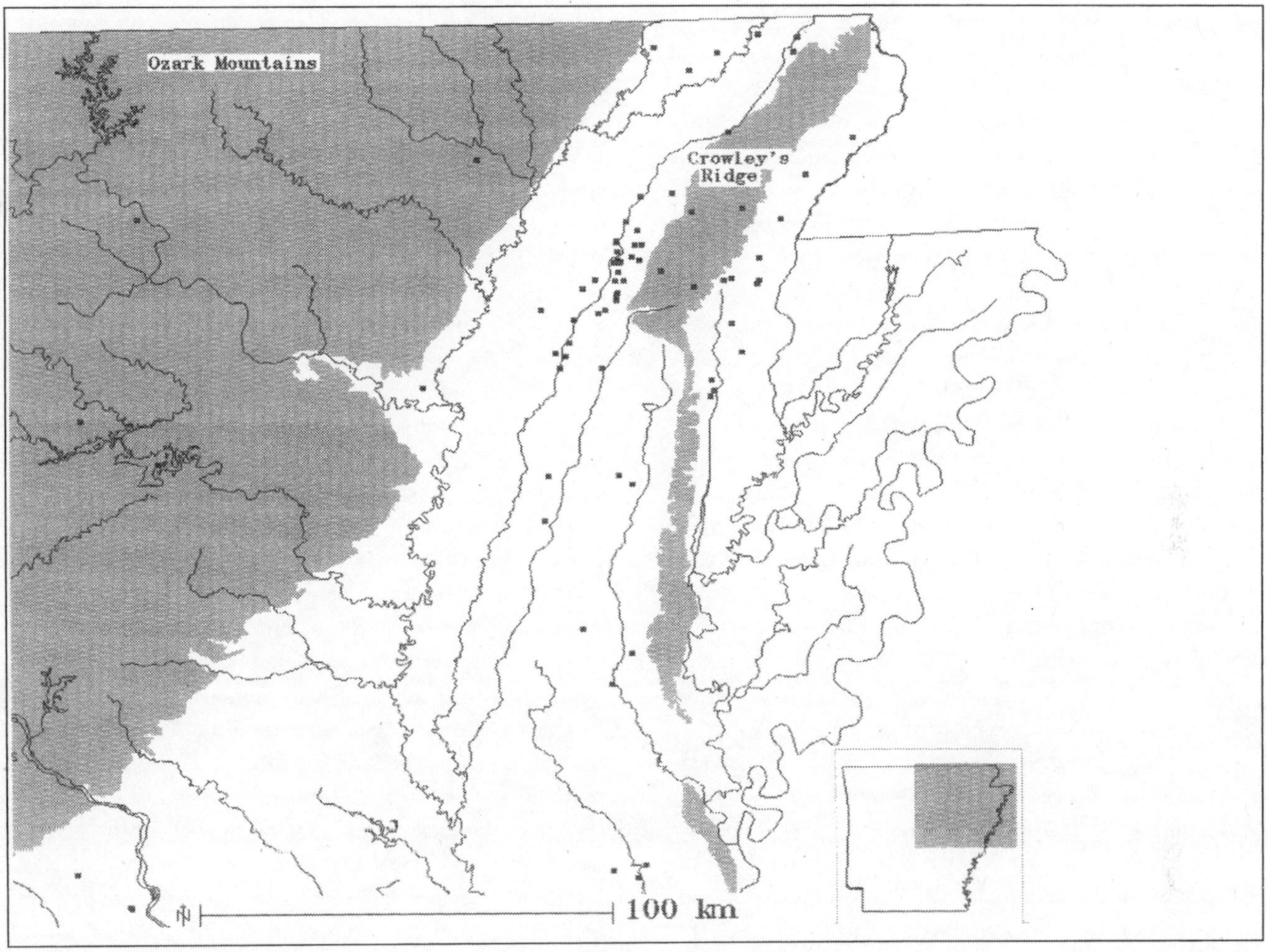

Figure 9.5 Distribution of pre-Dalton fluted points in northeastern Arkansas.

tion looks like a group of people focusing on two primary areas, located near the two sides of Crowley's Ridge. If a third expected concentration existed near the Ozark Escarpment, that concentration could be masked by Holocene alluvial deposits related to the modern Black River system. This supposition is supported by the reporting of traditional Clovis-like fluted points from a late Pleistocene land remnant at the edge of an alluvial fan created by the Black River near the Arkansas-Missouri border (Morse and Morse 1983:61).

There is an accelerator radiocarbon date of 10,890 ± 130 yr B.P. (NZA-1100) on a portion of the femur of a *Paleolama mirafica* found south of Senath, Missouri, just in the bootheel of Missouri (Morse and Graham 1991). This date demonstrates that the associated braided surfaces were available to Dalton hunters and to pre-Dalton hunters. However, the environment was varied but probably pretty swampy in many areas and not attractive to long-term occupation until the very end of the Pleistocene. The few Dalton points recovered from the eastern braided terrace that includes the town of Senath appear to be very late varieties thought to date right around 10,000 yr B.P.

Conclusions, admittedly based on very minimal data, are that pre-Dalton Paleoindians spent most of their time near Crowley's Ridge and near the Ozark Escarpment. The Eastern Lowlands were mainly characterized by active braided stream surfaces. A band or local group lived primarily on an escarpment 5 meters high located along a major channel. Hunting excursions eastward were rare and short-term and probably did not involve the hunting of megafauna, animals that would be difficult to transport to the more permanent settlement near the ridge. It appears that the more permanent settlements shifted along Crowley's Ridge, perhaps seasonally or perhaps just intermittently to take advantage of renewed resources.

On the west side of Crowley's Ridge evidently was another local group who concentrated their main settlements along the high terraces of a combined Cache–St. Francis–Black meandering river that flowed essentially within the present-day Cache River floodplain. An expected third local group would have similarly exploited the Ozark Escarpment. Whether two or more groups existed there of course is not known because of the masking of alluvial deposits. Gillam (1995) concluded that primary consideration was the availability of chert sources.

My current basic view of Paleoindians in northeastern Arkansas is as follows. Three early Paleoindian local groups expanded into six local groups by late Paleoindian times. The main settlement change was a doubling of population, with each local group having a slightly smaller, more manageable territory to exploit. At about 11,000 yr B.P. there may have been 75–150 Paleoindians in northeastern Arkansas. By around 10,500 yr B.P., the number of people may have increased to around 150–300.

Post-Dalton remains are difficult to assess in northeastern Arkansas. The early notched-point horizon (Morse and Morse 1983:104) is a relatively new concept, and we have no contextual data. If we assume that the Cache River point is the major component of an early notched-point horizon, we can accumulate a basic data base for a distributional map. These data can be supplemented by obvious early notched examples such as San Patrice, St. Johns variety, and Kirk corner-notched varieties. The early Archaic stemmed-point horizon is represented by the Hardin point, and Hardin point location data can be added if insufficient data are present for the early Archaic distribution using only Cache River points. Virtually every northeastern Arkansas informant has heard of Dalton, Cache River, and Hardin points and have usually reported their presence where applicable when reporting a site. Figure 9.6 is a GIS distribution map of Cache River and Hardin point locations as represented by our files and collection.

THE DATING OF THE DALTON PERIOD

In chronological order in northeastern Arkansas there are now recognized three late Pleistocene Paleoindian fluted-point expressions and an early Holocene notched-point horizon followed in turn by an early Holocene stemmed-point horizon. There are no datable deposits, nor are there any stratified sites to prove this sequence. Two Dalton-period sites have been excavated, and both contained extensive Dalton remains in tight context. The Dalton period in northeastern Arkansas is obviously an exclusive one (i.e., only Dalton points were present in both excavations). The Brand-site Dalton deposit was capped by a wind-blown deposit thought to date near the end of the Pleistocene (chapter 7). Many of the artifacts were recovered from living floors below the wind-blown deposits or just within the lowest portion of that deposit. There were no other point styles in the deposits containing Dalton points. The Sloan-site Dalton deposits consisted of clusters of Dalton artifacts buried within a sand dune dating to about 18,000 yr B.P. Most of the Dalton artifacts were recovered lying on a flat plane, indicating that there was minimal disturbance involved and that the artifacts were deliberately buried, almost certainly in human graves. No other point styles were recovered as part of any of these deposits. This means that early notched points were not part of a Dalton complex and dated to a different period. It also means that Sedgwick and Crowley's Ridge/Clovis points also dated to a different time period. Based on the Clovis to Folsom continuum, Sedgwick points should date later than Clovis-like points, but pre-Dalton. Both Dalton and Sedgwick seem to have developed directly out of a Clovis-like (Crowley's Ridge) base, and the view of Sedgwick as a transitional style is now questioned. Notched and stemmed points stratigraphically always date later than Clovis-Folsom points and should date later than Dalton points because notched and stemmed points do not appear to be contemporaneous with Dalton points. No Dalton points appear to be associated with early notched points at Dust Cave in Alabama, for instance.

There is a curious physical attribute that changes through time: length of lateral grinding. Crowley's Ridge/Clovis, Sedgwick, and Pelican points are minimally laterally ground for approximately 40% of their length. There was little difference between the measured whole points (twenty-seven Sedgwick, 42%; twenty-two Crowley's Ridge, 40%; three Pelican, 40%). Many of the Sedgwick points had been resharpened after tip loss and their percentages may be exaggerated by this fact. The Dalton points found at the Brand site had an average of about 26% of the point length exhibiting lateral grinding (Goodyear 1974:table 1, p. 23). The average percentage

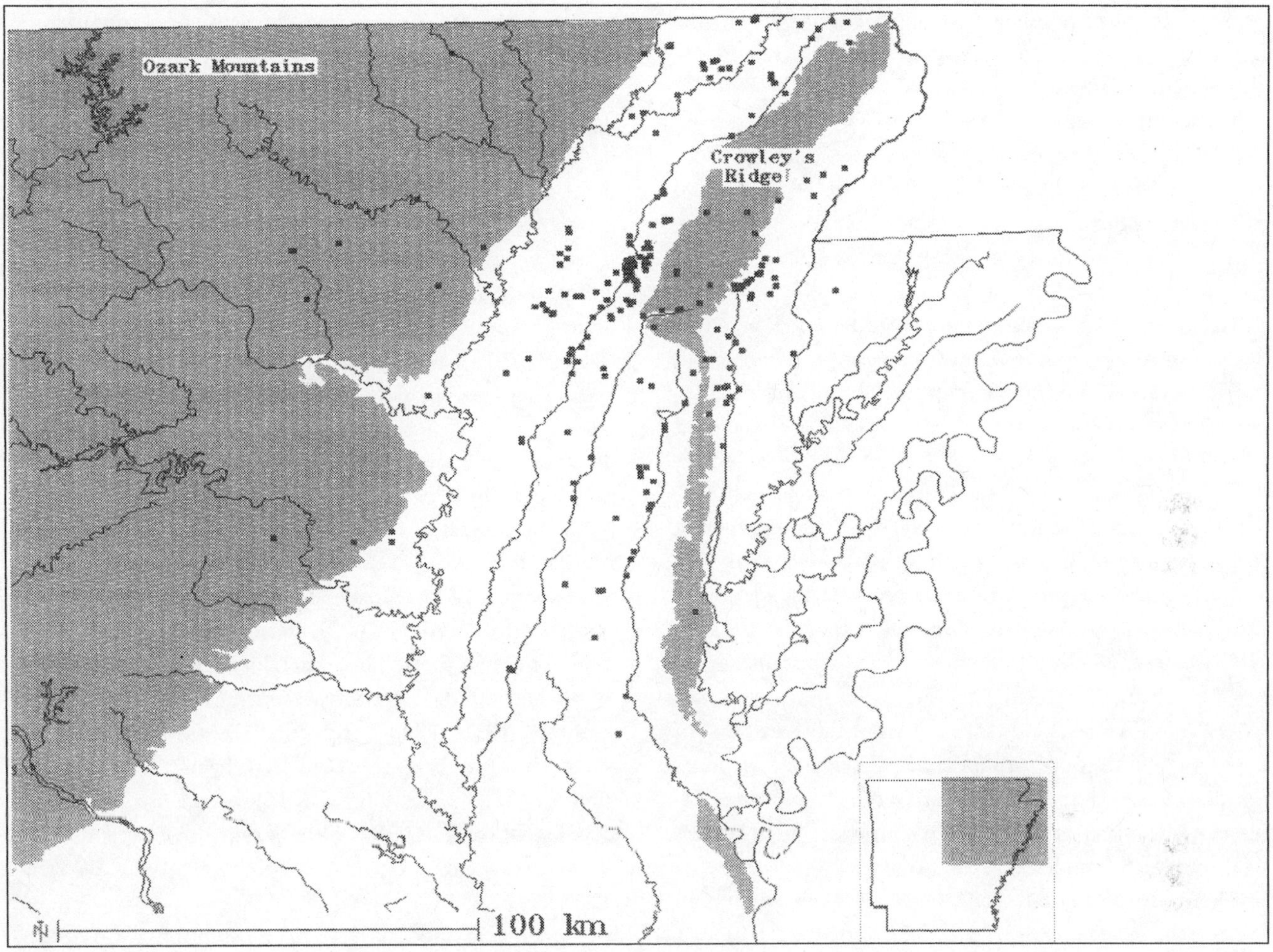

Figure 9.6 Distribution of early notched and stemmed points in northeastern Arkansas.

decrease in length of lateral grinding probably is due to a shift from a primary function as a penetrating projectile tip to a primary function as a butchering knife.

Lateral grinding is thought to have been done to provide a more secure binding and hence is an indication of hafting length. Waisted points tend to be laterally ground to a shoulder that is usually the widest part of the point. Titmus and Woods (1991) hypothesized another technological function for lateral grinding: to strengthen the point. In any case, the earlier fluted points were constructed in such a way that the tip was emphasized. Later Dalton points were constructed in such a way that the lateral edges were maximized and emphasized, indicating a primary function as a skinning/butchering knife. A primary function as a knife is also evident in later point styles based on beveling as a lateral retouch technique to rejuvenate lateral edges. Hardin, Kirk, and St. Charles points were so treated although like late-Dalton points the beveling was on the opposite (left) side from earlier Dalton points. This means that the Dalton point might have been resharpened with the point held tip in and later styles with the tip out. Bradley (chapter 4) believes this difference in beveling may be due to differences in cutting.

However, Cache River and Palmer-like points do not seem to have been consistently resharpened laterally. Many are simply too small. The makers of those points may have had other bifaces (and unifaces?) hafted as knives. For instance, the Edgefield scraper with a beveled cutting edge is characteristic of Taylor and San Patrice assemblages (Perino 1985:119). Did the appearance of early notched points with corresponding very short hafting areas have any association with the appearance of or increased sophistication of the atlatl?

It might be argued that Dalton points gradually became side-notched points about 10,000 yr B.P. Many of those points are beveled. Cache River points made from small triangular preforms may date circa 10,000–9,500 yr B.P. Like Palmer points, they are small. Unlike Palmer points, they are not serrated.

There is another possible major difference between fluted-point and notched-point complexes. The Dalton uniface industry continues a tradition begun with the earlier Clovis-like complexes, in turn based on the Upper Paleolithic of Eurasia. Early notched points do not appear to be consistently associated with an Upper Paleolithic–like uniface assemblage in the East. We do not know if this is true or not in northeastern Arkansas.

There are no appropriate radiocarbon dates in northeastern Arkansas. There are problems with the dates outside Arkansas. Much of the difficulty lies with not having a good stratigraphic sequence to date. In many cases where good deposits exist there is no datable carbon. In deposits where good carbon samples exist, the deposits themselves are open to questions of temporal mixture. Table 9.1 is a listing of the major radiocarbon dates known to us on early complexes in the Southeast.

There are no "good" dates for Clovis-related sites in the Southeast. The early Clovis dates shown in Table 9.1 need to be checked by accelerator dates on either older or new samples. This is being done (John Broster, personal communication). Kimmswick needs to be dated. There are now plans to try to date mastodon bone associated with the Clovis-like points found there (Russell Graham, personal communication). The final date of major megafaunal extinction is about 10,800–10,900 yr B.P. There is association with mastodon at Kimmswick, and mammoth in Florida where about eighty proboscidean ivory foreshafts have been found. Therefore there were widespread fluted-point makers before about 10,900–10,800 yr B.P. and probably several centuries before then.

Dalton remains are not associated with now-extinct megafauna. Dalton must date after 10,900–10,800 yr B.P. An apparent transitional complex known as Sedgwick now is considered partly contemporaneous and not ancestral to Dalton technology.

The two northeastern Arkansas excavations make it obvious that Dalton predates early notched points. The radiocarbon dates on early notched points, particularly at Dust Cave in Alabama and at the Page-Ladson site in Florida, make it clear that Dalton dates earlier than 10,000 yr B.P. and possibly earlier than 10,300–10,200 yr B.P.

Two dates at Rodgers Shelter may confirm an early date for Dalton. However, these dates need to be checked by accelerator dates either on new samples and/or the older samples. This process is in motion (Marvin Kay, personal communication). For now Dalton seems to date somewhere within the period of 10,700–10,200 yr B.P.

THE DALTON PERIOD IN THE SOUTHEAST

In 1926–1928 the controversy over whether people had inhabited the New World before the end of the Pleistocene was solved to everyone's satisfaction. Folsom points were found in close association with an articulated butchered extinct form of bison thought to be of Pleistocene age (Wormington 1957:23). That discovery was quickly reinforced by others. The initial discovery in the Southeast of an excavated "Folsom" was a fluted point at Macon, Georgia (Kelly 1938:7, fig. 5). In addition, blades, end scrapers, and what appears to have been a broken fluted preform (Kelly 1938:figs. 4–15) were also recovered. Somewhat later (1938–1940) fluted points and unifaces were excavated at Parrish in Kentucky (W. S. Webb 1951:434, fig. 11).

During the 1930s, "Folsom, Folsomoid, and Folsom-like" points were being reported throughout most of the eastern United States, including Arkansas (Fischel 1939). In total, twelve points (40% of those from the East) are included in Fischel's tables for the Southeast. By 1990, 9,253 fluted points had been recorded in eastern North America; about 60% of them were from the Southeast (Anderson 1990:169). Fluted points were being recorded in record numbers after about 1960, and today there is little doubt that the southeastern United States represents the single major late Pleistocene concentration in the New World. However, we have no idea what this means in terms of population or of length of occupation.

By some time in the twelfth millennium B.P., Paleoindians were present throughout the Southeast. Until a large sequence of radiocarbon dates associated with good contextual data exists, we can only speculate on the broad outline. There are at least eighteen named non-Dalton fluted point "types" and 39 Paleoindian "types" published in the eastern United States literature (Perino 1985, 1991).

Table 9.1
Selected radiocarbon dates in the Southeast

Period	Site	Date (yr B.P.)	Laboratory No.
Paleoindian	Little Salt Spring (Florida)	12,030 ± 200	TX-2636
Clovis	Johnson (Tennessee)	11,980 ± 110	TX-7454
		11,700 ± 980	TX-7000
Dalton	Rodgers Shelter (Missouri)	10,530 ± 650	ISGS-48
		10,200 ± 330	M-2333
Dalton	Puckett (Tennessee)	9,790 ± 160	Beta 48045
Dalton/Big Sandy I	Stanfield-Worley (Alabama)	9,640 ± 450	M-1152
		9,440 ± 400	M-1346
		9,340 ± 400	M-1347
		9,040 ± 400	M-1348
		8,920 ± 400	M-1153
Dalton/Graham Cave	Graham Cave (Missouri)	9,700 ± 500	M-130
		9,470 ± 400	M-1928
		9,290 ± 300	M-1889
Early Side-Notched and Late Lanceolate	Dust Cave (Alabama)	10,490 ± 360	Beta 40681
		10,390 ± 80	Beta 65179
		10,345 ± 80	Beta 40680
		10,330 ± 120	Beta 41063
		10,310 ± 230	Beta 65181
		9,990 ± 140	Beta 65177
		9,190 ± 130	Beta 65183
Bolen	Page-Ladson (Florida)	10,280 ± 110	Beta 21752
		10,000 ± 120	Beta 21750
		9,730 ± 120	Beta 11905
		9,450 ± 100	Beta 15089
Palmer	Thunderbird (Virginia)	9,900 ± 340	W-2816
Kessel/Kirk	St. Albans (West Virginia)	9,850 ± 500	M-1827
Kirk	Patrick (Tennessee)	9,410 ± 290	GX-4122
Kirk	Icehouse Bottom (Tennessee)	9,435 ± 270	GX-4126
		9,350 ± 215	GX-4125
		9,175 ± 240	GX-4127
		8,715 ± 140	I-9138
		8,525 ± 355	I-9137
Kirk	Rose Island (Tennessee)	9,330 ± 250	GX-3564
		9,110 ± 145	GX-3565
Kirk	St. Albans (West Virginia)	8,930 ± 160	Broyles 1971[a]
		8,850 ± 320	Broyles 1971[a]
		8,800 ± 320	Broyles 1971[a]

[a]Laboratory numbers not published.

Presumably older fluted points are more Clovis-like. Some of the eastern varieties are known as "Ross County" and "Kimmswick." At the Kimmswick site, located south of St. Louis, Missouri, fluted points were associated with deposits containing peccary, sloth, and mastodon (Graham et al. 1981). There are no radiocarbon dates, but these animals should predate about 10,900–10,800 yr B.P. The earliest eastern dates for Clovis were obtained at a site in West Tennessee (Broster and Norton 1992). They need to be reinforced with fresh dates because they both are several centuries earlier than expected and one has a standard error of about 1,000 years. Other dates on fluted-point deposits in the East are mostly very late Pleistocene and early Holocene. It is apparent that fluted points continued to be made until the end of the Pleistocene.

An artifact evidently associated with the earlier fluted points is the single-platform polyhedral blade core and its companion blades. This core-blade industry has been associated with the New Mexico Blackwater Draw Clovis horizon (Green 1963). They also occur with fluted points in Missouri (C. H. Chapman 1975:75–83), in Illinois (Tankersley and Morrow 1993), in Kentucky (Tankersley and Smith 1992), and in Tennessee (Broster et al. 1996), where fifty-three cores and 465 blades have been recovered as of this writing. Dalton is not associated with a strictly single-platform polyhedral blade-core industry, but with a disk-core industry, which can result in blades. The presence or absence of true blades from Clovis cores may help make an early or late Paleoindian determination.

The shift from early to late Paleoindian may correspond with the time of extinction of major megafauna, including tapir, llama, camel, horse, mastodon, sloth, and others. This is essentially when Clovis and Folsom separate, around 10,900–10,800 yr B.P. (Haynes 1984). The simplistic scheme of only Clovis and Folsom as the Paleoindian West is rapidly becoming more complex (Frison and Bonnichsen 1996), and one needs no longer feel alone in the eastern hodgepodge of styles. The problem, however, remains the lack of good dates. Good dates are precisely why the older western scheme is now undergoing change.

The eastern typological problem centers around several unanswered questions: Are stylistic differences real or more reflective of a combination of expected local group and temporal variation? If real, are the stylistic differences geographical or temporal or perhaps technological? Do stylistic differences reflect social distance and hence settlement and economic differences?

Given a Clovis-like base before about 10,900–10,800 yr B.P., there are some possible regional "late Paleoindian" traditions that can be outlined (Table 9.2). Along the western fringe of the East from Ontario into northeastern Arkansas occurs a point style named, respectively, from north to south Barnes, Illinois Folsom, and Sedgwick (Perino 1991:17). The spruce forest connecting these diverse regions was replaced in the lower Mississippi Valley about 12,500 yr B.P. (P. A. Delcourt and Delcourt 1981:147–149). The Great Lakes were not ice-free until about 10,000 yr B.P., but the area of Barnes points was free a half millennium or more earlier. The similarity of these three named styles may just be coincidence. However, Munson (1990) argued that the Illinois Folsom is part of an eastern extension of Folsom points that matches a late Pleistocene–early Holocene distribution of bison.

Sedgwick points occur immediately southeast of Munson's (1990) distribution map. There are late Pleistocene bison remains in that area, but it is not known if they date as late as the Sedgwick point must. In addition, the vegetation was basically cypress-gum with mixed hardwoods, not prairie. However the presence of llama at 10,900 yr B.P. hints at some prairie conditions. The horse and camel remains known in the area also may date this late. Dalton points, however, developed directly out of a Clovis technology (Bradley, chapter 4), and Dalton and Sedgwick points could be partially contemporaneous.

Barnes points occur immediately northeast of Munson's (1990) distribution map. Before 10,600 yr B.P., the region was characterized by an open tundra parkland dominated by spruce (Deller and Ellis 1992:8). Barnes points (Parkhill complex or industry) extend into upstate New York (Deller and Ellis 1992:125), and similar complexes exist to the east. Caribou might have been a major focus.

Cumberland points are characteristic in Kentucky, Tennessee, southern Ohio, northern Alabama, northern Mississippi, and northern Georgia (Perino 1985:94; Ledbetter et al. 1992; McGahey 1992). Probably, they are contemporaneous with the Barnes-Sedgwick continuum. Certainly they are distinctive and geographically concentrated. For instance, a Cumberland point has never been reported west of the Mississippi River. Cumberland points are essentially associated with a mixed-hardwood forest (P. A. Delcourt and Delcourt 1981:147, fig. 7).

Along the coastal plain from the Florida panhandle through South Carolina are found Suwannee and (rarely) Simpson points (Anderson et al. 1990; T. Charles and Mi-

Table 9.2
Late Pleistocene–early Holocene sequence chart for the Southeast

Years B.P.	Arkansas Missouri Mississippi Northern Louisiana	Tennessee Kentucky Northern Alabama	Southern Louisiana East Texas	Florida	North Carolina South Carolina Georgia	Eastern Great Lakes
9,000						
9,100						
9,200						
9,300						
9,400						
			Kirk Horizon			
9,500						
9,600						
9,700	Cache River		San Patrice		Palmer/	
9,800		Dust/			Taylor	
9,900		Hester		Bolen		
			Holocene/Pleistocene Border			
10,000						
10,100		Dalton			Hardaway/	
10,200	Dalton				Dalton	Holcombe
10,300			Hope			
10,400				Simpson		
10,500		Quad				Barnes
10,600	Dalton					
10,700	Sedgwick	Cumberland	Pelican	Suwannee		
10,800						Bull Brook
			Final Megafauna Extinction			
10,900						
11,000						
11,100	Kimmswick	Ross Co.				
11,200						
11,300						
			Clovis Base			

chie 1992; Dunbar and Waller 1992). Similar forms are present through Mississippi (McGahey 1992:fig. 20.4), and in Louisiana are known as Pelican points (C. H. Webb et al. 1971).

All of these areas appear to have had a basic Clovis-like initial occupation with the exception of portions of the Great Lakes area and the extreme Northeast, which were initially represented by the late Paleoindian Bull Brook point, probably immediately ancestral to the Barnes point and related point styles. Dating of the post-Clovis points just discussed (including Bull Brook) probably is around 10,900–10,800 to 10,600–10,500 yr B.P., based on just about everyone's current guess.

Around 10,600–10,500 yr B.P., Dalton points appeared in a very wide region (Figure 9.7). By about 10,000 yr B.P., points were notched over the majority of the eastern

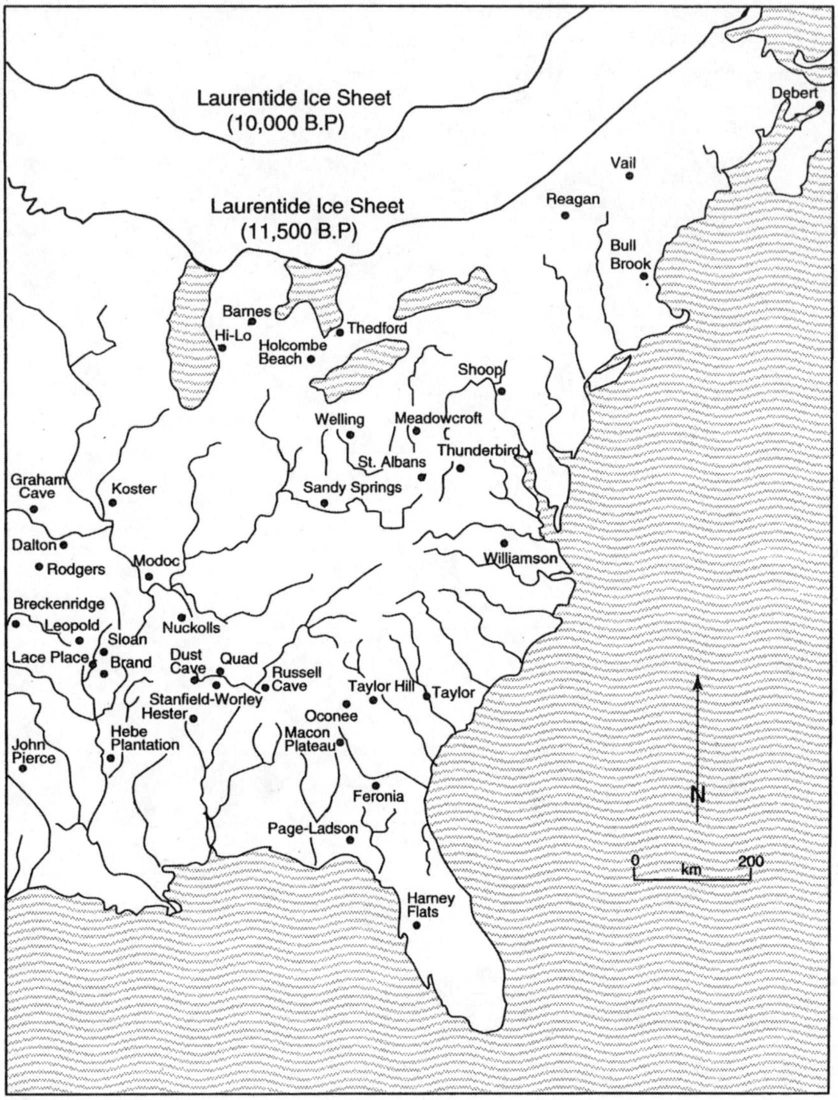

Figure 9.7 Major Dalton-period sites in the eastern United States (after Anderson and Sassaman [1992:fig. 4.1] and P. A. Delcourt and Delcourt [1981:fig. 7]).

United States. The non-Dalton regions of the north, the Great Lakes and the Northeast, were characterized by more traditional fluted points. These two broad areas reflected two distinct hunting strategies and game, and two basic kinds of environment. Dalton was associated with deer and oak-hickory forests. The northern fluted-point traditions were associated with caribou and boreal forests. By 10,000–9,500 yr B.P. the entire region once again was unified by a similar notched-point tradition. White-tailed deer and new hunting techniques, together with the end of the Pleistocene and increased population, contributed to this apparent unification. Apparent, because there are at least twenty-three published point types to contend with in the study of early Holocene archaeology in the eastern United States, not counting Hardin and other early stemmed varieties (Perino 1985, 1991).

Dalton points are said to occur throughout the eastern United States and as far west as the Rocky Mountains (Perino 1985:97). This misconception is based on the fact that most lanceolate points when resharpened resemble Dalton points. Dalton points in relatively large numbers occur in the following states: Missouri, Arkansas, Tennessee, Mississippi, Alabama, South Carolina, Georgia, Illinois, and Kentucky.

In Louisiana, the Dalton equivalent is San Patrice, Hope variety (Perino 1985:337). In Florida the Dalton equivalent is often thought to be Tallahassee (Perino 1985:373) [and the "Santa Fe" (Perino 1985:195)]. However, many or even perhaps all of the examples of the Tallahassee point may be late Holocene in date. In North Carolina the equivalent is the Hardaway Dalton (Coe 1964). In Florida, the Simpson point may have dated into the Dalton period. Part of the coastal plain may have been occupied relatively late. This is logical, assuming that the initial eastern United States occupation was by Clovis point makers in the midcontinent. However, until we have a clearer picture of the now-submerged coast we cannot be certain. Recent data from California indicate that fluted points do exist there despite the prevailing notion that occupation in California was essentially Holocene in time. Of course, we know that the karst portion of the Florida Gulf coast was occupied before the extinction of megafauna because about eighty proboscidean ivory foreshafts have been found there.

In Kentucky, Tennessee, and northern Alabama where the Cumberland point was most prevelant, Beaver Lake and Quad points occur in substantial numbers (Rolingson 1964). These two styles, which obviously are related to Cumberland, may date to an early Dalton time period. In the central Mississippi River Valley and the lower Missouri River Valley, the development of Dalton out of Clovis-like points seems to have taken place with a minimum of outside influence. Dalton points as a style diffused to the south and east. At the extreme eastern limits of the Southeast, Dalton style influence was both very late and in anticipation of the hafting shift from waisted lanceolate to notched. To the east Hardaway notched developed out of Hardaway lanceolate. To the south, San Patrice notched styles developed out of San Patrice lanceolate forms. To the southeast (Florida), lanceolate forms may have developed into Dalton-like Tallahassee points before the appearance of the Bolen complex.

The uniformity of the Kirk horizon at about 9,400 yr B.P. may be similar to what the East experienced in Clovis times. Immediately afterward, the Hypsithermal Climatic Period began. Microclimatic changes evidently resulted in increased localized foraging economies and more dispersed populations and settlements. Regional styles were once again characteristic in the Southeast.

10
Summary

DAN F. MORSE

Around 10,500 yr B.P. a local group of Native Americans, made up of about twenty-five to fifty individuals, lived at the edge of Crowley's Ridge in the center of the Cache River drainage in northeastern Arkansas. In 1974 a cemetery was excavated that contained some of the remains of these earliest Americans. Although fragments of the biological remnants were just barely preserved, the stone artifacts buried with those remains provided a wealth of information about the Cache River local group.

The excavation took place during 15 March–15 April 1974. In total, 439 Dalton-period artifacts including 146 points, forty-two adzes, ninety-five other bifaces, thirty-three end scrapers, sixty-eight other unifaces, thirty-five abraders, and twenty other stone artifacts were recovered and precisely plotted. In addition, 211 small fragments of bone and a large series of soil samples were collected.

The bone fragments were so minuscule and chalky that it was only with great care that the bone could be classified as human (63.9%), probably human (18.4%), indeterminate (7.8%), possibly nonhuman (9.9%), and nonhuman (0%). Both human adult and subadult remains were present in the assemblage. The Sloan site was indeed a cemetery and included representative members of the entire local group.

The specific artifact descriptions present a great amount of new raw data. The artifacts are representative of a brief (less than 100 years?) period of time and a single local group. Raw material not only includes local Crowley's Ridge Chert but the more distant Ozark cherts, most of which outcrop about 75 kilometers to the southwest. Burlington and Crescent Quarry Cherts, also used for points and especially the larger ones, outcrop near St. Louis, Missouri, almost 300 kilometers northeast of the Sloan site. There are classic Dalton sites throughout this area of chert sources and an extension of classic sites up the Missouri River an additional 150 kilometers to where the type Dalton site was discovered about 1948.

Technically, the points were fluted, a characteristic of points made during the Paleoindian Period of the United States. Dalton fluted-point technology developed out of an earlier Clovis fluted-point technology. The points at Sloan did not exhibit wear, further confirmation that they were grave associations. Points examined from other Dalton sites were used as projectiles and to cut meat and hide. Points resharpened into drill-like shapes were used to puncture hide.

Adzes were made from carefully selected chert cobbles from the Crowley's Ridge gravels. Adzes were used to cut charred wood and seasoned wood. They were hafted to seasoned-wood or antler handles and bound with leather. Adzes recovered at Sloan had not been used as much as those recovered from living sites.

End scrapers were made from flakes removed during biface reduction. These scrapers were used to scrape hide. Other unifaces examined were used to cut and scrape meat and hide, including a curious hafted and backed spokeshave-like specimen. Two gravers had been used to engrave bone or antler. A *pièce esquillée* was used to cut meat.

Bifaces are now considered a basic Paleoindian artifact. All but four of those recovered at Sloan could not have been preforms based on size alone. One biface examined (but not from Sloan) had been used to butcher meat.

A biface from Sloan had green and red pigment on its surface. This pigment is noteworthy because red ocher was recorded associated with several of the grave deposits. An adze preform may have been wrapped in a "greasy" hide. The microwear analysis has provided hints of ceremonial behavior beyond the technological function of stone tools.

Abraders were centrally grooved and/or laterally notched. They appear to have been used to grind the basal edges of adzes and points, possibly for strength. Distinctive discoid chert hammerstones were probably used to knap chert tools. An edge-abraded cobble possibly demonstrates that vegetable food was as important to the diet of the local group as was meat.

Artifact provenience indicates the possibilty of about thirty graves. The basic tool kit is oriented primarily toward butchering, hide working, woodworking, and tool production. Soil chemistry experiments indicate a high probability that even more definite grave information is extractable.

The estimated date of the cemetery is around 10,500 yr B.P. The current rule-of-thumb date for the Pleistocene-Holocene border is 10,000 yr B.P. The late Pleistocene climaxed at 18,000 yr B.P., and the early to middle Holocene Hypsithermal climaxed at about 7,000 yr B.P. The Dalton period in the central Mississippi Valley was a time of abundance, with mixed hardwoods and cypress-gum forests and with deciduous forest fauna. Temperature was warm and temperate. Seasonal temperature and precipitation extremes may not have been as pronounced as today. Relict braided stream channels provided numerous incidences of forest edges, ideal for white-tailed deer. Backswamps and streams would have been abundant with fish and waterfowl.

Except for Crowley's Ridge, which is about 75 meters higher, there was relatively little topographic variation (less than 7 meters). The late Pleistocene surface was essentially the same as the modern surface. Stablized sand dunes, which provided the setting for the Sloan site, date about 18,000 yr B.P. The site is situated on a slough between the floodplain of the largest regional permanent stream and Crowley's Ridge, and is central to the Cache River Basin. The environment included at least some of the plants that were domesticated after around 6,000 yr B.P., such as *Chenopodium, Polygonum,* and slightly later *Iva.* Bald cypress was present, an important fact because of the abundance of hafted stone adzes in the Dalton period. The Ozarks were characterized by a closed-canopy forest and consequently may have not been as attractive to long-term exploitation as the more savannalike lowlands. Diversity from upland to lowland would have been of great importance to human hunters and wild-plant gatherers.

The Paleoindian Period in the Americas is noted for controversies concerning the date of initial migration from Asia. Many investigators accept a general 11,300–10,000 yr B.P. dating for the period. On the early side, most of these investigators assume that the earliest date approaches 12,000 yr B.P. On the late side, western United States archaeologists often view Paleoindian as continuing into the Holocene, to 8,000 yr B.P. This period (10,000–8,000 yr B.P.) is included in the "early Archaic" by most eastern United States archaeologists. They have a tendency to equate the end of Paleoindian with the end of the Pleistocene.

The importance of the Sloan site is its demonstration of the higher-than-expected level of sophistication for a Paleoindian group. Everyone expects that points and scrapers are well made and attractive in the Paleoindian Period, but many are unaware of the technological sophistication of tool manufacture and function. Points were beveled to increase the number of possible resharpenings and to make the points more efficient knives. Adzes were used to form wooden objects, most commonly probably cypress dugout canoes.

These earliest hunters also processed and ate vegetable foods, including some of those their descendants domesticated 150 generations later. They used red (and possibly green?) pigment. Most important, the Sloan Paleoindians buried their dead in cemeteries. We did not expect to find a cemetery dating earlier than the middle Holocene in the central United States. Not only was their life ceremonially rich, but the number of well-crafted grave goods also indicate a certain richness of social-political life. Obviously, this local group was relatively stable and did not merely wander about in search of food and stone outcrops. The number of large tools is a kind of waste that can only exist in a stoneless environment if there is in place a system of sophisticated trade between local groups within a band network. The environment must be part of the answer. The Sloan site is not only pretty artifacts, but a window into the past that was different from what was expected when we approached the site in early 1974.

References Cited

Akridge, David Glen

1994a The Sloan Site Revisited: A Preliminary Report on the Soil Samples. *Field Notes, Newsletter of the Arkansas Archeological Society* 260:5–9.

1994b A Trace Element Soil Analysis of the Sloan Site: A 10,500 Year Old Cemetery in Northeast Arkansas. Chemistry 4273: Special Problems, Spring 1994. Manuscript on file, Arkansas Archeological Survey, Jonesboro.

Akridge, David Glen, and Dan F. Morse

1994 A Trace Element Soil Analysis of the Sloan Site: A 10,500 Year Old Cemetery in Northeast Arkansas. In *Arkansas Undergraduate Proceedings 1994,* 1–2. Arkadelphia, Arkansas: Henderson State University.

Anderson, David G.

1990 The PaleoIndian Colonization of Eastern North America: A View from the Southeastern United States. In *Early PaleoIndian Economies of Eastern North America,* edited by Barry Isaac and Kenneth Tankersley, 163–216. *Journal of Economic Anthropology Supplement* 5.

Anderson, David G., and Kenneth Sassaman

1992 Modeling Paleoindian and Early Archaic Settlement in the Lower Southeast: An Historical Perspective. In *PaleoIndian and Early Archaic Period Research in the Lower Southeast: A South Carolina Perspective,* edited by David G. Anderson, Kenneth E. Sassaman, and Christopher Judge, 19–49. Columbia: Council of South Carolina Professional Archaeologists.

Anderson, David G., Hazel R. Delcourt, Paul A. Delcourt, John E. Foss, and Phyllis A. Morse

1989 Cultural Resource Investigations in the L'Anguille River Basin: Lee, St. Francis, Cross and Poinsett Counties, Arkansas. Garrow & Associates, Inc., Contract No. DACW66-87-C-0046. Final Report submitted to the Department of the Army, Memphis District, Corps of Engineers.

Anderson, David G., R. Jerald Ledbetter, and Lisa O'Steen

1990 *Paleoindian Period Archaeology of Georgia.* Georgia Archaeological Research Design Paper No. 6, Laboratory of Archaeology Series Report No. 28. Athens: University of Georgia.

Anonymous

1948 From the Irvin Peithman Collection. *Journal of the Illinois State Archaeological Society.* V(4): cover.

Anonymous

1965 Obituary of Judge S. P. Dalton. *Central States Archaeological Journal* 12(3): 108.

Autin, W. J., S. F. Burns, B. J. Miller, R. T. Saucier, and J. I. Sneed

1991 Quaternary Geology of the Lower Mississippi Valley. In *Quaternary Non-Glacial Geology: Conterminous U.S.,* edited by R. B. Morrison, 547–582. *The Geology of North America,* K-2. Boulder: Geological Society of America.

Barbour, Erwin H., and C. Bertrand Schultz
1932 The Mounted Skeleton of *Bison Occidentalis,* and Associated Dart-Points. *Bulletin of the Nebraska State Museum* 1(32).

Behm, Jeffery A.
1985 Identification and Analysis of Stylistic Variation in Hardin Barbed Points. Ph.D. diss., Department of Anthropology, University of Wisconsin, Madison.

Bettison, Cynthia A.
1985 An Experimental Approach to Sickle Sheen Deposition and Archeological Interpretation. *Lithic Technology* 14:26–32.

Binneman, Johan, and Janette Deacon
1986 Experimental Determination of Use Wear on Stone Adzes from Bloomplaas Cave, South Africa. *Journal of Archaeological Science* 13:219–228.

Birks, H. J. B.
1976 Late-Wisconsinan Vegetational History at Wolf Creek, Central Minnesota. *Ecological Monographs* 46:395–429.

Boom, B. M.
1979 Systematic Studies of the Genus *Isoetes* in the Southeastern United States. Master's thesis, Department of Botany, University of Tennessee, Knoxville.

Bradley, Bruce A.
1974 Comments on the Lithic Technology of the Casper Site. In *The Casper Bison Kill Site,* edited by George C. Frison, 191–197. New York: Academic Press.
1991 Flake Stone Technology in the Northern High Plains. In *Prehistoric Hunters of the High Plains,* 2d ed., edited by George C. Frison, 369–396. New York: Academic Press.

Bradley, Bruce A., and George C. Frison
1996 Flaked-Stone and Worked-Bone Artifacts from the Mill Iron Site. In *The Mill Iron Site,* edited by George C. Frison, 43–69. Albuquerque: University of New Mexico Press.

Brain, Jeffrey P.
1970 Early Archaic in the Lower Mississippi Alluvial Valley. *American Antiquity* 35:104–105.

Branson, E. B.
1944 *The Geology of Missouri.* University of Missouri Studies 19(3), Columbia, Missouri.

Brätter, P., D. Gawlik, J. Lausch, and U. Rösick
1977 On the Distribution of Trace Elements in Human Skeletons. *Journal of Radioanalytical Chemistry* 37:393–403.

Braun, E. Lucy
1950 *Deciduous Forests of Eastern North America.* New York: Hafner Press.

Broecker, W. S., M. Andree, W. Wolfli, H. Oeschger, G. Bonani, J. Kennett, and D. Peteet
1988 The Chronology of the Last Deglaciation: Implications to the Cause of the Younger Dryas Event. *Paleoceanography* 3:1–19.

Broster, John B., and Mark R. Norton
1992 Paleoindian Projectile Point and Site Survey in Tennessee: 1988–1992. In *Paleoindian and Early Archaic Period Research in the Lower Southeast: A South Carolina Perspective,* edited by David G. Anderson, Kenneth E. Sassaman, and Christopher Judge, 263–268. Columbia: Council of South Carolina Professional Archaeologists.

Broster, John B., Mark R. Norton, Dennis J. Stanford, C. Vance Haynes Jr., and Margaret A. Jodry
1996 Stratified Fluted Point Deposits in the Western Valley of Tennessee. In *Proceedings of the 14th Annual Mid-South Archaeological Conference,* edited by Richard Walling, Camille Wharey, and Camille Stanley, 1–11. Special Publication 1. Memphis, Tennessee: Panamerican Consultants, Inc.

Brown, Calvin S.
1926 *Archaeology of Mississippi.* University, Mississippi: Mississippi Geological Survey.

Brown, James A.
1985 Long-Term Trends to Sedentism and the Emergence of Complexity in the American Midwest. In *Prehistoric Hunter-Gatherers,* edited by T. D. Price and J. A. Brown, 201–231. New York: Academic Press.

Brown, James A., ed.
1971 Approaches to the Social Dimensions of Mortuary Practices. *Memoirs of the Society for American Archaeology,* No. 25.

Broyles, Bettye J.
1971 Second Preliminary Report: The St. Albans Site, Kanawha County, West Virginia. *Report of Archeological Investigations* 3. Morgantown: West Virginia Geological and Economic Survey.

Butler, B. Robert
1962 *Contributions to the Prehistory of the Columbia Plateau: A Report on Excavations in the Palouse and Craig Mountain Sections.* Occasional Papers of the Idaho State College Museum, No. 9. Pocatello, Idaho.
1966 *A Guide to Understanding Idaho Archaeology.* Idaho State University Museum Special Publication. Pocatello, Idaho.

Call, R. Ellsworth
1891 *The Geology of Crowley's Ridge.* Annual Report of the Geological Survey of Arkansas for 1889, Vol. 2. Little Rock, Arkansas: Woodruff Printing Company.

Cambron, James W., and David C. Hulse

1960 The Transitional Paleo-Indian in North Alabama and South Tennessee. *Journal of Alabama Archaeology* 6:7–33.

Carneiro, Robert L.

1979 Tree Felling with the Stone Ax: An Experiment Carried Out Among the Yanomano Indians of Southern Venezuela. In *Ethnoarchaeology,* edited by C. Kramer, 22–58. New York: Columbia University Press.

Chapman, Carl H.

1948 A Preliminary Survey of Missouri Archaeology Part IV: Ancient Cultures and Sequence. *The Missouri Archaeologist* 10(4).

1952 Recent Excavations in Graham Cave. *Memoir: Missouri Archaeological Society* 2:87–101.

1975 *The Archaeology of Missouri, I.* Columbia: University of Missouri Press.

Chapman, Jefferson

1975 *The Rose Island Site and the Bifurcate Point Tradition.* Department of Anthropology, University of Tennessee, Reports of Investigations 14.

Chapman, R., I. Kinnes, and K. Randsborg, eds.

1981 *The Archaeology of Death.* Cambridge: Cambridge University Press.

Charles, D. K., and J. E. Buikstra

1983 Archaic Mortuary Sites in the Central Mississippi Drainage: Distribution, Structure, and Behavioral Implications. In *Archaic Hunters and Gatherers in the American Midwest,* edited by J. L. Phillips and J. A. Brown, 117–145. New York: Academic Press.

Charles, Tommy, and James L. Michie

1992 South Carolina Paleo Point Data. In *Paleoindian and Early Archaic Period Research in the Lower Southeast: A South Carolina Perspective,* edited by David G. Anderson, Kenneth E. Sassaman, and Christopher Judge, 242–247. Columbia: Council of South Carolina Professional Archaeologists.

Coe, Joffre

1964 The Formative Cultures of the Carolina Piedmont. *Transactions of the American Philosophical Society* 54(5).

Condon, Keith Warren

1981 Correspondence of Developmental Enamel Defects Between the Mandibular Canine and First Premolar. Master's thesis, Department of Anthropology, University of Arkansas, Fayetteville.

Crabtree, Don

1972 *An Introduction to Flintworking.* Occasional Papers of the Idaho State University Museum, 28.

Crabtree, Don, and Earl H. Swanson Jr.

1968 Edge-Ground Cobbles and Blade-Making in the Northwest. *Journal of the Idaho State University Museum* 11(2): 50–58.

Dalton, S. P.

1960 Experience of an Amateur. *Central States Archaeological Journal* 7(3): 106–110.

1961 Experience of an Amateur. *Central States Archaeological Journal* 8(2): 77–79.

Daniel, I. Randolph, Jr., and Michael Wisenbaker

1987 *Harney Flats: A Florida Paleo-Indian Site.* Farmingdale, New York: Baywood Publishing Company.

Dean, W. E., Jr.

1974 Determination of Carbonate and Organic Matter in Calcareous Sediments and Sedimentary Rocks by Loss on Ignition: Comparison with Other Methods. *Journal of Sedimentary Petrology* 44:242–248.

DeJarnette, David L., Edward B. Kurjack, and James W. Cambron

1962 Stanfield-Worley Bluff Shelter Excavations. *Journal of Alabama Archaeology* 8(1&2).

Delcourt, Hazel R.

1979 Late-Quaternary Vegetation History of the Eastern Highland Rim and Adjacent Cumberland Plateau of Tennessee. *Ecological Monographs* 49:244–280.

Delcourt, Hazel R., and Paul A. Delcourt

1988 Final Report of Palynological and Plant-Macrofossil Analysis, Hood Lake, Poinsett County, Arkansas. In *Cultural Resources Survey and Geomorphic Examination of the L'Anguille River Channel Cleanout, Arkansas,* edited by D. Anderson. Report submitted to the Department of the Army, Memphis District, Corps of Engineers.

1994 Postglacial Rise and Decline of *Ostrya virginiana* (Mill.) K. Koch and *Carpinus caroliniana* Walt. in Eastern North America: Predictable Responses of Forest Species to Cyclic Changes in Seasonality of Climates. *Journal of Biogeography* 21:137–150.

Delcourt, H. R., P. A. Delcourt, G. R. Wilkins, and E. N. Smith Jr.

1986 Vegetational History of the Cedar Glades Regions of Tennessee, Kentucky, and Missouri During the Past 30,000 years. *Association of Southeastern Biologists Bulletin* 33:128–137.

Delcourt, Paul A., and Hazel R. Delcourt

1981 Vegetation Maps for Eastern North America: 40,000 Yr B. P. to the Present. In *Geobotany II,* edited by R. C. Romans, 123–165. New York: Plenum Press.

1984 Late-Quaternary Paleoclimates and Biotic Responses in Eastern North America and the Northwestern Atlantic Ocean. *Palaeogeography, Palaeoclimatology, Palaeoecology* 48:263–284.

1987 *Long-Term Forest Dynamics in the Temperate Zone.* New York: Springer-Verlag.

1996 Quaternary Paleoecology of the Lower Mississippi Valley. *Engineering Geology* (in press).

Delcourt, P. A., O. K. Davis, and R. C. Bright
1979 Bibliography of Taxonomic Literature for the Identification of Fruits, Seeds, and Vegetative Plant Fragments. *Environmental Sciences Division, Publication* 1328. Oak Ridge, Tennessee: Oak Ridge National Laboratory.

Delcourt, P. A., H. R. Delcourt, R. C. Brister, and L. E. Lackey
1980 Quaternary Vegetation History of the Mississippi Embayment. *Quaternary Research* 13:111–132.

Delcourt, P. A., H. R. Delcourt, and J. L. Davidson
1983 Mapping and Calibration of Modern Pollen-Vegetation Relationships in the Southeastern United States. *Review of Palaeobotany and Palynology* 39:1–45.

Deller, D. Brian, and Chris J. Ellis
1992 Thedford II: A Paleo-Indian Site in the Ausable River Watershed of Southwestern Ontario. *Memoirs, Museum of Anthropology, University of Michigan,* No. 24.

Dubes, R. C.
1993 Cluster Analysis and Related Issues. In *Handbook of Pattern Recognition and Computer Vision,* edited by C. H. Chen, L. F. Pau, and P. S. P. Wang, 3–32. Singapore: World Scientific.

Dunbar, James S., and Benjamin I. Waller
1992 Resource Orientation of Clovis, Suwannee, and Simpson Age Paleoindian Sites in Florida. In *PaleoIndian and Early Archaic Period Research in the Lower Southeast: A South Carolina Perspective,* edited by David G. Anderson, Kenneth E. Sassaman, and Christopher Judge, 279–294. Columbia: Council of South Carolina Professional Archaeologists.

Dunbar, James S., Michael K. Faught, and S. David Webb
1988 Page/Ladson (8Je591): An Underwater Paleo-Indian Site in Northwestern Florida. *The Florida Anthropologist* 41:442–452.

Dunbar, James S., S. David Webb, and Dan Craing
1989 Culturally and Naturally Modified Bones from a Paleoindian Site in the Aucilla River, North Florida. In *Bone Modification,* edited by Rob Bonnichsen and M. Sorge, 473–497. Orono, Maine: Center for the First Americans.

Enlow, Donald H., and Sidney O. Brown
1956 A Comparative Histological Study of Fossil and Recent Bone Tissues. Part I. *The Texas Journal of Science* 8:405–442.
1957 A Comparative Histological Study of Fossil and Recent Bone Tissues. Part II. *The Texas Journal of Science* 9:186–214.
1958 A Comparative Histological Study of Fossil and Recent Bone Tissues. Part III. *The Texas Journal of Science* 10:187–230.

Faegri, K., and J. Iversen
1975 *Textbook of Pollen Analysis,* 3d rev. ed. New York: Hafner Press, Macmillan.

Fernald, M. L.
1950 *Gray's Manual of Botany.* New York: D. Van Nostrand.

Fischel, Hans E.
1939 Folsom and Yuma Culture Finds. *American Antiquity* 4:232–264.

Fisk, Harold
1944 *Geological Investigations of the Alluvial Valley of the Lower Mississippi River.* U.S. Army Corps of Engineers, Mississippi River Commission, Vicksburg, Mississippi.

Flenniken, J. Jeffrey
1978 Reevaluation of the Lindenmeier Folsom: A Replication Experiment in Lithic Technology. *American Antiquity* 43:473–480.

Fowells, H. A.
1965 *Silvics of Forest Trees of the United States.* U.S. Forest Service Agricultural Handbook 271:1–762.

Fowke, Gerard
1928 Archeological Investigations. In *44th Annual Report for 1926–1927,* 399–555. Washington, D.C.: Bureau of American Ethnology.

Frison, George C.
1991 *Prehistoric Hunters of the High Plains,* 2d ed. New York: Academic Press.

Frison, George C., and Robson Bonnichsen
1996 The Pleistocene-Holocene Transition on the Plains and Rocky Mountains of North America. In *Humans at the End of the Ice Age,* edited by Lawrence G. Straus, Berit V. Eriksen, Jon M. Erlandson, and David R. Yesner, 303–318. New York: Plenum Press.

Frison, George C., and Bruce A. Bradley
1980 *Folsom Tools and Technology at the Hanson Site, Wyoming.* Albuquerque: University of New Mexico Press.

Frison, George C., and Dennis J. Stanford
1982 *The Agate Basin Site: A Record of the PaleoIndian Occupation of the Northwestern High Plains.* New York: Academic Press.

Gaertner, Linda M.
1990 Microwear Analysis of Dalton "Wood-working Adzes" from Early Archaic Sites in Northeastern Arkansas. B. A. (Honors) thesis, Department of Anthropology, The Ohio State University, Columbus.

Giles, Albert W.
1930 *St. Peter and Older Ordovician Sandstones of Northern Arkansas.* Arkansas Geological Survey, Bulletin 4.

Gillam, J. Christopher
1995 Paleoindian Settlement in the Mississippi Valley of Arkansas. Master's thesis, Department of Anthropology, University of Arkansas, Fayetteville.

Gilliland, Marion Spjut

1975 *The Material Culture of Key Marco, Florida.* Gainesville: The University Presses of Florida.

Gleason, H. A., and A. Cronquist

1963 *Manual of Vascular Plants of Northeastern United States and Adjacent Canada.* Princeton: D. Van Nostrand.

Goldman-Finn, Nurit, and Boyce N. Driskell, eds.

1994 Preliminary Archaeological Papers on Dust Cave, Northwest Alabama. *Journal of Alabama Archaeology* 40(1&2).

Goldstein, L. G.

1981 One-Dimensional Archaeology and Multi-Dimensional People: Spatial Organization and Mortuary Analysis. In *The Archaeology of Death,* edited by R. Chapman, I. Kinnes, and K. Randsborg, 53–69. Cambridge: Cambridge University Press.

Goodyear, Albert C.

1974 *The Brand Site: A Techno-Functional Study of a Dalton Site in Northeast Arkansas.* Arkansas Archeological Survey, Research Series 7.

1982 The Chronological Position of the Dalton Horizon in the Southeastern United States. *American Antiquity* 47:382–395.

Graham, Russell W., C. Vance Haynes, D. Johnson, and Marvin Kay

1981 Kimmswick: A Clovis-Mastodon Association in Eastern Missouri. *Science* 213:1115–1117.

Graham, R. W., H. A. Semken Jr., and M. A. Graham, eds.

1987 *Late Quaternary Mammalian Biogeography and Environments of the Great Plains and Prairies.* Springfield: Illinois State Museum.

Green, Frank E.

1963 The Clovis Blades: An Important Addition to the Llano Complex. *American Antiquity* 29:145–165.

Gregg, S. A., K. W. Kintigh, and R. Whallon

1991 Linking Ethnoarchaeological Interpretation and Archaeological Data: The Sensitivity of Spatial Analytical Methods to Postdepositional Disturbance. In *The Interpretation of Archaeological Spatial Patterning,* edited by E. M. Kroll and T. D. Price, 149–196. New York: Plenum Press.

Griffin, James B.

1952 Prehistoric Cultures of the Central Mississippi Valley. In *Archeology of Eastern United States,* edited by James B. Griffin, 226–238. Chicago: University of Chicago Press.

Harding, Anthony, and Robert Young

1979 Reconstruction of the Hafting Methods and Function of Stone Implements. In *Stone Axe Studies: Archaeological, Petrological, Experimental, and Ethnographic,* edited by T. H. McK. Clough and W. A. Cummins, 102–105. Council for British Archaeology, Research Report 23.

Haynes, C. Vance

1984 Application of Accelerator Dating to Fluted Point Paleoindian Sites. *Archaeology of Eastern North America* 12:184–191.

Hester, James J.

1972 *Blackwater Locality No. 1: A Stratified, Early Man Site in Eastern New Mexico.* Fort Burgwin Research Center, Southern Methodist University.

House, John H.

1975 A Functional Typology for Cache Project Surface Collections. In *The Cache River Archeological Project: An Experiment in Contract Archeology,* edited by Michael B. Schiffer and John H. House, 55–74. Arkansas Archeological Survey, Research Series 8.

Ives, David J.

1975 *The Crescent Hills Prehistoric Quarrying Area.* Museum Briefs 22. Museum of Anthropology, University of Missouri-Columbia.

Jacobson, G. L., Jr., T. Webb III, and E. C. Grimm

1987 Patterns and Rates of Vegetation Change During the Deglaciation of Eastern North America. In *North America and Adjacent Oceans During the Last Deglaciation,* edited by W. F. Ruddiman and H. E. Wright Jr., 277–288. Boulder: Geological Society of America.

Jain, A. K., and R. C. Dubes

1988 *Algorithms for Clustering Data.* Englewood Cliffs, New Jersey: Prentice Hall.

Keeley, H. C. M., G. E. Hudson, and J. Evans

1977 Trace Element Content in Human Bones in Various States of Preservation: The Soil Silhouette. *Journal of Archaeological Science* 4:19–24.

Keeley, Lawrence H.

1980 *Experimental Determination of Stone Tool Uses: A Microwear Analysis.* Chicago: University of Chicago Press.

1982 Hafting and Retooling: Effects on the Archaeological Record. *American Antiquity* 47:798–809.

Kelly, A. R.

1938 *A Preliminary Report on Archeological Explorations at Macon, Ga.* Smithsonian Institution Bureau of American Ethnology, Anthropological Papers, No. 1.

Kennett, J. P., and N. J. Shackleton

1975 Laurentide Ice Sheet Meltwater Recorded in Gulf of Mexico Deep-Sea Cores. *Science* 188:147–150.

King, James E.

1973 Late Pleistocene Palynology and Biogeography of the Western Missouri Ozarks. *Ecological Monographs* 43:539–565.

King, James E., and W. H. Allen Jr.

1977 A Holocene Vegetation Record from the Mississippi

River Valley, Southeastern Missouri. *Quaternary Research* 8:307–323.

Kintigh, Keith W., and Albert J. Ammerman

1982 Heuristic Approaches to Spatial Analysis in Archaeology. *American Antiquity* 47:31–63.

Knuttson, Kjel

1988 *Patterns of Tool Use: Scanning Electron Microscopy of Experimental Quartz Tools.* Aun 10. Uppsala, Sweden: Societas Archaeologica Upsaliensis.

Kutzbach, J. E.

1987 Model Simulations of the Climatic Patterns During the Deglaciation of North America. In *North America and Adjacent Oceans During the Last Deglaciation,* edited by W. F. Ruddiman and H. E. Wright Jr., 425–446. Boulder: Geological Society of America.

Kutzbach, J. E., and H. E. Wright Jr.

1985 Simulation of the Climate 18,000 years B.P.: Results for the North American/North Atlantic/European Sector and Comparison with the Geologic Record of North America. *Quaternary Science Reviews* 4:147–187.

Lambert, J. B., C. B. Szpunar, and J. E. Buikstra

1979 Chemical Analysis of Human Bone From Middle and Late Woodland Sites. *Archaeometry* 21:115–129.

Lambert, J. B., S. V. Simpson, J. E. Buikstra, and D. K. Douglas

1984 Analysis of Soil Associated with Woodland Burials. In *Archaeological Chemistry III,* edited by J. B. Lambert, 96–113. Washington, D.C.: American Chemical Society.

Ledbetter, R. Jerald, David G. Anderson, and Lisa D. O'Steen

1992 Paleoindian Research in Georgia. In *Paleoindian and Early Archaic Period Research in the Lower Southeast: A South Carolina Perspective,* edited by David G. Anderson, Kenneth E. Sassaman, and Christopher Judge, 248–262. Columbia: Council of South Carolina Professional Archaeologists.

Leventer, A., D. F. Williams, and J. P. Kennett

1982 Dynamics of the Laurentide Ice Sheet During the Last Deglaciation: Evidence from the Gulf of Mexico. *Earth and Planetary Science Letters* 59:11–17.

Levi Sala, Irene

1986 Use Wear and Post-Depositional Surface Modification: A Word of Caution. *Journal of Archaeological Science* 13:229–244.

Lindsay, Debra

1993 *Science in the Subarctic: Trappers, Traders, and the Smithsonian Institution.* Washington, D.C.: Smithsonian Institution Press.

Logan, Wilfred D.

1952 Graham Cave: An Archaic Site in Montgomery County, Missouri. *Memoir: Missouri Archaeological Society* 2:1–86.

Mainfort, R. C., Jr.

1985 Wealth, Space, and Status in a Historic Indian Cemetery. *American Antiquity* 50:555–579.

Martin, John F.

1973 On the Estimation of the Sizes of Local Groups in a Hunting-Gathering Environment. *American Anthropologist* 75:1448–1468.

Mathis, Mark A.

1980 The Spatial Characteristics of Prehistoric Lithic Resource Procurement and Utilization: A Study Using Surface Artifact Collections in the Village Creek Basin of Northeast Arkansas. Master's thesis, Department of Anthropology, University of Arkansas, Fayetteville.

McGahey, Samuel O.

1992 Paleoindian and Early Archaic Data from Mississippi. In *Paleoindian and Early Archaic Period Research in the Lower Southeast: A South Carolina Perspective,* edited by David G. Anderson, Kenneth E. Sassaman, and Christopher Judge, 295–321. Columbia: Council of South Carolina Professional Archaeologists.

McGimsey, Charles R., III

1956 Cerro Mangote: A Preceramic Site in Panama. *American Antiquity* 22:151–161.

Medford, Larry D.

1972 Agricultural Destruction of Archeological Sites in Northeast Arkansas. In *Sites Destruction Due to Archeological Practices,* edited by J. L. Ford and M. A. Rolingson. Arkansas Archeological Survey, Research Series 3.

Mercer, Henry C.

1975 *Ancient Carpenters' Tools.* 5th ed. New York: Horizon Press, The Bucks County Historical Society.

Meserve, F. G., and Erwin H. Barbour

1932 Association of an Arrow Point with *Bison occidentalis* in Nebraska. *Bulletin of the Nebraska State Museum* 1(27).

Michie, James L.

1973 A Functional Interpretation of the Dalton Projectile Point in South Carolina. *South Carolina Antiquities* 5(2): 24–36.

Milligan, G. W., and M. C. Cooper

1985 An Examination of Procedures for Determining the Number of Clusters in a Data Set. *Psychometrika* 50:159–179.

Mitchell, S. R.

1959 The Woodworking Tools of the Australian Aborigines. *Journal of the Royal Anthropological Institute* 89:191–200.

Morse, Dan F.

1969 Introducing Northeastern Arkansas Prehistory. *Arkansas Archeologist* 10:12–28.

1970 Preliminary Notes on a Recent Mastodon and Tapir Find in Northeastern Arkansas. *Arkansas Archeologist* 11: 45–49.

1971a Recent Indications of Dalton Settlement Pattern in Northeast Arkansas. *Southeastern Archaeological Conference Bulletin* 13:5–10.

1971b The Hawkins Cache: A Significant Dalton Find in Northeast Arkansas. *Arkansas Archeologist* 12:9–20.

1973 Dalton Culture in Northeast Arkansas. *Florida Anthropologist* 25:28–38.

1975 Paleo-Indian in the Land of Opportunity: Preliminary Report on the Excavations at the Sloan Site (3GE94). In *The Cache River Archeological Project: An Experiment in Contract Archeology,* edited by Michael B. Schiffer and John H. House, 135–143. Arkansas Archeological Survey, Research Series 8.

1976 An Analysis of the Dalton Complex in the Central Mississippi Valley. *Habitats Humains Antérieurs A L'Holocène En Amérique,* direction by James B. Griffin. Nice, France: Union Internationale Des Sciences Préhistoriques et Protohistoriques.

1982 A Paleo-Indian/Early Archaic Cemetery Possibility in Arkansas. In *Peopling of the New World,* edited by J. E. Ericson, R. E. Taylor, and R. Berger, 147–162. Los Altos, California: Ballena Press.

1991 The Sloan Dalton Site. *Pictures of Record.* Weston, Connecticut: Hammerslough.

Morse, Dan F., and Albert C. Goodyear III

1973 The Significance of the Dalton Adze in Northeast Arkansas. *Plains Anthropologist* 18(62): 316–321.

Morse, Dan F., and Russell Graham

1991 Searching for *Paleolama. Field Notes, Newsletter of the Arkansas Archeological Society* 239:10–12.

Morse, Dan F., and Phyllis A. Morse

1983 *Archaeology of the Central Mississippi Valley.* New York: Academic Press.

1990 The Spanish Exploration of Arkansas. In *Columbian Consequences,* edited by David Hurst Thomas, 197–210. Washington, D.C.: Smithsonian Institution Press.

Morse, Dan F., David G. Anderson, and Albert C. Goodyear

1996 The Pleistocene-Holocene Transition in the Eastern United States. In *Humans at the End of the Ice Age,* edited by Lawrence G. Straus, Berit V. Eriksen, Jon M. Erlandson, and David R. Yesner, 319–338. New York: Plenum Press.

Munsell Color

1975 *Munsell Soil Color Charts.* Baltimore: Macbeth Division, Kollmorgaen Corporation.

Munson, Patrick J.

1990 Folsom Fluted Projectile Points East of the Great Plains and Their Biogeographical Correlates. *North American Archaeologist* 11:255–272.

Murray, P. D. F.

1936 *Bones: A Study of the Development and Structure of the Vertebrate Skeleton.* Cambridge: Cambridge University Press.

Odell, George H., and Frank Cowan

1986 Experiments with Spears and Arrows on Animal Targets. *Journal of Field Archaeology* 13:195–212.

Olausson, Deborah Seitzer

1983 Lithic Technological Analysis of the Thin-Butted Flint Axe. *Acta Archaeologica* 53:1–87.

O'Shea, J. M.

1984 *Mortuary Variability: An Archaeological Investigation.* New York: Academic Press.

Perino, Gregory

1967 The Cherry Valley Mounds and Banks Mound 3. *Central States Archaeological Societies Memoir* 1.

1985 *Selected Preforms, Points and Knives of the North American Indians,* Vol. 1. Idabel, Oklahoma: Points and Barbs Press.

1991 *Selected Preforms, Points and Knives of the North American Indians,* Vol. 2. Idabel, Oklahoma: Points and Barbs Press.

Phillips, Philip

1970 Archaeological Survey in the Lower Yazoo Basin, Mississippi, 1949–1955. *Papers of the Peabody Museum, Harvard University,* 1.

Phillips, Philip, James Ford, and James B. Griffin

1951 Archaeological Survey in the Lower Mississippi Alluvial Valley, 1940–1947. *Papers of the Peabody Museum, Harvard University,* 25.

Price, J. E.

1978 The Settlement Pattern of the Powers Phase. In *Mississippian Settlement Patterns,* edited by B. D. Smith, 201–231. New York: Academic Press.

Price, James E., and James J. Krakker

1975 *Dalton Occupation of the Ozark Border.* Museum Briefs 20, Museum of Anthropology, University of Missouri-Columbia.

Redfield, Alden

1971 *Dalton Project Notes, Volume One.* Museum of Anthropology, University of Missouri.

Redfield, Alden, and John H. Moselage

1970 The Lace Place, a Dalton Project Site in the Western Lowland in Eastern Arkansas. *Arkansas Archeologist* 11:21–44.

Rigaud, J. P., and J. F. Simek

1991 Interpreting Spatial Patterns at the Grotte XV: A Multiple Method Approach. In *The Interpretation of Archaeological Spatial Patterning,* edited by E. M. Kroll and T. D. Price, 199–220. New York: Plenum Press.

Ritchie, J. C.

1987 *Postglacial Vegetation of Canada.* New York: Cambridge University Press.

Robertson, P. A., G. T. Weaver, and J. A. Cavanaugh

1978 Vegetation and Tree Species Patterns Near the Northern Terminus of the Southern Floodplain Forest. *Ecological Monographs* 48:249–267.

Rolingson, Martha Ann

1964 *Paleo-Indian Culture in Kentucky.* Studies in Anthropology, No. 2. Lexington: University of Kentucky Press.

Royall, P. D.

1988 Late-Quaternary Paleoecology and Paleoenvironments of the Western Lowlands, Southeast Missouri. Master's thesis, Department of Geological Sciences, University of Tennessee, Knoxville.

Royall, P. D., P. A. Delcourt, and H. R. Delcourt

1991 Late-Quaternary Paleoecology and Paleoenvironments of the Central Mississippi Alluvial Valley. *Geological Society of America Bulletin* 103:157–170.

Saucier, Roger T.

1968 A New Chronology for Braided Stream Surface Formation in the Lower Mississippi Valley. *Southeastern Geology* 9:65–76.

1974 *Quaternary Geology of the Lower Mississippi Valley.* Arkansas Archeological Survey, Research Series 6.

1978 Sand Dunes and Related Eolian Features of the Lower Mississippi River Alluvial Valley. *Geoscience and Man* 19:23–40.

1981 Current Thinking on Riverine Processes and Geologic History as Related to Human Settlement in the Southeast. *Geoscience and Man* 22:7–18.

Schiffer, Michael B.

1975a Some Further Comments on the Dalton Settlement Pattern Hypothesis. In *The Cache River Archeological Project: An Experiment in Contract Archeology,* edited by Michael B. Schiffer and John H. House, 103–112. Arkansas Archeological Survey, Research Series 8.

1975b An Alternative to Morse's Dalton Settlement Pattern Hypothesis. *Plains Anthropologist* 20:253 266.

Schiffer, Michael B., and John H. House, eds.

1975 *The Cache River Archeological Project: An Experiment in Contract Archeology.* Arkansas Archeological Survey, Research Series 8.

Scott, L. J., and D. K. Aasen

1987 Interpretation of Holocene Vegetation in Northeastern Arkansas. In *A Cultural Resources Survey: Testing, and Geomorphic Examination of Ditches 10, 12, and 29, Mississippi County, Arkansas* by R. H. Lafferty III, M. J. Guccione, L. J. Scott, D. K. Aasen, B. J. Watkins, M. C. Sierzchula, and P. F. Baumann, 133–150. Mid-Continental Research Associates Report No. 86–5 to the Department of the Army, Memphis District, Corps of Engineers.

Semenov, Sergei A.

1964 *Prehistoric Technology,* transl. by M. W. Thompson. London: Cory, Adams, and Macay.

Smith, E. N., Jr.

1984 Late-Quaternary Vegetational History at Cupola Pond, Ozark National Scenic Riverways, Southeastern Missouri. Master's thesis, Department of Geological Sciences, University of Tennessee, Knoxville.

Smith, F. L., and R. T. Saucier

1971 Geological Investigation of the Western Lowlands Area, Lower Mississippi Valley. *U.S. Army Corps of Engineers Waterways Experiment Station, Technical Report* S-71-5.

Steyermark, J. A.

1963 *Flora of Missouri.* Ames: Iowa State University Press.

Tankersley, Kenneth B., and Julie E. Morrow

1993 Clovis Procurement and Land-Use Patterns in the Confluence Region of the Mississippi, Missouri, and Illinois Rivers. In *Highways to the Past: Essays on Illinois Archaeology in Honor of Charles J. Bareis,* edited by Thomas E. Emerson, Andrew C. Fortier, and Dale L. McElrath, 119–129. *Journal of the Illinois Archaeological Survey* 5(1&2).

Tankersley, Kenneth B., and Edward E. Smith

1992 Clovis in Kaintuckee. In *Paleoindian and Early Archaic Period Research in the Lower Southeast: A South Carolina Perspective,* edited by David G. Anderson, Kenneth E. Sassaman, and Christopher Judge, 322–330. Columbia: Council of South Carolina Professional Archaeologists.

Titmus, Gene L., and James C. Woods

1991 A Closer Look at Margin "Grinding" on Folsom and Clovis Points. *Journal of California and Great Basin Anthropology* 13:194–203.

Wakefield, Elmer G., and Samuel C. Dellinger

1936 The Probable Adaptation of Utilitarian Implements for Surgical Procedures by the "Mound Builders" of Eastern Arkansas. *The Journal of Bone and Joint Surgery* 18:434–438.

Webb, Clarence H.

1982 The Poverty Point Culture, 2d ed., rev. *Geoscience and Man* 17:1–85.

Webb, Clarence H., Joel L. Shiner, and E. Wayne Roberts

1971 The John Pearce Site (16CD56): A San Patrice Site in Caddo Parish, Louisiana. *Bulletin of the Texas Archeological Society* 42:1–49.

Webb, William S.

1951 The Parrish Village Site: Site 45, Hopkins County, Kentucky. *The University of Kentucky, Reports on Anthropology* 6:407–451.

Williams, Stephen

1954 An Archeological Study of the Mississippian Culture in

Southeast Missouri. Ph.D. diss., Yale University. Ann Arbor: University Microfilms.

Williams, Stephen, and James B. Stoltman

1965 An Outline of Southeastern United States Prehistory with Particular Emphasis on the Paleo-Indian era. In *Quaternary of the United States,* edited by Henry Wright Jr. and David G. Frey, 669–683. Princeton, New Jersey: Princeton University Press.

Wilmsen, Edwin N.

1970 *Lithic Analysis and Cultural Inference: A Paleo-Indian Case.* Anthropological Papers 16, University of Arizona, Tucson.

Wood, W. Raymond, and R. Bruce McMillan

1976 *Prehistoric Man and His Environments.* New York: Academic Press.

Wormington, H. Marie

1957 *Ancient Man in North America.* Denver Museum of Natural History, Popular Series 4. Denver: Peerless.

Wright, H. E., Jr.

1967 A Square-Rod Piston Sampler for Lake Sediments. *Journal of Sedimentary Petrology* 37:975–976.

1968 History of the Prairie Peninsula. In *The Quaternary of Illinois, Special Report 14,* edited by R. E. Bergstrom, 78–88. Urbana: University of Illinois.

Yerkes, Richard W.

1987 *Prehistoric Life on the Mississippi Floodplain.* Chicago: University of Chicago Press.

Yerkes, Richard W., and Albert M. Pecora III

1990 The Introduction of the Bow and Arrow. In *Late Woodland Archaeology at the Parkline Site (46PU99) Putnam County, West Virginia,* edited by C. M. Niquette and M. A. Hughes, 95–108. Contract Publication Series 90–93. Lexington, Kentucky: Cultural Resource Analysts, Inc.

Contributors

The extent of knowledge needed in a book of this scope is far beyond the capabilities of just one person. I have endeavored to bring together a research team that includes the best individuals known to me in the specific disciplines or subdisciplines of a variety of physical, biological, and social sciences:

Glen Akridge (Ph.D. candidate in Chemistry/Biochemistry, University of Arkansas). Cosmochemistry, geochemistry.

Bruce A. Bradley (Ph.D. in Archaeology, University of Cambridge, 1977). Flint knapping, stone technology, Paleoindian, North America, eastern Europe, southwestern United States. Senior Research Archaeologist, Crow Canyon Archaeological Center, Cortez, Colorado.

Keith W. Condon (Ph.D. in Anatomy, University of Illinois Chicago, 1987). Biological anthropology, neuromuscular development. Assistant Professor, Department of Biological Sciences, Florida International University, Miami.

Hazel R. Delcourt (Ph.D. in Ecology, University of Minnesota, 1978). Quaternary paleoenvironments of the nonglaciated eastern United States, plant ecology. Associate Professor of Ecology and Evolutionary Biology and Co-Director, Center for Quaternary Studies, University of Tennessee, Knoxville.

Paul A. Delcourt (Ph.D. in Geology, University of Minnesota, 1978). Quaternary paleoecology, Quaternary paleoenvironments of the nonglaciated eastern United States. Professor of Geology and of Ecology and Evolutionary Biology and Co-Director, Center for Quaternary Studies, University of Tennessee, Knoxville.

Linda M. Gaertner (Ph.D. candidate in Anthropology, University of Wisconsin, Madison). Microwear analyses on lithics.

Jami J. Lockhart (M.A. in Geography, University of Arkansas, 1988). Resource management and planning, environmental dynamics, geographic information systems and integrated data management, cartographic theory. Coordinator, Computer Services Program, Arkansas Archeological Survey. University of Arkansas Research Associate.

Robert C. Mainfort Jr. (Ph.D. in Anthropology, Michigan State University, 1977). Mortuary studies, ranked societies, multivariate data analysis, eastern United States. Administrator, Sponsored Research Program, Arkansas Archeological Survey; Assistant Professor of Anthropology, University of Arkansas, Fayetteville.

Dan F. Morse (Ph.D. in Anthropology, University of Michigan, 1967). Paleoindian, complex societies, contact, technology, eastern United States. Archeologist, Arkansas Archeological Survey; Professor of Anthropology, University of Arkansas, Fayetteville.

Phyllis A. Morse (M.A. in Anthropology, University of Michigan, 1958). Complex societies, Historic, eastern United States archaeology. Research Associate, Arkansas Archeological Survey, Jonesboro.

Jerome C. Rose (Ph.D. in Anthropology, University of Massachusetts, Amherst, 1973). Bioarchaeology of the Mississippi Valley, dental anthropology. Professor, Department of Anthropology, University of Arkansas, Fayetteville.

P. Daniel Royall (Ph.D. candidate in Geography, University of Tennessee, Knoxville). Watershed dynamics, geomorphology, geohydrology.

Roger T. Saucier (Ph.D. in Geography, Louisiana State University, 1968). Quaternary geology of the lower Mississippi Valley, alluvial and coastal geomorphology, paleoenvironments. Physical Scientist, Geotechnical and Environmental Laboratories, U.S. Army Engineer Waterways Experiment Station, Vicksburg, Mississippi.

Richard Yerkes (Ph.D. in Anthropology, University of Wisconsin, 1984). Environmental archaeology, microwear analyses on lithics. Associate Professor, Department of Anthropology, Ohio State University, Columbus.

Index

Note: asterisk (*) indicates figure.

abraders, cobble, 44*, 51, 88, 90, 141
abraders, sandstone: in clusters, 86, 88, 89, 90, 91–92; co-occurrence with other artifacts of, 91; grooved, 44*, 46–48; grooved and notched, 49, 50; notched, 44*, 48–49; other, 49, 50; use of, 45–46, 48, 49–50, 141
adzes, 22–23, 30, 32*; in clusters, 88, 89, 90, 91–92; co-occurrence with other artifacts of, 91; distribution of, 93*; edge grinding of, 49; experiments with, 63*; as grave offerings, 70–71; hafting of, 59, 63, 65–66; heat-treated, 71; measurement plots and correlations for, 23, 34*; measurements of, 33; microwear analysis of, 59, 60, 63, 64*, 65*, 70; pigments on, 66; preform for, 60, 66, 71; use of, 23, 59, 60, 63–65, 66, 70, 71, 140–41
Akridge, Glen, 3
Ammerman, A. J., 83, 84
Anderson, David, 22, 23
Archaic period, 30, 52, 101, 135
Arkansas Archeological Survey, 1, 126
Arkansas State University, 1–2
artifacts: clusters of, 83–84, 85*, 86*, 88, 89*, 90–93, 132; lack of disturbance of, 73, 87*, 132; lack of use of, 69–71; provenience of, 72, 73*, 74–82, 83*, 84*, 85*. *See also individual artifact names*
atlatl, 134
awls: bone, 46. *See also* Dalton awls
axes, 23

backed unifaces, 40*, 41; in clusters, 88, 89, 90, 92; co-occurrence with other artifacts of, 92; use of, 61, 68, 141
Barnes Cordmarked, 52
Barnes Plain, 52
Barnes point, 136, 137
Beaver Lake point, 139
Bell City/Oran Gap, 105, 114, 119
beveling. *See* Dalton points: beveled
bifaces, 30–31, 35*; caches of, 30–31, 73, 85; in clusters, 85, 86, 87, 88, 89, 90; fragments reused as tools, 31, 38; manufacture process for, 57; measurement plots and correlations for, 22, 31*; measurements of, 36–37; microwear analysis of, 61, 63, 68; pigment on, 141; use of, 61, 68, 141
Big Creek point, 52
Big Lake, 105
Big Sandy I point, 124
bison, 125, 134, 136
Black River, 97–98, 99, 100
Blackwater Draw, 136
blade industry/technology, 50, 136
bladelike flakes, 43
Bolen point, 125, 139
Bone, human, 13*, 72; distribution, 73*; histological examination of, 8, 11, 12; provenience of, 9–11; soil chemistry evidence for, 93–95
bone working, 46, 48, 49, 50, 68, 71
Boone Chert. *See* Ozark Chert
Bradley, Bruce, 22, 56*
Brand site (3PO139), 125, 126; abraders from, 47; adze fragments from, 59; artifact summary, 14; backed unifaces lacking from, 41; bifaces from, 30; Dalton burin from, 61; Dalton points from, 60, 61, 66, 67*, 132; dating of, 132; depositional context of, 98; end scrapers from, 31, 34, 62, 69; gravers from, 43; microliths from, 62, 68–69; pebble cores from, 45; *pièce esquillée* from, 62, 69, 70*
Brown, Calvin, 123–24
Buffalo Head Slough, 100, 101*
Bull Brook point, 137
burials: no. 1 (post-Dalton), 7, 52, 94, 95. *See also bone, human; cemetery; grave offerings*
burins. *See* Dalton burins
Burlington Chert. *See* Crescent Quarry Chert
Butchering tools: bifaces as, 68; Dalton points as, 66, 67*, 71, 133
Butler, B. R., 50, 51

Cache River Archeological Project, 1, 2
Cache River Basin: archaeological work in, 1; Dalton sites in, 127*, 128, 132; depositional units in, 97; dune formation in, 99; formation of, 99–100; meander belt of, 98. *See also* Western Lowlands
Cache River points, 52, 132, 133, 134
Cahokia site, 15
Cambron, James W., 124
camel, 136
canoes, dugout, 59, 66, 121
caribou, 136, 138
cemetery, 141–42; age of individuals in, 12–13; depth of burials in, 101–2; graves indicated by artifact concentrations, 84, 86*, 91, 92, 93; soil chemistry evidence for, 93–95. *See also* bone, human; grave offerings
ceramics, 52
Chapman, Carl, 124
chert sources, 14–15, 16*. *See also individual source names*
chopper/core, 44*, 45, 88, 90
Clinski-Harabasz index, 84–85

Clovis points: Dalton development out of, 132, 136, 139; dating of, 134, 136, 137; technology of, 57
Coldwater point, 124
collectors, relic, 1, 4, 6–7, 125, 128
Conine, Mike, 2
cores, pebble, 45
Cotter Chert, 17, 21, 30
Crescent Quarry Chert (Burlington Chert), 15–16; in artifact clusters, 92; backed uniface of, 41; biface of, 30, 31; Dalton points of, 17, 21; Sloan point of, 17
Crowley's Ridge, 96, 98, 128–29; ironstone, 45, 47, 48
Crowley's Ridge Chert, 15, 16; adzes of, 23; backed unifaces of, 41; bifaces of, 30, 57; Dalton points of, 21; end scrapers of, 34; pebble cores of, 45; perforator of, 42; retouched flakes of, 42; utilized flakes of, 43
Crowley's Ridge points, 130, 132
Cumberland points, 136, 139
Cupola Pond, 103–4, 119

Dalton, S. P., 124
Dalton adzes. *See* adzes
Dalton awls, 21, 22★, 67; in clusters, 88, 90, 91; co-occurrence with other artifacts, 91
Dalton burins, 21, 22★, 71; in clusters, 88, 91; microwear analysis of, 61; use of, 67–68
Dalton period: band size, 129–30; band territories, 14–15, 93, 128, 129★; dating of, current, 125, 132, 134, 137; dating of, past, 123–24; distribution in Arkansas of, 126★, 127★; distribution in eastern US of, 138★; origin of term, 124; relation to Meserve, 125; research in Arkansas, 125–32; settlement pattern, 128–29, 130★; social differentiation in, 93; tool kit, 58, 71, 83, 91, 141
Dalton points, 16–17; basal grinding of, 17, 21; beveled, 17, 19★, 20–21, 54, 55, 56, 133; in clusters, 85, 86, 87, 88, 89–91; compared to Clovis, 57; compared to Folsom, 57; development out of Clovis, 132, 136, 139; early recognition of, 124; edge grinding of, 49, 132–33; fluting, 54–55; as grave offerings, 70, 71, 140; impact fractures on, 21, 66, 68, 71; large, 17, 18★, 70, 91, 92★; measurement plots and correlations for, 22, 30★, 31★; measurements of, 22, 24–29; microwear analysis of, 60, 61, 66, 67★, 68, 69–70; preform for, 22★, 30, 54, 60, 66; production sequence of, 53–54, 55★, 56; reworked, 21, 22★, 61, 67–68, 71; serration of, 20, 21, 54; unbeveled, 20★, 21; use of, 60, 61, 66, 67★, 71, 132–33
Dalton scraper, 22★
Dalton site, 124
Davidson, Bill, 5
Davis, Hester, 3, 5, 7
deer, 125, 129, 138
discoid hammers, 43, 44★, 141
Dust Cave, 125, 132, 134, 135

Eastern Lowlands. *See* St. Francis Basin
edge-abraded cobble, 44, 50–51
Edgefield/Albany scrapers, 41, 133
end scrapers, 31, 34, 38★, 39–40; in clusters, 88, 89, 90, 91; co-occurrence with other artifacts of, 92; measurements of, 39; microwear analysis of, 62, 68, 69★; use of, 62, 68, 69★, 141
Everton Chert. *See* Ozark Chert

fire-cracked rock, 52
Fisk, Harold, 124
fluted points. *See individual point names*
Folsom points, 57, 125, 132, 134; Illinois, 136
Ford, James A., 123, 125
Ford-Redfield Survey, 125, 127
foreshafts, ivory, 134, 139
Forkum site (3GE3), 127, 128
Frison, George, 56

Goodyear, Albert C.: on adzes, 59, 63, 64, 65; on end scrapers, 68; on Dalton points, 22, 66; on source of abrader raw material, 47
Goshen/Plainview points, 54, 57
Graham Cave, 124, 135
grave offerings: adzes and adze preforms as, 70–71; biface caches as, 30–31; defining lots of, 91–93; large Dalton points as, 70; unused and little-used tools as, 70–71
gravers, 31, 43, 62, 68, 141
Griffin, James B., 123

hammers. *See* discoid hammers
Hanson site, 51
Hardaway Dalton points, 139
Hardin points/complex, 34, 52, 132, 133, 138
Hawkins Cache (3LW654), 2, 59, 126, 127–28
Haynes, Vance, 3
heat-treatment, 71
hide working, 66–67, 68, 69★, 70★, 71
hoes, 65
Hoffrichter, Norma, 7
Holocene: artifacts at Sloan site, 51–52; landscape and vegetation, 100, 104, 105, 109–14, 115, 116–18, 119–21
Hood Lake: environmental setting, 105, 106★; lithology and chronology, 108, 109★; plant macrofossils, 111–12, 113–14; pollen assemblage zones, 109, 110★, 111★, 112–14; sampling and analysis methods at, 108; vegetation history, 117–18, 121
Hopewell, 31
horse, 136
House, John, 1, 2, 64, 65, 68
Hulse, David C., 124
Hypsithermal, 100, 118, 139

Icehouse Bottom site, 135
impact fractures, 21, 66, 68, 71
ironstone objects, 45, 51, 88, 89

Johnson site, 135

Kimmswick site, 134, 136
Kintigh, K. W., 83, 84
Kirk corner-notched points, 132, 133, 139
K-means clustering, 83, 85, 91
knapping: of Dalton points, 53–55, 56★; handedness and resharpening in, 20–21; tools for, 46, 48, 49–50, 51
Koldehoff, Brad, 16

Lace site (3PO17), 58, 125, 127; adzes from, 59; Dalton points from, 60, 67; end scrapers from, 62; gravers from, 62, 68
Lamotte Sandstone, 48
Little Salt Spring site, 135

Livingstone, Frank, 3
llama, 131, 136

Macon, 134
maize, 117, 120
mammoth, 134
mastodon, 124, 134, 136
McGimsey, Bob, 3
Medford, Larry, 1
Meserve, F. G., 125
Meserve points, 124, 125
microliths, 62, 68–69
Million, Michael, 2
Mississippi Alluvial Valley, central: Dalton sites in, 14; early Holocene vegetation, 121★; late Pleistocene vegetation, 100; physiography and landforms, 96, 97★, 104★. *See also* Cache River Basin; St. Francis Basin; Western Lowlands
Mississippian period, 14, 42, 52
Mississippi Plain, 52
Missouri Historical Society, 123
Morse, Dan, M.D., 3, 5
Morse, Dan F.: on adzes, 59, 63, 64, 65; on Dalton awls, 67; on Dalton burins, 67–68; on Dalton points, 53, 55; on end scrapers, 68; excavation of Sloan site by, 1–2, 6, 7; on gravers, 68
Morse, Phyllis, 7, 56, 68
mortars, 50
Moselage, John, 125
Munson, P. J., 136

Nodena points, 52, 128
Nonconnah Creek, 104–5

ocher, 51, 129, 141
Old Field, 105
orthoquartzite, 48
Ozark Chert, 15, 16; backed unifaces of, 41; bifaces of, 30; Dalton points of, 17, 21, 22; end scrapers of, 34; perforator of, 42; retouched flakes of, 42
Ozark Escarpment: chert resources, 15; pre-Dalton settlement of, 132
Ozark Plateaus/uplands, 48, 104, 118, 120

Page-Ladson site, 134, 135
Paleoindian: dating of, 141; point types, 57, 134; sequence chart, 137★; uniface assemblages, 34. *See also individual point names*
Palmer points, 51–52, 133, 134
Parrish site, 134
Patrick site, 135
peccary, 136
Pelican points, 130, 132, 137
Pemiscot Bayou, 105
Penters Chert. *See* Ozark Chert
perforators, 40★, 41–42, 88, 90
Perino, Gregory, 125
Phillips, Philip, 123, 124
pièces esquillées, 44★; in cluster, 88, 90; microwear on, 62, 69, 70★; use of, 44, 62, 69, 141
Pitkin Chert, 15, 16; bifaces of, 30; chopper/core of, 44; Dalton points of, 1, 2, 21; end scrapers of, 34; *piece esquillee* of, 44★; retouched flakes of, 42, 43; utilized flakes of, 43
Pleistocene: dune formation, 99, 107; megafauna, 124, 134, 136, 139; river channel changes, 99–100; sedimentation rates, 114, 115★; terraces, 98; vegeta-

tion changes, 100, 103–5, 109, 110*, 111*, 112, 116*, 117, 119; woodworking, 23. *See also* Dalton period; Paleoindian
Pollen: from Hood Lake, 109–14, 117–18; from Powers Fort Swale, 115–17, 119–20; sampling and analysis methods, 108
Pomme de Terre River Valley, 103
post-Dalton occupation, 51–52, 132, 133*
Poverty Point site, 41–42
Powers Fort, 107–8
Powers Fort Swale, 105; environmental setting of, 106, 107*; lithology and chronology of, 114, 115*; pollen assemblage zones of, 115, 116*, 117; sampling and analysis methods of, 108; vegetational history of, 119–20, 121
Powers Phase, 107–8, 120
pre-Dalton occupation, 130, 131*, 132. *See also* fluted points; Paleoindian; *individual point names*
preforms. *See* adzes; Dalton points
provenience. *See* artifacts
Puckett site, 135

Quad points, 139
quartzite, 34
Quina retouch, 68

radiocarbon dates: of Clovis-related sites, 134; of Dalton sites, 125; of Paleoindian and Early Archaic sites, 135; of *Paleolama,* 131; of plant-fossil locations, 105
Redfield, Alden, 125
retouched flakes, 40*, 42, 43; in clusters, 88, 89, 90, 92; microwear analysis of, 61, 68
Rodgers Shelter, 125, 134, 135
Rose Island site, 135
Roubidoux Sandstone, 48

St. Albans site, 135
St. Charles points, 133
St. Francis Basin/River (Eastern Lowlands); glacial outwash in, 99, 114; Holocene vegetation in, 120; meander belt, 98; physiography and landforms of, 97*, 104*; plant-fossil sites in, 105
St. Johns points, 132
St. Peter sandstone, 45
sandstone, 45, 46–48. *See also* abraders, sandstone
San Patrice points, 132, 133, 138, 139
Saucier, Roger, 3, 5, 124
Scallorn points, 52
Scanlon, Charles, 7
Scheel, Charley, 125
Schiffer, Michael, 2, 128
scrapers, 31, 42. *See also* backed unifaces; Dalton scraper; Edgefield/Albany scrapers; end scrapers
Sedgwick points/complex, 130, 132, 134, 136
Shugtown side-notched points, 52
Simpson points, 136, 139
Sloan, Frank, xvii, 1, 2*, 4–5
Sloan, Mary Ann, 1
Sloan points, 17, 18*, 88, 90
Sloan site (3GE94; Dalton Hill): aerial photographs of, 5*, 7; bioturbation at, 73; Dalton sites near, 126, 127*; dating of, 132, 141; delay in publishing, xvi; discovery and excavation of, 1–3, 4–7; relic collectors at, 1, 4, 6–7; setting, 3, 5, 6*, 7, 97, 100, 101*, 141; significance, xv–xvi, 126; soils, 100; summary of findings at, 140–42; vegetation, 100, 120–21; water availability, 100
sloth, 124, 136
Smith, Jim, 2, 6
Smith, Sam, 7
soil samples, 93–94, 95*
Soto, Hernando de, 128
Spears, Carol, 3, 7, 94
spokeshaves, 41, 42
Stanfield-Worley shelter, 124, 125, 135
Suwannee points, 136

Tallahassee points, 139
tapir, 124, 136
Taylor points, 133
3CG71, 61, 68
3CG485, 61
3GE3, 4
3GE26, 128
3GE58, 61, 68
3GE93, 61, 68
3GE94, 128
3LW13, 127, 128
3LW89, 129
3PO27, 61, 68
3PO53, 60, 124
3PO81, 60
3PO161, 62
Thunderbird site, 135

unifaces, 34, 134. *See also* backed unifaces; scrapers
Upper Paleolithic, 134
utilized flakes, 40*, 43; in clusters, 85, 88, 90; co-occurrence with other artifacts of, 92

vegetation: history at Hood Lake, 117–18, 121; history at Powers Fort Swale, 119–20, 121; Holocene changes in, 100, 120–21; map for central Mississippi Alluvial Valley, 121

Western Lowlands: glacial outwash in, 114; historic drainage of, 107, 109; Holocene vegetation in, 100, 119, 120–21; landforms and geographic processes of, 98–99, 104*; paleogeographic reconstruction of, 99–100, 118; physiography of, 96, 97*, 98; sand dune fields of, 3, 98–99. *See also* Cache River Basin
White River, 97, 98, 99
Williams, Stephen, 125
Wisconsin glaciation, 99
Woodland period, 52
woodworking: with adzes, 23, 59, 63, 64, 65, 66, 70, 71; associated with burial activities, 71; woods available for, 121, 141
Wormington, Marie, 3, 124

Zebree site, 15